Lecture Notes in Computer Science

Edited by G. Goos, J. Hartmanis and J. van Leeuwen

1958

Lecture Notes in Computer Science 1938

Springer

Berlin
Heidelberg
New York
Barcelona
Hong Kong
London
Milan
Paris
Singapore
Tokyo

Simone Fischer-Hübner

IT-Security
and Privacy

Design and Use of
Privacy-Enhancing Security Mechanisms

 Springer

Series Editors

Gerhard Goos, Karlsruhe University, Germany
Juris Hartmanis, Cornell University, NY, USA
Jan van Leeuwen, Utrecht University, The Netherlands

Author

Simone Fischer-Hübner
Karlstad University
Department of Computer Science
Universitetsgatan 1, 651 88 Karlstad, Sweden
E-mail: simone.fischer-huebner@kau.se

Cataloging-in-Publication Data applied for

Die Deutsche Bibliothek - CIP-Einheitsaufnahme

Fischer-Hübner, Simone:
IT-security and privacy : design and use of privacy enhancing security
mechanisms / Simone Fischer-Hübner. - Berlin ; Heidelberg ; New York ;
Barcelona ; Hong Kong ; London ; Milan ; Paris ; Singapore ; Tokyo :
Springer, 2001
  (Lecture notes in computer science ; Vol. 1958)
  ISBN 3-540-42142-4

CR Subject Classification (1998): C.2, D.4.6, K.6.5, E.3, H.2.0, K.4

ISSN 0302-9743
ISBN 3-540-42142-4 Springer-Verlag Berlin Heidelberg New York

Springer-Verlag Berlin Heidelberg New York
a member of BertelsmannSpringer Science+Business Media GmbH

http://www.springer.de

© Springer-Verlag Berlin Heidelberg 2001
Printed in Germany

Typesetting: Camera-ready by author
Printed on acid-free paper   SPIN 10781014   06/3142   5 4 3 2 1 0

Foreword

In public debates about **potential impacts** of contemporary Information and Communication Technologies (ICTs), **invasion of "privacy" and misuse of personal data** are often regarded as being amongst the most evident negative effects of ICTs which should be carefully analysed and controlled. Computing experts and informaticians often use the term **"data protection"** as synonymous with "privacy" although this usage is somewhat misleading: the main task is NOT to protect the data but it is the **task to protect the personal sphere** represented by the data and their relations associated with a person (sometimes called the "data shadow" of a person's privacy).

Indeed, the term "data protection" tends to hide basic problems which have to be solved to technically protect the "data shadow" of a person's "private sphere". While "data protection" assumes that data have been taken and stored, an analysis of person's privacy concerns may require that related data should on no account be taken and stored. Therefore, the term "data protection" is too technically reductive to be used synonymously for privacy.

The consistent inadequate usage of the term "data protection" is another illustration of the validity of Joseph Weizenbaum's metaphor (in his book "Computer Power and Human Reasoning") according to which computer scientists tend to search for some solutions in the light of a lantern, whereas the key lies in the shadow. Indeed, it is comparably easy to describe how to technically protect data, whether related to a person, an enterprise or any other entity. Several models exist for restricting access to any data, either on a "discretionary" or "mandatory" basis (DAC, MAC), either built into the kernel of an operating system ("Reference Monitor") or into some outer shell. Some models may also distinguish between the roles a user of stored data actually plays (RBAC), and a refined model may also include tasks which a user actually has to perform upon such data (a valuable contribution of the author of this book). "Auditing" provides adequate means to control whether personal data are used according to prescriptions, such as rights of users or capabilities of related IT processes. All these models are quite easily implemented (although it is also easy to switch such technical protection off).

Beyond such technical methods, models, and tools, it is significantly more difficult to describe **basic requirements and means to protect the "data shadow" of a person**. Some such requirements can be found in the privacy laws which have been passed in several countries, though on different levels. Some degree of harmonization is available in the European Union, based on its Data Protection Directive, but there still exist many problems in the exchange of personal data with areas with different (or no) legal requirements.

Requirements for privacy protection may depend upon the legal basis of privacy in a particular country. In Germany where privacy is regarded as some quasi-constitutional **"right for informational self-determination"**, such requirements are concerned with the **necessity** of data collection and processing, **purpose specification** and **purpose binding**, and **the transparency** of personal data protection. In addition, directives of the European Union and OECD also require **lawfulness and fairness**. Based on the different legal systems, there are sufficient stipulations on the legal side regarding which requirements must be legally fulfilled to store, process, and communicate personal data.

For a long time, these legal requirements were almost disregarded by the ICT community. Until very recently, there was no basic model for privacy-related requirements which implementations and usage of related information systems must fulfill. It is the specific **value of Simone Fischer-Hübner's work** (published in this book covering her habilitation thesis), that a first model is now available which permits the description of requirements derived from legal concepts.

Moreover, the author does not simply present her suggestions as a collection of principles and technical requirements. Besides developing a "privacy-friendly concept of data protection", she also presents it as a formal model, the implementation of which (when done properly) may help to prove that privacy requirements have indeed been implemented in some software. The demonstration of the model presented in this book is also embedded in contemporary concepts of IT Security, as seen by the description of its realization within LaPadula's Generalized Framework for Access Control. Consequently, implementations of her model will - if done correctly - make the related software not only adaptable to contemporary ITSEC concepts but at the same time "**conforming with law**" and "**privacy-friendly**". She also convincingly counters any argument that such models are "just theoretical and hardly to be implemented": she demonstrates that and how her model can be implemented on a relevant platform.

This book can – and hopefully will – become the foundation of a new way to model and consequently implement user requirements into ICT systems which conform better than before with human principles (starting but not ending with privacy). In this sense, it is my sincere hope that this book becomes really successful.

November 2000   Dr. Klaus Brunnstein
                                      Professor for Application of Informatics
                                                   University of Hamburg

Preface

In the Global Information Society, the individual's privacy is seriously endangered and is becoming more and more an international problem. An international harmonisation of privacy legislation is needed but is hardly achievable due to cultural differences. Therefore, privacy commissioners are demanding that privacy should be a design criterion and that more privacy-enhancing technologies have to be designed, implemented and used. In addition to privacy technologies for the protection of users, there is also a need for privacy enhancing technologies for protecting the data subjects, who are not necessarily system users.

In this thesis, the related areas of privacy, IT-security and privacy-enhancing technologies are presented, elaborated, analysed and discussed. The central part of this thesis is the presentation of a formal task-based privacy model, which can be used to technically enforce legal privacy requirements such as the necessity of personal data processing and purpose binding. In addition, it is specified how the privacy model policy has been implemented together with other security policies according to the Generalized Framework for Access Control (GFAC).

This thesis was submitted as a habilitation thesis at Hamburg University in Germany, where it was accepted by the habilitation committee in December 1999. Subsequently, updates have been made to reflect recent developments.

A number of persons have supported me during the time in which I wrote and completed this thesis. I would like to give my thanks to all of them:

I am especially grateful to Prof. Dr. Klaus Brunnstein, who introduced me to the field of IT security and taught me the importance of taking an holistic view. The discussions I had with him, his ideas, motivating spirit and practical support have been very valuable to me.

I also want to express my gratitude to my colleagues at the Copenhagen Business School (CBS). In particular, I thank Prof. Gert Bechlund, who invited me to be a Guest Professor at the Institute of Computer and System Sciences (DASY) at CBS from fall 1994 to spring 1995, and Prof. Lars Frank, for the interesting discussions we had while we were working together at CBS. I also thank CBS for having funded my research during the time of my guest professorship.

I also owe special thanks to my colleague Dr. Louise Yngström, who has always been a valuable discussion partner and good friend to me. I especially want to thank her for initiating my invitation as a Guest Professor at the Department of Computer and System Sciences (DSV) at Stockholm University / KTH, which was financed by the Swedish Research Council. At DSV, I also found time for completing this thesis. Therefore I also want to thank DSV for all of its support and for providing a very pleasant working atmosphere.

I also want to thank my former student and colleague Amon Ott, with whom I worked closely during the phase of specification and implementation of my privacy policy. He was mainly responsible for RSBAC system implementation and discussed with me my system specification. I have enjoyed working with him very much.

I would also like to thank Dr. Michael Sobirey for stimulating discussions and cooperation. Furthermore, I thank my colleagues Dr. Kathrin Schier, Fredrik Björck and Kjell Näckros for discussions, support and friendship, as well as all my other colleagues from IFIP Working Group 9.6 for having been knowledgeable discussion partners.

I am also grateful to a friend of my family, William Watts, who has polished my English. Any mistakes that I might have introduced by modifying the text after he had done his corrections are entirely my own.

I also want to thank the members of the habilitation committee at Hamburg University, and also in particular the external evaluators Prof. Dr. Dr. Gerald Quirchmayr (Univ. Vienna), Prof. Dr. Waltraut Gerhardt (TU Delft) and Prof. Dr. Andreas Pfitzmann (TU Dresden) as well as Prof. Dr. Klaus Brunnstein, who acted as an internal evaluator, for all the work and time they had to spend reading and evaluating this thesis.

Last but not least, I would like to thank my family to whom I dedicate this work. I am most grateful to my beloved parents Hermann and Helga Fischer-Hübner, who have always supported and motivated me. My father as a dedicated lawyer, who was committed to his profession and clients, raised my interest in law and taught me the importance of justice. Finally, I want to express my special thanks to my dear husband Etamar, who was always there for me with love, patience and care.

September 2000   Simone Fischer-Hübner

Table of Contents

1. Introduction 1

2. Privacy in the Global Information Society 5

  2.1 Definition of Privacy and Data Protection 5

  2.2 Historical Perspective on Data Protection Legislation 6

  2.3 Privacy Principles of the German Census Decision 8

  2.4 Basic Privacy Principles... 10

  2.5 The EU Directive on Data Protection.. 11

  2.6 German Data Protection Legislation 14

    2.6.1 The German Federal Data Protection Act
        (Bundesdatenschutzgesetz) 14

    2.6.2 Data Protection Regulations for Information and
        Telecommunication Services 17

  2.7 Threats to Privacy in the Global Networked Society 18

    2.7.1 Privacy Threats at Application Level 18

    2.7.2 Privacy Threats at Communication Level 20

    2.7.3 Insecure Technologies... 23

  2.8 Problems of an International Harmonisation of Privacy Legislation 24

  2.9 The Need for Privacy Enhancing Technologies.............................. 30

  2.10 The Importance of Privacy Education... 31

  2.11 Conclusions... 32

3. IT-Security 35

  3.1 Definition... 35

  3.2 Security Models 38

    3.2.1 Harrison-Ruzzo-Ullman Model.. 40

    3.2.2 Bell LaPadula Model 41

    3.2.3 Unix System V/MLS Security Policy.. 46

    3.2.4 Biba Model... 47

    3.2.5 Lattice Model of Information Flow... 49

3.2.6   Noninterference Security Model 51
3.2.7   Clark-Wilson Model... 52
3.2.8   Chinese Wall Model... 56
3.2.9   Role-Based Access Control Models... 58
3.2.10   Task-Based Authorisation Models for Workflow 65
          3.2.10.1 Workflow Authorisation Model (WAM)............................. 66
          3.2.10.2 Task-Based Authorisation Controls (TBAC) 68
3.2.11   Security Models for Object-Oriented Information Systems.......... 68
          3.2.11.1 The Authorisation Model by Fernandez et al. 69
          3.2.11.2 The Orion Authorisation Model 69
          3.2.11.3 The DORIS Personal Model of Data 70
          3.2.11.4 Further Relevant Research... 71
3.2.12   Resource Allocation Model for Denial of Service Protection 72
3.2.13   Multiple Security Policies Modelling Approaches....................... 75
          3.2.13.1 The Generalised Framework for Access Control (GFAC) 75
          3.2.13.2 The Multipolicy Paradigm and Multipolicy Systems 78

3.3   Basic Security Functions and Security Mechanisms.............................. 78
      3.3.1   Identification and User Authentication 78
      3.3.2   Access Control 79
      3.3.3   Auditing... 80
      3.3.4   Intrusion Detection Systems.. 81
      3.3.5   Object Reuse Protection 83
      3.3.6   Trusted Path 83
      3.3.7   Cryptography... 83
                3.3.7.1   Foundations 83
                3.3.7.2   Symmetric Algorithms 85
                3.3.7.3   Asymmetric Algorithms 87
                3.3.7.4   Hash Functions 88
                3.3.7.5   Certificates.. 88

3.4   Security Evaluation Criteria... 90
      3.4.1   The Rainbow Series (Orange Book et al.)............................... 91
      3.4.2   European Initiatives.. 93
                3.4.2.1   Overview 93
                3.4.2.2   The German Green Book....................................... 94
                3.4.2.3   The Information Technology Security Evaluation Criteria
                          (ITSEC) 94
      3.4.3   North American Initiatives.. 96
                3.4.3.1   CTCPEC.. 96
                3.4.3.2   MSFR 96
                3.4.3.3   Federal Criteria... 97
      3.4.4   International Harmonisation.. 97
                3.4.4.1   ISO Initiatives (ISO/IEC-ECITS)............................. 97
                3.4.4.2   The Common Criteria... 97
      3.4.5   Shortcomings of IT Security Evaluation Criteria..................... 101

3.5   Conflict between IT Security and Privacy 102
      3.5.1   Privacy Implications of IT Security Mechanisms 102

3.5.2   A Holistic Approach to a Privacy-Friendly Design and Use
        of Security Mechanisms 104

4. Privacy-Enhancing Technologies **107**

4.1 Privacy-Enhancing Security Aspects 107
  4.1.1   Privacy-Enhancing Security Aspects for Protecting the
          User Identities 107
    4.1.1.1 Anonymity 108
    4.1.1.2 Unobservability 109
    4.1.1.3 Unlinkability 110
    4.1.1.4 Pseudonymity 110
  4.1.2   Privacy-Enhancing Security Criteria for Protecting the
          Usee Identities 112
    4.1.2.1 Depersonalisation 112
    4.1.2.2 The Risk of Re-identification 113
  4.1.3   Privacy-Enhancing Security Aspects for Protecting
          Personal Data 119

4.2 System Concepts for Protecting User Identities 120
  4.2.1   The Identity Protector 120
  4.2.2   Protecting User Identities at Communication Level 121
    4.2.2.1 Recipient Anonymity through Message Broadcast and
             Implicit Addresses 122
    4.2.2.2 Dummy Traffic 122
    4.2.2.3 DC-Nets 123
    4.2.2.4 Mix-Nets 127
    4.2.2.5 Crowds 134
  4.2.3   Protecting User Identities at System Level 135
    4.2.3.1 Pseudonymous System Accounts 135
    4.2.3.2 Anonymous System Access and Use through Authorisation
             Certificates 135
  4.2.4   Protecting User Identities at Application Level 137
    4.2.4.1 Prepaid Cards 137
    4.2.4.2 Untraceable Electronic Money through Blind Signatures 137
  4.2.5   Protecting User Identities in Audit Data through
          Pseudonymous Auditing 141
    4.2.5.1 Functionality of Pseudonymous Auditing 142
    4.2.5.2 Pseudonymisation of User Identifying Data in
             Audit Records 143
    4.2.5.3 Pseudonymisation Techniques 145
  4.2.6   Protecting User Identities from other Users and Services 145
  4.2.7   The Need for Anonymity and the Problem of Its Potential
          Misuse 146

4.3 System Concepts for Protecting Usee Identities - Inference Controls
     for Statistical Database Systems 147

4.4 System Concepts and Mechanisms for Protecting Personal Data 152
    4.4.1 Steganographic Systems 153
    4.4.2 Access Control Models for Personal Data Protection 156
        4.4.2.1 Privacy Criteria for Security Models 156
        4.4.2.2 Privacy Evaluation of Security Models 157

4.5 Privacy Evaluation of IT Security Evaluation Criteria 163

4.6 Conclusions 164

5. A Task-Based Privacy Model 167

5.1 Introduction 167

5.2 Model Description 167
    5.2.1 Model Elements (State Variables) 167
    5.2.2 Model Invariants and Constraints (Privacy Properties) 174
        5.2.2.1 Privacy Invariants 174
        5.2.2.2 Privacy Constraints 175
    5.2.3 Model Rules (State Transition Functions) 175
        5.2.3.1 General Transition Functions 176
        5.2.3.2 Privileged Transition Functions 178

5.3 Information Flow Control 186

5.4 Revocation of Authorisations 194

5.5 Example: Application of the Privacy Model in a Hospital Information
    System 198

5.6 Analysis of the Privacy Model 199

6. Specification and Implementation of the Privacy Policy Following
    the Generalised Framework for Access Control-Approach 201

6.1 Introduction 201

6.2 The Specification of the Privacy Policy Rules Component 203
    6.2.1 Access Control Information (ACI) 204
    6.2.2 Access Control Enforcement Facility (AEF) and Its Interface
        to ADF 210
    6.2.3 Access Control Decision Facility (ADF) 227

6.3 Implementation 253
    6.3.1 RSBAC Implementation 253
    6.3.2 Integration of Heuristic Policy Rules 254

6.4 Outlook 256

7. Concluding Remarks 259

Appendix A: Formal Mathematical Privacy Model 261

1. Model Components.. 261

2. Privacy-Oriented System 264

3. Theorems 268

4. Formal Definition of the Model Rules.. 289

5. Proofs 304

**Appendix B: Implementation of a Hospital Scenario
as a Demonstration Example** 325

References...331

1 Introduction

Since the Clinton government in the United States has started the National Information Infrastructure Programme [US Government 1993], most other technologically developed countries have issued information infrastructure programmes for the further development of information highways and to strengthen the information and communication industry. A group of representatives, mainly from industry, under the chair of the vice-president of the European Union (EU) commission at that time, Martin Bangemann, elaborated a report and an action plan for the EU [Bangemann 1994] to carry Europe forward into the global information society.

The various national and global information infrastructure programmes promote different initiatives such as teleworking, distance teaching, research networks, road and air traffic management systems, electronic commerce, health care networks and network access to all households with applications such as video on demand. They are motivated mainly by economic interests and hold great promises, such as the generation of new jobs, economic growth, better chances for people constrained by geography or disability, possibilities to overcome structural problems such as in traffic or in health care. On the other hand, the new information infrastructure will change our lives completely, and it bears different risks for society [CPSR 1994], [Fischer-Hübner/Schier 1996a], [Fischer-Hübner/Schier 1996b], [Fischer-Hübner 1997a].

The Internet as a contemporary data highway on which the global information society may be built is known for many security risks. Thus, the vast development of new information infrastructures will increase our dependability and might lead us to a vulnerable information society based on insecure technologies.

Besides, individual privacy is seriously endangered and is becoming increasingly an international problem. The global information society is evolving rapidly and many new information highways and applications are being developed. For these applications, there is a growing amount of personal data, such as sensitive medical data, business data and private data that are collected and processed. For example, health care networks are planned and developed based on common standards (e.g., standardised electronic patient case files) linking general practitioners, hospitals and social centres on national and European scales. While modern health care networks can improve costs and effectiveness of the health care system, the patient´s privacy is affected and has to be protected. With the development of new health care networks, an increasing amount of sensitive medical data will be collected, stored, shared among different health care professionals and transferred to different sites in the world. Hence, it has to be guaranteed that only authorised personnel can have access to the patient´s medical information. In particular, it has to be guaranteed that users can only access/process personal data, if it is necessary for their authorised tasks (*privacy principle of necessity of data processing*) and if the purpose of data processing is compatible with the purposes for which the data is obtained (*privacy principle of purpose binding*). Besides, due respect has to be paid to the privacy principle of transparency so that patients still know who has access to their data and for what purposes.

Moreover, in the Global Information Society an increasing amount of transactional data for network services will be available and can be collected at different sites around the world. This data can be used to generate consumer and communication profiles. Privacy as a fundamental human right has to be protected in a democratic society. Recent surveys and polls show that users are concerned about privacy threats, and regard privacy as one most important issue facing the Internet (e.g., see Harris Poll/Business Week, March 16/1998, or the Graphic, Visualization, & Usability Center's (GVU) 8th WWW User Survey). In fact, according to opinion polls, concern about privacy violations is now greater than at any time in recent history [Davies 1997], [PI/EPIC 1999].

The final report on "Germany´s Way to the Information Society" of the Enquete-Commission of the German Parliament "The Future of the Media in Economy and Society", stresses the importance of efficient privacy protection also for economic reasons [BT-Drucksache 1998]. According to the report, most consumers would not use the new technologies if they had to fear that personal data about them would be collected and used for purposes others than they have consented to.

The EU Directive on Personal Data Protection [EU Directive 1995] is aimed at enforcing a relatively high standard of data protection and will probably not only be an instrument for harmonisation within Europe. It also has a coercive effect on countries outside Europe to enact efficient data protection laws based on the EU Directive. Since Art. 25 of the EU Directive restricts personal data transfer only to such countries outside the EU that have enforced an appropriate level of data protection, several mainly Eastern European states fearing trade barriers have meanwhile drafted data protection legislation according to the European model. Nevertheless, a global international harmonisation of privacy legislation in addition to the EU-Directive on data protection is hardly achievable due to cultural, political and historical differences. The recent EU - US privacy dispute, in which the US position has been opposed to set up an omnibus effective privacy legislation covering also the private sector and instead has favoured means of self-regulation, demonstrates this problem.

In conclusion, in the networked society privacy is seriously endangered and is becoming more and more an international problem. Privacy cannot be sufficiently protected solely by legislation. Thus, privacy should also be enforced by technologies and should be a design criterion for information and communication systems. More privacy enhancing technologies, which can technically enforce legal privacy requirements, have to be designed, implemented and used.

Within the last years, data protection commissioners (e.g., the Dutch Data Protection Authority (The Registratiekamer) in cooperation with the Information and Privacy Commissioner (IPC) for the Province of Ontario/ Canada [Registratiekamer/IPC 1995] and a working group of German data protection commissioners [DS-Beauftragte 1998] have elaborated reports on privacy enhancing technologies that protect personal privacy by minimising or eliminating the collection of identifiable data. Also the Privacy Class of the Common Criteria [CC 1999] is focused on anonymity, pseudonymity, unlinkability and unobservability of users.

Such privacy technologies for protecting user identities are important means to protect the users from traffic analysis and the creation of communication and user profiles.

Nevertheless, in addition to privacy technologies for the protection of users, there is also a need for privacy enhancing technologies to protect data subjects (the so-called usees[1]) that are not necessarily acting as system users at the same time (e.g., bank customers, patients). Personal data has to be protected by adequate IT security mechanisms. In particular, security mechanisms such as access control or encryption are needed to protect the confidentiality and integrity of personal data, if personal data has to be stored, processed or transmitted.

However, the following problems and misconceptions exist: First, security mechanisms can also affect the user´s privacy, because security mechanisms are control mechanisms that often have to collect and process personal control data about the users, which could be misused, e.g. for performance monitoring. This results in a conflict between security and privacy. Moreover, today´s security models for access control are mainly not appropriate to enforce basic privacy requirements, such as necessity of data or purpose binding.

For this reason, a formal task-based privacy model has been developed, which can be used to technically enforce legal privacy requirements, such as necessity of data processing or purpose binding, in a system. The privacy model is defined as a state machine model and it has been formally proven that the model is consistent with its axioms. Furthermore, it has been specified how the privacy policy can be enforced according to the Generalized Framework for Access Control (GFAC) approach in Unix System V. In a further project, this (top-level) specification was then used and adapted for the implementation and integration of the privacy policy according to the GFAC-approach together with other security policies in the Linux operating system.

According to the task-based privacy model policy, access control decisions are dependent on the current tasks that users are performing and not on the user identities. With the help of authorisation certificates, the task-based privacy model can be used to enforce access control also for anonymous users. If it is used for anonymous access control, the collection and use of user-related control information will be avoided. Thereby, it can also support the user´s privacy protection and can hence effectively address the conflict between security and privacy.

A central part of this thesis (habilitation thesis) is the presentation of the formal task-based privacy model and the top-level specification of the privacy model policy rules component as part of a security kernel designed according to the GFAC-approach. The privacy model can be used as the basis for a privacy enhancing design and use of access control mechanisms.

Besides, the author wants to present, elaborate, analyse and discuss (and thereby also contribute to) the related areas of privacy, IT-security and privacy-enhancing technologies. General approaches to a privacy enhancing system design and further approaches to a privacy-friendly design and use of security mechanisms (e.g., anonymous access control, pseudonymous auditing) are discussed in particular.

The second Chapter "Privacy in the Global Information Society" of this thesis defines privacy and basic privacy principles and discusses privacy risks in the global

---

[1] A usee is a person about whom the IT-System produces and processes data, and who has usually no control over this process

information society. It also compares and critically analyses the approaches to privacy protection of different countries that have issued information infrastructure programmes. The difficulties for a common harmonised legal approach to privacy protection, due to cultural differences, are analysed. Thus, the need for data protection by IT security mechanisms and particularly the need for privacy-enhancing technologies is illustrated.

The third Chapter "IT-Security" discusses well-known security models and gives an introduction to basic security functions and IT-Security Evaluation Criteria. This discussion provides the basis for a subsequent analysis on how far state of the art security models and techniques are adequate and capable to protect personal data. Two key problems concerning the relation between security and privacy are addressed. The first problem, which is discussed in Chapter 4 in more detail, is that today's security models are more or less inadequate for personal data protection. The second problem, the conflict between security and privacy, is discussed at the end of Chapter 3 and an holistic approach to a conflict resolution is proposed.

Chapter four "Privacy-Enhancing Technologies" first provides definitions for privacy-enhancing security aspects for protecting user identities, for protecting usee identities and for protecting personal data. It then gives an overview to and classification of system concepts for protecting user identities at communication level, at system level and at application level. Furthermore system concepts for protecting user identities are briefly addressed. Finally, system concepts and mechanisms for protecting personal data are discussed. In particular, the security models for access control, which were introduced in Chapter 3, are evaluated according to certain privacy criteria and it is shown that none of them is capable to meet all those basic privacy criteria.

Then, in Chapter five "A Task-based Privacy Model" the formal task-based privacy model is presented by defining its state variables, privacy invariants, privacy constraints and state transition functions.

Chapter six "Specification and Implementation of the Privacy Policy following the GFAC-Approach" provides a top-level specification of the privacy policy rules component, which is part of a Unix system security kernel designed according to the GFAC approach. Besides, it briefly outlines how this specification was used and adapted for the implementation of the privacy policy in combination with further security policies in the Linux operating system.

In Chapter seven "Concluding Remarks", the most important results are summarised and an outlook is given.

Appendix A presents the formal mathematical privacy model as a state machine model. It gives a definition of a privacy-oriented system and formally proves that the system defined by the formal privacy model is privacy-oriented.

Appendix B provides an example how a system implementing the privacy model could be used to protect personal patient data in a hospital information system.

2 Privacy in the Global Information Society

Privacy as a social and legal issue has for a long time been a concern of social scientists, philosophers, and lawyers. With the arrival of the computer and increasing capabilities of modern IT-systems and communication networks, individual privacy is increasingly endangered. Especially on the way to a Global Information Society with different national programmes for the further development of data highways, there are severe privacy risks. Privacy as a fundamental human right recognised in the UN Declaration of Human Rights, the International Convenant on Civil and Political Rights and in many other international and regional treaties [PI/EPIC 1999] has to be protected in a democratic society.

In general, privacy protection can be undertaken by

- privacy and data protection laws promoted by government

- self-regulation for fair information practices by codes of conducts promoted by businesses

- privacy-enhancing technologies adopted by individuals

- privacy education of consumers and IT professionals.

In this Chapter, privacy risks and means of privacy protection are discussed and analysed. In the first part, a definition of privacy and an overview to privacy legislation is given. Then, privacy risks in the Global Information Society are discussed, and it is shown that privacy is becoming more and more an international problem. For this reason, an international harmonisation of privacy legislation besides the EU Directive on data protection is needed. However, it shows that, due to cultural, political and historical differences, there are significant deviations in the EU approach to privacy protection from the privacy regulations of other countries, which have developed information infrastructure programmes. Although the EU Directive on Data Protection might have a coercive effect also on countries outside the EU to enact efficient data protection legislation based on the EU Directive, a common international harmonised approach seems hardly feasible. Therefore, it is argued that besides privacy protection by legislation and code of conducts, privacy enhancing technologies as a means to technically enforce legal privacy requirements are becoming increasingly important. Finally, the importance of privacy education complementary to privacy enhancing technologies is pointed out.

2.1 Definition of Privacy and Data Protection

The first definition of *privacy* was given by Samuel D. Warren and Louis D. Brandeis in their famous article "The Right to Privacy", which appeared in the Harvard Law Review [Warren/Brandeis 1890]. The two American lawyers defined privacy *as "the right to be alone".* The reason for this publication was the development of new forms of technologies that was coupled with other developments. Photography used by the yellow press was in the view of the authors an attack on personal privacy in the sense of the right to be alone.

The most common definition of privacy in current use is the one by Alan Westin:

> *"Privacy is the claim of individuals, groups and institutions to determine for themselves, when, how and to what extent information about them is communicated to others"* [Westin 1967].

According to Westin's definition, natural (individuals) as well as legal persons (groups and institutions) have a right to privacy. In some countries, like France, Austria, Denmark, the juridical concept of privacy protection is extended to groups and institutions, whereas in most others, like in Germany, the USA or the U.K., it is restricted to individuals.

In general, the concept of privacy can be given three aspects [Rosenberg 1992]; [Holvast 1993]:

* *territorial privacy* (by protecting the close physical area surrounding a person, i.e. domestic and other environments such as the workplace or public space);

* *privacy of the person* (by protecting a person against undue interference, such as physical searches, drug testing or information violating his/her moral sense); and

* *informational privacy* (by controlling whether and how personal data can be gathered, stored, processed or selectively disseminated).

Personal data means any information concerning the personal or material circumstances of an identified or identifiable person (the data subject). The emphasis of this Chapter and of this thesis is on the discussion of informational privacy of individuals. Individual informational privacy has also been defined by the German Constitutional Court in its Census Decision of 1983 as the term *right of informational self-determination*, meaning *the right of an individual to determine the disclosure and use of his personal data on principle at his discretion.*

Data protection is the protection of personal data in order to guarantee privacy and is only a part of the concept of privacy. Privacy, however, is not an unlimited or absolute right, as it can be in conflict with other rights or legal values, and because individuals cannot participate fully in society without revealing personal data. Privacy and Data Protection laws shall help to protect privacy rights, if personal data is collected, stored or processed.

2.2 Historical Perspective on Data Protection Legislation

The interest in privacy increased in the 1960's and 1970's with the advent of Information Technology and its obvious surveillance potential.

In 1970, the very first modern Data Protection Act was adopted by the Parliament of the West German state Hesse and served as a basis for the adoption of similar laws by other German states, the West German Federal government as well as governments outside Germany. Sweden's Data Act, which was passed in 1973, was the first national data protection act in the world. The development of the German Federal Data Protection Act (Bundesdatenschutzgesetz: BDSG) started in 1973, when potential abuses arising from the automatic data processing of personal data and the need of legal privacy regulations had become obvious. In 1977, the German Parliament, the Bundestag, adopted the German Federal data protection act (BDSG). It was amended in 1990 to meet the privacy requirements, which had been set up by the German constitutional court in its census decision. These data protection acts were followed in Europe by laws enacted in France, Austria, Denmark and Norway in 1978 and in Luxembourg in 1979.

In the USA, the Privacy Act was adopted by the Congress in 1974 as an acknowledgement that the development of complex information systems posed a threat to personal privacy, especially after abuses by Federal Government had been experienced during the McCarthy era. The US Congress also passed the Fair Credit Reporting Act in 1970.

The Organization for Economic Cooperation and Development (OECD) had early recognised privacy problems and implications of transborder flows of personal data. In 1980, the OECD adopted its *Guidelines on the Protection of Privacy and Transborder Flows of Personal Data*, which should help to harmonise the different national laws and enforce some minimum degree of privacy protection amongst member countries. The OECD Guidelines helped to raise the international awareness of the importance of data protection. However, the OECD Guidelines are advisory in nature and not legally binding on its members. The OECD Guidelines were open for adoption by companies and organisations in the member states as a means of self-regulation [Madsen 1992].

In 1981, the Council of Europe adopted the *Convention for the Protection of Individuals with Regard to Automatic Processing of Personal Data*, which is legally binding on any member state that ratifies it. The adoption of the convention forced members, such as the UK and Ireland, to pass data protection legislation in order to permit ratification.

The Council of Europe Convention and the OECD Guidelines have a profound effect on the adoption of laws around the world. The rules within these documents form the core of data protection laws of dozens of countries [PI/EPIC 1999].

The United Nations (UN) considers the adoption of international data protection guidelines as a natural extension of the 1966 International Covenant on Civil and Political Rights. The *Guidelines Concerning Computerized Personal Data Files* were adopted by the General Assembly on 14 December 1990.

In July 1990, the European Community issued the first draft proposal for a Directive on Personal Data Protection, which was later revised. At that time, only seven EC members had adopted effective data protection legislation, while the remaining five had failed to comply with the Council of Europe Convention [Madsen 1992]. Besides the privacy protection of individuals, another objective of the Directive was to require a uniform minimum standard of privacy protection to prevent restrictions on free flow of personal data between EU member states for reasons of privacy protection.

The final *EU Directive 95/46/EC on the protection of individuals with regard to the processing of personal data and on the free movement of such data* [EU Directive 1995] was formally adopted in 1995 by the European Council. EU member states were supposed to revise their respective national laws (where necessary) to comply with the requirements of the directive by October 1998.

The *EU Directive 97/66/EC on Dataprotection in Telecommunications* [EU Telecommunications Directive 1997] was adopted in December 1997. It should harmonise privacy regulations in the telecommunication sector in the EU and should ensure privacy of user´s communications.

2.3 Privacy Principles of the German Census Decision

Important privacy principles were formulated in the Census Decision (Volkszählungsurteil) of the German Federal Constitutional Court (Bundesverfassungsgericht) in December 1983 (see [BVerfG, NJW, 1984, p. 419]). The German Census Law was ruled unconstitutional by the Constitutional Court, because basic privacy principles derived from the German constitution, especially the privacy requirement of purpose binding, were not considered in the plans for the census. In order to enforce the privacy principles formulated in the Census Decision, the German Federal Data Protection Act, data protection acts of the states as well as further laws with privacy regulations had to be amended and further more specific privacy regulations had to be passed.

The German Constitutional Court postulates privacy as the *right of informational self-determination*, which is derived from the basic rights formulated in Art. 1 I (principle of human dignity) and Art. 2 I (right of free development of personality) of the German Constitution (Grundgesetz: GG). This constitutional right of informational self-determination guarantees the permission of an individual to determine on principle himself on the disclosure and use of his personal information. The Human dignity of a person, who can freely develop as a part of a free society, is regarded as the highest legal value of the German constitutional system (see [BVerfGE 45, pp. 187]). Therefore, also the right of informational self-determination belongs to the highest legal values.

Furthermore, the Constitutional Court argued that this constitutional right is essential to protect the individual as well as the free democratic basic order:

"Who cannot certainly overlook which information related to him is known to certain segments of his social environment, and who is not able to assess to a certain degree the knowledge of his potential communication partners, can be essentially hindered in his capability to plan and to decide. The right of informational self-determination stands against a societal order and its underlying legal order in which citizens could not know any longer who what and when in what situations knows about them."

If it is not transparent to someone who else is knowing what about him and whether any deviant behaviour is monitored and registered, this person might try to behave so as not to attract attention. For example, if someone does not know if he is monitored while participating in a political meeting, he might prefer not to attend this meeting. This, however, also affects the free democratic order, which is based on free actions, social and political collaboration of the citizens.

However, the right of informational self-determination is not an absolute right and cannot be guaranteed unlimited, as it can be in conflict with other constitutional rights or legal values. Therefore, exemptions from this right of informational self-determination are permitted in case of a predominant public interest. Such exemptions have to be permitted by a constitutional law, which has especially to follow the *principle of clarity of the law* (*"Gebot der Normenklarheit"*) and the *principle of proportionateness* (*"Verhältnismäßigkeitsgrundsat"*). Both principles are derived from the *principle of the rule of law* (*"Rechtsstaatsprinzip"*). The privacy principles of necessity of data collection and processing, purpose binding and informational separation of power are in turn derived from the principle of proportionateness.

According to the principle of clarity of the law, the restricting law has to make clear under which conditions and to what extent restrictions on the constitutional right are permitted.

According to the principle of proportionateness, any measure affecting a constitutional basic right has to be suitable (*principle of suitability* – *"Geeignetheit"*) to achieve its objective and has to be necessary for its purpose (*principle of necessity* – *"Erforderlichkeit"*). Besides, restrictions imposed on the citizens have to be in proper relations to the significance of the purpose (*principle of proportionateness in the stricter sense* – *"Verhältnismäßigkeit im engerem Sinne"*).

The principle of **necessity of data collection and processing** (which is part of the principle of proportionateness) is satisfied, if there is no alternative means, which can achieve the objective of the data collection and processing just as good, but is less affecting the right of informational self-determination. For example, in the census decision the constitutional court discussed whether a mandatory statistical survey collecting information on the whole population is necessary, or whether a voluntary statistical survey or a survey collecting information on a sample of the population, could be just as effective.

The principle of proportionateness of data collection or processing in the stricter sense, depends among others, on the sensitivity of the personal data to be collected or processed. However, the sensitivity of personal data does not only depend on how „intimate" the details are, which the personal data is describing. The sensitivity of personal data is also mainly influenced by its purpose and context of use. In its census decision the German Constitutional Court proclaimed that there was no non-sensitive data, as dependent on the purpose and context of use all kinds of personal data can become sensitive. There is personal data that *per se* already contain sensitive information (e.g. medical data), but dependent on the purpose and context of use, such sensitive data can become even more sensitive and data that seems to be non-sensitive (e.g. addresses) can become highly sensitive as well.

For example, audit data, which an operating system is recording to detect and to deter intruders, could be (mis-)used for monitoring the performance of the users (see also Chapter 3.6). Thus, if audit data was used not only for security purposes, but also for work place monitoring, the audit data would become more sensitive.

Therefore, the Constitutional Court requires that the privacy principles of **purpose specification** and **purpose binding** ("Zweckbindung") have to be enforced: If personal data is to be collected or processed, the law maker has to specify the purposes which the data is to serve precisely for each application area. Personal data has to be suitable and necessary for these purposes. Personal data may then only be collected and used for these legitimate purposes as specified by the law.

The principle of **informational separation of power** is derived from the requirement that purposes of use have to be specified for each application area and from further restrictions placed on the passing on and further processing of personal data, as formulated in the census decision. According to the informational separation of power principle, personal data should be divided among different authorities and should not be linked. By this means, the individual shall be protected against total registration and classification of his personality.

As discussed above, the Constitutional Court has argued that a society, in which citizens could not know any longer who, what and when, and in which situations knows about them, would be contradictory to the right of informational self-determination. Thus, the privacy principle of **transparency of personal data processing** has to be guaranteed for the data subjects. Therefore, data subjects should have extensive information and access rights.

Furthermore, the Constitutional Court demands **adequate organisational and administrative measures** to protect the right of informational self-determination. In particular, organisational and technical security mechanisms have to be taken to protect the confidentiality and integrity of personal data.

2.4 Basic Privacy Principles

In order to protect the right of informational self-determination, national privacy laws, codes of conduct, codes of ethics of different computer societies, as well as, international privacy guidelines or directives, require basic privacy principles to be guaranteed when personal data is collected or processed.

In this Section, the most essential privacy requirements are summarised. Most of these privacy requirements were also formulated by the German Constitutional Court and are required by the German Federal Data Protection Act, by most other western data protection acts and by the EU-Directive on Data Protection, the UN Guidelines, and (for the most part) by the OECD-Guidelines:

- **Principle of lawfulness and fairness:** Personal data should be collected and processed in a fair and lawful way;

- **Principle of the purpose specification and purpose binding (also called purpose limitation):** The purposes for which personal data is collected and processed should be specified and legitimate. The subsequent use of personal data is limited to those specified purposes, unless there is an informed consent by the data subject;

- **Principle of necessity of data collection and processing:** The collection and processing of personal data should only be allowed, if it is necessary for the tasks falling within the responsibility of the data processing agency;

- **Information, notification and access rights of the data subjects:** Data subjects have the right to information, to notification and the right to correction, erasure or blocking of incorrect or illegally stored data. These rights should not be excluded or restricted by a legal transaction. Information and notification rights help to provide transparency of data processing;

- **Principle of security and accuracy:** Appropriate technical and organisational security mechanisms have to be taken to guarantee the confidentiality, integrity, and availability of personal data. Personal data has to be kept accurate, relevant and up to date;

- **Supervision and sanctions:** An independent data protection authority (also called supervisory authority, data protection commissioner or ombudsman) has to be designated and should be responsible for supervising the observance of privacy provisions. In the event of violation of the provisions of privacy legislation, criminal or other penalties should be envisaged.

According to the privacy principle of necessity of data collection and processing, personal data should not be collected or used for identification purposes when not truly necessary. Consequently, information systems should guarantee, if possible, that users can act anonymously. The best design strategy to enforce this requirement is the **avoidance or** (at least) **minimisation of personal data**. Thus, the requirement for privacy enhancing technologies is actually derived from the basic privacy principle of necessity of data collection and processing.

2.5 The EU Directive on Data Protection

The *EU Directive on the protection of individuals with regard to the processing of personal data and on the free movement of such data* [EU Directive 1995] was formally adopted in October 1995 by the European Council. Member states of the EU were supposed to amend their respective national laws (where necessary) to conform with the directive by October 1998. The main objective of the Directive is the protection of privacy as a fundamental right, which is increasingly endangered in the networked society. Another objective of the EU Directive is to require a uniform minimum standard of privacy protection to prevent restrictions on free flow of personal data between EU member states for reasons of privacy protection. The EU Data Protection Directive aims for a high level of protection. In October 1995, there were still two EU member states (Greece, Italy), that had not enacted a data protection act. Difference in levels of data protection in the member states may prevent the transmission of personal data from the territory of one member state to that of another member state and may therefore be an obstacle to the implementation of the European market.

The Directive contains a combination of concepts, which are enforced by the data protection legislation of different member states. For example, the concept of registration of processing operations (Art. 18) is enforced in the British, French and Scandinavian data protection legislation (among others). The concept of a data protection official inside an organisation (Art. 18, 20) was taken from the German Federal data protection act and the concept of special protection of special categories of data (Art. 8) was taken from the French, Irish and Scandinavian legislation. Rules for industrial self-regulation of personal data systems (Codes of conduct, Art. 27) were taken from the Dutch system. However, the EU Directive was mainly influenced by the German system and is most similar to the German legislation (see also [Walz 1998]).

The EU Directive is divided into seven chapters:
Chapter I provides definitions and covers the scope of the Directive. The EU Directive makes no differentiation between rules applied in the public and in the private sector. According to Article 3 (1), the Directive applies "to the processing of personal data wholly or partly by automatic means, and to the processing otherwise

than by automatic means of personal data which forms part of a filing system or is intended to form part of a filing system". A filing system is defined as "any structures set of personal data " (Art. 2. (c)). However, processing in the course of activities falling outside Community law is exempted (Art. 3 (2)), including "Processing operations concerning public security, defence, State security and activities of the State in the areas of criminal law". Processing by a natural person in the course "of a purely personal and household activity" is exempted as well (Art, 3 (2)).

Chapter II ("General rules on the lawfulness of the processing of personal data") sets out privacy principles, which were partly mentioned above in section 2.4. "Principles relating to data quality" formulated in Art.6 are enforcing the privacy principles of lawfulness and fairness, of purpose specification and purpose binding and of accuracy. The "Criteria of making data processing legitimate" (Art.7) is enforcing the privacy principle of necessity of data processing. According to Art.7, personal data may be processed if the data subject has consented or if the processing is necessary for the performance of a contract with the data subject, for compliance with legal obligations, for the protection of vital interests of the data subject, for the performance of a task carried out in public interest or if it is necessary for the purpose of legitimate interests by the controller unless these interests are overridden by the data subject´s privacy interest. According to Article 8, the processing of special categories of personal data revealing racial or ethnic origin, political opinions, religious or philosophical beliefs, trade union membership or aspects of health or sex life is generally prohibited, subject to exemptions. Extensive information and access rights of the data subjects as well as the right of the data subjects to object are formulated in Art. 10-14. The data subject´s right of access must also include a right to know the "logic involved" in any such automated decisions (Art. 12 (1)). The principle of security of processing is formulated in Art. 17. The national supervising authority must be notified in advance of any automated processing operations (Art. 18-19). Simplification or exemption from notification is allowed, where the organisation concerned has appointed an independent data protection official (Art. 18 (2)). The notified data is to be used so that a register can be kept by the supervisory authority or by the data protection official, and may be inspected by any person (Art. 21). Besides, prior checks of processing operations likely to present specific risks shall be carried out by the supervisory authority or by the data protection official following receipt of a notification.

These general rules could be used to enforce a relatively good level of data protection in Europe. However, it has also been criticised that some rules (especially the criteria for making data processing legitimate - Article 7) are very general and allow a variety of specific implementations in national laws. These differences in interpretation could hinder the goal of reducing divergences between national laws.

Besides, it is criticised that many rules of the EU Directive include exceptions that are mandatory and may hinder states in providing a stricter standard of privacy protection [Greenleaf 1995].

The methods by which these general rules defined in *Chapter II* are to be enforced in national law and by the EU are set out in *Chapter III* ("Judicial remedies, liabilities and penalties"), *Chapter V* ("Codes of Conduct"), *Chapter VI* ("Supervisory authority and Working Party...") and *Chapter VII* ("Community implementing measures"). According to Art. 27 of *Chapter V*, codes of conduct are to be encouraged, and national laws are to make provisions for trade associations and other bodies to submit them to the national supervisory authorities for opinion as to whether they comply with national laws. Such codes of conduct allow businesses to promote self-regulation for fair information practices. However, such codes are to "contribute to the proper implementation of the national provisions" (Art. 27 (1)), but they cannot in themselves satisfy the requirements of the Directive.

According to Art. 28 of *Chapter VI*, one or more public authorities must be responsible for monitoring the application of the Directive ("supervisory authority"). The supervisory authorities must be independent, must have investigative powers, effective powers of interventions, and powers to take court action where national legislation implementing the Directive is infringed (Art. 28 (3)). Besides, member states are to consult the supervisory authorities when developing administrative measures or regulations with privacy implications. In total, these provisions require a greater range of powers and responsibilities for the supervisory authorities than exist within most European data protection regimes [Bennett 1997].

Chapter IV ("Transfer of personal data to third countries") contains provisions for the transfer of personal data to third countries outside the EU. According to Article 25 (1), the export of personal data to third countries, which do not provide an adequate level of protection, is generally prohibited, subject to exemptions formulated in Art. 26. Only an "adequate" and not an equivalent protection is required. The question of adequacy of the level of protection afforded by a third country depends on the nature of the data, the purpose and duration of the proposed processing operations, the country of origin and the country of final destination, the rules of law in the third country in question and the professional rules and security measures which are complied within that third country (Art. 25 (2)).

Since in the USA, there is no national comprehensive privacy law for the private sector and there is no independent supervisory authority designated to monitor the observance of privacy provisions, it can be argued that the USA does not provide an adequate level of data protection. However, the Directive allows the possibility that adequate "professional rules and security mechanisms" may be sufficient or that satisfactorily agreed upon procedures may do as well. Thus, special arrangements could be made between US companies and the EU for the protection of personal data. In the present US political climate, there seems to be little inclination to enact comprehensive privacy legislation (see also [Rosenberg, 1997]). US American decision makers are favouring means of self-regulation and specific sectoral laws in the private sector instead of comprehensive legislative privacy regulations (see also Section 2.8). Besides, there is the fundamental problem that in open and free networks, such as the Internet, with no central agency of control, it is technically difficult and even virtually impossible to enforce this requirement [Koch 1995].

The EU Telecommunications Directive [EU Telecommunications Directive 1997] imposes obligations on carriers and service providers to protect the privacy of users´ communication. The new rules severely restrict marketing activities as well as access to billing data. Besides, it is required that Caller ID technology must incorporate an option for per-line blocking of number transmission. Furthermore, information collected in the delivery of communication must be destroyed once the call is completed.

2.6 German Data Protection Legislation

2.6.1 The German Federal Data Protection Act (Bundesdatenschutzgesetz)

The Federal Republic of Germany was the second European nation to adopt a comprehensive data protection law. The interest in Germany for privacy and data protection was in large part due to Germany's past history of personal data abuses. The German public realised that the new information processing technologies generated severe risks of potential personal data abuses. The result of these concerns was the introduction of data protection legislation in the German parliament, the *Bundestag*.

The Federal Data Protection Act (*Bundesdatenschutzgesetz*, BDSG) was passed by the *Bundestag* on January 27, 1977 and entered into force on January 1, 1978. Some years later, the BDSG had to be revised, as it did not satisfy all privacy principles, which had been formulated in the Census Decision of German Constitutional Court. In particular, the BDSG of 1978 only applied in so far as personal data was processed or used in or from data files, and there were no provisions for the collection of personal data. Besides, the fundamental privacy principle of purpose binding was not enforced. A revised German Federal Data Protection Law entered into force on June 1, 1991. After the adoption of the EU-Directive, further revisions were necessary to meet the requirements of the Directive (see below). A draft revision of the BDSG was approved by the German Government on June 14, 2000.

Important provisions of the BDSG enacted in 1991 that were kept by the draft BDSG of June 2000 include the following regulations:

According to § 1 I BDSG, the general purpose of the BDSG is "to protect the individual against violations of his personal right (*Persönlichkeitsrecht*) by handling person-related data".

The BDSG applies to Federal authorities and administrations, as well as to the private sector. Public authorities that come under the purview of the Federal states must comply with the requirements of the Data Protection law of each individual state (*Bundesland*). All of the 16 *Bundesländer* have their own specific data protection regulations that apply to the public sector of the *Länder* administration.

Other legal provisions of the Federation, which are applicable to personal data, shall take precedence over the provisions of the Federal Data Protection Act.

Part I of the BDSG sets out general provisions for data processing and data protection applying for both private and public sector. In particular, it contains rules on the general admissibility of data processing and use (§ 4 BDSG), inalienable rights of data subjects (§ 6 BDSG), compensation (§ 7, 8 BDSG), necessary technical and organisational measures to be taken when personal data is processed (§ 9 BDSG + Annex), as well as rules on the establishment of automated retrieval procedures (§ 10 BDSG) and rules on the commissioned processing or use of personal data (§ 11 BDSG).

Part II of the BDSG defines the legal basis for data processing by public bodies, whereas *Part III* defines regulations for the data processing by private bodies and public-law enterprises participating in competition.

Both parts set up differing rules for the admissibility of data processing, rights of the data subjects, as well as for the supervision of the data protection act.

Furthermore, *Part III* sets up different rules for the admissibility of personal data processing in dependence on whether personal data is processed for own purposes or in the normal course of business for the purpose of communication (e.g., personal data processing for market research, or personal data processing by credit reference agencies).

§§ 13 - 16 BDSG of *Part II* regulate the admissibility of data collection, storage, modification and use of data in the public sector as well as communication of data from the public bodies to public and to private bodies. These regulations are enforcing the privacy principles of purpose specification and binding, and of necessity of data collection and processing.

According to § 13 I BDSG, the collection of personal data shall be admissible if knowledge of it is needed to perform the duties of the bodies collecting it. According to § 13 II of the BDSG enacted in 1991, personal data, on principle, should be collected from the data subject with his knowledge and in this case he should be informed of the purpose of the collection. In the June 2000 draft the latter provision is replaced by § 4 II that also applies to the data processing by private bodies.

According to § 14 BDSG the storage, modification or use of personal data shall be admissible where it is necessary for the performance of the tasks of the controller of the data file and if it serves the purposes for which the data was collected. Some exceptions are formulated when the storage, modification or use for other purposes shall be admissible. One exception, for example, is made if the data subject has consented.

Also, the communication of personal data has to be necessary and the recipient may on principle only process or use the communicated data for the purposes for which they were communicated (§§ 15, 16 BDSG).

The Federal Data Protection Commissioner (*Bundesbeauftragter für den Datenschutz,* see §§ 22 -26 BDSG) is responsible for the supervision of the Data Protection Act. There are also Data Protection Commissioners (*Landesdatanschutzbeauftragte*) in each of the federal states (*Bundesländer)* who monitor compliance with the provisions of the Land data protection law (*Landesdatenschutzgesetze).* Supervision for the private sector, however, is carried out by a Supervisory Authority (§ 38 BDSG) in each *Bundesland* designated by the Land data protection law. Besides, according to the BDSG of 1991, private bodies who process personal data automatically and regularly employ at least five permanent employees for this purpose have to appoint a data protection officer (*Betrieblicher Datenschutzbeauftragter*), who is responsible for ensuring that data protection provisions are observed (§ 36). According to § 4 f of the June draft, both private and public bodies that process personal data automatically have to appoint a data protection officer.

Part IV of the BDSG contains special provisions, e.g. for the processing and use of personal data by research institutes and by the press. *Part V* defines criminal offences, administrative offences and sanctions for those who violate the data protection provisions.

As noted above, changes to the Federal Data Protection Law to make it consistent with the EU Directive became necessary. EU member states were supposed to amend and revise their data protection regulation to comply with the EU Directive by October 1998. For this purpose, the former German Christian Democratic/ Liberal Government had worked out a draft revised Federal Data Protection Act [BDSG-Referentenentwurf 1997] that was, however, criticised by the opposition and by members of the government. As it was impossible to come to an agreement, it was decided to postpone the discussion and enactment of a revised Federal Data Protection Act until after the German elections (that took place in autumn 1998).

As the EU Directive sets up equal rules for the private and the public sector, several amendments had to be done. Major changes were necessary to meet the requirements of the EU Directive and that were already proposed in [BDSG-Referentenentwurf 1997] include:

- Additional regulations for personal data collection also for the private sector
- New explicit restrictions for the processing of special categories of "sensitive" personal data
- New rules allowing the transfer of personal data to third countries outside the EU only if the third country in question has an appropriate level of data protection or if certain exceptions apply
- New requirement to appoint a data protection officer also for public authorities (*Betrieblicher und Behördlicher Datenschutzbeauftragter*)
- Exemption from the obligation of the controller to notify the data protection commissioner or supervisory authority before carrying out automatic data processing, if the controller has appointed a data protection officer.
- New rules for the prior checking and analysis of personal data processing operations to present specific risks
- New rules disallowing decisions which produce legal effects concerning a person or significantly affects him to be based solely on automated data processing
- More rights for the data subjects (e.g., right to object, right to notification also for personal data processing in the public sector)
- More rights and a better legal position for the data protection commissioner and supervisory authorities
- Review and modernisation of the annex to § 9 BDSG

A counter-proposal for an amendment of the BDSG, which had been worked out by the German Green Party [Bündnis90/die Grünen 1997], demands that the BDSG should be modernised to cope with privacy threats posed by modern technologies such as the Internet or other communication networks, CD-ROM collections, multifunctional chipcards and modern video technology. Also a position paper by the parliamentarian group of the Social Democratic Party [SPD-Bundestagsfraktion 1998] demanded that the required review of the BDSG should also be taken as a chance to react to new technological risks. Both proposals therefore formulated new regulations that were already enforced by *Federal Information and Communication Services Act* (Informations- und Kommunikationsdienste-Gesetz - IuKDG) and the *Interstate Agreement on Media Services* (Mediendienste-Staatsvertrag, MDStV) (see below). These included the requirement for a privacy-enhanced design of Information & Communication Technologies (particularly by enforcing the principle of data avoidance and data minimisation), as well as rules for a Privacy-Audit ("Datenschutz-Audit"). According to the rule for a Privacy-Audit, service providers and data processing agencies have the possibility to request the evaluation of their privacy concept and of their technical systems by an independent and authorised expert (see also below). Also the report "Germany´s Way to the Information Society" published by the Enquete-Commission "The Future of the Media in Economy and Society" of the German Parliament emphasised the necessity and importance of such regulations [BT-Drucksache 1998]. The proposal by the Green Party also included regulations for chipcards containing personal data, for video monitoring and surveillance and for the automatic publishing of personal data (e.g. on CD-ROMS or Web pages).

The Ministry of the Interior of the new Social-Democratic/Green Government worked out a new draft amendment of the Federal Data Protection Act, which was published in 1999 [BMI 1999]. This amendment was then revised and approved by the German Federal Government on June 14, 2000 [BDSG-Novellierungsentwurf 2000]. Besides revisions proposed in [Referentenentwurf 1997] and regulations for video monitoring, the June 2000 draft also includes regulations for

- **Data avoidance and minimisation (§ 3a):** The design and selection of data processing systems shall be oriented to the goal of collecting, processing and using either no personal data at all or as little data as possible. In particular, methods of anonymisation and pseudonymisation should be used, if the effort involved is reasonable in relation to the desired level of protection.

- **Privacy-Audit (§ 9b):** Service providers and data processing agencies should have the possibility to request the evaluation of their privacy concept and of their technical systems by an independent and authorised expert. Besides, they should have the possibility to publish the evaluation results (for advertisement purposes). Further procedures for evaluation and authorisation of experts have to be regulated by special law.

2.6.2 Data Protection Regulations for Information and Telecommunication Services

Recently, online services and multimedia applications have become increasingly widespread and pose specific privacy risks. Obviously, the BDSG as a general data protection law is not sufficient to effectively control the risks associated with the new technical possibilities and forms of use.

Therefore, the *Federal Information and Communication Services Act* (Informations- und Kommunikationsdienste-Gesetz - IuKDG) and the *Interstate Agreement on Media Services* (Mediendienste-Staatsvertrag, MDStV) were enacted, which both entered into force on 1 August 1997 and set out specific data protection provisions for Information and Telecommunication Services. IuKDG and MDStV were among the first laws that particularly demand to enforce the privacy principle of avoidance or minimisation of data collection, and, for this reason, shall be discussed in more detail in this Section.

The IuKDG consists of the Teleservices (Teledienstegesetz, TDG), the Teleservices Data Protection Act (Teledienstedatenschutzgesetz, TDDSG), the Digital Signature Act (SigG) and amendments of further acts.

The Federal IuKDG applies to all electronic information and communication services, which are designed for individual use, whereas the MDStV applies to electronic information and communication services, which are designed for general public use. Services designed for the general public were regulated by an Interstate Agreement, because according to the German Constitution, the German Federal states have supreme legislative authority for broadcasting. However, it is often hard to differentiate between services designed for individual use and services designed for public use. Therefore, the Federation and the Federal States have agreed upon almost literally corresponding privacy regulations, which are formulated in the TDDSG and in the MDStV.

Besides provisions enforcing the privacy principles of purpose binding and necessity of processing of contractual data, connection data and accounting data, as well as, the user´s right to information, TDDSG and MDStV contain the following regulations:

- The provider shall not make the use of tele- or multimedia services conditional upon the consent of the user to the effect that his personal data may be processed or used for other purposes (§ 12 (4) MDStV). According to TDDSG this obligation of the provider is only applicable if other accesses to these services are not or not reasonably provided to the user (§ 3 (3) TDDSG).

- The privacy principle of avoidance and minimisation of personal data is to be enforced: The design and selection of technical devices to be used for services shall be oriented to the goal of collecting, processing and using either no personal data at all or as little data as possible (§ 3 (4) TDDSG, § 12 (5) MDStV)
- The provider shall offer the user anonymous use and payment of services or use and payment under a pseudonym to the extent technically feasible and reasonable. The user shall be informed about these options (§ 4 (1) TDDSG, § 13 (1) MDStV).
- User profiles are only permissible, if pseudonyms are used. Profiles retrievable under pseudonyms shall not be combined with data relating to the bearer of pseudonyms (§ 4 (4) TDDSG, §13 (4) MDStV)

Moreover, § 17 MDStV defines and sets out the possibility of a so-called Privacy-Audit ("Datenschutz-Audit").

2.7 Threats to Privacy in the Global Networked Society

In the global information society, privacy is seriously endangered. A key problem is that the traffic on a global network (for example on the Internet) crosses international boundaries and is not centrally managed. On the Internet, there is no overall responsibility assigned to a certain entity, and there is no international oversight mechanism to enforce legal obligations (especially data protection legislation), as far as they exist [Budapest Draft 1996].

There are severe privacy risks, because personal data about the users or other data subjects are available and can be intercepted or traced at different sites around the world. Major risks are discussed in the following sub-sections (see also [Fischer-Hübner 1998], [Fischer-Hübner 2000]).

2.7.1 Privacy Threats at Application Level

The Bangemann report [Bangemann 1994] and most other Information Infrastructure Programmes promote initiatives such as teleworking, distance teaching, research networks, telematic services for enterprises, road and air traffic management systems, health care networks, public administration networks, network accesses for all households through applications such as telebanking and video on demand. Meanwhile, the global information society is evolving rapidly and many new information highways and applications for the health sector, public administration, research, electronic commerce and private life are being developed. For these applications, there is a growing amount of personal data, such as sensitive medical data, business data and private data that is collected, processed and are also communicated through networks across state borders.

Example: Health Care Networks:
Information Infrastructure Programmes promote the development of Health Care Networks at national and international scale. For example, according to the Bangemann report, European healthcare networks for less costly and more effective health care systems for Europe's citizens are planned. A direct communication "network of networks" based on common standards (e.g., standardised electronic patient case files) linking general practitioners, hospitals and social centres on a European scale shall be developed. These heath care networks shall improve diagnosis through on-line access to European specialists, on-line reservation of analysis and hospital services by practitioners extended on European scale, transplant matching, etc. A complete electronic medical patient case file, which can be shared between specialists and can be interchanged between hospitals and with G.P.s, can help to diagnose diseases correctly, to avoid duplicative risky and expensive tests, and to design effective treatment plans.
However, medical patient case files may contain some most sensitive information about topics such as abortions, emotional and psychiatric care, sexual behaviours, sexually transmitted diseases, HIV status, genetic predisposition to diseases. Privacy and the confidentiality of medical records have to be especially safeguarded, because access to medical information may cause social embarrassment, affect our insurability, or limit our ability to get and hold a job. Without broad trust in medical privacy, patients may avoid needed health care (see also [Rindfleisch 1997]).
In conclusion, due to the development of new health care networks at national and global scale and the growing use of telemedicine and telecare, more and more sensitive medical data will be collected, electronically stored, shared among different healthcare professionals and transferred to different sites in the world. The privacy of medical data is thus seriously endangered and has to be safeguarded. It has to be guaranteed that only authorised personnel can have access to the patient's medical information. In particular, users should only be able to access/process personal data, if it is necessary for their authorised tasks (privacy principle of necessity of data processing) and if the purpose of data processing is compatible with the purposes for which the data was obtained (privacy principle of purpose binding). Besides, due respect has to be paid to the privacy principle of transparency so that patients still know who has access to their data and for what purposes.

Furthermore, there are severe privacy risks, since more and more sensitive personal data can easily be communicated to and is often routed via different countries, which do not necessarily have an appropriate privacy level. Messages transmitted in plain text could be intercepted or modified at each site of the communication path.

2.7.2 Privacy Threats at Communication Level

A side-effect of global communication is that connection data is available at different sites around the world revealing details about communication partners, time of communication, services used, connections, and so on. This transactional data may reveal who communicated with whom, when, for how long, and who bought what for what price. Users leave an electronic trace, which can be used to create consumer or communication profiles.

Every electronic message contains a header with information about the sender and recipient, as well as the routing and subject of the message. This information could be intercepted at each site passed and could be used for traffic analysis. There is normally no anonymity of communication, because the recipient of an electronic mail (even if the e-mail is encrypted) can determine the sender's identity through the sender's e-mail address, which normally contains information about the user's name, background (for example, university or company), and location.

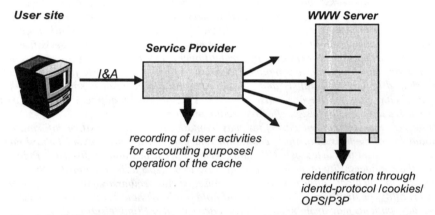

Fig. 2.1: Collection of communication data (see also [Köhntopp/Köhntopp 1996])

If a user is connected to the Internet by ISDN or modem, communication data will already have been obtained by the telephone company.

Besides, communication profiles could be created by the service provider to whom the user is connected (like Internet or mailbox providers). Service providers store personal user data about their subscribers (such as user name, login name, address, bank connection, and status). Users are normally identified and authenticated by the service providers, and their communication behaviour (for example, accesses to news or world wide web (WWW) sites) could be easily traced and supervised by the providers. Normally, service providers are recording the use of services to create accounting data for billing purposes. Besides, the service provider has to collect connection data for operation of the cache. Also, personal data about users can be recorded at remote servers. A recent study by the Electronic Privacy Information Center (EPIC) showed that none of the most frequently visited web sites on the Internet meet basic standards for privacy protection [EPIC 1997].

A WWW server can record the Internet Protocol (IP) addresses of requesting systems, which often reveals the user´s Internet domain name, workplace and/or approximate location. Furthermore, a requesting user may be re-identified by the identd-protocol, which operates by looking up specific TCP/IP connections and returning the user name of the process owning the connection. Besides, techniques, such as so-called "cookies", could be used by the remote WWW servers to monitor and track the user's accesses to web pages.

Cookies are blocks of ASCII texts that a server can store and later retrieve from the local WWW browser of the user. Cookies, which were introduced by Netscape to allow user-side customisation of Web information, are a mechanism that allows a Web site to record the user's comings and goings, usually without his knowledge or consent. If a user is identified by the server as having ordered goods or registered for software, the cookies of this user revealing his interests and his recent, common or preferred activities on the web sites can be related to his name or e-mail address by the server.

```
# Netscape HTTP Cookie File
# http://www.netscape.com/newsref/std/cookie_spec.html
# This is a generated file! Do not edit.

.doubleclick.net  TRUE  /  FALSE  1920499140  id  5e47d2c
.excite.com  TRUE  /  FALSE  946641600  UID  7A152CF333943ED8
.nrsite.com  TRUE  /  FALSE  946598400  NRid  iafC-yaFExOAgSq49wLzNq
.infoseek.com  TRUE  /  FALSE  897052931  InfoseekUserId
056BEAA0F18BCF114413D6815EF2E721
.netscape.com  TRUE  /  FALSE  946684799  NETSCAPE_ID
10010408,11761a29
www.aztech.com.sg  FALSE  /  FALSE  1293753600  EGSOFT_ID
134.100.7.163-3531300016.29139179
.yahoo.com  TRUE  /  FALSE  915145200  Y  v=1&n=btderttbe9r7k
www.geocities.com  FALSE  /  FALSE  937399384  GeoId
13424395874327384530
.linkexchange.com  TRUE  /  FALSE  942191999  SAFE_COOKIE
341d2eea1807d56e
.imgis.com  TRUE  /  FALSE  1032612266  JEB2  -1869117967|
.focalink.com TRUE  /  FALSE  946641600  SB_ID
0877534349000007387708891 95370
.amazon.comTRUE  /  FALSE  2082787201  ubid-main  3826-5903423-539594
www.csc.dk  FALSE  /  FALSE  1293753600  EGSOFT_ID
134.100.7.163-724676368.29159492
www.uk.uu.net  FALSE  /  FALSE  946684799  INTERSE
134.100.7.16322729879443306351
www.hgs.se  FALSE  /  FALSE  946511999  RoxenUserID 0x801292b9
www3.haaretz.co.il  FALSE  /  FALSE  1293753600  EGSOFT_ID
134.100.7.163-2616727280.29163945
.preferences.com  TRUE  /  FALSE  1182140421  PreferencesID
e9NFtWp8ioK5eo100BWHMa
.amazon.comTRUE  /  FALSE  885196800  session-id  9947-8202030-317488
.amazon.comTRUE  /  FALSE  885196800  group_discount_cookie F
.amazon.comTRUE  /  FALSE  885196800  session-id-time  885196800
```

Fig. 2.2: Example of a Netscape cookie file

Netscape soon modified its browsers so that cookies from one site could not be given to another site. However, web developers and Internet advertising companies (namely DoubleClick Network) soon found a way to use cookies to correlate users' activities between many different web sites to track the user's usage history and preferences. This could be done by adding cookies to GIF images that were served off third-party sites (see [Garfinkel/Spafford 1997]). Cookies may also permit third parties to investigate the activities of an individual if they have access to their computer and to their cookie files.

The current cookie usage is violating the provisions of the EU-Directive on data protection and of other national data protection legislation (see also [Mayer-Schönberger 1996]): First of all, because of their expiration date option, cookies may violate the "accuracy" and "timeliness" principles of Art.6. Furthermore, the average user is unaware of cookie storage and access. However, to meet Art. 7 of the EU Directive, a user has to give his informed consent to a cookie transfer, since the other alternative conditions of Art. 7 (a legal obligation, vital interests and or contractual arrangements) cannot be assumed. Browsers need to be specifically configured to disallow cookies or to display a cryptic warning that a cookie is going to be stored. The average user has not the technical knowledge to configure his system accordingly or to view or delete the cookie file and he can hardly make an informed decision based on such cryptic warnings. Consequently, there is no informed consent by the user and cookie technology is therefore violating Art. 7 of the Directive. Besides, the provisions of extensive information and access rights granted to the user by Art. 10-12 of the EU Data Protection Directive are violated.

OPS (Open Profiling Standard) and P3P (Platform for Privacy Preferences) are recent approaches to privacy preference management that give the user the ability to manage which information gets disclosed or withheld from a particular web site.

In May 1997, the American companies Netscape, Firefly Networks and Verisign announced the "Open Profiling Standard" (OPS). It was defined by Netscape as "a standard that enables personalisation of Internet services while protecting user's privacy" and was submitted to W3C (World Wide Web Consortium) [OPS].

Although OPS gives the user the ability to manage which information gets disclosed or withheld from a particular site, OPS could on the contrary also have the effect to severely endanger the user's privacy. In contrast to cookies, OPS uses standardised personal profiles, which can be shared by different sites and can contain user identifying data and many more personal attributes (such credit card number or personal prefreneces). Even if the user has to give his consent for the disclosure of information in his profile, he could be forced in practice to do so. This could for example be the case, if a user is relying on access to a service or to resources, and the access is only permitted to him, if he is providing access to information in his personal profile ([Brunnstein/Fischer-Hübner/Schaar 1998]).

OPS has subsequently been superseded by the P3P standard of the W3C [P3P]. The P3P standard should enable Web sites to express their privacy practices and should enable users to exercise preferences over those practices. P3P is a protocol designed to help users to reach a semi-automated agreement with on-line merchants with regard to the processing of individual's personal data.

P3P has been harshly criticised by privacy advocates to fail to comply with baseline standards for privacy protection. It is regarded as "a complex and confusing protocol that will make it more difficult for Internet users to protect their privacy. It builds on the "notice and choice" privacy approach and fails to ensure the observance of Fair Information Practices and lacks any means to enforce privacy practices [EPIC 2000]. Also P3P will in practice push or even force users to give up their privacy.

Thus, OPS and P3P actually can be used as privacy invasive rather than privacy enforcing technologies.

According to the German Multimedia legislation (§ 3 (3) TDDSG, § 12 (4) MDStV), the provider may not make the use of services conditional upon the consent of the user to the effect that his data may be processed or used for other purposes, if other access to these services is not or is not reasonably provided to the user. However, since the Internet has no national boundaries and personal data used for multimedia services often crosses national borders, corresponding international privacy regulations for multimedia services are needed as well.

A further serious privacy issue that had recently been under discussion was Intel´s initial plans to ship its newest generation of Pentium-III microprocessors with an embedded serial number that could be used to identify a computer - and by extension, its user. Moreover Mircosoft had conceded that a unique identifying number had been used by its Window98 OS, which has the potential to be even more evasive.

Transactional data can reveal sensitive information about the user´s communication behaviour and interests. For example, the choice of a news group or access to Web sites of a political magazine could reveal information about the political opinion of a user.

Marketing companies usually have a strong interest in such transactional data revealing the user´s preferences. Users have reasons to be concerned over the distribution of their transactional data for financial gains, and the (mis-) use for purposes other than the purposes for which it was collected: A noted case in the USA is the recent example of America Online (AOL) selling its subscriber contact information, financial information, and Internet activities.

As pointed out in [Goldberg/Wagner/Brewer 1997], privacy threats in the Internet are actually two-fold: The user´s online actions could be (1) monitored by unauthorised parties and (2) logged and preserved for future access many years later. Long-term databases and powerful search engines make it easy to build a comprehensive profile of individuals and thus contribute to the Internet´s "dossier effect". For example, "it is technically quite easy to collect information (such as a compendium of all posts you have made to electronic newsgroups) and store it for years or decades, indexed by your name for easy retrieval. If you are looking for a job twenty years from now, do you want your employer to browse through every Usenet posting you have ever made?" [Goldberg/Wagner/Brewer 1997].

2.7.3 Insecure Technologies

Another problem of the global information society is whether the requirements of appropriate technical and organisational security mechanisms to protect the personal data on the information highways and to provide network reliability can be guaranteed sufficiently. The Internet, an important contemporary information highway that consists of several thousand computer networks with several million users, is known for a lot of critical security holes [Brunnstein/Schier 1997]. Accidents, such as worm and chain letter attacks (e.g., the Internet worm, VBS/LoveLetter worm), hacking attacks (such as the KGB hacking incident), sniffer-password attacks, address spoofing, malicious agents and denial of service attacks have demonstrated the insecurity of Internet technology.

The user´s Privacy is especially endangered by technologies that uses downloaded code, such as JavaScript, Plug-Ins or ActiveX. Malicious downloaded programs can through a security hole scan the end user's hard disk or network for personal data (such as e-mail files) and then smuggle the data to the outside world using the computer's network connection (see [Garfinkel/Spafford 1997]).

In conclusion, in the global information society, privacy is at risk and is becoming more and more an international problem. Consequently, internationally harmonised privacy regulations are needed for an adequate level of privacy protection. Furthermore, data protection commissioners demand that privacy protection should be technically enforced and should already be integrated in the system design.

2.8 Problems of an International Harmonisation of Privacy Legislation

In the Bangemann report it is written:

'...Without the legal security of a Union-wide approach, lack of consumer confidence will certainly undermine the rapid development of the information society. Given the importance and sensitivity of the privacy issue, a fast decision from Member States is required on the Commission's proposed Directive setting out general principles of data protection.'

In the EU, privacy protection should be enforced by the EU Data Protection Directive. Nevertheless, even if the EU Directive can help to enforce a relatively high standard of data protection in Europe, it will not be able to protect privacy sufficiently in the global information society. As discussed above, personal data can easily be transferred or routed across state boundaries to countries without any data protection legislation, where its information content or communication data can be intercepted. Privacy is therefore an international problem, and an international harmonisation of privacy regulations is needed.

However, a hope is that the EU Directive will not only be an instrument for harmonisation within Europe. It can also, for the following reasons, have a coercive effect on countries outside Europe to enact efficient data protection laws based on the EU Directive: The Directive represents the "most modern international consensus on the desirable content of data protection rights" and "it may be a valuable model for countries currently without data protection laws" [Greenleaf 1996]. Besides, due to the restrictions of Art. 25 for the data transfer to third countries, there is an economic pressure on non-EU countries to enact efficient data protection acts. For these reasons, some states have already issued new data protection acts: For example, the 1993 Quebec data protection law (the first North American legislation to enact private sector data protection) was based on the earlier EC Directive Draft and was drafted explicitly to protect business from the possible blockage of data transfer from Europe. Also Canada has in 2000 adopted new laws to ensure that trade will not be affected by the requirements of the EU Directive. Besides, most countries in Eastern Europe, who hope to join the EU in the near future, are adopting new laws based on the EU Directive. For example Hungary, who is seeking EU membership, had in 1996 as the first country in Eastern Europe, passed data protection legislation and established a data protection commissioner. Countries outside the EU will increasingly use the EU Data Protection Directive as a model in devising or updating their legislation (see also [Bennett 1997]).

Nevertheless, the critical question remains whether a common harmonised approach to privacy will be possible due to cultural, historical, and political differences. Anthropologists have stated that, on a low level, privacy (especially privacy of the person and of the close surroundings) is a human physiological need. But, on higher organisational levels, privacy is basically a cultural construction and there are considerable cultural variations in privacy needs and interests [Lundheim/Sindre 1994]. In addition, experiences from World War II, especially the practice of the Nazi government in amassing and misusing great amounts of personal details about the population, have caused a greater sensitivity to privacy in western European states [Madsen 1992]. Another problem can be seen in non-democratic societies, where individual privacy is normally not protected by legislation. On the contrary, in these countries privacy is often invaded by the state.

In the following sections, the privacy approaches of technologically developed states that have set up information infrastructure programmes are compared with the EU approach. Thereby, considerable distinctions in the different national approaches to privacy protection are shown. Furthermore, all the approaches are critically analysed to determine the insufficiencies of privacy legislation (see also [Fischer-Hübner 1998], [Fischer-Hübner 2000]).

Singapore

Singapore was one of the first countries in the world that had issued a national information infrastructure programme. The information infrastructure plan *IT2000 - A Vision Of An Intelligent Island* was formulated by the Singapore government in August 1991 [Singapore 1991]. By 2000, Singapore, the Intelligent Island, should be among the first countries with an advanced information infrastructure that will link government, business, and people. *Singapore ONE (One Network for Everyone)* is a national initiative to deliver a new level of interactive, multimedia applications and services to all homes, businesses and schools throughout Singapore. So far, Singapore has worldwide the highest rate of Internet connections per household. However, Singapore, like most other Asian states, does not have any privacy protection laws so far. In September 1998, The National Internet Advisory Board proposed an industry-based self-regulatory "E-Commerce Code for the Protection of Personal Information and Communications of Consumers of Internet Commerce", which obliges providers to ensure confidentiality of personal user information, requires providers not to intercept communications unless required by law, and defines consumer rights. The code would be enforced by an industry-run Compliance Authority [PI/EPIC 1999]. However, it would have no legal force.

In January 2000, also the Infocomm Development Authority of Singapore issued Privacy Guidelines regulating the scanning of computers by Internet service providers after the Ministry of Home affairs had initiated a controversial scanning of 200.000 SINGNET (Singapore's Internet sub-network) user's computers.

In fact, privacy does not seem to be an important issue. Intensive surveillance of telephone conversations and Internet use by security services has for some time already been justified by Singapore's Internal Security Act. While promoting the use of the SINGNET, the government is trying to control the content of the information transmitted over the net at the same time [Madsen 1995].

Japan

In June 1993, the Information Industry Committee of the Industrial Council in Japan issued a report stating the need for the government to promote information technology. In May 1994, the Ministry of International Trade and Industry (MITI) published a *Programme for Advanced Information Infrastructure*. In this programme under the topic *Improvement of Environment for Realizing Advanced Information Society*, only security measures, and not privacy issues, are discussed [Japan 1994].

Japan, on the other hand, is one of the few Asian countries to have implemented a data protection act. The awareness of privacy in Japan has resulted more from economic self-interest than from any longstanding tradition of ensuring individual privacy [Madsen 1992]. The Japanese *Act for Protection of Computer Processed Personal Data* held by Administrative Organs was made official in December 1988. It governs the use of personal data in computerised files held by government agencies and is based on the OECD Guidelines. In addition, cities, towns, and villages have also enacted local privacy regulations. However, the Japanese data protection act only applies to national government organisations. Moreover, it does not install an independent data protection authority to control data processing. In 1989, MITI issued formal guidelines entitled *Protection of Personal Data Processed by Computers in the Private Sector* to encourage self-regulation in the private sector on privacy, information integrity, and information quality. These guidelines for privacy in the private sector as a means of self-regulation are not mandatory and can only be adopted internally by private companies. Nevertheless, the Japanese Information Processing Development Center -a joint public/private agency- has since April 1998 been offering a "privacy mark" system to companies and organisations which successfully submit to an examination of their data protection methods.

A government advisory panel suggested in an interim report in November 1999 that the government should introduce a law in 2001 that stipulates basic rules for dealing with personal information and called for both self-governing rules and laws for the credit research, medical and telecommunications industries, on an industry-by-industry basis [PI 1999].

United States of America

In 1993, the Clinton/Gore government presented the *National Information Infrastructure (NII) Programme - Agenda for Action* [US-Government 1993]. So far, the US have been criticised for being the first in technology but the last in data protection [Madsen 1992]. The US Privacy Act of 1974 only covers the federal public sector. Besides the Privacy Act, there is only a non-uniform patchwork of various privacy and computer security legislation. Thus, the US have avoided general data protection rules for the private sector in favour of specific sectoral laws governing, for example, video rental records, credit reports and financial privacy. Moreover, the US does not have a data protection authority to oversee privacy protection and to act if there are complaints from data subjects about unfair or illegal use of their personal data. Consequently, the only way for data subjects to fight against data misuse is through the courts.

It has been realised that the NII does not only promise many benefits, but is also increasing risks to privacy. Therefore, the Information Infrastructure Task Force's (IITF) Working Group on Privacy has developed privacy principles with the goal of providing guidance to all participants in the National Information Infrastructure [IITF 1995]. They are intended to be applied to governmental and private sectors, and are based on the idea that all participants (information providers, collectors, users, and data subjects) of the NII, have a shared responsibility for the proper use of personal information.

General Principles for All Participants require that all NII participants should ensure and respect information privacy, information integrity, and information quality.

Principles for Users of Personal Information require information users to assess the impact on privacy of current or planned activities and to use personal information only for these activities or for compatible uses. Data subjects will be informed by the data collector about the reason and purpose of data collection and about their rights. Information users should use appropriate security mechanisms to protect the confidentiality and integrity of personal data. Information users should not use information in ways that are incompatible with an individual's understanding. Furthermore, they should educate themselves about how privacy can be maintained.

According to the *Principles for Individuals Who Provide Personal Information*, individuals should obtain information about what data is being collected and for what reason, and how it will be protected. Individuals will have a responsibility to understand the consequences of providing personal data to others and will make intelligent choices on whether to provide or not to provide their personal data. Individuals will be able to safeguard their own privacy by having the means to obtain their data, to correct it, to use appropriate technical safeguards (for example, encryption), and to remain anonymous when appropriate. Furthermore, data subjects will have means of redress, if harmed by an improper disclosure or use of personal data.

The IITF privacy principles could raise the level of data protection in the US, especially if applied in the private sector. Unfortunately, the principles only offer guidelines for those who are drafting laws and regulations but they do not have the force of law. Although the IITF privacy principles are intended to be consistent with international guidelines such as the OECD guidelines, they do not, in some respect, offer the same level of privacy protection as the EU directive. In practice, the idea of shared responsibility of equal partners will not always work, because data subjects (such as employees) often depend on services provided by the data processing agencies (for example, employers), so that they hardly have the chance to enforce their rights themselves. Consequently, besides the right of redress, the control of an independent data protection authority is necessary to protect data subjects efficiently. In [IITF 1997] it is argued that the establishment of a data protection authority could reduce the likelihood that unfair information practices are prosecuted. However, in practice it is normally more cumbersome and risky for a citizen to go to court than to appeal to a data protection authority, which acts as the citizen's lawyer. Besides, with a data protection authority that monitors and checks the observance of data protection regulations, it is much more likely that personal data abuses are detected.

Currently, the US and EU are discussing how the EU Directive might affect transatlantic data flow, and whether Art. 25 will restrict the data flow from the EU to the USA and will thus have consequences on the transborder electronic commerce. A main question in the discussion is whether "adequacy" will be judged against the principles of the Directive or also against the methods of enforcement and oversight.

The European side tends to demand the enforcement of clear requirements of legitimacy (esp. purpose specification and binding) as well as an independent oversight authority that can act on complaints of the data subjects and can deal with non-compliance. Currently, the US American side is opposed to enact general data protection legislation, covering also the private sector according to the European model and instead favours means of self-regulation for the private sector.

A recent comprehensive report "*Privacy and Self-Regulation in the Information Age*" by the US Department of Commerce [US Dept. Commerce 1997] explored the benefits and challenges of self-regulatory privacy regimes. According to this report, effective self-regulation must involve substantive rules as well as means to ensure that consumers know the rules, that companies actually do what they promise to do, and that consumers can have their complaints heard and resolved fairly.

The Department of Commerce has also, first in 1998, proposed "Safe Harbors" for U.S. companies that would allow US firms to continue exchanging data if the firms choose voluntarily to adhere to certain privacy principles [US Dept. of Commerce 1998], [US Dept. of Commerce 2000]. The International Safe Harbor Privacy Principles are self-regulatory privacy guidelines that shall prevent US companies' data transfer from being cut off by the EU. After more than two years of high level discussions between the United States and the European Union, which have ended in several revisions of the proposal, EU member states approved the Safe Harbor agreement on May 31, 2000, although the Safe Harbor Principles were criticised by the Working Party (Data Protection Working Group of the EU according to Art.27 EU Directive) [European Commission 2000] and the Transatlantic Consumer Dialog [TACD 2000].

On July 5, 2000 the EU Parliament voted against Safe Harbor and adopted a resolution by the Committee on Citizen's Freedom and Rights, Justice and Home Affairs on the inadequacy of Safe Harbor calling on the European Commission to reopen the Safe Harbor negotiations. The European Commission on July 26, however, announced that it would go forward with the Safe Harbor agreement despite the opposition of the Parliament.

The private sector has already responded with technological tools like P3P and TRUSTe supporting self-regulation. As described above, P3P (The Platform for Privacy Preferences Project) developed by W3C (World Wide Web Consortium) allows Internet users to set default preferences for the collection, use, and disclosure of personal information on the Web. TRUSTe is a "seal of approval" that uses a standardised icon to link to an organisation's privacy practices and indicates that these practices are monitored by outside auditors. However, recently the European Commission evaluated P3P and OPS and stated that these technologies would not replace a legal framework. A main criticism was the following aspact: "Use of P3P and OPS in the absence of such a framework risks shifting the onus primarily onto the individual user to protect himself, a development which would undermine the internationally established principle that it is the 'data controller' who is responsible for complying with data protection principles (OECD Guidelines 1980, Council of Europe Convention No.108 1981, UN Guidelines 1990, EU Directives 95/46/EC and 97/66/EC). Such an inversion of responsibility also assumes a level of knowledge about the risks posed by data processing to individual privacy that cannot realistically be expected of most citizens" [European Commission 1998].

In the USA, voluntary privacy codes have generally been developed in conformity with the OECD Guidelines, whereby some of these codes embody external mechanisms for complaints and oversight and others are merely statements of good intention [Bennett 1997]. However, although several hundred USA companies signed to the OECD Guidelines, few adopted their provisions in practice [Madsen 1992].The record of self-regulatory codes has been disappointing, with little or no evidence that the aims of the codes are regularly fulfilled. The major problems with self-regulatory approaches are adequacy and enforcement [PI/EPIC 1999].

The United States argue that an omnibus privacy legislation is a feature of a continental legal system, and that the Anglo-American system based on Common Law dictates a less regulatory regime. According to the US tradition of self-help and judicial enforcement, more responsibility is placed on the individual to demonstrate damage and make a claim through the court. However, in contradiction to this argument, in the USA there are several application-specific acts regulating privacy aspects in the private sector, such as the *Fair Credit Reporting Act* or the *Video Rental Act*. Moreover, there are other states with an English common law tradition that enforce or plan to enforce an omnibus data-protection legislation. For example, the United Kingdom passed its data protection act covering the public and private sectors in 1984, and Canada has recently extended its data protection legislation also to the private sector (see below).

Canada

Until recently, privacy in Canada had only been regulated for most but not all of the federal public sector by the Privacy Act enacted in 1982. The Canadian Privacy Act in contrast to the US legislation established the Office of Privacy Commissioner. Besides, provincial privacy legislation covering government bodies exist in almost every Canadian province. However, only the province of Quebec has enacted privacy legislation for the private sector.

Voluntary privacy codes and standards have generally been the preferred approach of Canadian business and industry associations. The diversity of codes of practice in Canada was one reason for the Canadian Standards Association (CSA) to negotiate a Model Code for the Protection of Personal Information in the private sector with business, government, and consumer groups. Besides, the CSA was motivated by the EU-Directive and the fear of the possible blockage of personal data transfer from Europe.

In September 1995, the Canadian Information Highway Advisory Council presented the final report *Connection Community Content: The Challenge of the Information Highway* [Canada 1995]. In contrast to most other information infrastructure programmes, which were mainly influenced by input from representatives of the IT industry, the advisory council also included members from artistic, creative, and educational communities, and from consumer and labour organisations. It was chaired by David Johnston, professor of law at McGill University's Centre for Medicine, Ethics and Law.

Privacy protection and network security was one of five principles that were set up by the Information Highway Advisory Council. The council recommended that the government should continue to collaborate with the CSA, business, and consumer organisations, and other levels of government in order to implement the CSA code and develop effective independent oversight and enforcement mechanisms in order to "legislate" the standard. This recommendation was accepted by the Federal government in May 1996, which committed itself to having enforceable privacy legislation in Canada's private sector by the year 2000.

In the fall of 1998, the government introduced Bill C-54, the Personal Information Protection and Electronic Documents Act, which extended privacy legislation also to the commercial sector. After extensive hearings the act was revised, re-introduced as Bill C-6, amended and finally approved by Parliament on April 4, 2000. The law will go into force on January 1, 2001.

In conclusion, the EU Directive will undoubtfully lead to a further harmonisation of privacy protection legislation inside as well as outside Europe. Nevertheless, as the analysis in this Section showed, there will still be considerable divergences in the privacy approaches of the EU, the USA and other countries. Mainly cultural and political differences will probably hinder the further process of privacy harmonisation.

2.9 The Need for Privacy Enhancing Technologies

In a fully networked society, privacy is seriously endangered and cannot be sufficiently protected by privacy legislation or privacy codes of conduct alone. Data protection commissioners are therefore demanding that privacy requirements should also be technically enforced and that privacy should be a design criterion for information systems. The Dutch Data Protection Authority (the Registratiekamer) and the Information and Privacy Commissioner (IPC) for the Province of Ontario, Canada, have collaborated in the production of a report [Registratiekamer/IPC, 1995] exploring Privacy Enhancing Technologies (PET) that safeguard personal privacy by minimising or eliminating the collection of identifiable data.

The report on privacy enhancing technologies by the Registratiekamer and IPC, and a prior study of the Registratiekamer on how to design and model privacy technologies, [Registratiekamer 1995] mainly focussed on privacy technologies that permitted transactions to be conducted anonymously. A recent report by a working group of German data protection commissioners also addressed privacy enhancing technologies for protecting user identities. Nevertheless, in addition to privacy technologies for the protection of the users, there is also a need for privacy technologies to protect data subjects that are not necessarily acting as users at the same time.

Thus, extended security criteria for systems with high privacy requirements should cover a diversity of privacy enhancing security aspects such as (see also Chapter 4.1):

- *Privacy-Enhancing Security Aspects for protecting user identities providing Anonymity, Pseudonymity, Unlinkability, Unobservability of users:* The principles of minimisation and avoidance of personal data are derived from the legal principle of necessity of data collecting and processing, which requires that personal data should not be collected or used for identification purposes when not truly necessary. Consequently, if possible, the system should allow users to act anonymously.

- *Privacy-Enhancing Security Aspects for Protecting usee identities providing Anonymity and Pseudonymity of data subjects:* If personal data (about data subjects that are not necessarily users at the same time) has to be collected, it should be rendered anonymous or pseudonymous as soon as the purposes for which the data was collected permit this. In some cases, some users still need to access the personal data attributes, while other users only need statistical (anonymous) access. Inference controls for instance can be used to restrict users to statistical accesses only and can prevent those users deducing confidential information about some individual.

- Security mechanisms, such as access control or encryption, are necessary to *protect the confidentiality and integrity of* personal data, if (non-anonymous) personal data has to be stored, processed or transmitted. Such security mechanisms can also be classified as data protection technologies. Especially the privacy requirements of *purpose binding and necessity of data processing of personal data of users and data subjects* can be technically enforced through appropriate security policy and access control mechanisms.

Some of these privacy technologies (e.g., encryption tools, use of remailers) are in the hands of the individual user, who can decide to use them to protect themselves. Other privacy enhancing technologies are implemented by a privacy-enhanced system design, which is for instance avoiding or minimising the collection and use of personal data.

Privacy enhancing technologies are valuable tools for privacy protection in addition to privacy legislation. However, as also stated recently by a working group of the EU Commission [EU Commission 1998], they cannot replace a legal framework and should be applied within the context of enforceable privacy rules.

Privacy enhancing security criteria and the concept of an identity protector are discussed in Chapter 4 in more detail. Existing privacy enhancing technology systems or concepts are classified according to those criteria. Besides, it is analysed how far IT-Security Evaluation Criteria (TCSEC, ITSEC and the Common Criteria) are covering those privacy criteria. Moreover, privacy criteria are used for a privacy evaluation of security models. The emphasis of the second part of this thesis (Chapters 5 and 6) is on a formal privacy enhancing security model (the so-called task-based privacy model), which can technically enforce the legal privacy requirements of purpose binding and necessity of data processing.

2.10 The Importance of Privacy Education

The report of the Registratiekamer and IPC [Registratiekamer/IPC, 1995] concludes that, if privacy technologies are to play a more significant role, it will be necessary to create more public awareness as well as consumer demand for them. If there is a demand, providers will probably try to respond to market forces.

Generally, privacy education is important to raise the awareness of the users, the usees, the system designers, the IT professionals and of the management.

Most Privacy-Enhancing Technologies themselves are not necessarily an effective means to technically enforce privacy aspects, unless users or customers have sufficient technical knowledge to apply them. Thus users and customers need information and education about their rights, about the value of their personal data, about privacy risks and the possibilities of self-protection by the use of PET.

Moreover, privacy should be an important part of the education of computer scientists, because computer scientists are responsible for a lawful and ethically acceptable system design and system administration. IT systems often introduce new threats to privacy or sharpen privacy concerns. Many privacy problems could be prevented from the start, if privacy aspects were considered sufficiently from the beginning and during the system design process. Many privacy threats can be reduced or eliminated by a privacy-enhancing system design. Unfortunately, usees normally do not participate in the system design process and consequently their privacy interests are often neglected. Computer scientists should therefore represent the interests of the data subjects and be responsible for a privacy-friendly and privacy-acceptable system design. They should know how to assess privacy risks of IT-systems, as well as, how to technically enforce privacy requirements (see also [Nothdurft 1994], [Fischer-Hübner 1996a]).

Besides, for a lawful system administration and operation, the legal requirements of the data protection acts (esp. requirements for data security, as for example, defined in Art. 17 of the EU Data Protection Directive or § 9 BDSG) have to be fulfilled. Computer scientists should therefore be familiar with the enforcement of such legal requirements for data protection. This is especially important, as many German companies appoint computer scientists as data protection officers, who shall be responsible for ensuring that the data protection act and provisions are observed. Only persons who possess the specialised knowledge and demonstrate reliability shall be appointed as data protection officers. Since the EU Data Protection Directive also contains provisions for the appointment of data protection officials in organisations, the role of qualified data protection officials will become more relevant also in the European context.

However, although privacy can be regarded as an important topic for the qualification of computer scientists, it is taught as a part of the computer science curriculum only at few universities in Germany. In [Fischer-Hübner 1996a], an overview to privacy courses at computer science departments of German universities and Polytechnic Schools is given and course structures for a privacy education is recommended.

In conclusion, privacy education of participants is an important means of protection complementary to privacy regulations and privacy enhancing technologies.

2.11 Conclusions

On the way to the Global Information Society, privacy is at risk and is increasingly becoming an international problem. Thus, an international harmonisation of privacy legislation is needed. The EU Directive on data protection will lead to a further harmonisation of privacy protection legislation inside as well as outside Europe. Still, some countries such as the United States are opposed to a comprehensive data protection legislation according to the European model and are instead favouring self-regulatory codes for the private sector. Besides, there are also still many (mainly third-world or non-democratic) countries without any data protection regulations at all. Hence, it will be hardly possible to reach to an internationally harmonised high level of data protection legislation.

Major problems of self-regulation by codes of conduct are adequacy and enforcement. Besides, the enforcement of privacy legislation is a problem in practice and also in countries with comprehensive and sophisticated privacy legislation, still many privacy breaches are reported and occur in practice.

Hence, privacy cannot be sufficiently protected solely by legislation or codes of conduct. Thus, privacy should also be enforced by technologies and should be a system design criterion. In addition, the privacy education of consumers and IT professionals is becoming increasingly important.

In the next chapters, we will discuss security technologies that can be used for technical data protection and privacy enhancing technologies in general.

3   IT-Security

3.1. Definition

IT (Information Technology) Security mechanisms are needed to protect personal data and thus IT Security is often regarded as the technical side of privacy.

IT Security can be defined by different layers [Fischer-Hübner 1995]: it can be defined by the perspective or view on it, by the different security and safety aspects that shall be guaranteed, by models that shall enforce those different aspects, by basic security functions used by the models and security mechanisms that implement these security functions (see Figure 3.1). Security mechanisms can be divided into internal mechanisms that are enforced by the IT system and external mechanisms that are implemented outside of the system.

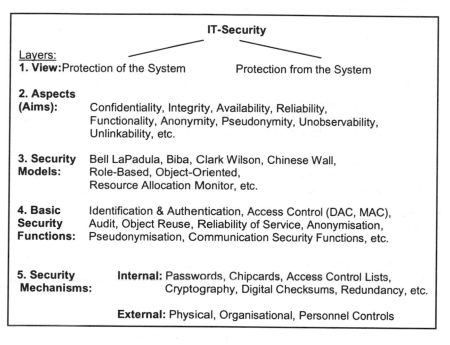

Fig. 3.1: IT-Security Layers

Normally, there is a n:m mapping between the components of subsequent layers. At each layer, the various security aspects, functions or mechanisms can overlap, may even be mutually exclusive (for example, protection of confidentiality can severely restrict availability), may have dependencies or can be independent from each other.

The meaning of the term IT - Security has evolved in the recent years. For a long time, research and development of secure systems had been concentrated on security aspects to protect the IT-system and its information against unauthorised or inappropriate use. Having been funded primarily by the government, the emphasis of IT-security research and development was initially on confidentiality in the meaning of secrecy of classified information. This tradition has persisted even in commercial applications, where integrity, not secrecy, is the primary goal [Gasser 1988, p.4].

Since the late eighties, IT security has been defined by at least the following aspects:

- *Confidentiality:* prevention of unauthorised or improper disclosure of data.

- *Integrity:* goal of ensuring that data continues to be a proper physical and semantic representation of information, and that information processing resources continue to perform correct processing operations [IDA 1990]. Integrity involves three overlapping goals:

  1. Preventing unauthorised users from making modifications

  2. Preventing authorised users from making improper modifications

  3. Maintaining internal data consistency (self-consistency of interdependent data) and external data consistency (consistency of data with the real-world environment that the data represents).

Important integrity principles and policies are the principle of well-formed transactions and the policies of authorised actions, separation of duties, rotation of duties, separation of resources, and of encapsulation (see [IDA 1990]).

- *Availability:* prevention of the unauthorised withholding of data or resources. Goals of availability are timely response, fair allocation, fault tolerance, utility or usability, controlled concurrency [Pfleeger 1997, p.6].

In contrast to confidentiality and integrity, which can be mainly protected by means of access control, protection of availability is technically much harder to achieve and will probably not be possible until some time in the future ([Gasser, p.4], [Pfleeger, p.6]).

Further security aspects can be defined besides these three "traditional" security aspects. The Canadian and the ISO/IEC Security Evaluation Criteria (see Chapter 3.4) use *accountability* (ensuring that users can be made accountable for their actions) as a security facet besides confidentiality, integrity, availability. However, it could be argued that accountability is already included in the three traditional security aspects.

Besides the *protection of the IT-system*, another perspective on IT security focuses on the *protection of the environment, the users and usees from the system*. Especially computer-based accidents in high-risk areas (e.g. medical application, control of life-sensitive transportation systems) and incidents of personal data abuses have demonstrated the need for protection against the malfunctioning of the system or system misuses.

Also according to [Dierstein 1997], there are two complementary views on IT security: security of the system and security of the usees.

In the English language, a distinction is made between "security" and "safety". Important aspects of safety are *functionality* (the system performs its functions always "as required") and *reliability* (all functions performed on a system are always equally performed under equal constraints). In the German language, the central term "Sicherheit" includes both security and safety. In [Brunnstein 1997] it is stressed that a holistic view including traditional IT security and safety aspects is needed.

For the protection of the usees from the IT-system against personal data abuse, the confidentiality, integrity and availability of personal data have to be guaranteed. Thus, privacy can partly be protected by the IT-security aspects confidentiality, integrity, and availability and should therefore be seen as a part of these security aspects. Nevertheless, the best strategy to protect the usees is the avoidance or minimisation of personal data, if possible. This strategy is derived from the privacy principle of necessity of data collection. Therefore, further important privacy-enhancing security aspects are:

- *Anonymity:* information concerning personal or material circumstances can no longer or only with a disproportionate amount of time, expense and labour be attributed to an identified or identifiable individual. Anonymity of a user means that the user may use a resource or service without disclosing the user's identity.

- *Pseudonymity:* personal information is modified by a substitution function, so that it cannot be attributed to an individual without use or knowledge of this function. Pseudonymity of a user means that the user may use a resource or service without disclosing its user identity, but can still be accountable for that use.

- *Unobservability:* ensures that a user may use a resource or service without others, especially third parties, being able to observe that the resource or service is being used.

- *Unlinkability:* ensures that a user may make multiple uses of resources or services without others being able to link these uses together.

The term "Multilateral Security" is defined as an approach aiming at a balance between the different security requirements of different parties (system owners, operators, as well as, usees) protecting in particular users in a way privacy regulations demand it [Rannenberg 1994]. Privacy-enhancing security aspects will be defined and discussed in Chapter 4 in more detail.

This Chapter gives an introduction to well-known security models, basic security functions and IT-Security Evaluation Criteria. Two key problems concerning the relation between IT security and privacy will be pointed out:

The first problem is that the well-known security models are mainly not addressing privacy. This problem will be discussed in more detail in Chapter 4. Subsequently, in

Chapters 5 and 6, a formal task-based model that addresses privacy aspects will be presented.

Another problem is that there is a conflict between IT security and privacy. This conflict and a holistic approach to conflict resolution are discussed in the last section of this Chapter.

3.2 Security Models

For the design of a secure system, the system's security policy has to be defined. A security policy is a set of rules that regulate how an organisation manages, protects and distributes information. A (formal) security model is a (mathematically) precise statement of the security policy. Thus, the purpose of a security model is to express precisely the system's security requirements. A security model should be simple and abstract. It should therefore only model security properties of the system and should not include too many functional properties of the system that are irrelevant to the security policy.

Security models are useful to test a particular security policy for completeness and consistency, to document a security policy, to help conceptualise and design an implementation, to check whether an implementation meets its requirements [Pfleeger 1997, p. 277].

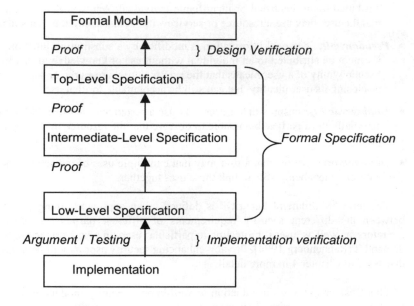

Fig.3.2: Formal System Development Path

Formal security models that are written in a formal mathematical notation, play an important role in the formal system development process to increase the assurance that the implementation corresponds to the model, i.e. that the system will meet its security requirements.

Figure 3.2 shows a formal system development path using specification layers (see [Gasser 1988, pp. 204]). One step in the formal system verification is proving the consistency (design verification) between the formal specification of a system and a formal security model, which means that it is proven that the specification conforms to the functions, invariants, and constraints of the model. Another step in the verification consists of proving the consistency (implementation verification) between the formal specification and its program implementation. However, unlike the design verification, a complete formal implementation verification is not possible with today's technology. State of the art in verification today only permits to show the correspondence between implementation and formal specification by informal argument. A formal specification may consist of several layers. The top layer (top level specification) is most resembling the model and the bottom layer (low level specification) is most resembling the implementation code. The correspondence proof or argument has to take place between each pair of layers.

Besides the proof that the system implementation corresponds to the security model, it has to be shown that the security model enforces the stated security policy. A state-machine type model, which describes a system as an abstract mathematical state machine allows to prove its security policy by mathematical induction.

A state machine model is developed by the following steps [Gasser 1988, p.138]:

1. Definition of security-relevant state variables, which represent the system state (e.g., subjects, objects, security attributes, access rights).

2. Definition of conditions for a secure state (invariants, security properties).

3. Definitions of state transition functions (also called rules of operation) which describes changes to state variables that may take place.

4. Proof that the functions maintain the secure state. For each state transition function it has to be proven that if the system is in a secure state prior to the operation, the system will remain in a secure state after the operation (i.e. the security properties will be preserved).

5. Definition of the initial state

6. Proof that the initial state is secure, i.e. the initial state satisfies the security properties.

If it can be proven that the initial state is secure and that all functions preserve security, mathematical induction tells us that the system will always be in a secure state, regardless of the order in which the functions are invoked. Moreover, it might be necessary to add constraints to state machine models that specify security properties about state transitions. A constraint differs from an invariant, because it addresses the relationships between variables in two successive state transitions.

However, as for invariants, it has to be proven for constraints as well that they are satisfied by each function.

The formal task-based privacy model, which is presented in Chapter 5 and 6 of this thesis, as well as most of the security models described in this Chapter are state machine models.

While formal methods are regarded as important means to establish assurance (the confidence that may be held in the system security), they also have their limitations.

Today there are no practical tools for proving complete code correspondence of a large system and for checking the correctness of such a proof. Thus code correspondence proofs have to be supported by a huge manual effort, which is an error prone process.

Moreover, formal system verification can only prove that the system enforces the model´s security properties, which does not mean that the system is really secure in a broader sense (see also [Fischer-Hübner 1992]).

In [Abrams/Zelkovitz 1994], M.Abrams and M.Zelkowitz discuss limitations of formal methods and state. Their résumé is: "All known methods contributing to correctness have shortcomings that make it impossible to establish correctness beyond reasonable doubt. That is, establishing correctness is a matter of belief, not proof."

The most important and well-known security models, which will be presented and discussed in the next sections, are the HRU-Model, the Bell LaPadula Model, the Biba Model, the Lattice Model, the Chinese Wall Model, the Clark Wilson Model, as well as Role-Based and Task-based Access Control Models. Besides, new security models for object-oriented database systems and the DORIS personal model of data, which has been designed to support privacy as the individual's right of informational self-determination, will be presented. Finally we briefly present the Resource Allocation Model for Denial of Service Protection as one of the few models addressing availability aspects. In Chapter 4, the most relevant models will be evaluated under privacy aspects, and it will be shown that most of them are more or less inappropriate to enforce privacy aspects.

3.2.1 Harrison-Ruzzo-Ullman Model

Harrison, Ruzzo and Ullman [Harrison/Ruzzo/Ullman 1976] introduced an access matrix model for protection systems (HRU model) that is a variation of a model introduced by Graham and Denning [Graham/Denning 1972]. With the revised model they proved limitations of general protection systems.

In the HRU model, a configuration (or state) of a protection system is defined as a triple (S,O,A), where S is the set of current *subjects*, O is the set of current *objects*, S $\subseteq$ O, and A is an *access matrix*, with a row for every subject in S and a column for every object in O. A[s,o] is a subset of R, the finite set of *generic rights*, and gives the rights to object o possessed by subject s.

Changes to the states of a system are modelled by a set of *commands*. Commands, which are specified by a sequence of *primitive operations* and are conditioned on the presence of certain access rights in the access matrix, have the following form:

```
command name (o₁,o₂,...,oₖ)
    if r₁ in A[s₁,o₁] and
       r₂ in A[s₂,o₂] and
       .....
       rₘ in A[sₘ,oₘ]
    then
       op₁
       op₂
       ..
       opₙ
    end
```

The following six primitive operations are identified:

- **enter** r into A[s,o]
- **delete** r from A[s,o]
- **create subject** s
- **create object** o
- **destroy subject** s
- **destroy object** o.

Harrison, Ruzzo and Ullman defined an unsafe state to be one in which a generic right could be leaked into A. They then showed that the general safety problem for such protection system is undecidable by showing how the behaviour of an arbitrary Turing machine can be encoded in a protection system such that leakage of a right corresponds to the Turing machine entering a final state. Whereas the safety problem is in general undecidable, it is decidable for certain specific protection systems. For example, Harrison et al. also show that if commands are restricted to a single operation each (in so-called mono-operational protection systems), the safety problem is decidable. Thus, the general undecidability of the safety problem does not rule out constructing individual protection systems and proving they are secure.

One consequence of this result is that if complex systems are designed that can only be described by complex models, it becomes difficult to find proofs of security. Hence for verifiable security properties, the complexity of the security model should be limited [Gollmann 1999, p.53].

3.2.2 Bell LaPadula Model

The Bell LaPadula model was published in 1973 by D.Elliott Bell and L.J.LaPadula at the Mitre Corporation [Bell LaPadula 1973], as one of the first and most often used security models. A refined model and its interpretation for the Multics security kernel was published in 1976 [Bell LaPadula 1976]. The Bell LaPadula model specifies a so-called multilevel security policy, which is mainly appropriate for military and governmental applications.

The Bell LaPadula model represents abstractly the security-relevant elements of a system: **Subjects**, denoted individually S_i , are active entities, whose access to **objects** (passive entities, denoted O_j) have to be controlled.

The modes of access are represented by **access attributes** $\underline{x}$. The following four different access modes are defined in the model:
- $\underline{e}$ (execute-access, neither observation nor alteration)
- $\underline{r}$ (read-access, observation with no alteration)
- $\underline{a}$ (append-access, alteration with no observation)
- $\underline{w}$ (write-access, both observation and alteration).

The system state is defined by the 4-tuple (b, M, f, H), which consists of the following four components:

1. The current access set **b**: A current access by a subject to an object is represented by a triple (S_i, O_j, x) meaning that S_i has current $\underline{x}$-access to O_j in the state. The current access set b is a set of such triples representing all current accesses.

2. The hierarchy **H**: Structure imposed on objects, which allows directed, rooted trees and isolated objects. The hierarchy was introduced to model Multics' hierarchically structured file directory system.

3. The Access Matrix **M**: The access matrix represents the current access permission structure. Its component M_{ij} records the modes in which subject S_i is permitted to access object O_j. Thus entries of M are sets of access attributes.

4. The Level Function **f**: Each subject and each object receive a security level, which is a pair (classification, set of categories). Classifications are sensitivity levels, for which an ordering relation is defined. For military or governmental applications usually the classifications unclassified, confidential, secret, top secret are used, which are listed in increasing order of sensitivity. Categories, which are often representing projects or departments in an organisation, could have the values Nuclear, NATO, or Crypto. Categories help to enforce the *need-to-know principle* by granting users current access only to information that they need to perform their duties. For security levels a dominance ordering is defined, which is a partial ordering.
One level dominates another:
(classification-1, category-set-1) dominates (classification-2, category-set-2) $\Leftrightarrow$
(classification-1 $\geq$ classification-2) $\wedge$ (category-set-1 $\supseteq$ category-set-2).

The level function f is a triple of security level assignment functions (f_S, f_O, f_C). The (maximum) security level of a subject S_i is denoted $f_S(S_i)$. Similarly, the security level of an object is denoted $f_O(S_i)$. Besides, a current security level is defined for subjects, which allows a subject to operate at less than its maximal security level. The current security level of a subject S_i is denoted $f_C(S_i)$. It is required that $f_S(S_i)$ dominates $f_C(S_i)$.

In the Bell LaPadula model, "security" is defined by the following three properties, which have to be satisfied in every system state:

1. Simple security property (no read-up):
If a subject S_i has current "observe" access to an object O_j, then the security level of the subject dominates the security level of the object:
$(S_i, O_j, \underline{x}) \in b, \underline{x} \in \{\underline{r}, \underline{w}\} \Rightarrow f_S(S_i)$ dominates $f_O(O_j)$.

2. *-property (confinement-property, no write-down):
If a subject S_i has simultaneous current "observe" access to an object O_1 and current "alter" access to an object O_2, then the security level of the object O_1 is dominated by the security level of object O_2:
$(S_i, O_1, \underline{x}) \in b, \underline{x} \in \{\underline{r}, \underline{w}\} \wedge (S_i, O_2, \underline{y}) \in b, \underline{y} \in \{\underline{a}, \underline{w}\} \Rightarrow$
$f_O(O_1)$ is dominated by $f_O(O_2)$.

The *-property can be refined in terms of the current security level of a subject:
In any state, a current access $(S_i, O_j, \underline{x})$ implies:
$f_O(O_j)$ dominates $f_C(S_i)$ if $\underline{x} = \underline{a}$
$f_O(O_j) = f_C(S_i)$ if $\underline{x} = \underline{w}$
$f_O(O_j)$ is dominated by $f_C(S_i)$ if $\underline{x} = \underline{r}$.

The *-property does not apply to trusted subjects, which are subjects guaranteed not to consummate a security-breaching information transfer even if it is possible.

3. ds-property (discretionary security property):
A state satisfies the ds-property provided that every current access is permitted by the current access matrix M:
$(S_i, O_j, x) \in b \Rightarrow x \in M_{ij}$.

The simple security property is used to prevent that a subject can read-access an object with a higher security level ("read-up"). It shall guarantee that the security level of a subject receiving information must be at least as high as the security level of the information.

The *-property is used to prevent "write-down", which occurs when a subject with access to high-level data transfers that data by writing it to a low-level object (see Figure 3.3).

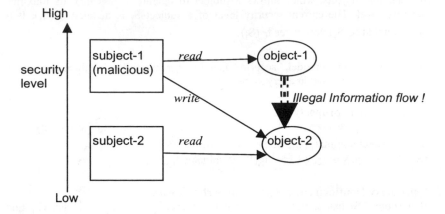

Fig. 1.3: Illegal information flow from object-1 to object-2 allows subject-2 to read information with a higher security level

Since in the military or governmental environment, the enforcement of security levels is mandated by executive order, directive and regulation, the simple security and the *-property are enforced by mandatory access control (MAC). A discretionary security policy allows a users to grant/revoke access to a document to another individual based on his own discretion. The capability to alter the permission structure M is included in the model, and thus the ds-property is enforced by discretionary access control (DAC).

Inputs to the system are requests R_k and outputs are decisions D_m. A system is defined by all sequences of (request, decision, state) triples with some initial state z_0, which satisfy a certain relation on successive states.

The Bell LaPadula model is a state machine-type model. The basic security theorem states that security (defined by the simple security-, *- and ds-property) can be guaranteed systemically when each alteration to the current state does not itself cause a breach of security, i.e. the security properties are preserved from one state to the next. Possible state alterations are defined by rules, which are functions for specifying a decision and a next state for every state and every request. In the model, rules for the requests to get and release current access, change security levels, give and rescind access permission, create an object and to delete a group of objects are defined and it is formally proven that these rules preserve security.

It is usually assumed that the security levels of objects cannot be changed (except by the security officer). This last assumption is known as *tranquility*.

Analysis of the Bell LaPadula model:

The Bell LaPadula model defines a policy for protecting the secrecy of classified information, which is most appropriate for military or governmental applications. However, it uses a very limited definition of "security", which is misleading. In the model definition, "security" is defined by the simple security-, *- and ds-property, although these security properties are only protecting some security aspects. Other confidentiality or security aspects (such as privacy or integrity) are not addressed by the model. Since the Bell LaPadula model is central to the Orange Book [DoD 1985], the public often misinterpreted security as defined by the Bell LaPadula model definition. The model has meanwhile been implemented in various so-called "trusted" or "secure" systems (e.g., Trusted Oracle, Trusted Solaris, Trusted Xenix, A&T System V/MLS). It has even been used in commercial applications, although in the commercial sector other security policies protecting integrity seem to be more appropriate.

Steven Lipner [Lipner 1982] demonstrated how the Bell LaPadula model might be used in commercial data processing. In particular, he showed how the security levels can be defined and used appropriately to protect integrity needs, such as the separation of the programming environment from the application environment. Nevertheless, since the emphasis of the model is on controlling of "observe"-accesses and not on the control of modifications, it is not appropriate to enforce essential integrity goals.

Indeed, the so-called blind write scenario may cause integrity problems [Amoroso 1994, p.114]: In a system defined to meet the Bell LaPadula model rules, the situation may arise that a subject is allowed to write up to an object, but is not allowed to observe the effect of this write to the object. Due to these potential integrity problems, most computer system designers have typically modified the rules of the Bell LaPadula model to a more restricted model such as disallowing read up and restricting writes to subjects and objects with the same security level.

Moreover, in [McCollum/Messing/Notargiacomo 1990], it was pointed out that special dissemination controls for DoD/Intelligence use, such as NOFORN (not releasable for foreign nations) and ORCON (originator controlled release) cannot be handled by the Bell LaPadula model. Thus, even for military applications, additional forms of access control are needed.

Further criticisms have arisen regarding the Bell LaPadula model: If an access request is rejected, the requesting subject can already derive information about the object. Covert channel attacks that exploit such possibilities of illegal information transfer are described in [McLean 1990]. Moreover, the fact that information can be stored in file names or status variables, which are not objects in the model, can as well be exploited by covert channel attacks.

Moreover, the privileges of "trusted subjects" could be exploited: The concept of trusted subjects, which are not constrained by the no-write-down restriction of the *-property, was introduced to perform various system administration functions (such as back-up, restoring services after crashes). Outside the model, a trusted subject should be shown "not to consummate the undesirable transfer of high level information that *-property constraints prevent untrusted subjects from making" [Bell LaPadula 1976]. However, it is in general hardly possible to guarantee that a process is a "trusted" process. Even processes that have been demonstrated to be trusted can be infected by malicious programs. However, when the policy enforced by a trusted subject is different from the policy described in the security model, the validity of the model is compromised [Abrams et al. 1990].

3.2.3 Unix System V/MLS Security Policy

A slightly modified version of the Bell LaPadula model is implemented in the System V/MLS system. System V/MLS (MLS stands for Multilevel Security) is a product based on the Unix operating system, developed by AT&T, which received a B1 rating from the National Computer Security Center in 1989. The mandatory access control (MAC) security policy of AT&T's System V/MLS (see [Flink/Weiss 1988]), Version 1.2.1, was one of the four security policies, which were implemented in the Generalized Framework for Access Control (GFAC) project, and is therefore briefly presented in this Section.

The Bell LaPadula model is implemented in System V/MLS with the following modifications: Instead of enforcing the ds-property, the discretionary access control of Unix System V is used. Besides, write-accesses to subjects and objects are restricted with the same security level to prevent blind writes.

Table 3.1: UNIX system operations involved in enforcing mandatory controls [Flink/Weiss 1988]

Symbol:	Represents:
R	Read (file, directory, etc.)
S	Search (directory)
E	Execute
W	Write (overwrite or append)
O	Overwrite
A	Append
C	Create
L	Link
U	Unlink
St	Read file/ i-node-status
Ch	Change status
K	Send a signal
Ripc	read IPC mechanism
Wipc	Write IPC mechanism

Subjects are assumed to be Unix processes, which inherit the security level of the process owner. Objects are assumed to be Unix files, directories, i-nodes, interprocess communication (IPC) structures, and processes (when they receive signals). In addition to the four access modes defined in the Bell LaPadula model (read, write, append and execute), further access types representing Unix system operations are defined. Table 3.1 shows all Unix system operations involved in enforcing the System V/MLS security policy.

Table 3.2 shows a summary of the System V/MLS mandatory access control policy. In this table, S stands for a subject, O for the object in question and Od stands for a directory object. The symbols >= (= =) stand for "dominates" (identical security levels).

Table 3.2: System V/MLS mandatory policy summary [Flink/Weiss 1988]

Operations:	Dominance Relation:
R/S/E	S >= O
W(O/A)	S == O
C/L/U	S == Od
St	S >= O
Ch	S == O
Ripc	S >= O
Wipc	S == O
K	S == O

3.2.4 Biba Model

The model defined by Biba in 1977 [Biba 1977] was the first security model to address integrity. Biba realised that in the military environment, integrity protection of sensitive information is an important issue. In [Biba 1977] he discusses four different integrity policies (*Low-Water Mark Policy, Low-Water Mark Policy for Objects, Ring Policy, Strict Integrity Policy*) as well as the application of these policies to the Multics' security kernel.

The following basic elements are used to mathematically define the Biba model:

  S: the set of subjects s;
  O: the set of objects o;
  I: the set of integrity levels; the set of integrity levels is defined (analogous to the security levels of the Bell LaPadula model) by the product of the set of integrity classes and the powerset of the set of integrity categories;

A partial ordering on the set of integrity levels is defined by the relation (subset of I × I) "≤" ("less than or equal").
Moreover, the following access modes are defined:

o: a relation (subset of S × O) defining the capability of a subject to observe an object

m: a relation (subset of S × O) defining the capability of a subject to modify an object

i: a relation (subset of S × S) defining the capability of a subject to invoke another subject.

  Of the four different integrity policies, the *Strict Integrity Policy* is by far the most accepted, so much that this policy is normally assumed when the Biba model is discussed. Therefore, only the Strict Integrity Policy of the Biba model is presented in the following passage. The Strict Integrity Policy is the mathematical dual of the Bell LaPadula policy/model and is defined by three properties:

1. **Simple Integrity-Property:**
   If a subject has the capability to observe an object, the subject's integrity level has to be less than or equal to the integrity level of the object (a subject cannot observe objects of lesser integrity):
   $$\forall s \in S, o \in O: s \underline{o} o \implies il(s) \leq il(o)$$

2. **Integrity *-Property:**
   If a subject has the capability to modify an object, the object's integrity level has to be less than or equal to the integrity level of the subject (a subject cannot modify objects of higher integrity):
   $$\forall s \in S, o \in O: s \underline{m} o \implies il(o) \leq il(s)$$

3. **Invocation Property:**
   If a subject has the capability to invoke a second subject, the integrity level of the second subject has to be less than or equal to the integrity level of the invoking subject (a subject may not send a message to subjects of higher integrity):
   $$\forall s_1, s_2 \in S: s_1 \underline{i} s_2 \implies il(s_2) \leq il(s_1)$$

Since invocation is a special case of modification, the invocation property follows directly from the integrity *-property.

The Biba model is based on the assumption that low integrity of a source object implies low integrity for any object based on the source object. Consequently, it is prohibited for a subject with a low integrity level to "write-up" information (of low integrity) to an object of higher integrity. Similarly, it is forbidden for a subject with a high integrity level to "read-down" information of lower integrity.

In addition to this **mandatory integrity policy**, which is defined by these axioms, Biba also defines a **discretionary integrity policy**, which is based on Multics' Access control list structure. According to the discretionary integrity policy, a subject may observe (modify) those objects specifically naming the user of the accessing subject as well as the observe (modify) access mode on its access control list.

Analysis of the Biba Model:

The Biba model addresses integrity, but ignores other security aspects. However, the model uses a limited definition of integrity and focuses only on specific integrity goals. Biba considers two types of integrity threats: internal threats, which are caused by a malicious or incorrect subsystem, and external threats, which are posed by one subsystem attempting to change the behaviour of another by the supplying of false data, improperly invoking functions, or direct modification. Integrity is defined as the guarantee that a subsystem, which has been initially determined to perform properly, will perform as it was intended to perform by its creator. The goal of the Biba model, which focuses on external threats, is thus to guarantee that the subsystem adheres to a well-defined code of behaviour. According to Biba, internal threats should be prevented by program verification and are not addressed by his model. Thus, the Biba model is inadequate to protect the integrity goal of data consistency effectively.

The model is thus primarily concerned with the protection from intentionally malicious attacks. The partially ordered integrity levels provide a hierarchical lattice for identifying authorised users and providing separation at the user type level. These attributes allow the Biba model to address the integrity goal of preventing unauthorised users from making modifications [IDA 1990].

Nevertheless, the Biba model does not prevent an authorised user to make improper modifications, because invalid information can still be written-down or transferred within an integrity level domain. For example, Fred Cohen has demonstrated that a system which has implemented the Bell LaPadula model and the Biba model is not resistant against virus attacks.

Since Biba's Strict Integrity policy is dual to the Bell LaPadula policy, its implementation is straight forward and well understood. Nevertheless, a problem is how to assign appropriate integrity labels. While the Bell LaPadula model perfectly fits with the government classification scheme, there are currently no corresponding criteria for determining integrity levels and categories [IDA 1990]. So far, the Biba model has only been implemented in a few system (e.g., in the VMM security kernel for the VAX architecture [Karger et al. 1990]).

3.2.5 Lattice Model of Information Flow

Dorothy Denning presented a Lattice Model of Information Flow [Denning 1976], [Denning 1982] to describe policies and channels of information flow and to guarantee that no unauthorised information flow is possible.

According to [Denning 1982], an information flow policy is defined by a lattice $(SC, \leq)$, where SC is a finite set of security classes, and $\leq$ is a binary relation partially ordering the classes of SC. For security classes A and B, the relation $A \leq B$ means class A information is lower than or equal to class B information. Class A information is permitted to flow into class B if and only if $A \leq B$ (within a class or upward).

A lattice is a structure consisting of a finite partially ordered set together with least upper and greatest lower bound operators on the set. Thus, $(SC, \leq)$ forms a lattice, if it is a partially ordered set and there exist least upper and greatest lower bound operators, denoted $\oplus$ and $\otimes$ respectively, on SC.

That $(SC, \leq)$ is a partially ordered set implies that $\leq$ is reflexive, transitive and antisymmetric.

That $\oplus$ is a least upper bound operator on SC implies for each subset of classes $S = \{A_1, A_2, ..., A_n\}$ of SC, there exists a unique class $\oplus S = A_1 \oplus A_2 \oplus ..... \oplus A_n$ in SC (the least upper bound of the subset) such that:
1. $A_i \in S$: $A_i \leq \oplus S$
2. $\forall C \subseteq SC$: $(\forall A_i \in S: A_i \leq C) \Rightarrow \oplus S \leq C$.

That $\otimes$ is a greatest lower bound operator on SC implies for each subset of classes $S = \{A_1, A_2, ..., A_n\}$ of SC, there exists a unique class $\otimes S = A_1 \otimes A_2 \otimes ..... \otimes A_n$ in SC (the greatest lower bound of the subset) such that:
1. $\forall A_i \in S$: $\otimes S \leq A_i$

2. $\forall\, C \subseteq SC$: $(\forall\, A_i \in S: C \le A_i)\ \Rightarrow C \le \otimes S$.

The highest security class, High, is High = $\oplus SC$. The lowest class, Low, is Low = $\otimes SC$.

Example:

An example for a lattice structure is a subset lattice $(2^M, \subseteq)$ of an arbitrary set M with set inclusion $\subseteq$ as an ordering relation on the set of all subsets 2^M. The least upper bound $\oplus$ corresponds to set union $\cup$, and the greatest lower bound $\otimes$ to set intersection $\cap$. High = M, and Low = $\varnothing$.

Figure 3.4 shows a subset lattice for M = {Medical, Financial, Criminal}, which can be used to model authorised information flow in a database containing medical, financial, and criminal information. Medical information, for example, is only allowed to flow to records containing medical information.

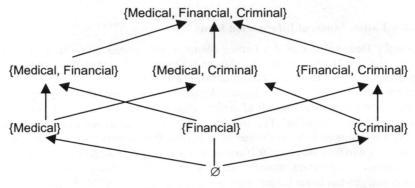

Fig. 3.4: Subset Lattice

The security classes of the Bell LaPadula model form a lattice determined by the Cartesian product of the linear lattice of the security classifications and the subset lattice of the categories.

The *information state* of a system is described by the value and security class of each object in the system, which may be a file, record, program variable or memory location, and register. Each object x has a security class x, which can be a fixed class ("static binding") or can be varying with its content ("dynamic binding"). *State transitions* are modelled by operations that create/ delete objects or change the value or security class of an object.

The information flow caused by operations can be measured by applying information theory:

Given an object x in state s and an object y in state s′. $H_{y'}(x)$ $(H_y(x))$ is the conditional entropy of x_s given the value y_s of y in state s ($y_{s'}$ of y in state s′).

Execution of command α in state s causes information flow from x to y :

$x_s \to_\alpha y_{s'}$ if $H_{y'}(x) < H_y(x)$.

Information flow can be either implicit, e.g. caused by an assignment $x:=y$, or implicit, e.g. caused by executing the if-statement `if x=1 then y:=1`.
A flow from x to y is authorised by a flow policy if and only if $\underline{x \leq y}$.

The transitivity of the relation $\leq$ implies that any indirect flow $x \to y$ resulting from a sequence of flows $x = z_0 \to z_1 \to .... \to z_{n-1} \to z_n = y$ is permitted if each flow $z_{i-1} \to z_i$ $(1 \leq i \leq n)$ is permitted.

Moreover, the existence of the least upper bound $\oplus$ and the greatest lower bound $\otimes$ operators simplify the design of verification mechanisms:
A set of flows $x1 \to y$, $x2 \to y$, ..., $xn \to y$ (e.g., in the statement $y:= x1 + x2$) is authorised if $\underline{x} = \underline{x1} \oplus \underline{x2} \oplus ....\oplus \underline{xn} \leq y$.
A set of flows $x \to y1$, $x \to y2$,....., $x \to ym$ (e.g., in the statement if x=0 then y1:= 0; y2:=O) is authorised if $\underline{x \leq y} = \underline{y1} \otimes \underline{y2} \otimes ....\otimes \underline{ym}$.

A state is authorised if it is derived from an initial state by the execution of commands causing only authorised information flow. By transitivity of the relation $\leq$, the state remains authorised if the flow caused by each state transition is authorised.

"Security", defined by the guarantee of only authorised information flow, can be enforced at execution time by validating flows as they occur (e.g. by access control), or before program execution by program certification verifying the information flow (e.g., by compiler-based mechanisms or program verification) (see [Denning 1982, pp. 279]).

Analysis of the Lattice Model:

The lattice model is an extension of the Bell LaPadula model. The lattice model, however, is more precise, as it describes exactly which information flow should be prevented, while the Bell LaPadula model disallows accesses which could (but do not have to) cause insecure information flow. Thus, it authorises more secure information flow. Moreover, there are examples of insecure information flow along storage channels, which are allowed by the Bell LaPadula policy, but can be detected by information flow analysis.

Nevertheless, the lattice model shares many drawbacks of the Bell LaPadula model. It also uses a very limited definition of security and thus addresses only some confidentiality aspects. Besides, it cannot be used to prevent covert channels either.

3.2.6 Noninterference Security Model

J. Goguen and J. Meseguer [Goguen/Meseguer 1982] from SRI International presented a security model addressing mainly confidentiality aspects, which is also known as the Noninterference Model.

Goguen and Meseguer sharply distinguish between a security policy, which defines the security requirements for a given system, and the system itself, which may be presented by a model.

Their security model has an ordinary state machine component, and also a capability machine component which keeps track of what actions are permitted to what users.

Besides, Goguen and Meseguer provide a simple requirement language for stating security policies, based on the concept of noninterference, where a noninterference security property is defined as:

"one group of users, using a certain set of commands, is noninterfering with another group of users if what the first group does with those commands has no effect on what the second group of users can see."

Their approach can also be used to express the Multilevel Security policy by defining that a system is noninterference secure if users with low security levels are completely unaffected by any activity of users with high or incompatible security levels. Specifically, the system is defined to be noninterference secure if for all users, their system output sequence is the same as the output sequence resulting from an input sequence with all input from users with high or incompatible security levels removed.

In contrast to information flow policy, which analyses what users (processes or variables) can potentially interfere with others, the Goguen and Meseguer model determines what users must not interfere with others. The information flow techniques may analyse a large number of cases that actually cannot occur. The Goguen and Meseguer claim that their model provides a more refined analysis based on noninterference, which contains explicit information about the operations invoked by users.

However, McCullough [McCullough 1988] showed that the noninterference property does not compose, which means that it is possible to connect two systems, both of which are judged to be secure, so that the composed system is not secure. Besides, he pointed out that the model only considers deterministic systems, because it assumes that the system output is a function of the input sequence. Moreover it only considers uninterruptable systems. Interrupts lead to nondeterminism, because time is not explicitly considered in the model.

The noninterference model has mainly raised attention in the scientific community, but had a lesser impact on the design and development on practical secure computer systems [Amoroso 1994, pp.123].

3.2.7 Clark-Wilson Model

D.Clark and D.Wilson [Clark/Wilson 1987] presented a model for achieving data integrity based on commercial data processing practices. Clark and Wilson pointed out that in the commercial data processing environment, distinct security policies, related to integrity rather to disclosure, were of highest priority. Second, some separate mechanisms were required for enforcement of these policies, disjointed from those of the Orange Book. The publication of the Clark Wilson model has initiated new interest in the computer security research community in the area of integrity protection and research.

The Clark and Wilson integrity policy is based on two key concepts:

1. **Well-formed transactions:** a user should not manipulate data arbitrarily, but only in constrained ways that preserve or ensure the internal consistency of data.

2. **Separation of duty:** all operations are separated into several subparts and it is required that each subpart be executed by a different person.

The elements of the Clark Wilson model are:

Constrained Data Items (CDIs):	data items within the system to which the integrity model must be applied.
Unconstrained Data Items (UDIs):	data items not covered by the integrity policy. New data is put into the system as UDIs and may subsequently be transformed into CDIs.
Integrity Verification Procedures (IVPs):	procedures that shall confirm that all of the CDIs in the system conform to the integrity specification at the time the IVPs are executed.
Transformation Procedures (TPs):	correspond to the concept of well-formed transactions mentioned above. The purpose of TPs is to change the set of CDIs from one valid state to another.

Beside, certification (C) and enforcement (E) rules that govern the interaction of the model elements are defined. Certification is done by the security officer, system owner, and system custodian. Enforcement is done by the system. The rules are stated as follows:

C1: (Certification) All IVPs must properly ensure that all CDIs are in a valid state at the time the IVP is run.

C2: All TPs must be certified to be valid. That is, they must take a CDI to a valid final state, given that it is in a valid state to begin with. The security officer must specify for each TP_i a relation (TP_i, (CDI_a, CDI_b,...)), where the list of CDIs defines a particular set of arguments for which the TP has been certified.

E1: (Enforcement) The system must maintain the list of relations specified in rule C2, and must ensure that the only manipulation of any CDI is by a TP, where the TP is operating on the CDI as specified in some relation.

E2: The system must maintain a list of relations of the form: (UserID, TP_i, (CDI_a, CDI_b,...)) (the so-called "access triples"), which relates a user, a TP, and the data items that TP may reference on behalf of that user. It must ensure that only executions described in one of the relations are performed.

C3: The list of relations in E2 must be certified to meet the separation of duty requirement.

E3: The system must authenticate the identity of each user attempting to execute a TP.

C4: All TPs must be certified to write to an append-only CDI (the log) all information necessary to permit the nature of the operations to be reconstructed.

C5: Any TP that takes a UDI as an input value must be certified to perform only valid transformations, or else no transformations, for any possible value of the UDI. The transformation should take the input from a UDI to a CDI, or the UDI is rejected.

E4: Only the agent permitted to certify entities may change the list of such entities associated with other entities: specifically, associated with a TP. An agent that can certify an entity may not have any execute rights with respect to that entity.

IVPs check that a system starts in a valid state that can only be changed by TPs. TPs are certified to preserve the validity of system states. Thus, the system will always stay in a valid state.

The Clark Wilson model is enforced by access controls that are mandatory in that the users of the system should not be able to modify the list of programs permitted to manipulate a particular data item or to modify the list of users permitted to execute a given program (see rule E4).

Analysis of the Clark Wilson model:

The Clark Wilson model effectively addresses all three goals of integrity (preventing unauthorised users from making modifications, preventing authorised users from making improper modifications, maintaining internal and external data consistency) [IDA 1990]:

An IVP verifies internal consistency as well as external consistency by periodically cross-checking internal data with the external reality that it represents.

Transformation Procedures (TPs) maintain internal consistency by taking the system from one valid state to another valid state. For example, in an accounting system, a TP would correspond to a double entry bookkeeping transaction. Double entry bookkeeping ensures internal data consistency by requiring that any modification of the books be comprised of two parts, which account for or balance each other.

The principle of separation of duty prevents authorised users from making improper modifications and supports external data consistency. For example, the process of purchasing and paying for some item might involve the following step which should each be performed by different persons in order to prevent fraud: authorising the purchase order, recording the arrival of the item, recording the arrival of the invoice, authorising the payment.

55

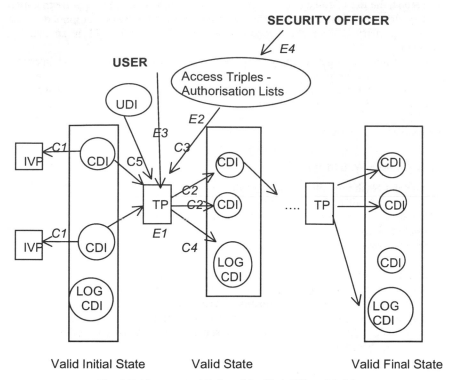

Fig. 3.5: Elements and Rules of the Clark Wilson Model

Access triples, as required by rule E2, are used to implement the separation of duty concept and to address the integrity goal of preventing unauthorised users from making modifications.

The primary advantage of the Clark Wilson model is that it is based on tested business methods that have worked in the paper world for many years. However, a disadvantage of the model is that IVPs and techniques for ensuring that a TP preserves integrity are not easy to implement on real IT-systems, because in practice limitations exist for potential software validation and verification techniques [Amoroso 1994, p.155].

Independently, Lee [Lee 1988] and Shockley [Shockley 1988] developed implementations of the Clark Wilson model enforcement rules using Biba model categories and trusted subjects.

In [Abrams et al. 1993] extensions to the Clark Wilson model are recommended:

First, user roles should be included and should be administrated by two different agents: one agent can assign roles to users, but will be constrained by information in the system that defines the roles. The other is the agent that can define roles. A way to support administration of roles is to store the access triples that define user´s authorisations in reserved CDIs encapsulated within vendor-supplied TPs.

Second, the use of so-called "primary CDIs" is recommended to support separation of duty. Primary CDIs have values that require corroboration by two or more different users. A primary CDI should change only as a result of the last TP in an enabling sequence.

Furthermore, in order to apply integrity to mechanisms that implement integrity, access triples can be protected from unauthorised modification by storing them in a CDI called "CDI-triples" and restricting access to this CDI to a Triples Manager by a role assignment. Similarly, TPs and IVPs can be protected from unauthorised modification by assigning roles and including TP/IVP-management TPs in appropriate access triples.

3.2.8 Chinese Wall Model

Brewer and Nash presented a model of the Chinese Wall policy [Brewer/Nash 1989]. The Chinese Wall policy arises in the financial segment of the commercial sector, which provides consulting services to other companies, and is used to prevent a conflict of interest. A conflict of interest exists when one person can obtain sensitive information on competing companies (e.g., two banks or two oil companies).

In the model, all corporate information objects are stored in a hierarchically arranged structure (see Figure 3.6): At lowest level are elementary objects, such as files. Each object contains information concerning only one corporation. At the intermediate level, objects concerning each corporation are grouped together in a company dataset. At highest level, datasets whose corporations are in competition, are grouped together in a conflict class.

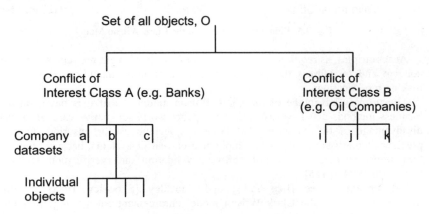

Fig. 3.6: The composition of company information objects in the Chinese Wall policy

The Chinese Wall policy requires that a user should not be able to read information for more than one company in any given conflict of interest class. For example, a consultant should not have read access to two or more banks or two or more oil companies.

In the model, a mandatory rule for restricting read accesses (read-rule) is defined as follows:
Subject S can read object O only if

1. O is in the same company dataset as an object already accessed by that subject (i.e. O is within the wall), or

2. O belongs to an entirely different conflict of interest class.

A matrix N with a column for every object and a row for every subject is used to record who accessed what. Initially, N is initialised everywhere false (no subject has accessed any object). Besides, it is defined that, given such an initiate state, the first ever access will be granted.
In the model, the following theorems are proven:

(1) Once a subject has accessed an object the only other objects accessible by that subject lie within the same company dataset or within a different conflict of interest class.

(2) A subject can at most have access to one company dataset in each conflict of interest class.

In order to prevent illegal information transfer by copying information from one company dataset to another company dataset, the following write-rule is defined:
Subject S can write object O only if

1. S can read O by the read-rule, and

2. no object can be read which is in a different company dataset to the one from which write access is requested and contains unsanitized information.

Sanitized information is public information relating to all corporations.

Moreover, according to a refined exposition of the Chinese Wall policy, it is required that users may only execute certain named processes and that those processes may only access certain objects. Thus a process is allowed to access an object if the user requesting it is allowed to execute it and that user, by the Chinese Wall policy, is allowed to access that object and that process is allowed to access that object.

Analysis of the Chinese Wall model:

The Chinese Wall model is a commercially inspired policy, which allows access permissions to change dynamically. It mainly addresses confidentiality aspects, but can also be used to enforce the integrity principle of separation of duty.
Due to this dynamic aspect, Brewer and Nash claim that the Chinese Wall policy cannot be represented by the Bell LaPadula model. However, it was pointed out that the Chinese Wall policy can be implemented using Bell LaPadula categories if the user's allowed category set is permitted to change dynamically, and if this ability is

used to vary the category set as a result of user accesses in accordance with the Chinese Wall policy [IDA 1990].

Ravi Sandhu [Sandhu 1992] pointed out that since the Brewer-Nash model does not distinguish between users and processes, the write-rule is applied to all users in the system. However, the write-rule of the Chinese Wall policy applied to users is too restrictive to be employed in a practical system, because it implies that a user who has read objects from two or more company datasets cannot write at all. Besides, the purpose of the write-rule is to prevent Trojan Horse infected processes from breaching the Chinese Wall. The write-rule cannot, however, address the threat of a malicious human user who can compromise the security policy by employing communication means outside the computer system.

Sandhu showed how the Chinese Wall policy can be employed in a practical system in a sensible way by applying the security rules to processes instead of human users. By maintaining a careful distinction between user, principals (corresponding to user accounts) and processes, he showed that the Chinese Wall policy is an interpretation of the lattice-based information flow policy which can be easily represented within the Bell LaPadula framework.

3.2.9 Role-Based Access Control Models

Recently, role-based access control models have emerged. The roots of role-based access control can be traced back to the earliest access control systems. Roles have been employed in several mainstream access control products of the 1970s and 80s, such as IBM´s RACF (see [Sandhu et al. 1994]). Besides, role- based systems have already been developed for some time by a variety of organisations. Often closely related concepts such as user groups were used to implement roles. Different research groups have conducted early research work on role-based modelling of access control. In [McLean/Landwehr/Heitmeyer 1984] a security model for military message systems was presented which already introduced the features of roles. Besides, the role-concept was used in the DORIS approach [Biskup/Brüggemann 1988], which is an information system that takes privacy issues into account (see Chapter 3.2.11.3). Role-based models for information systems that consider "duties" and "liberties" in addition to permissions and prohibitions to be an attribute of roles were presented by [Jonscher/Gerhardt 1991] and [Lubinski 1993].

As an approach to formally model role-based access control mechanisms, the RBAC (Role-Based Access Control) model was first presented by D. Ferrailo and R. Kuhn in 1992 [Ferraiolo/Kuhn 1992] and has since then raised considerable attention. NIST (National Institute of Standards and Technology) has conducted research in RBAC, RBAC systems are beginning to emerge, the first RBAC workshops were organised by the ACM, and a RBAC protection profile for the Common Criteria has been developed (the chapter 3.4.4.2). The revised RBAC model [Ferraiolo/Cugini/Kuhn 1995], which was presented by Ferrailo, Cugini and Kuhn in 1995, will be presented in the following Section.

The RBAC model:

A role based access control (RBAC) policy bases access control decisions on the functions a user is allowed to perform within an organisation. RBAC is a form of mandatory access control, because the security administrator is responsible for enforcing policies and users cannot pass access permissions on to other users.

A role can be defined by a set of operations (privileges) that a user or set of users can perform within an organisation. Authorised operations to objects are allocated to roles by a security administrator. Besides, membership of users in a role is also granted and revoked by a security administrator on the basis of the users´ specific job responsibilities and qualifications.

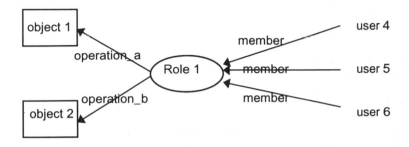

Fig. 3.7: RBAC role relationships

RBAC model elements:

The elements of the RBAC model are defined as follows: A *user* is a person, a *subject* represents an active user process, a *role* is a collection of job functions (set of privileges). Besides, an *operation* represents a particular mode of access to a set of one or more protected RBAC *objects*.

The following functions describe the mappings among users, subjects, and roles:

subject-user(s:subject) = the user associated with subject "s".

authorised-roles(s:subject) = {the roles associated with subject "s"}

role-members(r:role) = {the users authorised for role "r"}

user-authorised-role(u: user) = {the roles associated with user "u"}.

The consistent subject assumption requires that if a subject is authorised for a role, then this role has to be an element of the set of roles for which the subject is authorised:

$\forall$ s: subject, u: user, R, r: roles:

subject-user(s) = u $\wedge$ authorised-roles(s) = R $\wedge$ u $\in$ role-members(r) $\Rightarrow$ r $\in$ R.

The relationships between roles, operations, and objects are described by the following functions:

role-operations(r:role) = {the operations that are associated with role "r"}

operation-objects(op:operation) = {the authorised objects for which the operation "op" can be applied}.

RBAC properties:

The following security properties are required and used to define role hierarchies, role authorisation and role activation, operational separation of duty and authorised access to objects :

RBAC includes the concept of role hierarchies that allows roles to "contain" other roles. That is, one role may implicitly include the privileges and constraints that are associated with another role. For example, in a hospital information system, the role "doctor" contains the role "health-care provider" and thereby inherits the privileges from health-care provider. Role hierarchies are defined by the following property:

Property 1 (Role Hierarchy): If a subject is authorised to access a role and that role contains another role, then the subject is also allowed to access the contained role:

$\forall$ s: subject, ri, rj:roles: rj $\in$ authorised-roles(s) $\wedge$ rj > ri $\Rightarrow$ ri $\in$ authorised-roles(s).

The association of a user with a role should be subject to the principles of least privilege and static separation of duty. Besides, there is a constraint requiring that some roles can only be occupied by a certain number of employees at any given period of time.

Through the use of RBAC, least privilege can be easily achieved by granting only those operations to a role that need to be performed by members of this role.

The principle of static separation of duty requires means that by virtue of a user being authorised as a member of one role, the user is not authorised as a member of a second conflicting role. For example, in the bank the roles *teller* and *auditor* are mutually exclusive. Mutually exclusive roles and the static separation of duty properties are specified as follows:

mutually-exclusive-authorisation(r:roles) = {the list of roles that are mutually exclusive with "r"}.

Property 2 (Static Separation of Duty): A user is authorised as a member of a role only if that role is not mutually exclusive with any other roles for which the user already possesses membership:

$\forall$ u:user, ri, rj: roles: i $\neq$ j: u $\in$ role-members(ri) $\wedge$ u $\in$ role-members(rj) $\Rightarrow$ ri $\notin$ mutually-exclusive-authorisation(rj).

According to the RBAC model, it is possible to restrict the number of users allowed for a role at any given time. For example, only one user should act as a manager or as a department chair at any given time. The number of users allowed for a role and the existing number of users associated with a role is specified by the following two functions:

membership-limit (r:roles) = the membership limit (≥ 0) for role "r".

number-of-members (r:roles) = N (≥ 0) the number of existing members in role "r".

The Cardinality property is defined as:

Property 3 (Cardinality): The capacity of a role cannot be exceeded by an additional role member:
$\forall$ *r: roles: membership-limit(r)* $\geq$ *number-of-members(r).*

The RBAC model also defines properties for the role activation. The following functions define active roles for a subject which are the roles that the subject is currently using:

active-roles (s:subject) = {the current list of active roles for a subject "s"}

A role can be activated by a user, if the user is authorised for the proposed role. This is specified by the following property:

Property 4 (Role Authorisation): A subject can never have an active role that is not authorised for that subject:
$\forall$ *s: subject: active-role(s)* $\subseteq$ *authorised-role(s).*

Furthermore:

Property 5 (Role Execution): A subject can execute an operation only if the subject is acting within an active role:
$\forall$ *s: subject, op: operation: exec(s,op)* $\Rightarrow$ *active-role(s)* $\neq \emptyset$

Moreover, it is required that the activation of the proposed role is not mutually exclusive with any other active role(s) of the user. This requirement provides administrators with the capability to enforce dynamic separation of duty. In contrast to static separation of duty that places constraints on the role authorisations, dynamic separation of duty places constraints on the simultaneous activation of roles. For example, a user could be authorised for both the roles Payment Initiator and Payment Authoriser, but can dynamically assume only one of these roles at the same time. The mutually exclusive roles for the proposed active role is specified by the following function:

mutually-exclusive-activation (r:roles) = {the list of active roles that are mutually exclusive with the proposed role "r"}.

The property of dynamic separation of duty is defined by:

Property 6 (Dynamic Separation of Duty): A subject can become active in a new role only if the proposed role is not mutually exclusive with any of the roles in which the subject is currently active:

$\forall$ *s: subject, r_i, r_j : roles. i $\neq$j : r_i $\in$ active-roles(s) $\wedge$ r_j $\in$ active-roles(s)* $\Rightarrow$
r_i $\notin$ mutually-exclusive-activation(r_j).

Moreover, the proposed operation has to be authorised for a subject's active role.

The following function enables subjects to execute RBAC operations:

exec(s:subject, op:operation) = {TRUE iff subject "s" can execute operation "op", otherwise it is false}.

The property of Operation Authorisation is defined by the following property:

Property 7 (Operation Authorisation): A subject can execute an operation only if the operation is authorised for the role in which the subject is currently active:

$\forall$ *s: subject, op: operation $\exists$ r: roles: exec(s,op)* $\Rightarrow$
r $\in$ active-roles(s) $\wedge$ op $\in$ role-operations(r).

Furthermore, RBAC can be used by the system administrator to enforce a policy of Operational Separation of Duty which requires that for all the operations associated with a particular business function, no single user can be allowed to perform all operations. Operational separation of duty can be specified with the following function and property:

function-operations (f:function) = {the set of all operations required for a business function "f"}.

Property 8 (Operational Separation of Duty): For all the operations required for a particular business function, the authorised roles of no single user should be allowed to perform all operations:

$\forall$ *u: user, r: role, f: function :*
$\neg$ *(function-operations(f) $\subseteq$ $\cup$ role-operations(r)).*
r$\in$ user-authorised-roles(u)

Moreover, control of access to RBAC objects is specified with the following function and property:

access (s: subject,o:object) = {TRUE iff the subject can access the object, otherwise it is FALSE}.

Property 9 (Object Access Authorisation): A subject can access an object only if the role is part of the subject´s current active role set, the role is allowed to perform the operation, and the operation to access the object is authorised:

$\forall$ *s: subject, o:object: access(s,o)* $\Rightarrow \exists$ *r:roles, op:operation:*

r $\in$ *active-roles(s)* $\wedge$ *op* $\in$ *role-operations(r)* $\wedge$ *o* $\in$ *operation-object(op)*.

Further RBAC research:

The National Institute of Standards and Technology (NIST) has been conducting research in the area of RBAC. Descriptions of current NIST RBAC projects can be found at the NIST/ RBAC Web pages [NIST-RBAC].

One NIST research program led by R. Sandhu was set up to define RBAC and its feasibility. In [Sandhu et al. 1996], a first approach to define a family of four RBAC reference models was presented which can serve to guide product development and customer evaluation. In [Sandhu/Ferraiolo/Kuhn 2000], the NIST model for role-based access control (RBAC) is presented as the result of the approach to reach to a unified standard reference model for role-based access control. The NIST model focuses on those aspects of RBAC for which consensus is available and is organised into 4 main levels of increasing functional capabilities called flat RBAC, hierarchical RBAC, constrained RBAC and symmetric RBAC. Table 3.3 summarises the features of the levels of the NIST RBAC model.

Table 3.3: RBAC Variations organised as levels [Sandhu/Ferraiolo/Kuhn 2000]

Level	Name	RBAC Functional Capabilities
1	Flat RBAC	• users acquire permissions through roles • must support many-to-many user-role assignment • must support many-to-many permission-role assignment • must support user-role assignment review • users can use permissions of multiple roles simultaneously
2	Hierarchical RBAC	Flat RBAC + • must support role hierarchy (partial order) • **level 2a** requires support for arbitrary hierarchies • **level 2b** denotes support for limited hierarchies (such as trees, inverted trees
3	Constrained RBAC	Hierarchical RBAC + • must enforce separation of duties • **level 3a** requires support for arbitrary hierarchies • **level 3b** denotes support for limited hierarchies (such as trees, inverted trees)

4	Symmetric RBAC	Constrained RBAC + • must support permission-role review with performance effectively comparable to user-role review • **level 4a** requires support for arbitrary hierarchies • **level 4b** denotes support for limited hierarchies (such as trees, inverted trees)

Flat RBAC requires user-role assignment review whereby the roles assigned to a specific user can be determined as well as users assigned to a specific role. The similar requirement for permission-role review is deferred until level 4 because it can be intrinsically difficult to implement in large-scale distributed systems.

Besides, Ravi Sandhu showed that lattice-based access controls could be enforced by appropriate configuration of RBAC components [Sandhu 1996b]. Sandhu demonstrated that the concepts of role hierarchies and constraints were critical to achieving this result. A practical consequence is that lattice-based access control can be realised as a particular instance of RBAC.

Another NIST program was conducted to demonstrate how RBAC could be applied to health care systems [Barkley 1995]. Also in [Pangalos/Khair 1996], [Mavridis et al. 1999] it was shown how role-based access control can be used in combination with MAC to protect personal data in medical databases. One further current NIST project aims to design and implement RBAC features for networked web servers [Barkley et al. 1997], [Ferraiolo/Barkley/Kuhn 1999].

Analysis of Role-Based Access Control:

RBAC is an access control mechanism, which allows to express and to enforce enterprise-specific security policies and which simplifies the administration of access rights. Users can be made members of roles as determined by their responsibility and qualification and can be easily reassigned from one role to another without modifying the underlying access structure. Roles can be granted new permissions, or permissions can be revoked from roles as needed. RBAC can be used by the security administrator to enforce the principle of least privilege as well as static, dynamic, and operational policies of separation of duties.

An important characteristic of RBAC is that by itself it is policy neutral and can be used to articulate policy rather than embodying a particular security policy. Specifically, lattice-based access control can be realised as a particular instance of RBAC, as shown by Sandhu. Sandhu suggests that it might be better to develop systems that support general RBAC and specialise these to lattice-based access control, because RBAC has much broader applicability than lattice-based control, especially in the commercial sector.

In [Ramaswamy/Sandhu 1998], Ramaswamy and Sandhu analyse and compare RBAC features implemented in *INFORMIX Online Dynamic Server Version 7.2, Sybase Adaptive Server release 11.5* and *Oracle Enterprise Server Version 8.0*. A summary of the RBAC features that are supported or not supported in these three DBMS products is given in Table 3.4. Note that Informix and Oracle implement

RBAC features by a discretionary access control mechanism by enabling the role grantee to grant that role to other users. In Sybase only users in the role "System Security Officer" are authorised to grant roles to other users and hence Sybase implements a non-discretionary access control mechanism.

In such network operating systems as Novell´s NetWare and Microsoft´s Window NT roles are used for system administration. The ORACLE relational database management system supports role-based access control in its Version 7.0 product line [Notargiacomo 1995], [Oracle 1994] and in higher version product lines. Oracle´s approach to role-based access control was accepted into the SQL3 specification. Role-Based Access Control Features are also supported in the most recent versions of the commercial database management systems Informix and Sybase.

Table 3.4: Role-Based Access Control Features in Commercial Database Management Systems [Ramaswamy / Sandhu 1998]

Item	Feature	Informix	Sybase	Oracle
1	Ability for a role grantee to grant that role to other users	YES	NO	YES
2	Multiple active roles for a user session	NO	YES	YES
3	Specify a default active role set for a user session	NO	YES	YES
4	Build a role hierarchy	YES	YES	YES
5	Specify static separation of duty constraints on roles	NO	YES	NO
6	Specify dynamic separation of duty constraints on roles	(YES)	YES	NO
7	Specify maximum or minimum cardinality for role membership	NO	NO	NO
8	Grant DBMS System Privileges to a Role	NO	YES	YES
9	GRANT DBMS Object Privileges to a Role	YES	YES	YES

3.2.10 Task-Based Authorisation Models for Workflow

Workflows represent processes in manufacturing and office environments that typically consist of several well-defined activities, called tasks. Authorisation mechanisms have to ensure that these tasks are executed by authorised subjects only. Besides, subjects may gain access to required objects only during the execution of the task.

3.2.10.1 Workflow Authorisation Model (WAM)

In [Atluri/Huang 1996], a Workflow Authorisation Model (WAM) is proposed for synchronising the authorisation flow with the workflow. WAM ensures that authorisation is granted only when a tasks starts and revoked as soon as the task finishes.

Model elements are a set of subjects $S = \{s_1, s_2,...\}$, a set of objects $O = \{o_1, o_2, ..\}$, a finite set of objects types $\Gamma = \{\gamma_1, \gamma_2,...\}$, a finite set of privileges PR and a time set $T = \{r \in R^3 \mid r \geq 0\}$ and a time interval set $\{ [t_l, t_u] \in T \times T \mid t_l \leq t_u\}$ that represent the set of all closed intervals.

A workflow can be represented as a partially ordered set of tasks $\{w_1, w_2, ..., w_n\}$, where each task w_i in turn can be defined as a set Op_i of a partial or total order of operations $\{op_1, op_2,..op_n\}$ that involve manipulation of objects.

More precisely, a **task w_i** is defined as: $(OP_i, \Gamma_{IN_i}, \Gamma_{OUT_i}, [t_{l_i}, t_{u_i}])$, where OP_i is the set of operations to be performed in w_i, $\Gamma_{IN_i} \subseteq \Gamma$ is the set of object types allowed as inputs, $\Gamma_{OUT_i} \subseteq \Gamma$ is the set of object types as expected as outputs, and $[t_{l_i}, t_{u_i}]$ is the time interval during which w_i must be executed.

$[t_{l_i}, t_{u_i}]$ specifies temporal constraints stating the lower and upper bounds of the time interval during which a task is allowed to be executed.

Whenever a task w_i is executed, a task-instance will be generated.
A **task-instance w_{inst_i}** is defined as: $(OPER_i, IN_i, OUT_i, [t_{s_i}, t_{f_i}])$, where $OPER_i$ is the set of operations performed during the execution of w_i, IN_i is the set of input objects to w_i such that $IN_i = \{x \in O \mid \gamma(x) \in \Gamma_{IN_i}\}$, OUT_i is the set of output objects from w_i such that $OUT_i = \{x \in O \mid \gamma(x) \in \Gamma_{OUT_i}\}$, and $[t_{s_i}, t_{f_i}]$ is the time interval during which w_i has been executed.

An **authorisation** A_i is defined as a 4-tuple $A_i = (s_i, o_i, pr_i, [t_{b_i}, t_{e_i}])$, where subject s_i is granted access on object o_i with privilege pr_i at time t_{b_i} and is revoked at time t_{e_i}.

For a task w_i an **authorisation template $AT(w_i)$** is defined as a 3-tuple $AT(w_i) = (s_i, (\gamma_i, -), pr_i)$, where
(i) $s_i \in S$,

(ii) $(\gamma_i, -)$ is an *object hole* which can be filled by an object o_i of type γ_i, and

(iii) pr_i is the privilege to be granted to s_i on object o_i when $(\gamma_i,-)$ is filled by o_i.

$AT(w_i) = (s_i, (\gamma_i, -), pr_i)$ specifies that s_i is allowed to perform task w_i and that w_i can only process objects of type γ_i and requires a privilege pr_i on the objects.

A task w_i may have more than one authorisation template attached to it, if there are more than one type of object to be processed, or more than one subject is required to perform the processing.

The following rule ensures that authorisation is granted only when a task actually starts and is revoked when the task is completed:

Authorisation Derivation Rule:
Given an authorisation template $AT(w_i) = (s_i, (\gamma_i,-), pr_i)$ of task $w_i = (OP_i, \Gamma_{IN_i}, \Gamma_{OUT_i}, [t_{l_i}, t_{u_i}])$, an authorisation $A_i = (s_i, o_i, pr_i, [t_{b_i}, t_{e_i}])$ is derived as follows:
Grant Rule: Suppose object $o_i \in \Gamma_{IN_i}$ is sent to w_i at t_{a_i} to start w_i. Let the starting time of w_i be t_{s_i}.

If $t_{a_i} \leq t_{u_i}$, the $s_i \leftarrow s(AT)$, $pr_i \leftarrow pr(AT)$, $t_{e_i} \leftarrow t_{u_i}$, and

(if $t_{a_i} \leq t_{l_i}$, then $t_{b_i} \leftarrow t_{l_i}$; otherwise $t_{b_i} \leftarrow t_{a_i}$)

Revoke Rule: Suppose w_i ends at t_{f_i}, at which point o_i leaves w_i.

IF $t_{f_i} \leq t_{u_i}$, then $t_{e_i} \leftarrow t_{f_i}$.

Example:
The workflow of check processing consists of the three tasks: preparation, approval and issue of the check:
$w_1 = ($ {read request, prepare check}, {request, check}, {check}, [10, 50])
$w_2 = ($ {approve check}, {check}, {check}, [20, 60])
$w_3 = ($ {issue check}, {check}, {check}, [40,80])
Suppose the associated subjects for performing these processes are John, Mary, and Ken, respectively. The following authorisation templates could be generated instead of granting all the required privileges for the subjects involved in advance:
$AT_1(w_1) = ($John, (request, -), read), $AT_2(w_1) = ($John, (check, -), prepare)
$AT(w_2) = ($Mary, (check, -), approve), $AT(w_3) = ($Ken, (check, -), issue).

WAM can be extended to specify role-based authorisations, if s is replaced with a role R in AT: $AT = ((R, -) (\gamma, -), pr, [t_l, t_u])$.

(R,-) is a *"role hole"* and the actual authorisation is derived when it is filled by a subject performing a role R.

In [Atluri/Huang 1996], a model of implementation of WAM using timed and coloured petri nets is presented to show how synchronisation of authorisation flow and workflow can be achieved. According to Atluri et al., Petri nets were mainly used for the reason that the safety problem in authorisation models is equivalent to the reachability problem in Petri nets. Thus, reachability analysis techniques of Petri nets can be used to conduct the safety analysis of WAM.

3.2.10.2 Task-Based Authorisation Controls (TBAC)

In [Thomas/Sandhu 1997], R. Thomas and R. Sandhu present the concept of task-based authorisation controls (TBAC) as a new kind of active security models that are required for agent-based distributed computing and workflow.

TBAC has similar objectives as WAM. In contrast to traditional access controls and security models, one objective of TBAC is to approach security modelling and enforcement at the application and enterprise level. Besides, TBAC is taking a task-based, active approach to security, where permissions are constantly monitored and activated and deactivated in accordance with emerging context associated with progressing tasks. The authors claim that in TBAC an authorisation is more closely modelling the equivalent of an authorisation in the paper world, because an authorisation step is used to model and manage a set of related permissions. Moreover, the concept of TBAC additionally provides features such as usage tracking of permission, life-cycle management of authorisations, the ability to put permissions temporarily on hold without invalidating them, as well as support of composite authorisations (a composite authorisation is an abstraction and consists of a set of component authorisation steps which are not visible externally to other authorisation steps outside the composite authorisation).

In [Thomas/Sandhu 1997], a family of TBAC models is introduced which is currently further investigated in ongoing research projects.

Analysis Task-based Authorisation Models

The most obvious application of Task-based Authorisation Models is in secure workflow management. Traditional security models as well as more recent models, such as role-based or object-oriented authorisation models, are normally not addressing the synchronisation of authorisation flow and workflow.

Like RBAC, WAM and TBAC are application-oriented and policy neutral.

3.2.11 Security Models for Object-Oriented Information Systems

Object-oriented database systems have been studied in research projects for some years now and have already been developed in some commercial products. In spite of this, there has been relatively little work on security models for object-oriented systems, although some work does exist. In this section, we will present some initial work on authorisation models for object-oriented systems.

3.2.11.1 The Authorisation Model by Fernandez et al.

In [Fernandez/Gudes/Song 1989], [Larrondo/Gudes/Song 1990], [Fernandez/Gudes/Song 1994], an authorisation model for object-oriented database systems is presented that consists of a set of policies, a structure for authorisation rules, and algorithms to evaluate access requests against the authorisation rules. The model uses the concept of implied authorisation, where an authorisation defined at some level of the class hierarchy implies rights for the subclass. User access policies are thus based on the concept of inherited authorisations applied along the class structure hierarchy.

The following authorisation policies (P1 - P3) are to be enforced by the model:

P1 (inherited authorisation): a user who has access to a class is allowed to have similar type of access in the corresponding subclass to the attributes inherited from that class.

P2 (class access): access to a complete class implies access to the attributes defined in that class as well as to attributes inherited from a higher class (but only to the class-relevant values of these attributes). If there is more than one ancestor (multiple inheritance), access is granted to the union of the inherited attributes.

P3 (visibility): an attribute defined for a subclass is not accessible by accessing any of its superclasses.

In the model, an authorisation rule is defined as a tuple (U, A, AO) where U is a user or user group, A is an access type or set of access types, and AO is the set of attributes of the object O to be accessed.

Access validation starts by extracting a data request from a user query or from an executing program. This request has the structure (U', A', AO'), where U' (user, process) is the subject making the request, AO' is the requested object (set of attributes), and A' is the requested access type. This request is compared with the authorisation rules to decide if the request should be granted or denied. Thus, access validation requires a search along the class structure hierarchy for potentially authorising rules.

Furthermore, the model includes a set of administrative policies for the administration of authorisation, including delegation and revocation.

In [Larrondo/Gudes/Song 1990], policies were proposed for negative authorisation rules (stating denial of privileges), content-dependent restrictions (expressed as predicates) along the hierarchy, and for resolving conflicts between several implied authorisations.

3.2.11.2 The Orion Authorisation Model

The Orion model that enforces a discretionary protection policy was first presented in [Rabitti et al. 1991]. A revised version was later proposed in [Bertino/Origgi/Samarti 1994].

Elements of the revised model are subjects, objects and access modes.

Subjects can be either users or user groups. A group is defined as a set of other subjects (users or groups). Groups are not necessarily disjoint, i.e. a subject may belong to more than one group. The membership relation allows to structure subjects into a subject graph.

The set of *objects* is composed of databases, classes of the databases, and instances of the classes. Objects are organised into an object granularity hierarchy: a class is composed of a set of instances, a database is composed of a set of classes. The system in turn consists of a set of databases.

The set of *access modes* consists of privileges that users can exercise on objects (read, write, create, delete, read-definition), where the access modes applicable to an object depend on the type of object. Access modes are related by means of an implication relationship.

The Orion model supports the concepts of *positive/negative, strong/weak,* and *explicit/implicit* authorisations.

Authorisations specified by the users are called explicit, whereas authorisations derived by the system are called implicit. For the Orion model, the following kinds of implication rules are defined: implication rules for the propagation of authorisations along the subject graph, implication rules for objects based on the hierarchical structure of the set of objects, implication rules along the inheritance hierarchy and implication rules for access modes based on relationships among access modes.

For example, the authorisation of a group for the privilege to modify an object implies the following authorisations:

• the write privilege on the object for the direct members of the group (implication rule for subjects)
• the write privilege to the direct descendants of the object in the object granularity hierarchy (implication rule for objects)
• the read privilege on the object (implication rule for access modes).

A positive authorisation is used to specify that a subject may exercise an access mode on an object, whereas a negative authorisation is used to specify the denial of an access mode on an object. Negative authorisations are useful to override implied access rights and to specify precisely the required authorisation of subjects.

Strong authorisations cannot be overridden by other authorisations, whereas weak authorisations may be overridden, according to specified rules, by other strong or weak authorisations. Weak authorisations in combination with positive/negative authorisations are useful to model exceptions.

In [Bertino/Weigand 1994], the Orion model is further extended to include content-based authorisations to which implication rules are also applied.

3.2.11.3 The DORIS Personal Model of Data

The DORIS ("Datenschutz-orientiertes Informationssystem") personal model of data is designed to model privacy as defined by the right of informational self-determination in information systems [Biskup/Brüggemann 1988]. The model is basically object-oriented, while an application can be conveniently described by non-first normal form tuples. The data manipulation language is high level and relational.

In the model, persons (users, data subjects) are represented by encapsulated objects. Every person is created as an instance of a class that is called group. The groups form a hierarchy. The data part of an object corresponds to the knowledge of an individual (about him/her and his/her relationship to other persons), the operation part corresponds to the possible actions of the individual. A person holds two kinds of rights: His acquaintances (with other persons) which can be dynamically granted or revoked, and authorities on roles that are statically received during creation according to class membership.

The set of acquaintances constitutes the person's social environment. A person can only send messages to his/her acquaintances querying about their knowledge or asking them to perform an operation. Then an acquaintance reacts to the message if the sender exhibits an appropriate authority, i.e. if the sender is performing an appropriate role.

Thus, if a query or update expression in a user's transaction has to be evaluated then the system enforces the privacy policy by two rules: The evaluation of the expression is modified such that messages are sent only to his/her acquaintances. The evaluation of the expression is totally refused if the substitute is not able to exhibit one authority with respect to each involved group.

3.2.11.4 Further Relevant Research

Further authorisation models enforcing discretionary access control for object-oriented database systems have, for example, been presented in [Dittrich/Hartig/Pfefferle 1989] [Brüggemann 1992].

Besides, some work has been performed on enforcement of the Bell LaPadula policy by modelling mandatory access controls using the object-oriented approach. For example, Jajodia et al. present the concept of a message filter which corresponds to the reference monitor of the Bell LaPadula model [Jajodia/Kogan/Sandhu 1995]. The message filter model enforces access control by exploiting the encapsulation characteristics of object-oriented systems. Since in object-oriented systems messages are the only means through which information can be exchanged among objects, the model controls information flow by mediating (filtering) the messages exchanged between objects. Another mandatory access control model that enforces the Bell LaPadula principles was proposed in [Millen/Lunt 1992].

Samarti et al. present a model that also uses a message filter component which intercepts every message to enforce safe information flow [Samarti et al. 1996]. According to the model, information flow is safe only if there is information flow from object O_i to object O_j and all users that can read O_j (i.e. that are listed in an access list associated with O_j) can also read O_i. Their approach, however, requires the check and filtering of every message at run time what considerably increases the overhead in the system. Therefore, M.Gendler-Fishman and E.Gudes proposed a compile-time model for safe information flow in object-oriented databases [Gendler-Fishman/Gudes 1997].

In [Essmayr/Pernul/Tjoa 1997] the OOAC (object-oriented access controls) concept was presented, which is based on the assumptions that everything within the object-oriented environment is regarded as an object, particularly security subjects (e.g., users, roles) are regarded as first-class objects, and messages are the only means for communicating to other objects. An object authorisation language (OAL) has been proposed that allows to specify authorisations in a declarative manner. As claimed by the authors, one advantage of OOAC is that it can be used to implement any known access control policy (e.g., discretionary, mandatory, role-based), because the structure and behaviour of database objects exactly determine the ways an object can be protected against unauthorised access.

[Castano et al. 1995] provides a survey of authorisation models for object-oriented systems.

Analysis of Security Models for Object-oriented Information Systems:

The models illustrated above enforce different security policies and offer some solutions to the problem of protection object-oriented systems. Discretionary security models have the disadvantage that they are vulnerable to Trojan Horse attacks. Mandatory models, which enforce the Bell LaPadula policy, have most of the disadvantages of the Bell LaPadula model.

One of the main characteristics of object-oriented systems is the encapsulation property. Hence, authorisation models should exploit the encapsulation characteristics and should support the specification of authorisations to execute methods instead of authorisations to execute elementary read and write operations. Furthermore, authorisation models, which support implicit authorisations, should also support the specification of negative, as well as, positive authorisations. The concept of positive and negative authorisations allows to model exceptions to authorisations. However, a policy for solving possible authorisation conflicts has to be provided as well.

As pointed out in [Castono et al. 1995, pp. 434], the task of devising a formal authorisation model for object-oriented information systems is particularly difficult owing to the lack of a standard reference model for object-oriented systems. Although all models are based on a set of common concepts, object-oriented systems have different characteristics, which may affect the authorisation model.

3.2.12 Resource Allocation Model for Denial of Service Protection

While most security models focus on protecting confidentiality and/or integrity, there are only few formal models addressing availability issues.

J.Millen introduced a model for a resource allocation monitor for denial of service protection [Millen 1992] in the face of certain kinds of deliberate attacks.

A denial of service protection base is characterised as a resource monitor closely related to a Trusted Computing Base, supporting a waiting-time policy for benign processes. Resource monitor algorithms and policies can be stated in the context of a state transition model of a resource allocation system.

Basic elements and state structure:

Basic elements of a resource allocation model consist of a set of *processes P* and a set of *resource types R*.

A process can be in one of two states: running or asleep. Each process type r has a capacity $c(r)$ and a maximum (virtual) holding time (MHT), denoted $h(r)$, that this resource r may be requested for exclusive use.

The current state of the resource allocation system is represented by a 4-tuple (A, T, S_Q, T_Q), where:

- A: $P \times R \rightarrow IN$ is the *allocation matrix* and A(p,r) is the number of units of resource type r that are currently allocated to process p. The *allocation vector* A_p for a process p is one row of the matrix, defined by $A_p(r) = A(P,r)$.

  It is defined:
  running(p) if $A_p(CPU) = 1$, and asleep(p) if $A_p(CPU) = 0$.

- T: $P \rightarrow IN$ is the *time vector*. Its value T(p) represents the system real time at the last time it was updated.

- S_Q: $P \times R \rightarrow IN$ is the *space requirement matrix*. Each value $S_Q(p,r)$ is a non-negative integer representing resource units needed by a process to complete its task. Each process p has a *space requirement vector* S_{Q_p} that corresponds to a row of the space requirement matrix.

- T_Q: $P \times R \rightarrow IN$ is the *time requirement matrix*. Each value $T_Q(p,r)$ is a non-negative integer representing the real time (number of "ticks") needed by a process to complete its task. Each process p has a *time requirement vector* T_{Q_p} that corresponds to a row of the time requirement matrix.

State transitions:

A possible state transition is denoted by $(A', T', S_Q', T_Q') \rightarrow (A', T', S_Q', T_Q')$. In the model, primed state components will always refer to a state that may follow the state referred to by unprimed components.

State changes are due to a reallocation of resources. A transition is a *deactivate transition*, if running(p) and asleep'(p). Transitions that p begins as asleep are called *reallocation transitions* for p. A reallocation transition that allocates the CPU (i.e. asleep(p) and running'(p)), is an *activate transition* for p.

Model Rules:

The eight rules (or better: properties) that comprise the resource allocation model are defined as follows:

(R1) *The total amount of currently allocated units of any resource must not exceed the system capacity for it:*

$$\sum_{p \in P} A_p \leq c$$

(R2) *The space requirement vector must be all-zero for a running process:*

$$\text{If running (p) then } S_{Q_p} = 0$$

(R3) *No reallocations affect a process that remains running:*
$$\text{if running}(p) \text{ and running}'(p) \text{ then } A'_p = A_p$$

(R4) *The time vector changes only on activate and deactivate transitions:*
$$\text{If } A'_p(CPU) = A_p(CPU) \text{ then } T'(p) = T(p)$$

(R5) *When a time vector value is updated, the new value is greater than any previous value:*
$$\text{if } A'_p(CPU) \neq A_p(CPU) \text{ then } T'(p) > T(p)$$

(R6) *Space requirements are updated in reallocation transitions:*
$$\text{if asleep}(p) \text{ then } S_{Q'_p} = S_{Q_p} + A_p - A'_p$$

(R7) *Time requirement vectors do not change during reallocation transitions:*
$$\text{if asleep}(p) \text{ then } T_{Q'_p} = T_{Q_p}$$

(R8) *The only reallocation in a deactivate transition is to revoke the CPU:*
$$\text{if running}(p) \text{ and asleep}'(p) \text{ then } A'_p = A_p\text{-CPU.}$$

In order to specify a denial of service protection base (DPB), the states and transitions are further constrained, both structurally, and by imposing conditions expressing the denial of service policy:

A **Denial of Service Protection Base (DPB)** is characterised by:

- A resource allocation system

- A resource monitor algorithm (resource monitor controls changes in the allocation set and the time at which a state change may occur).

- A waiting time policy (e.g., Maximum Waiting Time Policy, Finite Waiting Time Policy)

- User agreements (additional constraints on requirement vector changes during deactivate transitions. If these constraints are respected by a process, the process is called benign)

The DPB must satisfy the following conditions:

1. Each benign process will make progress in accordance with the waiting time policy

2. No non-CPU resource is revoked from a benign process until its time requirement is zero: If $r \neq CPU$ and $A_p(r) \neq 0$ and $A'_p(r) = 0$ then $T_{Q_p}(r) = 0$.

Analysis of the resource allocation model:

Millen's resource allocation model addresses denial of service attacks undertaken by malicious processes. It offers a detailed approach to specifying space and time requirements towards avoiding denial of service. In practice, however, the job of proving DPB properties can be quite difficult.

Protection against denial of service attacks is an important availability aspect. In addition to denial of service protection, availability has to be protected by fault tolerance services, robustness services and recovery services. These availability services, however, cannot be formally stated by a state transition model approach.

3. 2.13 Multiple Security Policies Modelling Approaches

As discussed in this Chapter, most security models are designed for special security needs of certain applications, and are more or less neglecting other important security aspects. However, the real world has multiple coexistent security policies. Thus, the necessity of multiple policy components has become obvious. In this Section, two similar approaches of modelling multiple security policies will be presented: the Generalised Framework for Access Control (GFAC) which was proposed by Marshal Abrams et al., and the Multipolicy Paradigm.

3.2.13.1 The Generalised Framework for Access Control (GFAC)

The GFAC project directed by Marshall Abrams started in the early nineties (see [Abrams et al. 1990], [Abrams et al. 1991a], [Abrams et al. 1991b], [LaPadula 1995]). GFAC provides an improved framework for expressing and integrating multiple policy components.

The main objectives are [LaPadula 1995]:
- Make it easy to state, formalise, and analyse diverse access control policies
- Make it feasible to configure a system with security policies chosen from a vendor-provided set of options with confidence that the system's security policy makes sense and will be properly enforced.
- Construct the model in a manner that allows one to show that it satisfies an accepted definition of each security policy it represents.

GFAC is based on the premise that all access control policies can be viewed as rules expressed in terms of attributes by authorities.

Authorities: An authorised agent that defines security policies, identifies relevant security information, and assigns values to attributes.

Attributes: Characteristics or properties of subjects and objects defined within the computer system for access control decision making

Rule: A set of formalised expressions that define the relationships among attributes and other security information for access control decisions in the computer system, reflecting the security policies defined by authority.

GFAC refers to security attributes and other access control data as access control information (ACI) and the rules that implement the trust policies of a system as access control rules (ACR).

A system function consists of two parts: adjudication and enforcement. In GFAC, "rule" means the portion of a system function that adjudicates access control requests. Nevertheless, GFAC explicitly recognises the two parts of access control: adjudication and enforcement. The agent that adjudicates access control requests is called access control decision facility (ADF), whereas the agent that enforces the ADF's decision is called access control enforcement facility (AEF). The ADF uses the security policies defined by authority and a metapolicy to decide whether a subject's request to access an object satisfies these security policies. In a trusted computer system, the AEF corresponds to the system functions of the trusted computing base (TCB) and the ADF corresponds to the access control rules within the TCB that embody the system's security policy. The ADF and AEF together encompass the reference validation mechanism. Figure 3.9 illustrates the Generalised Framework in terms just described.

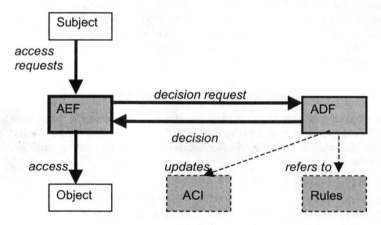

Fig. 3.9: Overview of GFAC (see [Abrams et al. 1991b], [LaPadula 1995])

The GFAC project motivated the Rule-Set Modelling approach, which is a new approach to formal modelling of a trusted computer system. In traditional security modelling approaches, the security model rules describe both access policy and system behaviour. The rule set modelling approach separates the decision criteria (access rules) from the state transition (system operations). AEF corresponds to a model of the system operations, called state-machine model, which abstractly defines the interface of processes to the TCB. ADF corresponds to a policy model, called the rule-set model, which defines the security policies of the trusted computer system. Figure 3.10 illustrates the rule-set modelling approach.

In a project directed by Marshall Abrams, the ORGCON policy and two other supporting policies (FC, SIM) were prototyped in the style of the Generalised

Framework for Access Control (see [Abrams et al. 1991b]). AT&T System V/MLS was selected as the platform on which the GFAC project would prototype the policies.

ORGCON (Originator-Controlled Access Control) is a controlled-distribution information handling policy (*read, no copy* policy, see [Abrams et al. 1993]). The ORCON policy was implemented by adding TCB software on top of, but making use of, the existing System V/MLS security mechanisms.

The FC (Functional Control) policy uses system roles of users and categories of objects. The system roles are *user, security officer,* and *administrator.* The categories are *general, security,* and *system.* The FC policy allows access of a process whose owner is in role R to an object having category C only if R "is compatible with" C. The relation "is compatible with" is defined as follows:
– *user* is compatible with *general*
– *administrator* is compatible with *general* and *system*
– *security officer* is compatible with *general* and *security.*

The SIM (Security Information Modification) policy uses types of data and system roles of users. If the data object contains security information, its data type is *si.* The SIM policy allows modifying access to data of type *si* only if the system role of the owner of the process is *security officer.*

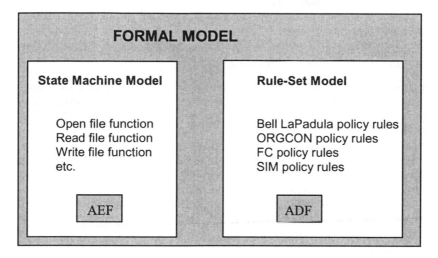

Fig. 3.10: Parts of the Formal Model according to the Rule-set Modelling Approach (see [Abrams et al. 1991b])

Leonard LaPadula later specified how the Bell LaPadula policy, the Clark Wilson policy, the FC policy and the SIM policy could be implemented according to the GFAC concept in Unix System V/MLS [LaPadula 1995]. We have used this draft top level specification that LaPadula presents in his publication, to model and implement a formal privacy policy, in the style of GFAC (see Chapter 6).

3.2.13.2 The Multipolicy Paradigm and Multipolicy Systems

The Multipolicy Paradigm proposed by Hilary Hosmer [Hosmer 1992b] is based on an approach that is very similar to GFAC. The Multipolicy Paradigm permits a multilevel secure system to enforce multiple, sometimes contradictory, security · policies. As GFAC, it also suggests to separate the system policy from the enforcement mechanism, so that it is possible to change policies without reevaluation of the system. Policy domain codes on data are used to indicate which security policy to enforce on the data, and multiple label segments supply the attributes needed for each policy. Metapolicies, policies about policies, coordinate the enforcement of multiple security policies. Metapolicies coordinate the interaction between policies, explicitly specifying order, priority, and conflict resolution strategies (see also [Hosmer 1992a]).

In [Kühnhäuser 1995], the Custodian Model for supporting multipolicy systems in distributed applications was presented.

3.3 Basic Security Functions and Security Mechanisms

In this Section, we will give a brief overview of basic security functions and mechanisms, which can be used to implement a security policy. The emphasis is put on important security functions and mechanisms that can enforce confidentiality and integrity aspects.

3.3.1 Identification and User Authentication

In order for a system to make meaningful decisions about whether a user should be allowed to access the system and to subsequently use services or resources, the user has to identify himself and the system has to authenticate the user (establish the validity of the claimed identity).

The verification of a person´s identity can rest on the following four principles (see [Everett 1992]):
- Something a person knows (e.g., a password)
- Something a person owns (e.g., a token such as a smart card)
- Some physical property of a person (e.g., his/her fingerprint)
- Some trait a person exhibits (e.g., the way he/she writes his/her signature or key stroke dynamics).

The last two characteristics belong to a class of recognition parameters generally referred to as Biometrics.

Password mechanisms are widely used in the computer world. However, password mechanisms are generally considered to be the weakest form of identity verification. Passwords are vulnerable due to their predictability and can, for example, be determined by disclosure of the user, disclosure at the host, sniffing attacks, password guessing or exhaustive search. The security of a password mechanism is heavily dependent on the used criteria for password selection and management.

Tokens are subject to transferability, with or without the agreement of the genuine token holder.

Biometrics are often put forward as the salvation of the identity verification problem. However, biometrics is still an emerging technology. All biometrics are subject to the false reject and the false accept error rate (see [Everett 1992]). Besides, biometrics can be vulnerable to interception and replay.

A further characteristic that can be used for authentication is the user´s geodetic location. Geodetic location, as calculated from a location signature, can be used to determine whether a person is attempting to log in from an approved location or to ensure that users can perform sensitive operations only from approved physical locations. GPS-based technology can be used to achieve Location-based Authentication. Location-based Authentication can be performed continuously and transparent to the users [Denning/MacDoran 1998]. However, Location-based Authentication systems are based on rather expensive technology and are vulnerable to attacks to the base systems.

A secure approach to user authentication should combine different techniques. For example, a combination of password, identity token and/or biometrics techniques could be used.

3.3.2 Access Control

Traditionally, Access Controls have been divided into two classes: Discretionary Access Control (DAC) and Mandatory Access Control (MAC).

Discretionary Access Control:

Discretionary access control is defined
> "as a means of restricting access to objects based on the identity of the subjects and/or groups to which they belong. The controls are discretionary in the sense that a subject with a certain access permission is capable of passing that permission (perhaps indirectly) on to any other subject" [TCSEC 1985].

DAC permits the granting and revoking of access privileges to be left to the discretion of the individual user, without the intercession of a security administrator. DAC is based on the "owner"-principle: A user that creates a file is regarded as the "owner" of the files and is controlling accesses to it.

Two major types or discretionary access control mechanisms are capability lists and access control lists (ACLs). Capabilities are associated with subjects. The system maintains a list of capabilities for each user. A capability is a key to a specific object, along with a mode of access. A subject possessing a capability may access the object in the specified way. Subjects might be allowed to grant (revoke) access to objects by passing copies of their own capabilities to other users (taking away capabilities from others). Access Control Lists are associated with objects. The ACL of an object identifies the individual users or group of users who may access the object.

DAC plays an important role in supporting security requirements of many organisations, especially within engineering and research environments

[Ferraiolo/Gilbert/Lynch 1993]. Within these environments, the discretionary sharing of access and exchange of information is important. Besides, DAC is appropriate if the need for users to access information is dynamic and changes rapidly over short periods.

However, discretionary access controls have the major drawback that they are, by their very nature, subject to Trojan horse attacks. With discretionary controls, programs acting on the user's behalf are free to modify access control information for files that the user owns (see also [Gasser 1988, pp. 74] for further discussion of Trojan horse attacks).

Mandatory Access Control:

Under mandatory controls, special security attributes are assigned to subjects and objects, either by the security administrator or automatically by the system. The system decides whether a subject can access an object by comparing their security attributes. These security attributes cannot be changed on request as can discretionary access control attributes such as access control lists. Thus, mandatory is the complement of discretionary.

Mandatory access controls prevent such types of Trojan horse attacks by imposing access restrictions that cannot be bypassed. A program operating on behalf of a user cannot change the security attributes of itself or of any object.

The TCSEC [TCSEC 1985] definition of mandatory access control refers to the Bell LaPadula policy. According to this definition, mandatory security works by associating security attributes with objects to reflect their sensitivity (as represented by a label). Similar security attributes are associated with subjects to reflect their authorisations (i.e., clearances).

Marshall Abrams uses the term non-discretionary to identify situations in which authority is vested in some users, but there are controls on delegation and propagation of authority [Abrams 1993].

3.3.3 Auditing

Auditing is a basic security function, which allows for the recording and review of all security-relevant events and provides an additional level of user assurance that misuse will not go undetected [Seiden/Melanson 1990]. The primary purpose of auditing is to detect and deter penetration of a computer system and to reveal usage that identifies misuse [NCSC 1987]. The information used to maintain a log of activity (the so-called audit trail) should be constructed in well-defined blocks of information called audit records.

Auditing is generally performed at user/operating system interface and from within the operating system itself. Nonetheless, trusted application are also often granted the right to perform their own auditing. Application level auditing reduces the level of audit data collected, and makes the audit trail easier to comprehend [Picciotto 1987].

According to [TCSEC 1985] and [ITSEC 1991], an auditing mechanism should at least be able to record the following types of events: use of identification and authentication mechanisms, introduction of objects into a user's address space (e.g., file open, program initiation), deletion of objects, actions by authorised users affecting the security of the system, and other security relevant events (e.g., the use of covert channels). For each recorded event, the audit record shall identify: data and time of the event, user, type of event, and success or failure of the event. For identification/authentication events the origin of the request (e.g., terminal ID) shall be recorded as well and for events that access or delete an object the audit record shall include the name of the object.

Auditing should have a minimal impact on system performance and a high degree of reliability. The confidentiality and integrity of the audit data have to be protected by technical and organisational means. For systems with high security requirements, the role of an auditor is introduced to enforce the principle of separation of duties. Besides, security precautions have to be taken to protect against the loss of audit data (e.g., in case of an overflow of the audit trail medium) (see [Seiden/Melanson 1990]).

3.3.4 Intrusion Detection Systems

Audit controls in traditional auditing systems have the disadvantage of being very complex, and of being executed only *a posteriori*. Auditing usually generates a large amount of audit data. For example, a VMS system with 100 users could generate 100-Megabyte audit data in a week. Thus, the manual analysis of such large amounts of audit data is practically very limited and can only be performed from time to time. Consequently, attacks might be undetected or can only be detected a long time after they occurred.

Therefore, the necessity of providing automated tools for audit trail analysis arises. Intrusion detection systems provide a mechanism for real-time detection of security violations, whether they are initiated by outsiders who break into the system, or by insiders who attempt to abuse their privileges.

Currently, there are two different kinds of intrusion detection methods which are generally employed by intrusion detection systems (see also [Castano et al. 1995, p.343]):

- **Anomaly detection methods**. This intrusion detection method is taking the approach of Dorothy Denning's Intrusion-Detection Expert System (IDES) Model [Denning 1986]. The Intrusion Detection model is based on the hypothesis that security violations can be detected by monitoring the system's audit records for abnormal patterns of system usage. The model includes profiles for representing the behaviour of subjects with respect to objects in terms of metrics and statistical models, and rules for acquiring knowledge about this behaviour from audit records and for detecting anomalous behaviour. Anomaly detection systems enable the statistical profiles of a user's normal behaviour to be compared with parameters of the current user's session. 'Significant' deviation from the normal behaviour is reported to the security officer, where 'significant' is defined by thresholds which were set for each profile. The advantage of the anomaly detection approach is that it is independent of any particular system, application environment, system vulnerability or type of intrusion.

- **Misuse detection systems.** This second type of intrusion detection method uses so-called a priori expert system rules that encode information about known system vulnerabilities, reported attack scenarios, as well as intuition about suspicious behaviour.

In general, an intrusion detection system accepts audit information from one (or several) target system(s), and matches it against statistical profiles and/or a misuse database to determine whether the behaviour is suspicious. Each target system is responsible for collecting audit data and putting it into the intrusion detection system's generic format.

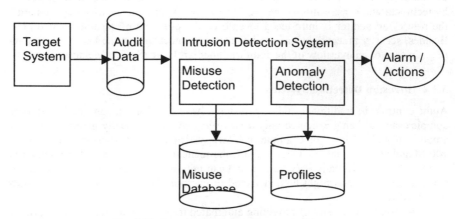

Fig. 3.11: Intrusion Detection System Architecture

Audit information sources for intrusion detection system tools are mainly operating system audit trails, accounting data, system logs or network packets.

Examples of some early intrusion detection systems are SRI International's *Intrusion Detection Expert System* (IDE*S*) [Lunt et al 1992], National Security Agency's *Multics Intrusion Detection and Alerting System* (MIDAS) [Sebring et al. 1988], Haystack Laboratories *Haystack System* [Smaha 1988], Los Alamos National Laboratory's *Wisdom&Sense* (W&S) [Vaccaro/Liepens 1989]. One of the first concepts of an intrusion detection expert system to detect virus infections was proposed in [Brunnstein/Fischer-Hübner/Swimmer 1991]. An *Intrusion Detection and Avoidance System* (IDA) was presented in [Fischer-Hübner 1993]. At the beginning of the nineties first commercial intrusion detection systems became available such as AT&T's *ComputerWatch* [Dowell/Ramstedt 1990] or *Stalke*r from the Haystack Laboratories [Smaha/Winslow 1994]. More recent systems are *SRI International's Next-Generation Intrusion Detection Expert System* (NIDES) [Anderson/Frivold/Valdes 1995] and the NIDES successor system *Emerald* [Porras/Neumann 1997], the *Adaptive Intrusion Detection system* (AID) [Sobirey/Richter/König 1996], and ASAX (*Advanced Security audit trail Analysis on uniX*) [Mounji et al. 1995]. Web-sites with overviews of intrusion detection projects and products are offered by [Price] and [Sobirey].

3.3.5 Object Reuse Protection

Reuseable objects such as disk, tape or memory space have to be cleared (overwritten) by the operating system after they are released by a first process and before they are reassigned to a second process. Otherwise the second process could scan the assigned object for residual sensitive data.

3.3.6 Trusted Path

A trusted path is "a mechanism by which a person at a terminal can communicate directly with a Trusted Computing Base (TCB). This mechanism can only be activated by the person or Trusted Computing Base and cannot be imitated by untrusted software". [TCSEC 85].

A trusted path should prevent attacks where users are thinking that they are communicating directly with the Trusted Computing Base when, in fact, their keystrokes and commands are being intercepted by an attacker. On a trusted system, a trusted path could for instance be established by pressing a unique key sequence that, by design, is intercepted directly by the TCB.

3.3.7 Cryptography

Cryptographic techniques are used to protect data, whether this is transmitted as messages, or stored in a single place. In addition to confidentiality, cryptography can be used to provide *authentication* (reassurance to the recipient of the identity of the sender), *integrity* (reassurance to the recipient that the message has not been modified in transit), as well as *nonrepudiation* (the ability of the recipient to prove to a third party that the sender really did send the message). Furthermore, cryptographic techniques are used to implement major privacy enhancing technologies providing anonymity, pseudonymity, unlinkability and/or unobservability for the users.

3.3.7.1 Foundations

An encryption algorithm, also called a cipher, is a mathematical function which transforms meaningful data, known as *plaintext*, to a non-meaningful form, known as *ciphertext*. The decryption algorithm must transform the ciphertext back to the original plaintext. Both the encryption and decryption operations use a key, so that the ciphertext is a function of both the plaintext and the encryption key. The recipient of the message must have the corresponding decryption key in order to recover the correct plaintext.

The process of encryption and decryption is illustrated in Figure 3.12, where the encryption key is denoted k_e, whilst the decryption key is denoted by k_d.

The security of the encryption and decryption algorithms should depend only on the secrecy of the key(s) and not on the secrecy of the algorithms E and D.

In order to maintain the confidentiality of the message, the decryption key k_d must remain secret, known only by the recipient of the message.

There are two general types of encryption algorithms, depending on the relationship between the encryption and decryption keys: Symmetric algorithms, or secret-key algorithms, are algorithms where the encryption key can be calculated from the decryption key and vice versa. In this case, therefore, it is necessary for the encryption key k_e to be secret also. Asymmetric algorithms, or public-key algorithms, are designed, so that it is practically impossible (i.e. computationally infeasible) to obtain the decryption key k_d from knowledge of the encryption key k_e. The algorithms are called "public-key" because the encryption key can be made public. In these systems, the encryption key is often called the public key, whilst the decryption key is called private key.

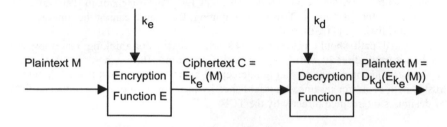

Fig. 3.12: The encryption and decryption process

Cryptanalysis is the science and study of methods of breaking ciphers. The basic attacks are known as *ciphertext only* (the attacker has only the ciphertext of several messages using the same encryption algorithm), *known plaintext* (the attacker knows some plaintext-ciphertext pairs) or *chosen-plaintext* (the attacker is able to acquire the ciphertext corresponding to selected plaintext).

An encryption algorithm is *perfectly*, or *unconditionally*, *secure*, if, no matter how much ciphertext a cryptanalyst has, there is no information to recover the plaintext.

Perfect secrecy was defined by Shannon [Shannon 1949] by the condition:

$p_C(M) = p(M)$;

Perfect secrecy means that the probability that message M was sent given that ciphertext C was received is equal to the probability of message M. Thus, intercepting the ciphertext C gives a cryptanalyst no additional information. Perfect secrecy requires that the number of keys must be at least as great as the number of possible messages. Otherwise there would be some message M such that for a given C, no key deciphers C into M, implying $p_C(M) = 0$. *One-time pads*, which are ciphers using a nonrepeating random key stream, are the only ciphers that achieve perfect secrecy given infinite resources. All other ciphers are breakable in a known-plaintext attack, simply by trying every possible key one by one. This attack is also called a *brute-force* attack.

An algorithm is considered *computationally secure*, if it cannot be broken by systematic analysis with available resources.

3.3.7.2 Symmetric Algorithms

Symmetric algorithms can be divided into two categories. *Stream algorithms* operate on the plaintext a single bit at a time, whilst *block algorithms* operate on the plaintext in groups of bits.

The following paragraph reviews some of the most prominent symmetric key encryption algorithms.

Data Encryption Standard (DES):

The Data Encryption Standard (DES) [NBS 1977] had been a worldwide standard for more than 20 years. DES was published in 1977 by the National Bureau of Standards for use in commercial and unclassified U.S. government applications. It was based on the Lucifer cipher algorithm designed by IBM.

DES is a block cipher, which maps a 64-bit input block into a 64-bit output block using a 56-bit key. The key is actually expressed as a 64-bit number, but every eighth bit is used for parity checking and is ignored. The algorithm, which is used both to encipher and to decipher, can be summarised as follows: An input block is first transposed under an initial permutation IP. After the algorithm has performed 16 iterations (called rounds) of a function that combines substitution and permutations, the block is transposed under the inverse permutation IP^{-1} to give the final result. DES embodies two concepts of Shannon´s theory of information secrecy [Shannon 1949]. Shannon identified two techniques to conceal information: confusion, which is provided by the substitutions, and diffusion, which is provided by the permutations.

The National Security Agency (NSA) had declared key elements of the algorithm design as "sensitive", not to be made public. The secrecy of the design had raised the fear that certain trapdoors had been imbedded in the DES algorithm. Recently, it has been admitted that the DES algorithm design was chosen in such a way as to defeat differential cryptanalysis attacks, a technique that was only introduced by Eli Biham and Adi Shamir in 1990 [Biham/Shamir 1990], (see also [Pfleeger 1997, pp. 112]).

The most serious objection raised against DES is the length of key, which is effectively only 56 bits long. It has always been pointed out that DES may be broken under a known-plaintext attack by exhaustive search.

In 1996, a report by an ad hoc group of prominent cryptographers published calculations to demonstrate the inadequacy of DES with 56-bit keys [Blaze et al 1996]. For example, a special purpose DES search machine using FPAG (Field Programmable Gate Array) technology could be built for $ 3000 Thousands, which could recover the right key on average in 19 days. A government agency willing to spend $10 Million to build a search machine using ASIC (Application-Specific Integrated Circuits) technologies could find the right key on average in 6 minutes. The authors concluded that the minimal key length for symmetric ciphers to protect information adequately for the next 20 years should be at least 90 bits long.

In January 1999, a worldwide coalition of computer users, worked with the Electronic Frontier Foundation's (EFF) "Deep Crack," a specially designed supercomputer, and a worldwide network of nearly 100,000 PCs on the Internet, to win RSA Data Security's DES Challenge III in a record-breaking 22 hours and 15 minutes. The worldwide computing team deciphered a secret message encrypted with the DES algorithm using commonly available technology.

Triple DES:

Triple DES is a technique by which the DES algorithm is applied three times to each plaintext block: A plaintext message M is enciphered as

$$C = DES_{k_1} (DES^{-1}_{k_2} (DES_{k_3} (M)));$$

That is, it is successively enciphered, deciphered, and then enciphered again, potentially using three different keys k_1, k_2, k_3.

Typical applications use two conventional DES keys k_1 and k_2, with k_1 being reused for the final encrypt. Triple DES with two keys gives the effect of a 112-bit key.

A triple DES device can interoperate with conventional DES encryption by using identical key values for k_1, k_2, k_3; using the same key in all three steps yields the same result as encrypting only once with that key.

International Data Encryption Algorithm (IDEA):

IDEA was developed by Xuejia Lai and James Maasey at the ETH Zurich in 1990 [Lai/Massey 1990].

IDEA is a block cipher, which operates on 64-bit plaintext blocks using a 128-bit key. As DES, IDEA also operates in rounds and uses both confusion and diffusion. The same algorithm is used for encryption and decryption.

IDEA was designed to be efficient to compute in software. Current software implementations of IDEA are about twice as fast as DES. The IDEA algorithm was designed to be immune against differential cryptanalysis. So far, no weaknesses of IDEA have been detected.

Advanced Encryption Standard:

Since DES cannot provide adequate security for sensitive applications any longer, NIST announced its intentions to develop a Federal Information Processing Standard (FIPS) for an Advanced Encryption Standard (AES) in January 1997. The major result of this effort should be "a FIPS specifying an Advanced Encryption Algorithm (AEA) - an unclassified, symmetric, block-cipher algorithm accommodating multiple key sizes, which is intended to be available royalty-free worldwide" and which "will have a usable lifetime of at least thirty years, and which will also be used extensively throughout the U.S. Government and private sectors" [Foti 1998].

NIST's "Request for Candidate Algorithm Nominations for the Advanced Encryption Standard" was announced in September 1997. On August 20, 1998, at the First AES Candidate Conference, NIST announced the fifteen official AES candidates, who have been submitted by researchers from industry or academia from different countries and are now under public evaluation and analysis (see [NIST-AES]). NIST was holding a Second AES Candidate Conference to discuss results of the public evaluation and analysis of the Round 1 AES candidate algorithms on March 22-23, 1999. Using the analysis and public comments received, NIST selected five AES finalist candidates, which were MARS by IBM Research, RC6 by RSA Laboratories, Rijndal by Joan Daemen and Vincent Rijmen, Serpent by Ross Anderson, Eli Biham, and Lars Knudsen and Twofish by Bruce Schneier, John Kelsey, Doug Whiting, David Wagner, Chris Hall, Niels Ferguson. At the Third AES Candidate Conference (AES3), which was held April 13-14, 2000 in New York, technical analysis of the finalists was presented and discussed, along with views as to which of the finalists should be selected as the AES winner(s). On October 2, 2000 NIST announced that Rijndael [Rijndael] has been selected as the proposed AES.

3.3.7.3 Asymmetric Algorithms

Symmetric encryption schemes suffer from the key distribution problem: before communication can take place, a secure communication channel is needed to send the secret keys to both the sender and the receiver. A solution to this problem is to use a public key encryption scheme. Each user has both a public and a private key, and two users can communicate knowing only each other's public key.

Another advantage of most public-key systems is that they are ideally suited to produce *digital signatures*. The RSA algorithm, for example, can easily be used to create a digital signature of a document by encrypting it using the private key. In practical implementations, since public-key algorithms are too inefficient to sign long documents, digital signature protocols are implemented with one-way hash functions: First a one-way hash of the document is produced, which is then encrypted (signed) with the private key.

The concept of public-key cryptography was invented by Whitfield Diffie and Martin Hellmann [Diffie/Hellmann 1976]. The most popular public key cryptographic algorithm is RSA [Rivest/Shamir/Adleman 1978], which is called after its inventors Rivest, Shamir, and Adleman. Another public key algorithm that relies on the difficulty of computing discrete logarithms over finite fields was, for example, suggested in 1984 by El Gamal [El Gamal 1984].

RSA Algorithm:

RSA is based on the hard problem to factor large numbers. To generate the keys, two large (100 or 200 digits large) prime numbers p and q are chosen, from which the value n = p * q is obtained.

Next e is chosen to be relatively prime to (p-1)*(q-1). Finally, Euclid's extended algorithm is used to compute the decryption key, d, such that

e*d mod (p-1) * (q-1) = 1. In other words: $d = e^{-1} \mod ((p-1) * (q-1))$.

The public encryption key is the pair (e,n) and the private decryption key is the pair (d, p, q). To encrypt a message m, the message is first divided into numerical message blocks m_i smaller than n.

Each message block m_i is encrypted by computing $c_i = m_i^e \mod n$.

The plaintext is recovered by $m_i = c_i^d \mod n$.

RSA has been subject to extensive cryptanalysis, however, no serious flaws have yet been detected. It is conjectured that the problem of recovering the plaintext from the public keys and the ciphertext is equivalent to the hard problem of factoring the product n of the two large primes. To successfully withstand factoring attacks, an appropriate key length has to be chosen. It is recommended to use a key length of at least 1024 bits for applications that have to be secure today and in the near future. To provide security within the next 20 years, a key length of at least 1536 bits is recommended (see [Schneier 1996, pp. 158] for further discussion of the key length).

Hybrid Cryptosystems:

Public-key algorithms have two disadvantages: First, they are slow. Symmetric algorithms are generally at least 1000 times faster than public-key algorithms. Second, they are vulnerable to chosen-plaintext attacks, because a cryptanalyst can use the public key to perform trial encryptions.

Thus, in most practical implementations (so-called hybrid cryptosystems) public key encryption and symmetric encryption are combined: public-key cryptography is used to secure and distribute session keys. These session keys are used with symmetric encryption to secure the message transfer. Since a session key is created when it is needed to encrypt communications of a session and destroyed after the session, the risk and profitability of compromising the session key is drastically reduced.

3.3.7.4 Hash Functions

A hash (also known as a message digest) is a one-way function h that takes a message m of arbitrary length and computes from it a fixed-length (short) number h(m). For practical reasons, for any number m, it has to be relatively easy to compute h(m). For a hash function to be considered cryptographically secure, it must be computationally infeasible to find a message that has a given prespecified message digest (pre-image resistance), and it similarly should be impossible to find two messages that have the same message digest (collision resistance). Examples of hash functions that are regarded as secure with a 160 bit hash result are, for instance, RIPEMD-160 [RIPEMD] or SHA-1 (Secure Hash Algorithm) [NIST-SHA 1995].

3.3.7.5 Certificates

Key distribution is easier with public key cryptography. Each node is responsible for knowing its own private key and all public keys can be made accessible in one or several places. While secrecy of the public keys is not required for secure communication or digital signatures, it is essential to maintain their integrity so they can be used to transmit messages in secrecy and validate digital signatures. Thus, the problem with public key cryptographic systems is to verify the claimed identity of the public key owner.

The typical solution is *certificates*, which were first proposed by Kohnfelder [Kohnfelder 1978]. Certificates are signed documents specifying a name of the public key owner and the corresponding public key. A higher level authority asserts the binding between the identity of the public key owner and the public key for the interval of the certificate validity by signing a document that contains user name, key, name of the issuing authority, expiry date, etc. Several proposals exist specifying the precise format of certificates, most notably X.509 certificates used in the X.509 Directory Framework.

In order to trust a public key from the certificate, the user must establish trust in the certificate issuer. Certificates could be issued by an official *Certification Authority* (CA) that may in turn have its certificate signed by another issuing CA. The system for the management of public keys and certificates, and establishment of trust in different public keys or certificates is called a *certification* or *public key infrastructure*. A certification infrastructure can be established as a hierarchy of Certification Authorities. Another approach is taken by PGP´s web-of-trust model, which is based on the users´ ultimate trust in themselves. (PGP –Pretty Good Privacy- is a freeware electronic-mail security program [PGP], originally designed by Philip Zimmermann).

Certificates can be stored on databases around the network. Users can send them to each other. Besides, the issuing CA has to maintain copies of the certificates.

Certificates of the above type are called **identity certificates**. However, certificates can be used for two purposes. They can identify a person associated with a public key or they can specify authorisations (e.g., access rights) to be given to the holder of a cryptographic key without identifying the holder´s identity. Recently, **authorisation certificates** have been specified that bind the public key to an authorisation given to the keyholder (i.e. the person that owns and controls the corresponding private key). The corresponding private key can be viewed as a capability equipped with the rights specified in the certificate [Gollmann 1999, p.219].

SPKI (Simple Public Key Infrastructure) **certificates** [SPKI] are a concrete type of authorisation certificates, which are currently being standardised by the IETF (Internet Engineering Task Force).

A SPKI certificate is a digitally signed record that may be expressed as a 5-tuple (I, S, D, A, V) where

- I is the public key or a hash of the public key of the certificate´s issuer

- S is the subject acquiring the authority (typically its public key, hash of a public key or a local name of the subject in the issuer´s local name space)

- D is the delegation bit indicating whether the subject has the right to further delegate the rights granted in this certificate

- A is the authorisation field (also called tag) specifying the permissions granted by the issuer to the subject

- V is the validity field of the certificate.

Two SPKI certificates $<I_1, S_1, D_1, A_1, V_1>$ and $<I_2, S_2, D_2, A_2, V_2>$ can be reduced if $S_1 = I_2$ and D_1 = true. The certification resulting from the reduction is $<I_1, S_2, D_2, A_1 \cap A_2, V_1 \cap V_2>$.

The purpose of SPKI structures is to communicate permissions or rights from one key holder to another. SPKI certificates can be chained together into sequences. Typically, the last certificate within a sequence is a permission certificate that expresses that a subject has a certain right. The final certificate is preceded by delegation certificates delegating authorisations. The first certificate within the sequence must be issued by the verifier of the sequence (see also [Nikander/Viljanen 1998]). Thus, the verifier of the certificate chain must be the source of the chain and all useful authorisation chains are therefore loops.

The issuer and subject are usually expressed as public keys and not as names as e.g. in X.509. This allows them to be relatively anonymous, if desired. In Chapter 4.2.3.2 we will show how SPKI certificates can be used to verify user´s access rights even when the user desires to stay anonymous.

If identity certificates are used for an identity-based access control in a distributed system environment, centralised or hierarchical certification authorities are needed. These CAs must all be trusted with respect to access control decisions that depend on the correct mapping between keys and names. A CA sees the certificates it issues, and typically sees them again later (e.g. in case of online certificate validation with the CA). Thus CAs are sites where profiles of the user´s activities can be created (see also [Brands 1999].

Authorisation certificates bind a key directly to an authorisation. Hence, there is no need to contact a CA for access control decisions, and consequently security and privacy risks in connection with CAs are avoided.

3.4 Security Evaluation Criteria

Most users and system purchasers do not have the knowledge to judge about the security or test reports provided by vendors and to decide whether offered systems are fulfilling their security requirements.

Since users need confidence in the security of the system that they are using, an independent third-party evaluation is desirable. Independent experts can assess an IT system against defined evaluation criteria. IT Security Evaluation Criteria also provide an objective yardstick for the users to compare the security capabilities of IT systems they are thinking of purchasing.

Meanwhile several IT security evaluation criteria exist, which are briefly discussed in this Section. Recently, legislation (§14 German Digital Signature Act, § 17 Digital Signature Ordinance) has been issued that requires the use of certified technical components fulfilling assurance requirements and refers to the European IT Security Evaluation Criteria (ITSEC).

An overview to the history of European and North American Security Evaluation Criteria is illustrated in Figure 3.12.

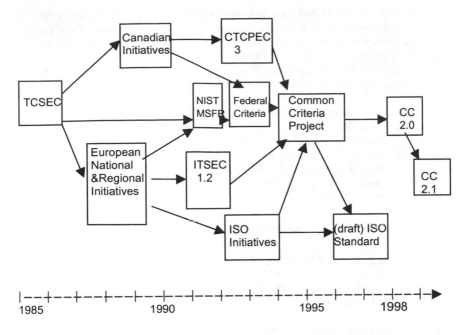

Fig. 3.12: History of IT Security Evaluation Criteria (see also [Troy 1996])

3.4.1 The Rainbow Series (Orange Book et al.)

In 1983, the U.S. Department of Defence published *the "Trusted Computer System Evaluation Criteria"* (TCSEC) document, which is also known as the Orange Book because of the colour of its cover. A second version with minor changes was published in 1985 [TCSEC 1985]. It had for a long time formed the basis for NSA product evaluations. TCSEC is oriented towards mainframe systems that were mainly in use during the eighties, i.e. stand-alone, multi-user operating systems without external connectivity. Besides, the TCSEC is mainly addressing military security needs and policies and is at the same time neglecting commercial security aspects. The emphasis of the TCSEC is on the protection of confidentiality, whilst other security aspects are hardly addressed (e.g., integrity is only addressed in form of label integrity).

Actual configurations of systems, particularly when networked, may result in vulnerabilities in spite of the evaluated ratings of individual components (e.g., passwords transmitted in clear between networked systems permit easy compromise). Thus it is important to consider complex systems (including networks, database management, applications) as a single system [Neumann 1990].

For this reason TCSEC was subsequently "interpreted" for both networks and databases: The *"Trusted Network Interpretation"* (Red Book), which was published by the National Computer Security Center (NCSC) in 1987 [NCSC 1987], provides interpretations of the TCSEC for network systems and describes a number of additional security services that arise in conjunction with networks. The *"Trusted Database Management System Interpretation"* of the TCSEC (Lavender Book) was issued by the NCSC in 1991 [NCSC 1991].

The Red Book and the Lavender Book should be considered in addition to the Orange Book, along with others in the "rainbow" series of documents [Neumann 1990].

TCSEC defines four basic divisions, A, B, C, and D, ordered in hierarchical manner, were A is the division with the highest degree of security. Within divisions there are a number of subdivisions known as classes, which are also ordered in hierarchical manner. The complete set of security classes from lowest to highest degree of security is D, C1, C2, B1, B2, B3, A1. Within each class, the four major sets of criteria "Security Policy", "Accountability", "Assurance" and "Documentation" are addressed. The security relevant portions of a system are referred to as the *Trusted Computing Base* (TCB). The following section summarises the minimal requirements of each security class:

Division (or Class) D: Minimal Protection
This division is reserved for those systems that have been evaluated but that fail to meet the requirements for a higher evaluation class. No security characteristics are needed for a D rating.

Division C: Discretionary Protection

Class C1: Discretionary Security Protection:
Class C1 systems are intended for an environment of cooperating users processing data at the same level(s) of sensitivity. C1 requires identification and authentication mechanisms. Besides, a C1 system provides separation of users and data and incorporates discretionary access controls, which allows users to specify and control sharing of those objects by named individuals or defined groups or both. Security testing shall assure that there are no obvious ways to defeat the security protection mechanisms.

Class C2: Controlled Access Protection:
C2 systems enforce a more finely grained discretionary access control than C1 systems, making users individually accountable for their actions through login procedures, auditing of security-relevant events, and resource isolation. Besides, measures for a secure object reuse have to be taken, guaranteeing that reassigned media must contain no residual data from previously contained objects.

Division B: Mandatory Protection

Class B1: Labeled Security Protection:
In addition to the requirements for C2 systems, an informal statement of the security policy model, data labeling, and mandatory access control over named subjects and objects must be provided. The mandatory access policy is the Bell-LaPadula model. Any flaw identified by testing must be removed.

Class B2: Structured Protection:
The TCB of a B2 system is based on a clearly defined and documented security model that requires discretionary and mandatory access control to be enforced on all objects and subjects, including devices. Analysis of covert channels is required. Authentication mechanisms are strengthened. The TCB must be carefully structured into protection-critical and non-protection-critical elements and well-defined largely independent modules. The TCB interface is well-defined. The design and implementation of a B2 system must enable a more thorough testing and review. A descriptive top-level specification of the TCB has to be maintained and it has to be demonstrated that the TCB implementation is consistent with the descriptive top-level specification. The system is "relatively resistant to penetration".

Class B3: Security Domains:
The TCB of a B3 system must satisfy the reference monitor that it mediates all accesses of subjects to objects, be tramperproof, and be small enough to be subjected to analysis and tests. The TCB should be minimised by excluding modules from the TCB that are not protection-critical. A security administrator is supported, audit mechanisms are expanded to signal security-relevant events and to take actions to terminate suspicious activities. System recovery procedures are required. The system is "highly resistant to penetration".

Division A: Verified Protection:

Class A1: Verified Design:
Class A1 systems are functionally equivalent to B3 systems in that no additional functionality requirements are added. However, A1 systems require the use of formal design specification and verification techniques in order to raise the degree of assurance that the TCB is correctly implemented. Important criteria for class A1 certification are: a formal security model and a mathematical proof of its consistency and adequacy, a formal top-level specification (FTLS) of the TCB, a (formal or informal) demonstration that the FTLS corresponds to the model, informal demonstration that the TCB implementation is consistent with the FTLS, and formal analysis of covert channels.

Beyond Class A1:
This section addresses additional assurance criteria for a formal implementation verification, which are beyond current technology.

3.4.2 European Initiatives

3.4.2.1 Overview

Developments in IT and the inflexibility of the TCSEC made several European nations begin their own criteria development efforts in the late 1980's. However, manufacturers, who are typically based multi-nationally, did not want different security criteria in different countries. Besides, it was recognised that there are common security requirements among nations. Therefore, the European efforts have been harmonised by the Commission of the European Communities into the "Information Technology Security Evaluation Criteria" (ITSEC). The first version 1.0 was published in 1990 and was mainly based on the following national criteria documents:

- The French Catalogue de Critéres Destinés á évaluer le Degré de Confiance des Systémes d´Information ("Blue-White-Red Book")[SCSSI 1989]
- The British UK Systems Security Confidence Levels [CESG 1989]
- The British DTI Commercial Computer Security Centre Evaluation Levels Manual ("Light Green Book") [DTI 1989a]
- The British DTI Commercial Computer Security Centre Functionality Manual [DTI 1989b]
- The German IT-Security Criteria ("German Green Book") [GISA 1989].

Besides, the Netherlands contributed to it. The Version 1.2 [ITSEC 1991] was published in June 1991 and became the basis for evaluations in EU member states for a trial period.

3.4.2.2 The German Green Book

The German Green Book was published in 1989 by the German Information Security Agency (GISA) as "a further development of the Orange Book". One of its major contributions is the decoupling of functionality and assurance requirements.

The German criteria identified the following eight basic security functions: identification and authentication, administration of rights, verification of rights, audit, object reuse, error recovery, continuity of service, data communication security. Ten predefined functionality classes, F1 through F10, are used to define functional requirements for the basic security functions. Classes F1 through F5 correspond to the functionality requirements of the TCSEC classes C1 through B3. Besides, the five additional functionality classes were defined to address the following security aspects: F6 (High Program and Data Integrity), F7 (High Availability), F8 (High Data Communication Integrity), F9 (High Data Communication Integrity), F10 (High Data Communication Integrity and Confidentiality).

Furthermore, eight quality levels, Q0 through Q7, were defined corresponding roughly to the assurance requirements of the TCSEC levels D through Beyond A1.

One or no functionality class from F1 –F5 can be combined with a subset of functionality classes from F6 - F10 and with a quality level in any way, producing 1536 different potential evaluation results, even though some combinations (e.g., F5/Q0) might be useless.

3.4.2.3 The Information Technology Security Evaluation Criteria (ITSEC)

According to the ITSEC, a Target of Evaluation (TOE) can be either a system or product. A system is defined as a specific IT installation with a particular purpose and operational environment, whilst a product is a package of IT software and/or hardware that can be used in a variety of environments. The TOE is considered in the context of the operational requirements and the threats it is to encounter. The sponsor of the evaluation determines the security target, which defines the security functions of the TOE, may describe threats or security mechanisms, and includes the evaluation level desired, specified in ITSEC terms.

Under the ITSEC, the evaluation factors are functionality and the assurance aspects of correctness and effectiveness. Like the German Green Book, the ITSEC also separates functionality and assurance criteria.

Functionality refers to the security enforcing functions of the security target, which may be individually specified or referenced by predefined functionality classes.

The following generic headings are recommended for specification of the security enforcing functions of the security target:

1. Identification and authentication
2. Access control
3. Accountability
4. Audit
5. Object reuse
6. Accuracy
7. Reliability of service
8. Data exchange

The Claims Language, which was provided by the U.K. Department of Trade and Industry's Light Green Book, is given as a particular example of a semiformal notation that has been successfully used in the definition of security targets. The Claims Language is a subset of English, which was designed to provide a structured way in which claims could be made about the security features of IT products.

Besides, ITSEC provides ten predefined example functionality classes (F-C1, F-C2, F-B1, F-B2, F-B3, F-IN, F-AV, F-DI, F-DC, F-DX) that are directly corresponding to the German functionality classes F1 through F10.

Evaluation of effectiveness assesses whether the security enforcing functions and mechanisms of the TOE will actually satisfy the stated security objectives. The assessment of effectiveness involves consideration of the suitability of the TOE's functionality, binding of functionality (whether individual security functions are mutually supportive and provide an integrated and effective whole), the consequences of known and discovered vulnerabilities, and ease of use.

In addition, evaluation of effectiveness assesses the strength of mechanisms, i.e. the ability of security mechanisms of the TOE to withstand direct attacks. The three strength levels basic, medium and high are defined.

Evaluation of correctness assesses whether the security enforcing functions and mechanisms are implemented correctly. Seven evaluation levels labelled E0 to E6 have been defined representing ascending levels in confidence in the correctness. E0 through E6 are corresponding roughly to the assurance requirements of the TCSEC levels D through A1 as well as to the German Q0-Q6 quality levels.

As already pointed out in this Section, ITSEC offers the following significant changes over the TCSEC: ITSEC separates functionality and assurance requirements. Besides, the ITSEC defines new functionality requirements classes that are also addressing integrity and availability aspects. Functionality can also be individually specified, which means that ITSEC is independent of a specific security policy.

Furthermore, ITSEC in contrast to TCSEC also supports evaluations by independent, commercial evaluation facilities.

ITSEC		TCSEC Class
E0	↔	D
F-C1, E1	↔	C1
F-C2, E2	↔	C2
F-B1, E3	↔	B1
F-B2, E4	↔	B2
F-B3, E5	↔	B3
F-B3, E6	↔	A1

Fig.3.13: Intended correspondence between ITSEC and TCSEC classes [ITSEC 1991]

Nevertheless, it was intended that ITSEC also corresponded to the TCSEC classes. The intended correspondence between the ITSEC and the TCSEC classes is shown in Figure 3.13.

3.4.3 North American Initiatives

3.4.3.1 CTCPEC

Canada began their own criteria development work in 1988, when the Canadian System Security Centre (CSSC) was formed to develop and work out criteria and to establish a Canadian evaluation capability, among other tasks. The Draft Version 3.0 of "The Canadian Trusted Computer Evaluation Criteria" (CTCPEC) was published in April 1992 and was followed by the final version of CTCPEC V3.0, which was published in January 1993 [CTCPEC 1993].

The CTCPEC addresses "monolithic systems, multi-processing systems, data bases, subsystems, distributed systems, networked systems, and others". CTCPEC also separates functionality and assurance requirements. Functionality consists of Confidentiality Criteria, Integrity Criteria, Availability Criteria, and Accountability Criteria. Each of the four "Functional Criteria" is divided into - altogether 18 - "Security Services". Besides, Assurance Criteria are applied across the entire product under evaluation. Nevertheless, the CTCPEC also considers dependencies between functionality aspects, between assurance aspects or between functionality and assurance aspects, which are documented by constraint relations.

3.4.3.2 MSFR

Partly in response to these criteria initiatives largely in Europe and Canada, NSA and NIST in the USA agreed to jointly re-work the TCSEC to bring it up to date technically and to meet also the needs of non-military, especially commercial IT applications. A first document was the Minimum Security Functional Requirements

(MSFR) [MSFR 1992], an update of the TCSEC's C2 requirements set intended to be more useful to private industry and civil government bodies. The MSFR was strongly influenced by the ITSEC's Security Target philosophy, which separated functional and assurance criteria and justified each against threats in the intended environment of use (see [Troy 1996]).

3.4.3.3 Federal Criteria

In December 1992, NIST and NSA published the draft version 1.0 of the "Federal Criteria for Information Technology Security" (FC) [FC 1992]. FC in turn was heavily influenced by the MSFR and by the CTCPEC.

The FC introduced the concept of a Protection Profile, which is an implementation-independent set of functionality and assurance requirements for a category of products that meet specific consumer needs. A protection profile also considers dependencies between security aspects. A vendor might produce a product that is intended to meet the requirements of the profile. The vendor would then map the requirements of the protection profile in the context of the specific product, onto a statement called a Security Target, which is similarly defined as a security target in ITSEC. A security target has a similar structure as a protection profile, and is a product-specific description, elaborating the more general requirements in a protection profile and including all evidence of how the product meets the security requirements of a given protection profile.

3.4.4 International Harmonisation

3.4.4.1 ISO Initiatives (ISO/IEC-ECITS)

ITSEC has also motivated and influenced ISO initiatives to work on a truly international standard that permits comparability between the results of independent security evaluations. In late 1990 the Joint Technical Committee 1 of the International Organisation for Standards and the International Electrotechnical Commission (ISO/IEC JCT1) established the project "Evaluation Criteria for IT Security" (ECITS) in Working Group 3 "Security Evaluation Criteria" of Subcommittee 27 "Security Techniques" (SC27/WG3). The draft ISO-ECITS included a multipart standard: Part 1 "Model", Part 2 "Functionality Classes" (which was also influenced by the CTCPEC), and Part 3 "Assurance".

3.4.4.2 The Common Criteria

In parallel to the work in ISO/IEC, the sponsoring organisations of the CTCPEC, FC, TCSEC and ITSEC started to develop their own set of criteria, the so-called "Common Criteria" (CC), whose draft Version 1.0 was published in January 1996 [CC 1996]. Its purpose was to resolve the conceptual and technical differences found in the source criteria and to deliver the results to ISO as a contribution to the international standard under development. In April 1996, the CC replaced the previous working drafts in ISO/IEC JCT1/SC27/WG3, when WG3 accepted Part 1 through Part 3 of the CC trial Version 1.0 as the basis for its further work.

After a period of trial-use and public review, The CC Version 2.0 [CC 1998] was published in the Spring 1998. The Common Criteria Project Sponsoring Organisations (the national security agencies of Canada, Germany, France, the Netherlands, UK, as well as NSA and NIST) have committed themselves to replacing their respective evaluation criteria with the CC Version 2.0. The ISO WG3 made a small number of editorial changes to CC V 2.0 text in October 1998 to create the "Final Draft International Standard" (FDIS) 15408. The CC Version 2.1 [CC 1999] was published in August 1999 and is a version that aligns it with International Standard ISO/IEC 15408.

Overview of the CC structure:

The CC consists of three major parts, following the original ISO criteria structure:

Part 1 *"Introduction and General Model"* consists of the introduction and presentation of the general model and concepts of IT security evaluation.

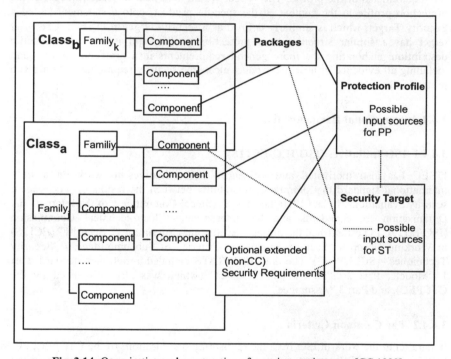

Fig. 3.14: Organisation and construction of security requirements [CC 1999]

Part 2 *"Security Functional Requirements"* establishes a set of functional components as a standard way of expressing the functional requirements. It catalogues the set of functional components, families and classes.

Part 3 *"Security Assurance Requirements"* is the catalogue of assurance requirements, consisting of a set of discrete assurance components, families and classes similarly to Part 2, plus a grouping of selected components into a series of seven increasingly rigorous packages called Evaluation Assurance Levels (EALs). Besides, Part 3 also contains evaluation criteria for Protection Profiles (PP) and Security Targets (ST).

Organisation and construction of requirements:

Thus, the CC presents security requirements under the distinct categories of functional and assurance requirements.

The CC defines a set of constructs that combine into meaningful assemblies of security requirements. These constructs can be used in defining security requirements for prospective products and systems. The relationships among the various constructs for requirements expression are illustrated in Figure 3.14 and explained below.

The CC security requirements are organised into the hierarchy of class – family – component to help consumers to locate specific security requirements.

The most general grouping of security requirements is a *class*. The members of a class, termed *families*, share security objectives but may differ in emphasis or rigour. A *component* describes a specific set of security requirements and is the smallest selectable set of security requirements.

Dependencies that may exist between components are described as a part of the CC component definitions.

Figure 3.15 illustrates the principle of the hierarchical decomposition of security requirement classes.

The CC defines three types of security requirement constructs: package, PP and ST. It preserves the concepts of protection profiles and security targets, which were introduced by the Federal Criteria.

A *package* is defined as a reusable set of either functional or assurance components (e.g. an EAL), combined together to satisfy sets of identified security objectives.

A *protection profile (PP)* is defined as an implementation-independent, reusable set of security requirements for a category of targets of evaluation (TOEs) that meet specific consumer needs. A PP can contain security requirements either from the CC, or stated explicitly, and should include an EAL (and possibly additional assurance components). A set of PP examples has been developed (see [CC-Project]). This set includes commercially oriented ones from previous criteria (CS1/C2 and CS3), a Draft Role-Based Access Control (RBAC) Protection Profile and Firewall Protection Profiles (traffic filter firewall profile, application level profile). It is envisioned that there will be a living catalogue or registry of PPs.

A *security target (ST)* contains a set of security requirements, which is used as the basis for evaluation of an identified TOE. This set of security requirements may be made by reference to a PP, directly by reference to CC functional or assurance components, or stated explicitly, and should be shown, by evaluation, to be useful and effective in meeting the identified security objectives.

The TOE security requirements can be constructed by using existing PPs, existing packages, existing functional and assurance requirement components, and/or additional functional and/or assurance requirements not contained in the CC.

Class	Family	Components

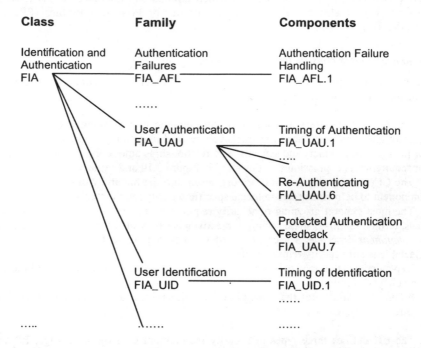

Fig. 3.15: Functionality Class FIA as an Example of a class – family – component hierarchy

Functional Security Requirements:

Part 2 contains the following eleven classes of CC Security Functional Requirements: FAU (Security Audit), FCO (Communication/Non-Repudiation), FCS (Cryptographic Support), FDP (User Data Protection), FIA (Identification and Authentication), FMT (Security Management), FPR (Privacy), FPT (Protection of the TOE Security Functions), FRU (Resource Utilisation), FTA (TOE Access), FTP (Trusted path/channels).

It is intended that these classes cover the known range of IT security functions. They are further subdivided into 66 families of related components.

Assurance Requirements:

Part 3 contains the following seven classes of specifiable assurance components covering the correctness of the TOE implementation and the effectiveness of the security functions: ACM (Configuration Management), ADO (Delivery and Operation), ADV (Development), AGD (Guidance Documentation), ALC (Life-Cycle Support), ATE (Tests), AVA (Vulnerability Assessment).

Besides, as already mentioned above, useful combinations of assurance components have been combined into seven Evaluation Assurance Levels (EALs):

EAL1 – functionally tested (new)
EAL2 – structurally tested (like C1 – E1)
EAL3 – methodically tested and checked (like C2 – E2)
EAL4 – methodically designed, tested, and reviewed (like B1 – E3)
EAL5 – semiformally designed and tested (like B2 – E4)
EAL6 – semiformally verified design and tested (like B3 – E5)
EAL7 – formally verified design and tested (like A1 – E6)

The seven EALs are increasingly strong packages of mutually supportive components covering requirements from each of the classes which have been developed for normal use in PPs and STs. Nevertheless, individual assurance components can be specified to augment these EALs for particular product needs.

3.4.5 Shortcomings of IT Security Evaluation Criteria

Some fundamental criticisms on the concept of IT Security Evaluation Criteria, especially on the inappropriate metrical approach of early evaluation criteria, have been raised in [Brunnstein /Fischer-Hübner 1990], [Brunnstein/Fischer-Hübner 1992].

A major shortcoming of the TCSEC, which has until recently been used for NSA certifications, is that it is only addressing military security needs and policies, and is neglecting commercial security aspects. When the TCSEC was introduced, there was an implicit contract between government and vendors, saying that if vendors built products and had them evaluated, the government would buy them [Pfleeger 1987, p.324]. Consequently, IT security development and research activities have concentrated on maintaining secrecy of classified data, funded by the US Government. This effect of promoting confidentiality aspects, was also encouraged by more recent security criteria, such as ITSEC, which intends to keep compatibility with TCSEC. While 5 of ITESC's predefined functionality classes refer to the functionality of the TCSEC security classes, only five additional classes address other security aspects, such as integrity or availability.

Nevertheless, ITSEC and other more recent security criteria are independent of a specific security policy and allow to define own functional security requirements. For example, the concept of protection profiles in the CC allows user groups and customers to state explicitly their security requirements. However, in contrast to early security criteria, the CC are criticised of being too voluminous and complex.

Another major criticism is that IT Security Evaluation Criteria are biased on providing security only for system owners and operators (see [Rannenberg 1994]). The protection of usees from the system, has not been considered by early criteria catalogues and is not really addressed by the CC, in due respect, either. This problem will be discussed in more detail in Chapter 4.

In addition to criticisms on the concepts of security criteria, there are also criticisms on organisational aspects of security evaluation and certification procedures. In particular, the process of evaluation and certification is very costly and still takes too long relative to a commercial computer product delivery cycle. A consequence is that there are normally no certificates for the latest product versions.

Alternatives to the current evaluation and certification procedures are discussed in [Stiegler 1998].

3.5 Conflict between IT-Security and Privacy

Technical security mechanisms are necessary to protect personal data against accidental or unauthorised access, modification or other illegal processing. They are required by many privacy acts, because they are regarded as technical means to protect privacy. Unfortunately, security mechanisms can also affect privacy.

Security mechanisms often require the collection and use of personal control data about users and usees. This personal control data can be misused, for example, for performance monitoring. This results in a conflict where security mechanisms can both help to protect the privacy of data subjects and at the same time can be used to invade the privacy of users and usees (see [Denning/Neumann/Parker 87], [Fischer-Hübner/Yngström/Holvast 92], [Fischer-Hübner 1993], [Ketelaar/Fischer-Hübner 94]).

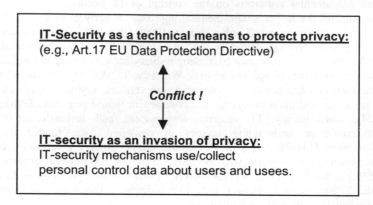

Fig. 3.16: Conflict between IT-Security and Privacy

3.6.1 Privacy Implications of IT Security Mechanisms

The following examples demonstrate how security mechanisms affect and endanger the privacy of the system's users and of other usees, who are not actively involved [Fischer-Hübner/Yngström/Holvast 92]:

Identification and Authentication mechanisms:

Identification and Authentication mechanisms produce and use information about the user's presence and location. Especially continuous authentication such as keystroke dynamics can be used to monitor the user's presence at his working place. If devices such as smartcards are used as employee authentication for access to certain security relevant areas, the employee's personal movements and his contacts with other employees can be tracked.

Besides, the use of location-based authentication and location signatures have the potential of being used to track the physical location of individuals.

Another problem arises if biometrics are used for identification and authentication purposes. Biometric technologies are based on the storage and use of personal data of such aspects of the body and/or its behaviour as the micro-visual pattern of the retina, the geometry of the hand or a finger, the aural pattern of the voice, the pattern of handwriting of signatures, and facial appearances. People, however, might feel de-humanised by being reduced to codes. Besides, in many western nations, the stigma of criminality is associated with fingerprinting, and, by association, with other biometric techniques [Davies 1994].

Access Control:

Discretionary access control mechanisms (DAC), such as access control lists, require the storage and usage of information about the user's access rights. Mandatory access control (MAC) that implement the policy of the Bell LaPadula model use security levels that are attached to users and to objects. This access control data reveals personal information about the user's status. Furthermore, in order to attach a security level (clearance) to a user, his trustworthiness and personal background has to be checked e.g. by surveillance. These procedures affect the user's territorial and informational privacy.

Auditing and Intrusion Detection:

Auditing produces information about the activities and behaviour of the users. If activities of users with respect to other people (usees) are audited, the audit trails may also contain critical information about these usees.

This problem is illustrated by the following example: In Germany, the police forces are allowed to have online access to the German traffic information system ZEVIS. A sample of these accesses is audited in order to check their legitimacy. These audit trails do not only contain personal information about the activities of the requesting police officers, but also reveal sensitive information about the car holders that are observed as suspects by the police.

Monitoring of unusual and security relevant activities on a system through system status information also means a continuous control of a user's actions.

Intrusion Detection Expert Systems that are based on Denning's Intrusion Detection Model [Denning 86] produce and use statistical profiles that store statistics about the behaviour of subjects (e.g. users) with respect to objects. These statistics can be directly misused for employee performance control [Denning/Neumann/Parker 87]. Studies have shown that the user's awareness of computerised performance monitoring at work may result in decreasing productivity, increasing stress and lower level of job satisfaction [Irving/Higgins/Safayeni 1996].

Back-up mechanisms:

Besides these security mechanisms that control the actions of users, backup-mechanisms can also endanger privacy rights. Backup files might contain personal data that was stored on the system at backup-time, but has become outdated and incorrect. According to most privacy acts, individuals have the right to have incorrect personal data corrected and to have illegally stored data deleted. Normally such corrections are only done on system's on-line data and not on the backup-files. The consequence is that after the correction or deletion of personal data in the system, backups may still store the incorrect personal data and may therefore be in conflict with the data subject´s privacy rights.

3.5.2 A Holistic Approach to a Privacy-Friendly Design and Use of Security Mechanisms

Security mechanisms should not only directly address privacy requirements, but should also be used in a privacy-friendly way to further approach the mentioned conflict between security and privacy. As invasion of privacy is not only a technical problem, but has also social, legal and psychological dimensions, a holistic approach to a privacy-friendly use and design of security mechanisms is necessary, which has to involve specialists from different disciplines. This approach should especially contain the following measures (see [Fischer-Hübner/Yngström/Holvast 92]):

a.) Educational means

Persons that are responsible for system security, such as system-designers, auditors, security administrators, should be taught about the privacy-interests and rights of the users and usees. An important countermeasure to vulnerability could be gained, if information and understanding is given to planners and practitioners of IT-security as well as to users and usees.

b.) Legal means

Basic privacy requirements such as purpose binding, necessity of data collection and processing, as well as the rights of data subjects to be informed have to be guaranteed with respect to security control data.

Usage for security purposes only:

The principle of purpose binding has also to be applied to personal data needed by security mechanisms. The German data protection act in § 14 IV BDSG therefore restricts the use of personal data collected for privacy protection controls, backup or operation maintenance only to those purposes.

Necessity of data collection and processing:

Applying the privacy principle of necessity of data processing, which is part of most data protection acts, should also protect privacy. Only that security control information should be used and retained, which is needed for a particular application. If for instance location-based authentication is used, even though a geodetic location can be known at the meter level, for many applications the location could be rounded, for example, to a country level for the purpose of controlling transborder data flow (see [Denning/MacDoran 1996]).

The right to be informed:

As data subjects, the users shall have the right to be informed and notified about their personal control data, in particular about all the kinds of activities that are audited or monitored. As specific expert knowledge is required to understand the different security audit events and classes, additional explanations should be provided to the users. This right to information and notification is part of most data protection acts. In particular, it is also formulated by the EU directive on data protection. Besides, according to Art. 12 of the EU Directive, data subjects shall also have the right to obtain from the controller knowledge of the logic in any automatic processing of data concerning him at least in the case of automated decisions. Consequently, if intrusion detection systems are used, data subjects should have the right to be informed about the general system functionality. However, knowledge about the logic of audit-based monitoring shall only be provided, as far as this information is not security-relevant. It would be irresponsible to reveal for instance the expert system rules that encode sensitive information about system vulnerabilities.

Participation of the works council:

According to the German workers legislation (§ 87 I No.6 Betriebsverfassungsgesetz) the workers representation (works council, "Betriebsrat") has the right to participate in the decision to introduce any system that can be used or misused for performance monitoring. Arrangements that are met without the participation of the works council are regarded as invalid. Therefore, security mechanisms which could potentially be misused must be accepted by the works council. If an intrusion detection system is accepted by the work council, the works council should also have influence over what actions are being monitored and the profiles used. Furthermore, the use of user profiles, which store information typically needed for performance control, should be prohibited.

c.) Technical means

In addition to legislative means, technical and organisational means to enforce a privacy-friendly use and design of security mechanisms are needed as well.

In particular, security policies that protect personal security control data from illegal and unnecessary accesses have to be implemented. An example of a formal privacy model, which is adequate to enforce such security policies, will be presented in Chapter 5.

Besides, security control data should be pseudonymised or anonymised if possible to balance the conflict between security and privacy. Techniques of a privacy-enhancing design and use of security mechanisms are for instance techniques of anonymous system use, which operate with anonymous control data, or pseudonymous auditing techniques where user-identifying audit data is pseudonymised. These technical means will be discussed in the next Chapter.

In this Chapter, we have discussed "traditional" security concepts, which are regarded as technical data protection means. However, as discussed above, we have shown that such security mechanisms can also be in conflict with the privacy rights of users and usees. Besides, traditional security models were not specifically designed for privacy protection and mainly address other security aspects.

In the next Chapter, we discuss security concepts that specifically aim at protecting privacy of users and usees. Such privacy enhancing technologies can be divided into privacy enhancing technologies for protecting user identities, for protecting usee identities and for personal data protection. As traditional security models are mostly inappropriate to enforce basic legal privacy requirements for personal data protection (-a problem that is also discussed in more detail at the end of the next Chapter-), a task-based privacy model for personal data protection is introduced in Chapter five.

4   Privacy-Enhancing Technologies

4.1 Privacy-Enhancing Security Aspects

As defined in [Registratiekamer 1995], privacy technologies refer to a variety of technologies that safeguard personal privacy by minimising or eliminating the collection of identifiable data. We extend the definition of privacy technologies to include also security technologies to protect the confidentiality, integrity and availability of personal data. Thus, extended security criteria for systems with high privacy requirements should cover a diversity of privacy enhancing security aspects such as:

- *Privacy-Enhancing Security Aspects for protecting the user identities providing Anonymity, Pseudonymity, Unlinkability, Unobservability of users:* The principles of minimisation and avoidance of personal data are derived from the legal principle of necessity of data collecting and processing, which requires that personal data should not be collected or used for identification purposes when not truly necessary.

- *Privacy-Enhancing Security Aspects for Protecting the usee identities providing Anonymity and Pseudonymity of data subjects:* If personal data (about data subjects that are not necessarily users at the same time) has to be collected, it should be rendered anonymous or pseudonymous as soon as the purposes for which the data was collected permit this. In some cases, some users still need to access the personal data attributes, while other users only need statistical (anonymous) access. Inference controls can be used to restrict users to statistical accesses only and can prevent those users can deduce confidential information about some individual.

- Security aspects, such as access control or encryption, are necessary to *protect the confidentiality, integrity and availability of* personal data, if (non-anonymous) personal data has to be stored, processed or transmitted. Security mechanisms for protecting personal data can also be classified as data protection technologies. Especially the privacy requirements of *purpose binding and necessity of data processing of personal data of users and data subjects* can be technically enforced through an appropriate security policy and access control mechanisms.

4.1.1 Privacy-Enhancing Security Aspects for Protecting the User Identities

A key component of the user's privacy is preserving the user's ability to remain anonymous. *Anonymity* ensures that a user may use a resource or service (e.g., may send or receive a message) without disclosing the user's identity. *Pseudonymity* can protect the user's identity in cases where anonymity cannot be provided, e.g. if the user has to be held accountable for his activities.

Besides, another key aspect is *unobservability* of the user, which ensures that a user may use a resource or service without others, especially third parties, being able to observe that the resource or service is being used. Furthermore, it has to be prevented that an attacker can link various information about a user to a profile that could finally be used to re-identify the user. *Unlinkability* ensures that a user may make use of resources and services without others being able to link these uses together.

The definitions of privacy-enhancing security criteria for protecting user identities given above are corresponding to the definitions given in the privacy functionality class of the Common Criteria [CC 1999]. In the following Section, anonymity, pseudonymity, unobservability and unlinkability will be defined more formally and in more detail.

Anonymity, pseudonymity, unobservability and unlinkability depend on the model of possible attackers [Pfitzmann/Waidner 1987], [Pfitzmann 1990]. Such an attack model defines how far a potential attacker can access or derive relevant information and what resources he can use. For instance, anonymity of communication depends on how far an attacker can control or observe network stations, communication lines and communication partners. The attackers might be eavesdroppers, who can observe some or all messages sent or received, collaborations consisting of some senders, receivers, and other parties, or variations of these.

4.1.1.1 Anonymity

A formal definition of anonymity is given in [Pfitzmann 1990]:

Let R_U denote the event that an entity U (e.g., a user) performs a role R (e.g., as a sender or receiver of a message) during an event E (e.g., communication event, business transaction). Let A denote an attacker, and let NC_A be the set of entities that are not cooperating with A.

According to [Pfitzmann 1990] an entity U is called **anonymous** in role R for an event E against an attacker A, if for each observation B that A can make, the following relation holds:

$$\forall \, U' \in NC_A: 0 < P(R_{U'} \mid B) < 1.$$

A less strict requirement could be that the above relation does not have to hold for all but at least for most non-cooperating entities from the set NC_A.

However, anonymity for an entity U in the role R can only be guaranteed if the value $P(R_U \mid B)$ is not too close to the values 1 or 0.

Thus, an additional requirement should be: $0 \ll P(R_U \mid B) \ll 1$. (A $\ll$ B means that A is much smaller than B).

There are different types of anonymous communication properties depending on the role that a user is performing during a communication event: **Sender anonymity** means that the user is anonymous in the role of a sender of a message, while the receiver might not be. **Receiver anonymity** similarly means that the user is anonymous in the role of a receiver of a message.

An entity U is defined as **perfectly anonymous** in role R for an event E against an attacker A, if for each observation B that A can make: $\forall\, U' \in NC_A$: $P(R_{U'}) = P(R_{U'} \mid B)$;that is, observations give an attacker no additional information.

Perfect sender (receiver) anonymity against an attacker means that the attacker cannot distinguish the situations in which a potential sender (receiver) actually sent (received) communications and those in which he did not.

In [Reiter/Rubin 1997], further degrees of anonymity of communication are introduced:

- **Beyond suspicion:** A sender's (receiver's) anonymity is beyond suspicion if even though the attacker can see evidence of a sent (received) message, the sender (receiver) appears no more likely to be the originator (recipient) of that message than any other potential sender (receiver) in the system.
- **Probable innocence:** A sender (receiver) is probably innocent (or better: not involved) if, from the attacker's point of view, the sender (receiver) appears no more likely to be the originator (recipient) than not to be the originator (recipient). This is weaker than beyond suspicion in that the attacker may have reasons to expect that the sender (receiver) is more likely to be involved than any other potential sender (receiver), but it still appears, at least as likely, that the sender is not responsible. That is, the probability that the sender (receiver) is involved is less or equal to 0.5.
- **Possible innocence:** A sender (receiver) is possible innocent if, from the attacker's point of view, there is a nontrivial probability that the real sender (receiver) is someone else.
- **Provably exposed:** The identity of a sender (receiver) is provably exposed if the attacker can not only identify the sender (receiver), but can also prove the identity of the sender to others.

4.1.1.2 Unobservability

An event E is **unobservable** for an attacker A [Pfitzmann 1990], if for each observation B that A can make, the probability of E given B is greater zero and less one:

$$0 < P(E \mid B) < 1.$$

A stricter requirement, which prevents that the value $P(E \mid B)$ is too close to either 1 or 0, could be: $0 \ll P(E \mid B) \ll 1$.

If for each possible observation B that A can make, the probability of an event E is equal to the probability of E given B, that is $P(E) = P(E|B)$, then E is called **perfectly unobservable**.

An event can only be unobservable for third parties that are not involved. A special form of unobservability, where the relation between the sender and recipient of a message is hidden, is called **unlinkability of sender and recipient**. Unlinkability of sender and recipient means that though the sender and recipient can both be identified as participating in some communication, they cannot be identified as communicating with each other.

4.1.1.3 Unlinkability

Let $X_{E,F}$ denote the event that the events E and F have a corresponding characteristic X. Two events, E and F, are **unlinkable** in regard of a characteristic X (e.g., two messages are unlinkable with a subject or with an transaction) for an attacker A [Pfitzmann 1990], if for each observation B that A can make, the probability that E and F are corresponding in regard of X given B is greater than zero and less than one:

$$0 < P(X_{E,F} \mid B) < 1.$$

A stricter requirement for unlinkability is: $0 \ll P(X_{E,F} \mid B) \ll 1$.
E and F are **perfectly unlinkable** if: $P(X_{E,F} \mid B) = P(X_{E,F})$.

4.1.1.4 Pseudonymity

Pseudonymity ensures that a user acting under one or more pseudonyms may use a resource or service without disclosing his identity. However, under certain circumstances it is possible to translate the pseudonyms into the user identities. Pseudonymity should be enforced if anonymity cannot be guaranteed, for instance because the user has to be still accountable for his actions.

Pseudonyms can be classified according to the degree of protection that they are providing [Pfitzmann/Waidner/Pfitzmann 1990] (see Figure 4.1):

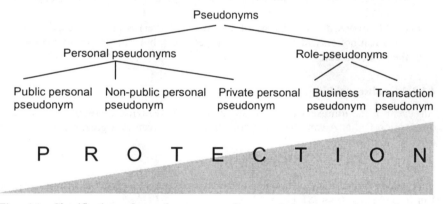

Fig. 4.1: Classification of pseudonyms according to their degree of protection (see [Pfitzmann/Waidner/Pfitzmann 1990])

A pseudonym is called a **personal pseudonym** if it is related to an individual and used by its holder for various business dealings and/or transactions over some time period. Thus, a personal pseudonym is an alias for a user's name. Personal pseudonyms can be divided into public personal pseudonyms, non-public personal pseudonyms and private personal pseudonyms. At the time a pseudonym is used for the first time, the translation *of public personal pseudonyms* (e.g., telephone numbers) to the real identities is publicly known, whereas the translation of *non-public* *pseudonyms* (e.g., bank account numbers without user names) is known only by certain parties, and the translation of *private personal pseudonyms* is only known by their holders. However, an individual usually uses a personal pseudonym for several business transactions, and the pseudonym thus allows all transaction records to be linked together into a profile of the individual, which can in turn be used to reveal the individual's identity.

A **Role pseudonym**, which is not related to the individual but to the role that the individual is currently performing, offers a higher degree of protection. A *business pseudonym* is a role pseudonym used for the various transactions of a business activity, whilst a *transaction pseudonym*, which offers the highest degree of protection, is only used for one single transaction.

Pseudonyms can also be classified according to the way that they are generated and translated to user identities (see also [DS-Beauftragte 1998]):

Self-generated pseudonyms are generated by the owner and are not stored together with identity data. Thus, only the owner should be able to translate his self-generated pseudonym directly into his real identity.

Reference pseudonyms can only be directly translated to real identities by the use of reference lists, which contain the mappings of pseudonyms to real identities. Reference pseudonyms are useful for applications where in exceptional cases the real user identities have to be revealed (e.g., in order to make the user accountable for his actions). The reference list should be kept separate from the pseudonymous data records, and should ideally be under control of a trusted third party. A higher degree of protection can be achieved, if the information that allows deriving the mapping of pseudonyms to real identities is divided, and is kept by different trusted third parties. In this case, pseudonyms can only be directly re-identified if the different trusted third parties are willing to cooperate.

Cryptographic pseudonyms are generated by encrypting the identity data. Thus, in order to directly translate cryptographic pseudonyms to real identities, the decryption function and decryption key have to be known. Cryptographic pseudonyms can for instance be used to implement pseudonymous auditing (see Chapter 4.2.5).

Applying a one-way function on the identity data creates **one-way pseudonyms**. Usually, these kinds of one-way functions are implemented by cryptographic one-way functions (e.g., one-way hash functions). The security of one-way pseudonyms should be based on the secrecy of used parameters, and not on the secrecy of the algorithm of the one-way function.

In contrast to cryptographic pseudonyms, one-way pseudonyms cannot be directly translated back to real identities through decryption. For this reason, one-way pseudonyms provide a higher decree of protection. However, in order to find the real identity of a one-way pseudonym, the one-way function has to be applied to the identity data of all individuals in question, and the results have to be compared with the pseudonym.

An advantage of cryptographic and one-way pseudonyms over reference pseudonyms is that they do not require the storage of identity data. Nevertheless, the decryption keys or parameters should also be kept separate from the pseudonymous data, and should be under control of one or several trusted third parties as well.

Examples for implementation techniques of pseudonyms are:

- *Hash functions:* Hash values of identity data can serve as pseudonyms. For the generation of pseudonyms, it is important that the hash algorithm can be trusted to be collision-free (that is, it must be computationally infeasible to find two values that hash to the same thing) to guarantee the one-way property.

- *Biometrics:* Biometric characteristics, stored in digital representation, can be used as a special form of a one-way pseudonym of an individual.

- *Public encryption keys* can serve as digital pseudonyms (as they are also called in [Chaum 1981], [Chaum 1985]). If they are generated under control of the users, they can be regarded as self-generated pseudonyms.

- *Certificates:* According to the German Digital Signature Act, a certificate can also be a signed message specifying a pseudonym (instead of the name/identity) of the public key owner and his public key.

- *Trusted Third Parties:* A trusted third party can keep track of the digital pseudonyms that a user uses in his relationship with a number of service providers. The user's trust is based on the assumption that the trusted third party keeps the relationship between his identity and pseudonym secret. The service-provider's trust, on the other hand, is based on the assumption that under certain circumstances the trusted third party will reveal the user's identity (e.g., to hold the user responsible for improper use).

4.1.2 Privacy-Enhancing Security Criteria for Protecting the Usee Identities

4.1.2.1 Depersonalisation

Personal data is often collected for research purposes. However, scientists conducting statistical research normally only need statistical access to the data and do not have to know the identities of the data subjects.

In such cases, the identities of the usees can be protected, if the data records are **rendered anonymous** (that is, depersonalised) or **rendered pseudonymous** (that is, transferred into a pseudonymous form) as soon as possible.

Perfect depersonalisation means that data is rendered anonymous in such a way that the data subject is no longer identifiable. The definition of the term "depersonalisation" in the data protection act of some German states (Saxony, Schleswig-Holstein, Mecklenburg-Vorpommern) corresponds to this definition.

However, in most applications perfect depersonalisation is practically almost impossible to achieve. Thus, the Federal German Data Protection Act defines depersonalisation as "the modification of personal data so that the information concerning personal or material circumstances can no longer or only with a disproportionate amount of time, expense and labour, be attributed to an identified or identifiable individual" (§ 3 VII BDSG). This form of depersonalisation is also called **practical depersonalisation** ("faktische Anonymisierung").

There are several legal requirements for a (practical) depersonalisation of personal data. In the Census Decision, the German Constitutional Court required an early practical depersonalisation of census data, as well as protection mechanisms against re-identification. Besides, according to § 40 III BDSG, personal data held by research institutes "shall be depersonalised as soon as the research purpose permits this". Until this time, user-identifying data should be stored separately. That is, it is required that the data is at least stored in a pseudonymous form.

Personal data records are rendered pseudonymous by replacing the directly (and if possible indirectly) user-identifying data with pseudonyms.

For some applications, there are user groups that have to access data records with their identity information, whilst other involved parties do not need to know the identity of the data subjects. In a hospital database, for example, the treating physicians have to have direct access to the patient's medical records, while researchers might only be permitted access to statistical summaries of the records. Such a general-purpose database has to provide both statistical and non-statistical access. An access control mechanism has to be used that renders the output of statistical queries anonymous; that is, data can only be accessed in anonymous form. Such inference controls for statistical databases are discussed in Chapter (4.3).

4.1.2.2 The Risk of Re-identification

Data records, which are collected for statistical purposes, normally contain the following types of data attributes (see also [Rauterberg 1984]):

- *Identity data* (e.g., name, address, personal number)
- *Demographic data* (e.g., sex, age, nationality, education, religion, marital status). These are data attributes of individuals whose values are normally known. Besides, the statistical distribution of these attributes is normally known.
- *Analysis data* (e.g., diseases, habits); that is, the data attributes for which the statistical analysis is conducted. These variables are usually not generally known.

Often, personal data records are depersonalised by removing the identity information from the records. However, an attacker with adequate supplementary knowledge about the demographic information of a data subject could use the knowledge to re-identify the data subject and to disclose sensitive information. Data subjects with a unique combination of demographic data values are especially exposed to such re-identification attacks.

Thus, in order to determine the degree of anonymity of a statistical database, a measure for the risk of re-identification is needed. A re-identification risk measure, which can also be used to estimate the percentage of data subjects that can be uniquely re-identified was proposed in [Fischer-Hübner 1987], and is presented in the following Section:

The degree of anonymity of a statistical database depends on the size of the database and the entropy of the demographic data attributes that can serve as supplementary knowledge of an attacker.

The entropy of the demographic data attributes depends on
- the number of attributes
- the number of possible values of each attribute

- frequency distribution of the values
- dependencies between attributes

Given m attributes $X_1,...X_m$, and let each attribute X_i have n_i values $x_{i1},...,x_{in_i}$, and

$$\sum_{j=1}^{n_i} p(x_{ij}) = 1.$$

According to Shannon [Shannon 1948], [Shannon 1949], the entropy of an attribute X_i is defined by the weighted average as:

$$H(X_i) = -\sum_{j=1}^{n_i} p(x_{ij}) * ld(p(x_{ij})) = \sum_{j=1}^{n_i} p(x_{ij}) * ld(1/p(x_{ij})).$$

where $p(x_{ij})$ is the probability of the value x_{ij}, and ld is the logarithmus dualis function.

If $p(x_{ij}) = 0$, then $p(x_{ij}) * ld(p(x_{ij})) = 0$, since $\lim_{x \to 0} x * ld(x) = 0$.

The entropy of an attribute measures its uncertainty in that it gives the number of bits of information that the attribute provides on the average and that can be used for re-identification attacks.

The entropy of an attribute X_i has the following two properties:
1. The entropy increases as the number n_i of possible values increases.
2. Given the number n_i of possible values, the entropy decreases as the distribution of attribute values becomes more and more skewed.

For a given number n_i of possible values, the entropy is maximal, if all values are equally likely. In this case: $H(X_i) = n_i * ((1/n_i) * ld(n_i)) = ld(n_i)$.

It reaches a minimum of $H(X) = 0$, when $p(x_{ij}) = 1$ for some value x_{ij} (if an attribute has the same value for each data record, it cannot be used to disclose any information about the data subject).

Example 4.1:
Given the attribute sex with two possible values "male" and "female", and p(male) = 0.469 and p(female) = 0.531. Then:
H(sex) =p(male) * ld (1/p(male)) + p(female) * ld (1/p(female)) = 0.469 * ld (1/0.469) + 0.531 * ld (1 / 0.531) = 0.997.

Given the attribute nationality with the two possible values G (German) and F (Foreigner), and p(G) = 0.9, p(F) = 0.1. Then:
H(nationality) = 0.9 * ld (1/0.9) + 0.1 * ld (1/0.1) = 0.465.

115

The attributes sex and nationality both have two possible values. However, since the distribution of the two values of the attribute nationality is more skewed, the entropy of nationality is much smaller.

Now, let the attribute nationality have the seven possible values: G (German), T (Turkish), I (Italian), J (Jugoslavian), GR (Greek), EU (other EU citizens), O (other nationalities), with p(G) =0.9, p(T) = 0.032, P(I) = 0.004, p(J) = 0.012, p(GR) = 0.004, p(EU) = 0.013, p(O) = 0.005. Then:

H(nationality) = 0.9 * ld(1/0.9) + 0.032 * ld (1/0.032) + 0.004 * ld(1/0.004) + 0.012 * ld(1 / 0.012) + 0.004 * ld(1/0.004) + 0.013 * ld(1/0.013) + 0.005 * ld(1/0.005) =0.529.

Thus, this example demonstrates that the entropy of nationality increases as the number of possible values increases. However, due to the unequal frequency distribution of its values, the entropy of nationality is lower than the entropy of sex, although the attribute sex only has two possible values.

The following function ANV (standing for "average number of values") defines a measure for the average number of values for an attribute X_i, which can actually be used for re-identification.

Definition 4.1:

$$ANV(X_i) = 2^{H(X_i)} = 1 / \prod_{j=1}^{n_i} p(x_{ij})^{p(x_{ij})}$$

For given X_i: $1 \leq ANV (X_i) \leq n_i$. $ANV(X_i) = n_i$, if all values are equally likely.

Example 4.2:
According to example 4.1, H(sex) = 0.997. Besides, the attribute nationality with seven possible values has an entropy of H(nationality) = 0.529. Thus:

$ANV(sex) = 2^{H(sex)} = 2^{0.997} = 1.996$.
Thus, on the average almost 2 of the two possible values can be used for re-identification.
$ANV(nationality) = 2^{0.529} = 1.443$.
Thus, for the attribute nationality, the average number of values that can be used for re-identification is much lower than the number of possible values.

For a combination of attributes $X_1,..., X_m$, the entropy is defined as [Shannon 1948] [Shannon 1949]:

$$H(X_1,...,X_m) = \sum_{j_1=1}^{n_1} .... \sum_{j_m=1}^{n_m} p(x_{1j_1},...,x_{j_m}) * ld(1/ p(x_{1j_1},...,x_{j_m})) \cdot$$

where $p(x_{1j_1}, \ldots, x_{mj_m})$ is the joint probability of $X_1 = x_{1j_1}$,and..., $X_m = x_{mj_m}$.

It can be shown that:

$$H(X_1, \ldots, X_m) = H(X_1) + H(X_2 \mid X_1) + \ldots + H(X_m \mid X_1, \ldots, X_{m-1}),$$

where $H(X_i \mid X_1, \ldots, X_{i-1})$ is the conditional entropy of X_i given $X_1, \ldots X_{i-1}$.

The conditional entropy is defined as [Shannon 1949]:

$$H(X_i \mid X_1, \ldots, X_{i-1}) = \sum_{j_1=1}^{n_1} \ldots \sum_{j_i=1}^{n_i} p(x_{1j_1}, \ldots, x_{ij_i}) * Ld(1 / p(x_{ij_i} \mid x_{1j_1}, \ldots, x_{i-1j_{i-1}})),$$

where $p(x_{ij_i} \mid x_{1j_1}, \ldots, x_{i-1j_{i-1}})$ is the probability of $X_i = x_{ij_i}$, given $X_1 = x_{1j_1}$, and ..., $X_{i-1} = x_{i-1j_{i-1}}$.

It can be shown that $H(X_i \mid X_1, \ldots, X_{i-1}) \le H(X_i)$.

If all attributes $X_1, \ldots, X_m$ are independent from each other, then $H(X_i \mid X_1, \ldots, X_{i-1})) = H(X_i)$ for i = 1..m, and $H(X_1, \ldots, X_m)$ is maximal with $H(X_1, \ldots, X_m) = H(X_1) + \ldots + H(X_m)$.

$H(X_1, \ldots, X_m) = 0$, if there is one combination of attribute values $X_1 = x_{1j_1}$,and..., $X_m = x_{mj_m}$ with $p(x_{1j_1}, \ldots, x_{mj_m}) = 1$.

Example 4.3:
The attributes marital status and sex are dependent from each other. The following table shows as an example the frequency distribution of these attributes for the population of a city (numbers in thousands):

Sex	Total Population	Single	Married	Widowed	Divorced
Male	754	333	352	24	45
Female	855	296	351	144	64
Total	1609	629	703	168	109

Thus, the entropy of the attribute sex and marital status is:
H(sex, marital status) = H(sex) + H(marital status / sex) =
[p(male) * ld (1/p(male)) + p(female) * ld(1/ p(female))] +
[p(single, female) * ld (1(p(single/female)) + p(single, male) * ld (1/ p(single/male))
+p(married, female) * ld (1/ p(married/female))
+ p(married, male) * ld (1/ p(married/male))
+ p(widowed, female) * ld (1/ p(widowed/female))

+ *p(widowed, male) * ld (1/ p(widowed/male))*
+ *p(divorced, female) * ld (1/ p(divorced/female))*
+ *p(divorced, male) * ld (1/ p(divorced/male))]* =
*[(754 / 1609) * ld (1609/754) + (855/1609) * ld(1609/855)]* +
*[(296/1609) * ld(855/296) + (333/1609) * ld(754/333) + (351/1609) * ld(855/351) +*
*(352/1609) * ld(754/352) + (144/1609) * ld(855/144) + (24/1609) * ld(754/24) +*
*(64/1609) * ld(855/64) + (45/1609) * ld(754/45)]* = *0.97 + 1.613* =*2.610.*

The following function ANVC (for "average number of value combinations") is defined to measure for the average number of value combinations for attributes X_1, ...,X_m, which can actually be used for re-identification.

Definition 4.2:

$$\text{ANVC}(X_1,...,X_m) = 2^{H(X_1,...,X_m)}$$

Since $0 \leq H(X_1, ..., H_m) \leq H(X_1) + ...+ H(X_m) \leq ld(n_1) +...+ ld(n_m) = ld(\prod_{i=1}^{m} n_i)$:

$$1 \leq \text{ANVC}(X_1,...,X_m) \leq \prod_{i=1}^{m} n_i$$

If there are no dependencies between the attributes $X_1,..., X_m$, then:

$$\text{ANVC}(X_1,...,X_m) = \prod_{i=1}^{m} \text{ANV}(X_i), \text{ where ANV}(X_i) \text{ is given by definition 4.1.}$$

If in addition, for each attribute X_i all possible values $x_{i1},..., x_{in_i}$ are equally likely, then:

$$\text{ANVC}(X_1,...,X_m) = \prod_{i=1}^{m} n_i .$$

Given a database with an overall size of N records (referring to N different data subjects), and demographic attributes $X_1,..., X_m$. Suppose an attacker has supplementary knowledge about the demographic attribute values of a data subject. We want to know how many records on the average the attacker can "filter" from the database with the help of his knowledge about the values for $X_1,...,X_m$; that is, the average seize of sets of records with identical values for the attributes $X_1,.., X_m$.

This value for the so-called *average query set seize* can be estimated by the function AQSS, which is defined by:

Definition 4.3:

$$\text{AQSS}(X_1, \ldots, X_m) = N / \text{ANVC}(X_1, \ldots, X_m).$$

It is:

$$0 < N / \prod_{i=1}^{m} n_i \leq \text{AQSS}(X_1, \ldots, X_m) \leq N.$$

We can now define a function RR to estimate the average risk of re-identification:

Definition 4.4:

$$\text{RR}(X_1, \ldots, X_m) = \begin{cases} \text{ANVC}(X_1, \ldots, X_m) / N & \text{if ANVC}(X_1, \ldots, X_m) \leq N \\ 1 & \text{else.} \end{cases}$$

It is:
$$1 / N \leq \text{RR}(X_1, \ldots, X_m) \leq 1.$$

Example 4.4:
Given a database with N= 100 records referring to N different data subjects, and given the demographic attributes marital status and sex. Then

$$\text{ANVC}(\text{sex}, \text{marital status}) = 2^{H(\text{sex}, \text{marital status})} = 2^{2.61} = 6.105$$

Thus, 6.105 of eight possible value combinations can be used on the average.
AQSS(sex, marital status) = 100 / 6.105 = 16.38;
that is, through the knowledge of the values for the attribute sex and marital status, an attacker can "filter" on the average 16.38 records from the database.
The re-identification risk can be estimated by:
RR(sex, marital status) = 6.105 / 100 = 0.0615.

For a given number N of database records referring to N different data subjects and attributes $X_1, \ldots, X_m$, the risk of re-identification is minimal with $\text{RR}(X_1, \ldots, X_m) = 1/N$, if $H(X_1, \ldots, X_m) = 0$.

In this case, the "re-identification risk" value 1/N corresponds to the likelihood of choosing by chance a certain record from the database consisting of N records.

The percentage of data subjects, which could be re-identified through the knowledge of $X_1, \ldots X_m$, can be estimated by: $\text{RR}(X_1, \ldots, X_m) * 100\%$.

A similar function DA ("**D**eanonymisierbare Personen") to estimate the percentage of re-identifiable individuals, was proposed by M. Rauterberg [Rauterberg 1984].

Rauterberg defines a so-called "Orwell Coefficient" OR by the product OR = Π ANV (X_i).

The value of DA is given by:

$$DA = \begin{cases} OR/N * 100\% & \text{if } OR \leq N \\ 100\% & \text{if } OR > N. \end{cases}$$

The function DA is not considering dependencies between attributes and is easier to calculate than the function RR, because the conditional entropies do not have to be calculated. If the attributes $X_1,...,X_m$ are independent from each other, then

$DA = RR(X_1,...,X_m) * 100\%$.

If, however, there are dependencies between $X_1,...,X_m$, then DA $>$ $RR(X_1,...,X_m)$; that is, the value of DA is an overestimation the real average risk of re-identification. An example of attributes that are highly dependent on each other, are the attributes nationality and religion.

4.1.3 Privacy-Enhancing Security Aspects for Protecting Personal Data

If (non-anonymous) personal data has to be collected, processed or transmitted, the EU Data Protection Directive as well as the data protection legislation of most western states require security safeguards to protect the confidentiality, integrity and availability of the personal data. Such security mechanisms, which can be used to protect personal data (e.g. encryption, access control mechanisms), can also be classified as data protection technologies.

Especially the legal privacy requirements of *purpose binding and necessity of data processing of personal data of users and data subjects* can be technically enforced through appropriate security policy and access control mechanisms.

In Chapter 4.4.2.2, we will examine how far well-known security models are addressing privacy aspects and show that most of the known security models are not appropriate to enforce the legal privacy requirements of purpose binding and necessity of data processing. For this reason, a formal task-based privacy model has been developed, which can be used to technically enforce these legal privacy requirements. The privacy model will be presented in Chapter 5.

In chapter 3.5 we have pointed out that security mechanisms that operate with personal control data can also affect the user's privacy. Thus, particularly privacy-enhanced security mechanisms that do not operate with personal control data or pseudonymised control data should be taken.

4.2 System Concepts for Protecting User Identities

4.2.1 The Identity Protector

The Dutch Data Protection Authority (the "Registratiekamer") and the Information and Privacy Commissioner (IPC) for the Province of Ontario, Canada, have collaborated in the production of a report [Registratiekamer/IPC 1995] exploring privacy enhancing technologies that safeguard personal privacy by minimising or eliminating the collection of identifiable data, and thus permit transactions to be conducted anonymously. This report and a prior study of the Registratiekamer [Registratiekamer 1995] introduced the concept of an "identity protector", which is a useful concept to classify information & communication systems providing anonymity, pseudonymity, unlinkability and/or unobservability for the users. In the following sections, we also refer to the concept of an identity protector (IP) to give an overview to system concepts protecting user identities.

As described in [Registratiekamer 1995], the system elements of an information & communication system are modelled by a user representation (i.e. user process), a service provider representation (person or parties responsible for systems such as a main frame computer, a server system, the system of an Internet provider), services (e.g., communication services, payments, access to data), an access control information database (storing the user's privileges) and an audit file (recording all security-relevant actions).

System elements of the information & communication system that have to operate with identity data have to be separated by technical means from parts that can operate with anonymous or pseudonymous data. This task of separation can be done by a so-called "identity protector". The identity protector (IP) can be seen as a system element that controls the exchange of the identity between the various system elements. The identity protector may take the form of a functional element within an information & communication system, a separate information system controlled by the user (e.g., smart-card), or another system that is under the supervision of a trusted third party.

The identity protector offers the following functions [Registratiekamer 1995]:
- reports and controls instances when identity is revealed
- generates pseudo-identities
- translates pseudo-identities into identities and vice-versa
- converts pseudo-identities into other pseudo-identities
- combats fraud and misuse of the system

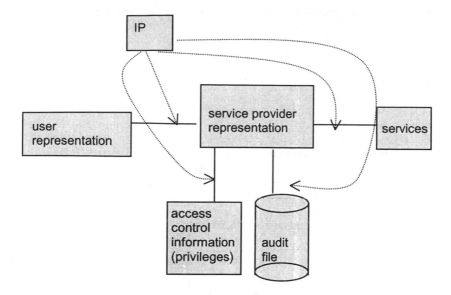

Fig. 4.2: Possible Installations of the Identity Protector (IP)

It is installed on one of the interaction lines in the information & communication system (see Figure 4.2) and creates two domains within the information system: the identity domain in which the user´s identity is known, and one or more pseudo domain(s) in which the user´s identity is secret (see Figure 4.3).

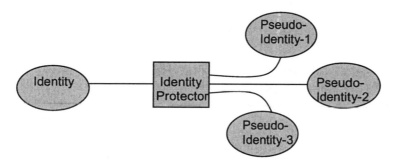

Fig. 4.3: The Identity Protector separates the identity and pseudo domains [Registratiekamer 1995]

4.2.2 Protecting User Identities at Communication Level

In this and in the following Section, we present privacy enhancing technologies that are protecting user identities in the entire information & communication system.

These system concepts correspond to installations where the identity protector is placed between the user representation and the service provider representation. Thus, the identity domain only contains the user representation; i.e. the user identities are unknown to all other system elements. This Section discusses system concepts for a complete protection of user identities at communication level, whilst the next Sections present some system concepts for a complete protection of user identities at system and application levels.

Important known system concepts providing unobservability and anonymity of the sender and/or recipient of a message are discussed below. Further security mechanisms for enhancing privacy in mobile communication by protection of the confidentiality of the current location of a mobile station and thereby preventing the generation of moving profiles will not be discussed. Location Management Strategies for preventing the generation moving profiles of the mobile phone subscribers are, for instance, discussed in [Kesdogan et al 1996]. The Application of Direct Sequence Spread Spectrum mechanisms in mobile communication to protect from locating and identifying a sending mobile station is discussed in [Thees/Federrath 1995].

4.2.2.1 Recipient Anonymity through Message Broadcast and Implicit Addresses

By delivering a message to all stations (broadcast), the receiving of the message can be made completely anonymous. Implicit addresses should be used to guarantee that only the intended recipient, the so-called addressee, can recognise that the message is addressesed to him [Pfitzmann/Waidner 1987].

In contrast to an explicit address, an implicit address does not describe a place in the network, but is an attribute which can only be used by the addressee to recognise that a message is addressed to him. An implicit address is called invisible, if it is only visible to its addressee, otherwise it is called visible. Invisible implicit addresses can be implemented by encrypting each message with the public key of the addressee. However, this implementation is quite costly, because every station has to decrypt all messages with each of its private keys and message redundancy has to be used to decide which messages are addressed to it. Visible implicit addresses could be realised less costly by using arbitrary transaction pseudonymous, which users can choose for themselves (or which can be generated by pseudo random number generators) and are used by the senders as message prefixes (see [Pfitzmann/Waidner 1987], [Federrath/Pfitzmann 1997]).

4.2.2.2 Dummy Traffic

Dummy messages are meaningless messages, which can be sent out at times of low network traffic to prevent traffic analysis. The anonymity of the sender can be protected, if an attacker controlling a network cannot determine any longer when and how many meaningful messages are sent.

4.2.2.3 DC-Nets

A DC-net (Dining Cryptographers Network) proposed by David Chaum [Chaum 1985], [Chaum 1988] allows participants to send and receive messages anonymously in an arbitrary network. It can be used to provide perfect sender anonymity.

Binary superposed sending:

The scheme proposed by David Chaum is based on binary superposed sending. Each user station shares a random bit stream with at least one other user station. These random bit streams serve as secret keys and are at least as long as the messages to be sent. For each single sending step (round), every user station adds modulo 2 (superposes) all the key bits it shares and its message bit, if there is one. Stations that do not wish to transmit messages send zeros by outputting the sums of their key bits (without any inversions). The sums are sent over the net and added up modulo 2. The result, which is distributed to all user stations, is the sum of all sent message bits, because every key bit was added twice (see Figure 4.4). If exactly one participant transmits a message, the message is successfully delivered as the result of the global sum to each participant. Detected collisions have to be resolved, for example, by retransmitting the message after a random number of rounds [Chaum 1988].

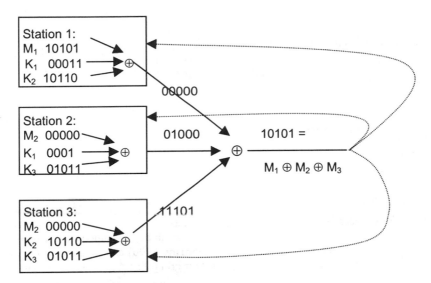

Fig. 4.1: Binary superposed sending in a DC-net [Pfitzmann/Waidner 1987]

Superposed sending guarantees perfect sender anonymity (unconditional sender untraceability). Even if an attacker controls all communication lines, he gets no information about the sender of the message. The only things the attacker gets to know about of the message bits transmitted by each station, is their parity sum, because the message bits (inversions) are hidden by a one-time pad, and only their parity is revealed, as only the parity of the pad is known [Chaum 1988]. Perfect recipient anonymity (unconditional recipient untraceability) can be guaranteed by reliable broadcast. In addition, message secrecy should be enforced by encrypting messages.

Formal Definition of the Generalised Approach:

Formally, the technique of superposed sending can be defined as follows (see [Waidner 1990], [Pfitzmann 1990]):
Let $P = \{P_1, ..., P_n\}$ be the set of all *participants*, and let $(F, +)$ be a finite abelian group. The set F is called the *alphabet* of the DC-net. The *key graph* G is defined as an undirected self-loop free graph with node P.
For each round, participants P_i, P_j who are directly connected by an edge of G choose a key $K_{ij} := K_{ji}$ from F at random.
Each participant P_i chooses a message character $M_i \in F$, outputs his local sum:

$$O_i := M_i + \sum_{j=1}^{i-1} K_{ij} - \sum_{j=i+1}^{n} K_{ij} \qquad (*)$$

and receives as input the global sum:

$$S := \sum_{i=1}^{n} O_i = \sum_{i=1}^{n} (M_i + \sum_{j=1}^{i-1} K_{ij} - \sum_{j=i+1}^{n} K_{ij})$$

Since each key is both added and subtracted exactly once, the global sum is equal to the sum of all message characters:

$$S = \sum_{i=1}^{n} M_i$$

If exactly one M_i has been chosen by a participant P_i unequal to 0, this message character is successfully delivered to all participants.
In [Chaum 1988], unconditional sender untraceability of superposed sending is proven if F is the Galois field GF(2). In [Pfitzmann 1990] and [Waidner 1990], the following Lemma is proven for any finite abelian group F:

Lemma (superposed sending):
Let A be a subset of participants controlled by the attacker, and assume that the graph $G \setminus (P \times A)$ is connected. Let $(O_1, ..., O_n) \in F^n$ be the output of a single round. Then for each vector $(M_1, ..., M_n) \in F^n$ which is consistent with the attacker's a priori knowledge about M_i

with $\displaystyle\sum_{j=1}^{n} O_j = \sum_{j=1}^{n} M_j$

the same number of key combinations exist which satisfy equation (*) and which is consistent with the attackers a priori knowledge about K_{ij}.

Thus, the conditional probability for $(M_1,...,M_n)$ given the output $(O_1,...,O_n)$ is equal to the conditional probability for $(M_1,...,M_n)$ given ΣM_i ; that is, an attacker gets no additional information about the characters M_i besides their sum.

Anonymity preserving multi-access protocols:

Superposed sending realises an additive multi-access channel with collision. A collision has to be resolved by a multi-access protocol that is preserving anonymity. Possible protocols are discussed in [Pfitzmann 1990], [Waidner 1990], [Chaum 1988].

These multi-access protocols combine a fixed number c of characters into a message. Each message is transmitted in c consecutive rounds, called slots.

A simple, but not very efficient protocol is slotted ALOHA [Roberts 1972]: If P_i wishes to send a message, he does so in the next slot. If a collision occurs, P_i detects the collision $(S \neq M_i)$ and retransmits its message after waiting a random number of slots.

More efficient protocols that avoid collisions use a reservation technique: A number of slots for real messages are preceded by a reservation frame, which is used to reserve them for specific participants.

Exchange of keys:

Superposed sending requires the exchange of a huge amount of randomly chosen keys. In [Chaum 1988], it is suggested that one member of each pair of participants that are supposed to share a secret key, generates a nonrepeating random key stream in advance, makes two identical copies of the key stream on separate optical disks, and then supplies one such disk to his communication partner. An alternative approach, with lower costs, uses key streams generated by cryptographic pseudo random-sequence generators. This approach, however, reduces information-theoretic security to complexity-theoretic security, since this system might be broken if the generators were broken.

Fail-stop broadcast:

In [Waidner 1990], it is shown how the sending of a specific participant X can be traced by an active attacker P_a who is able to alter the messages received by X and is controlling the current communication partners of X.

Such active attacks on untraceability are based on the fact that for services using two-way communication it is impossible to realise unconditional sender untraceability without unconditional recipient untraceability and vice versa: Assume that an attacker P_a communicates with some honest participant X, and that X will answer to a message M by sending message M′. If P_a is able to identify the sender of M′, he can identify the recipient of M and vice versa.

If the following active attacks are possible, a DC-net does not guarantee recipient untraceability, and thus it cannot guarantee sender untraceability: P_a succeeds to deliver a message M consecutively to a single participant only, and a meaningless message to all others. Thereby he can identify X by checking whether he receives M′ or not. If P_a delivers M to a subset of participants and successively partitions the set of participants, he can identify X in log(n) rounds on average.

In [Waidner 1990], DC^+-nets are proposed as a solution, and it is formally proven that DC^+-nets achieve unconditional untraceability in spite of active attacks. The DC^+-net uses a DC-net, but replaces the reliable broadcast network by a so-called *fail-stop broadcast* network.

A fail-stop broadcast prevents active attacks by stopping message transmission as soon as two honest participants receive different input characters. If such a difference is detected by an honest participant P_i, he will disturb the superposed sending in the subsequent rounds by choosing his output randomly from F instead of outputting his local sum according to equation (*).

In [Waidner 1990], [Lukat/Pfitzmann/Waidner 1991], it is suggested to implement fail-stop broadcast by fail-stop key generation schemes. If a deterministic fail-stop key generation scheme is used, the keys K_{ij} and K_{ji} used for superposed sending depend completely on the input characters I_i^s and I_j^s received by P_i and P_j in round s. Thus, a difference between I_i^s and I_j^s will automatically disturb superposed sending and thereby stop message transmission. Hence requirements for a deterministic fail-stop key generation scheme are:

Superposed sending: If for all rounds s=1,...,t-1 the equation $I_i^s = I_j^s$ holds, then the keys K_{ij}^t and K_{ji}^t for round t are equal and randomly selected from F.

Fail stop: If there exists an index s <t with $I_i^s \neq I_j^s$, then the keys K_{ij}^t and K_{ji}^t for round t are independently and randomly selected from F.

However, a deterministic fail-stop key generation scheme has to distinguish between all possible input character sequences, and thus has to store all input characters.

A probabilistic fail-stop key generation is more efficient, but guarantees only a *probabilistic version of the fail-stop requirement*:

If two honest participants receive two different input characters in round t, they will disturb superposed sending for the following d rounds (d∈ IN).

An example for a probabilistic fail-stop key generation scheme is defined by [Lukat/Pfitzmann/Waidner 1991]:

Let $(F, + , \bullet)$, and let $(a^1, a^2,...)$, $(b^3, b^4,...)$ be randomly and privately chosen from F^{IN}, let c be randomly and privately chosen from F, and let b^1, b^2, $K_{ij}^0, I_i^0 :=0$. Then define for all $r \in$ IN:

$$K_{ij}^r := a^r + (c + K_{ij}^{r-1}) \bullet (b^r + I_i^{r-1}).$$

In [Lukat/Pfitzmann/Waidner 1991], it is proven that the maximum number of d for which the probabilistic fail-stop requirement is satisfied, is a random variable with probability distribution $P(d) = 1/|F| (1- 1/|F|)^{d-1}$.

If t_{max} is the maximum number of rounds of superposed sending, the attacker's probability of a successful attack is: $P_A \leq t_{max} / |F|$.

Computationally secure servability:
Without any further measures, an attacker could untraceably and permanently disrupt the system, and thereby prevent others from sending messages. In [Waidner/Pfitzmann 1989], solutions for computationally secure servability are discussed, which can identify computationally restricted disrupters and remove them from the DC-net.

As discussed above, DC-nets provide perfect sender and recipient anonymity (unconditional sender and recipient untraceability). However, DC-nets require that each user station transmits at least as much data as all stations together want to send. Thus, DC-nets are costly to implement and due to performance reasons not an appropriate solution for channels with low bandwidth.

4.2.2.4 Mix-Nets

The technique of a Mix network, which was originally introduced by David Chaum [Chaum 1981], realises unlinkability of sender and recipient, as well as, sender anonymity against the recipient and optionally recipient anonymity. The concept of mix nets is further discussed in [Pfitzmann/Waidner 1987], [Pfitzmann 1990], [Pfizmann/Pfitzmann/Waidner 1991], [Cottrell 1995], [Gülcü 1996], [Franz/Jerichow/Pfitzmann 1997], [Franz/Jerichow/Wicke 1998].

A mix is a special network station, which collects and stores incoming messages, discards repeats, changes their appearance by encryption, and outputs them in a different order. By using one mix, the relation between sender and recipient is hidden from everybody but the mix and the sender of the message. To improve security, a message is sent over a mix net, which consists of a chain of independent mixes. The sender and/or recipient must perform cryptographic operations inverse to those of the mix, because the recipient must be able to read the message. A global attacker, who can monitor all communication lines, can only trace a message through the mix network, if he has the cooperation of all mix nodes on the path or if he can break the cryptographic operations. Thus, in order to ensure unlinkability of sender and recipient, at least one mix in the chain has to be trustworthy.

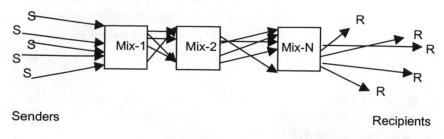

Senders   Recipients

Fig. 4.5: A chain of mixes hides the relation of incoming and outgoing messages

A mix path can either be chosen at random from the set of available mixes for each message or be fixed for all messages. Fixed-path systems are also called mix cascades.

Basic scheme for the protection of the sender:

Assume that sender A wants to send anonymously a message M to recipient B. A chooses a mix sequence Mix_1, Mix_2,..., Mix_m. Let for simplicity Mix_{m+1} denote the recipient. Each Mix_i with address A_i has initially chosen a key pair (c_i, d_i), where c_i is a public key of Mix_i and d_i is its private key. Let z_i be a random string.

Sender A recursively creates the following encrypted messages, where M_i is the message that Mix_i will receive:

$$M_{m+1} = c_{m+1} (M)$$
$$M_i = c_i(z_i, A_{i+1}, M_{i+1}) \text{ for } i=1,...,m$$

and sends M_1 to Mix_1.

Each Mix_i decrypts the incoming message $M_i = c_i(z_i, A_{i+1}, M_{i+1})$ with its private key d_i, discards the random string z_i, and finds the address A_{i+1} of the next mix Mix_{i+1} in the chain and the message M_{i+1}, which it forwards to Mix_{i+1}. The random string z_i is needed to prevent an attacker that can encrypt an outgoing message again with the public key of the mix, so that he can compare the result with the former input.

Protecting the recipient:

The technique just described does not prevent A from tracing B. The anonymity of the recipient can be protected by message broadcast and implicit addresses as described above. Another approach that is roughly analogous to the broadcast solution uses so-called indirect replies [Gülcü/Tsudik 1996]: instead of delivering a reply directly to the recipient, it is delivered to a local news group with a special number tag. The recipient can then scan this newsgroup for replies matching that number tag.

In [Chaum 1981], the technique of an untraceable return address for providing recipient anonymity was introduced: Assume that B wants to receive a message anonymously. B first chooses a sequence of Mixes $Mix_1,...,Mix_m$ and creates an untraceable return address according to the following scheme:

$$R_{m+1} = e$$
$$R_j = c_j(k_j, A_{j+1}, R_{j+1}) \quad \text{for } j=1,...,m$$
$$RA = (k_0, A_1, R_1),$$

where e is a label of the return address, k_j is a symmetric keys that is used by Mix_j to encode message, A_j is the address of Mix_j, c_j is a public key of Mix_j, and z_j is a random string (for j=1,...,m).

B is then sending anonymously this untraceable return address to A (see figure 4.6). It is now possible that A sends his reply message, while protecting the anonymity of the recipient B: A encrypts his reply message m with the symmetric key k_0 and sends $k_0(M)$ and R_1 to Mix_1.

B sends RA anonymously to A:

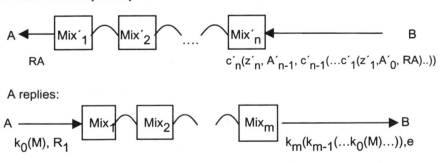

Fig. 4.6: Scheme for protecting the recipient (see also [Franz/Jerichow/Pfitzmann 1997])

Each Mix$_j$ receives $k_{j-1}(...k_0(M)..)$, R_j and decrypts $R_j = c_j (k_j, A_{j+1}, R_{j+1})$ with its private key d_j. It subsequently forwards $k_j(k_{j-1}(...k_0(M)...))$, R_{j+1} to Mix$_{j+1}$. The recipient B finally receives $k_m(k_{m-1}(...k_0(M)...))$, e. The label e indicates B which sequence of symmetric keys $k_0,..,k_m$ he has to use to decrypt the message M.

Two-way anonymous conversation:

The two schemes described above provide either sender or recipient anonymity. By combining both schemes, it is possible for two parties to communicate anonymously in both directions. Suppose that A sends anonymously a message including an untraceable return address RA to a news group. If B does not trust A, he can send his reply anonymously through a self-chosen sequence of Mixes to the first mix used in the untraceable return address (see Figure 4.7).

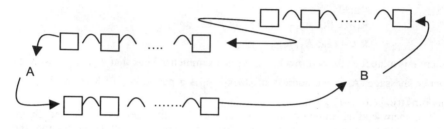

Fig. 4.7: B´s anonymous reply to A´s anonymous message (see also [Gülcü/Tsudik 1996])

Attacks and countermeasures:

In this section, we will discuss active and passive attacks on the mix technology as well as countermeasures. Passive attacks are those that can be carried out by merely observing message traffic, whilst active attacks use direct modifications of the message flow (see also [Gülcü/Tsudik 1996]):

Passive attacks:
Messages can be traced by content, seize or time.

To prevent **tracing by actual content**, all messages to and from a mix must be encrypted and must include random string as described above.

However, the basic mix scheme introduced above does not **prevent tracing by message size.** Each mix M_i in the chain decrypts its incoming messages and strips off the random string z_i and address A_{i+1} of the subsequent mix. Thus, messages are decreasing by size on their way through the mix network. To prevent size correlation, messages have to have a constant size throughout the entire mix network. A uniform message length can be achieved, if each mix is padding messages to a constant length with random data. A length-preserving coding scheme for mix networks is presented in [Chaum 1981], [Pfitzmann 1990].

Moreover, an attacker could trace messages by comparing their arrival and departure times at each mix of the chain. One solution to prevent **time correlation**, which delays and reorders messages, is to output messages in batches or message pools. If a batch is used, at least N messages are accumulated before being forwarded in random order (N is called the batch size). A message pool first collects N messages and then sends out one of the (N+1) messages in the pool (including the one that has just arrived) chosen at random. The techniques of batches and pools could also be combined, i.e., if the (N+1)th message arrives, m (m < N) arbitrary messages are chosen and forwarded.

So-called interval batching can be used to control the duration of message delays. In this advanced scheme, time is divided into equal periods of length T. If at the end of each time period the number of incoming messages is smaller than the batch seize N, the batch is filled with dummy messages. Thus, interval batching guarantees that a message will be delayed at most T time units by each mix.

Active attacks:
If a regular batch or pool is used, an attacker can fill the batch of a mix with only planted messages, which the attacker can recognise. Thus, if another message of an honest participant arrives to a batch, the entire batch will be forwarded and the attacker can simply trace the message that he did not generate. Similarly, if a pool is used, the attacker could send another number of messages after the arrival of message of a honest participant, so that this message will be flushed back out of the pool.

Such **isolate & identify** attacks can be prevented, if a certain number of dummy messages are sent out, even when the batch is full. In addition, it could be required that there should be enough messages in the batch or pool originating from different senders. Otherwise, sufficient dummy messages have to be added. However, digital signatures and a certification instance have to be used to implement this kind of control [Franz/Jerichow/Pfitzmann 1997].

Besides, **message replay attacks** can be used to follow a message to its final destination. If an attacker captures a message and sends many copies to the first mix, many messages, which look identical at each hop, will be forwarded through the same chain of mixes. Thus, the route of the message stream can easily be identified.

In order to prevent replay attacks, each mix has to keep track of incoming messages and discard replays. Replays can be detected by keeping a log of message IDs of sent messages. If a hybrid encryption scheme is used, the public-key encrypted form of a session key can serve as a message ID. If messages are time-stamped, message entries can be deleted from the log after some fixed system-wide time interval. Another solution is to require anonymous ecash postage in each layer. If the message is resent, then the ecash will be doubly spent and the mix would refuse to send it. Besides, anonymous payment schemes for mixes will also make replay attacks (as well as denial of service attacks) expensive and can enable the commercial operation of mix services [Cottrell 1995].

Since a mix-net relies on the security of a public-key system, it is at best computationally secure (in contrast to DC-nets that can provide perfect anonymity).

In addition to the basic mix concept, further means of protection have to be taken to prevent traffic analysis. However, in some environments, in particular if there is insufficient bandwidth for use of the broadcast approach, mix-nets can provide sender and recipient anonymity, where DC-nets cannot [Chaum 1988].

Applications:

There are several implementations or concepts of how to implement the technology of mix nets for different applications, such as:

- E-mail (Anoymous Remailers) [Cottrell 1995], [Gülcü/Tsudik 1996]
- ISDN [Pfitzmann 1990], [Pfitzmann/Pfitzmann/Waidner 1991]
- Mobile Computing [Cooper/Birman 1995]
- Mobile Communication [Federrath/Jerichow/Pfitzmann. 1996]
- Interactive Internet Communication: Web-Browsing, Remote Telnet, etc.
- (e.g., Anonymizer, Pipenet, Onion Routing, Freedom) [Boyan 1997], [Goldberg/Wagner/Brewer 1997], [Syverson/Goldschlag/Reed 1997], [Goldschlag/Reed/Syverson 1996], [Feedom]

In the following Section, we will briefly describe Anonymous Remailer technologies as well as implementations of Mix technology for interactive Internet services.

Anonymous Remailers:

A simple "type-0" remailer corresponds to a mix network consisting of one single mix. The most widely used one was the Finnish remailer service anon.penet.fi, which was closed down by its operator J.Helsingius, after it had been raided by the Finnish police in cooperation with the FBI. The anon.penet.fi – remailer performed the following operations: it stripped off all header information of an incoming message before forwarding it to its final destination. Then a pseudonym for the sender was created, if it was not already assigned, and in the outgoing message the address of the sender was replaced by the pseudonym. The pseudonym allowed the recipients of the message to reply to the real sender without knowing his identity.

However, the security of type-0 remailers is very weak. If they are not trustworthy, the anonymity of the users is not guaranteed. Worse still, the identity table kept by anon.penet.fi containing the mappings of pseudonyms and real user addresses, was a very sensitive point of attack. Besides, attackers who could eavesdrop on Internet traffic traversing the anon.penet.fi site could match up incoming and outgoing messages to learn about the identity of the pseudonymous users [Goldberg/Wagner/Brewer 1997].

So-called cypherpunk remailers (or type-1 remailers) enable to chain an encrypted message through a series of remailers. However, most cypherpunk remailers do not offer sufficient protection against tracing of message by seize or time correlation, or against replay or isolate & identify attacks.

A more sophisticated remailer technology, which can protect anonymity effectively and which was strongly influenced by Chaum´s concept of digital mixes, is Mixmaster (or Type-2 remailer) [Cottrell 1995]. Mixmaster also uses chaining of mixes and encryption at each link of the chain. Besides, it uses a length-preserving encoding scheme, sends messages as one or more packets of exactly the same length, includes defences against replay attacks and offers an improved message reordering code to stop passive correlation attacks based on timing coincidence.

Babel [Gülcü/Tsudik 1996] is another advanced remailer system that was developed at IBM Zurich Research Laboratory and allows both sending and receiving anonymous electronic messages and takes effective countermeasures against passive and active attacks. One special countermeasure against replay attacks, which is used by the Babel system, are Inter-Mix Detours. A mix in a chain normally forwards a message directly to the next hop in the chain. In the detour mode, however, a mix can anonymously forward the message to the next hop through a random path of mixes (called a detour). In order to avoid endless detour loops, detoured messages are tagged accordingly. The advantage of inter-mix detours is that even the originator of an anonymous message cannot recognise its own message as it leaves the mix.

In [EFGA], a current list of available remailer services for the Internet with an estimation of their reliability is offered.

Anonymous Interactive Internet Communication:

The Anonymizer [Boyan 1997] is a system corresponding to one single mix to provide anonymity protection for Web browsing. It is a web proxy that filters out identifying headers and source addresses from the web browser, as well as Java applets, JavaScript scripts and cookies. The connection itself, however, is not anonymised. The Anonymizer does not offer chaining or any effective countermeasures against passive and active attacks. Thus, it is a single point of trust with rather weak security features.

Further anonymising proxy servers are available, such as the Lucent Personalized Web Assistant (LPWA) [LPWA], [Gabber et al. 1999], which allows a user to use personalised services at web-sites by computing a different, but consistent pseudonyms for him for each web-site. As the Anonymizer, also LPWA has access to all user´s browser behaviour, and thus has to be trusted not to divulge this information.

A more secure solution is for instance provided by Onion Routing [Syverson/Goldschlag/Reed 1997], [Goldschlag/Reed/Syverson 1996], [Goldschlag/Reed/Syverson 1999]. Onion Routing is an architecture that provides anonymous socket connections by means of proxy servers. Onion Routing has been implemented at the Naval Research Laboratory with proxies for Web browsing, remote logins, and e-mail. An Onion is a layered object to produce an anonymous bi-directional virtual circuit between communication partners within link encrypted connections already running between routing nodes. The initiator´s proxy (for the service being requested) constructs a "forward onion", which encapsulates a series of routing nodes forming a route to the responder, and sends it with a create command to the first node. Each layer of the onion is encrypted with the public key of each node in the route and contains two function/key pairs as a payload. These "forward" and "backward" function/key pairs are applied by each node to crypt data that will be sent forward and back along the virtual circuit. After sending the onion, the initiator's proxy sends data through the anonymous connection. All information (onions, data, and network control) are sent through the Onion Routing network in uniform-seized cells. All cells arriving at an onion router within a fixed time interval are mixed together to reduce correlation by network insiders. Reply onions, which correspond to untraceable return addresses, allow for a responder to send back anonymously a reply after its original circuit is broken.

Onion routing is based on the concept of mix-networks. Since individual routing nodes in each circuit only know the identities of adjacent nodes, and since the nodes further encrypt multiplexed virtual circuits, traffic analysis is made difficult. However, if the first node behind the initiator's proxy and the last node of the virtual circuit cooperate, they will be able to determine the source and recipient of communication through the number of cells sent over this circuit (or through the duration for that the virtual circuit was used).

In [Berthold/Federath/Köpsell 2000], a so-called "adaptive chop-and-slice algorithm" is suggested to counteract such timing or message volume attacks: Large messages have to be "chopped" into short pieces of specific constant length, called "slices". Each slice is transmitted through an anonymous Mix channel. Besides, active users without an active communication request send dummy messages. Thus, the starting time and duration of a real communication is hidden, because all active users start and end their communication at the same time. Dependent on the traffic load, is throughput and duration of the anonymous channel is modified.

Another commercial system for anonymising Internet communication, which is based on the Mix concept, is the Freedom product by the Canadian company Zero-Knowledge System, Inc. [Freedom]. Freedom also provides a pseudonymous communication infrastructure where users can take virtual identities called "nyms".

4.2.2.5 Crowds

Reiter and Rubin developed Crowds – a system based on the idea that users can make anonymous Web transactions when they blend into a "crowd" [Reiter/Rubin 1997], [Reiter/Rubin 1998], [Reiter/Rubin 1999]. A crowd is a geographically diverse group that performs Web transactions on behalf of its members. Each crowd member runs a process on his local machine called "jondo". Once started, the jondo engages in a protocol to join the crowd, during which it is informed of the other current crowd members and in which the other crowd members are informed of the new jondo's membership. Besides, the user configures his browser to employ the local jondo as a proxy for all network services. Thus all http-requests are directly sent to the jondo rather than to the end Web-server and the jondo forwards the request to a randomly chosen crowd member. Whenever a crowd member receives a request from another jondo in the crowd, it makes a random choice to forward the request to another crowd member with a probability $p_f > \frac{1}{2}$ or to submit the request to the end Web server to which the request was destined. The server's reply is sent backward along the path, with each jondo sending it to its predecessor on the path. All communication between jondos is encrypted by a cryptographic key shared between the jondos involved.

Crowds provides sender anonymity against the end Web-server which is beyond suspicion, since the end server obtains no information regarding who initiated any given request. Second, since a jondo on the path cannot distinguish whether its predecessor on the path initiated the request or is forwarding it, no jondo on the path can learn the initiator of a request. Since all communication between jondos is encrypted, crowds also offers receiver anonymity against a local eavesdropper (e.g., local gateway administrator) that can observe the communication involving the user's machine unless the originator of the request ends up submitting the request itself. (However, the probability that an originator submits its own request decreases as the crowd seize increases).

Crowds enables very efficient implementations that typically outperforms mixes that uses layered encryption techniques. However, in contrast to mix-nets, crowds cannot protect against global attackers.

4.2.3 Protecting User Identities at System Level

In this Section we will discuss system concepts that allow a user to use a system anonymously or pseudonymously.

4.2.3.1 Pseudonymous System Accounts

Simple organisational measures, which allow a user to access a system under a name pseudonym, were suggested in [Registratiekamer 1995]: If a new employee enters a large organisation, the head of the department can draw up an access profile for him on the basis of the required access level. This profile, which should not contain data that can be associated with the new employee, is then sent to the system administrator. The system administrator checks the profile for authenticity and sets up a user account under a pseudonymous user-ID with authorisations in accordance with the employee's access profile. He then returns a form to the department head with the user-ID and a password for the new pseudonymous user account. Thus the new employee has now access to the system without the system administrator knowing who the employee is. If the employee is violating his access rights, he can still be identified through the department head.

4.2.3.2 Anonymous System Access and Use through Authorisation Certificates

In [Nikander/Viljanen et al. 1998], it has been pointed out that authorisation certificates such as SPKI-certificates can be used to implement distributed access control management with the option for a user to anonymously access systems and/or services and resources.

An authorisation certificate (see Chapter 3.3.7.5) binds a public key to an authorisation and is a proof of its holder's authority to act. By signing the certificate the issuer expresses her belief that the holder of the private key is authorised to act. A user can prove that he is the holder of a private key by using a conventional public key authentication protocol. Since an authorisation certificate does not have to include information about the subject's identity, it can be used to gain anonymous access.

SPKI-certificates can be chained into sequences, where the last certificate in the chain is typically a permission certificate, which is preceded by zero or more delegation certificates. The first certificate within the sequence must be issued by the verifier of the sequence.

Figure 4.8 shows a chain of SPKI-certificates, which allows verifying the user's access rights even when the user wishes to stay anonymous.

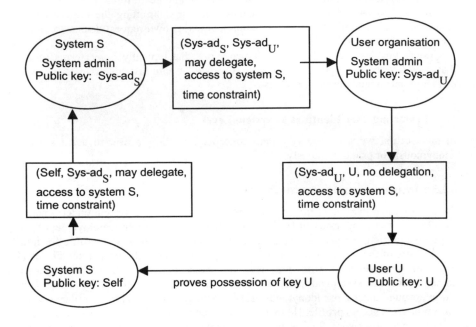

Fig. 4.8: Authorisation certificate chain (loop) for gaining anonymous system access (see also [Nikander/Viljanen et al. 1998])

In this example (which is similar to an example given in [Nikander/Viljanan 1998]), a system S is administrated by a system administrator Sys-ad, represented by the system administrator's public key Sys-ad$_S$. The fact that the system (owner) S (unconditionally) trusts the system administrator Sys-ad is represented digitally as a trust certificate signed with the system's secret key K_S. This system administrator, on his behalf, delegates a right to grant access to the system to the system administrator of the user's organisation (represented by the public key Sys-ad$_U$). Sys-ad$_U$ in turn grants the user U a right to access the system S. With this authorisation certificate chain and by execution of a public-key authentication protocol the user can now anonymously get access to the system.

If the access control policies implemented in the system S are not based on identities, but on certain user authorisations (e.g., roles in role-based access control), similar certificate chains can be used to authorise the (anonymous) user for further accesses. If the last certificate in the chain for instance is a permission certificate expressing the subject's authorisation for a certain role, the user can with this certificate be authorised for a role and by performing this role receive privileges defined for the role on the system.

Since only U's public key and not his identity is known, U can act anonymously in the system S. The user organisation, however, usually knows the identities of the users to whom it issues authorisation certificates. Thus, in cooperation with the issuers, users can be re-identified. Hence, strictly speaking authorisation certificates enable anonymity in the local system S and pseudonymity in the overall system environment.

However, keys are easily recognisable identifiers that can be used to combine data collected from different sources, which might finally lead to a reidentification of a user. One solution with more reliable privacy protection is to create temporary keys that do not reveal their owner. When a user wants his anonymity to be protected, he provides the issuer of a new certificate with a freshly generated public key. The temporary keys cannot be connected to the owner or to each other [Aura 1999].

4.2.4 Protecting User Identities at Application Level

In addition to infrastructures for anonymous communication and system use, privacy has also to be protected at application level. Major future applications on the new information infrastructures will be in the area of electronic commerce. Thus, in this Section we will concentrate on two different techniques to provide anonymous payment.

4.2.4.1 Prepaid Cards

Prepaid cards can provide a simple means for anonymous payments of services offered for information infrastructures. Prepaid cards are smartcards, on which an amount of money can be loaded. Anonymous prepaid cards are "one-way " cards on which money can only be loaded once (e.g., telephone cards), or cards on which anonymous ordinary cash can be loaded. Money can also be loaded anonymously from a customer's bank account to a card (The German "Geldkarte", however, is not anonymous [Schier/Fischer-Hübner 1998]. The "Geldkarte" is an Eurocheque card with an additional chip with the function of an electronic wallet. The loading of money to the card is logged in each clearing station. Besides, each transaction is logged at the merchant site and sent to the clearing station).

4.2.4.2 Untraceable Electronic Money through Blind Signatures

In this Section, we will briefly introduce David Chaum's concept of untraceable electronic money based on blind signatures. Chaum's Digicash scheme has not proved successful in the marketplace, although DigiCash's ecash is an example of a privacy technology for electronic payment applications with the strongest privacy protection of any deployed payment systems for the Internet.

David Chaum [Chaum 1985], [Chaum/Fiat/Naor 1988], [Chaum 1992], has invented protocols based on blind signatures, which allow electronic money to flow tracelessly from bank through consumer and merchant before returning to the bank. Blind signatures, which were invented by David Chaum, are an extension of digital signatures that provide privacy. They allow someone to sign a document without seeing its actual content. Blind signature scheme can also be used for other privacy-enhanced applications, such as anonymous voting schemes

In the basic "online " payment protocol (see Figure 4.9), electronic bank notes are messages signed by a bank using a particular private key indicating its value (e.g., one dollar).

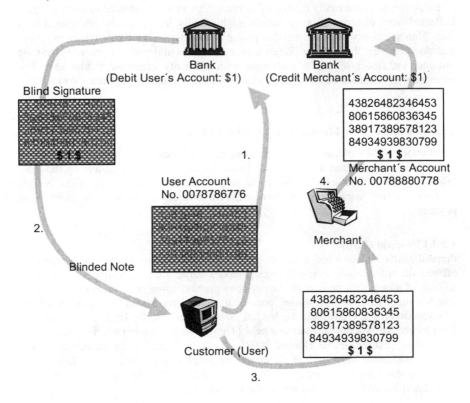

Fig. 4.9: Flow of ecash's untraceable electronic money [Chaum 1992]

The customer Alice (i.e., her computer) first generates a note number (of at least 100 digits) at random and in essence multiplies it by a blinding factor, which she has also chosen at random. She then signs the "blinded" note number with her private key and sends it to the bank.

The bank verifies and removes Alice's signature, signs the blinded note with its worth-one-dollar signature, debits her account and returns the note with the "blind signature". Besides, it sends Alice a digitally signed withdrawal receipt. Alice divides out the blinding factor and thereby receives the original note number signed by the bank. She can then use the money to pay for purchase at Bob's shop. Bob transmits the note to the bank after verifying the bank's signature. The bank verifies its signature, checks the note against a list of those already spent and credits Bob's account by one dollar. Besides, it sends a signed "deposit slip" to Bob. Bob hands the merchandise to Alice along with his own signed receipt.

The blind signature scheme allows creating "unconditionally untraceable" electronic money: even if the bank and the shop collude, they cannot determine who spent which notes. Since the bank does not know the blinding factors, it cannot correlate withdrawals from one account with deposits to another. (Note that, however, the anonymity of the customer is only protected, if he does not use ecash over non-anonymised IP connection and if he does not send a delivery address).

Cryptographic Protocol for Blind Signatures:

In this Section, the cryptographic protocol for the use of blind signatures to create and spend untraceable money [Chaum 1985], [Chaum/Fiat/Naor 1988] is given.

Let (e, n) be the bank's private key, and (d,n) the bank's public key.

f is a suitable one-way function. Money has the form $(x, f(x)^d \pmod n)$.
The protocol for issuing and spending such money [Chaum 1985] can be summarised as follows:

1. The customer Alice chooses at random x and r, and supplies the bank with :

   $B = r^e * f(x) \pmod n$
   where f(x) is the serial number of a bank note and r is a blinding factor

2. The bank signs the blinded note (and thereby creates the blind signature), returns

   $B^d \pmod n = (r^e * f(x))^d \pmod n = r * f(x)^d \pmod n$
   and withdraws one dollar from her account

3. Alice extracts $C = B^d / r \pmod n = f(x)^d \pmod n$
   from B

4. To pay Bob one dollar, Alice gives him the pair $(x, f(x)^d \pmod n)$

5. Bob immediately calls the bank, verifying that this note has not already been deposited

   The one-way function f has to be applied to prevent easy forgery of electronic money: Suppose $(x, x^d \bmod n)$ should be electronic money. Then it is easy to forge electronic money by first choosing a random y, and exhibiting $(y^e \bmod n, y)$. To forge money of the form $(x, f(x)^d \bmod n)$, a forger has to produce $(f^{-1}(y^e) \bmod n, y)$. However, since it should not be possible to invert the one-way function f, such an easy way of forgery is made impossible.

Blind Signatures and Perfect Crimes:

In [von Solms/Naccache 1992], S. von Solms and D. Naccache show how blind signatures can potentially be misused to commit a perfect crime (in financial terms), such as kidnapping and blackmailing. The strategy works as follows:

<u>Step 1</u>: Open a bank account with a bank which issues ecash and open an ecash account, kidnap the victim

<u>Step 2</u>:
2.1 Choose a set of xs $(x_1, x_2,...,x_p)$ and a set of rs $(r_1, r_2, ..., r_p)$

2.2 - Compute set B_j where $B_j = r_j^e * f(x_j) \pmod n$
   - Mail B_j to the authorities with the threat to kill the victim, if the following instructions are not complied with:
   a. For all j, compute the set $D_j = B_j^d \bmod n = r_j * f(x_j)^d \pmod n$
   b. Publish D_j in a newspaper

2.3 Buy the newspaper and compute $C_j = D_j / r_j \bmod n = f(x_j)^d \pmod n$.
   { (x_j, C_j) } represents legal authorised and untraceable money.

Note that if crimes are committed according to the above strategy, conditions are worse than in usual criminal (kidnapping) cases for the following reasons. First, the police cannot register the serial numbers of the bank notes that are handed over to the kidnapper. Furthermore, no physical contact between the kidnapper and the blackmailed persons or police is needed in order to hand over the blackmailed money. This example illustrates the conflict between privacy protection and possible misuses, which will be discussed below in more detail (see Chapter 4.2.7).

The protocol introduced above affords on-line clearing, which is a possible though rather expensive solution to prevent anyone from making several copies of electronic notes and using them at different shops. In such an "on-line" system, the merchant has to call the bank to check against a central list that the money has not been deposited before.

In [Chaum/Fiat/Naor 1988], D.Chaum, A.Fiat and M.Naor also present a protocol for "off-line" electronic money, where the merchant will no longer have to check with the bank to see if the money has already been spent. This method for generating blinded notes requires that the customer must answer a random numeric query about each note when making a payment in a shop. The customer's responses are used by the merchant to check the proper form of the money and are then sent to the bank, which stores this information. Spending a note once does not compromise unconditional untraceability. If, however, a note is spent twice, the bank will get enough information to trace the payer's account.

Another offline electronic payment scheme for untraceable electronic cash guaranteeing multi-party security was introduced by Stefan Brands [Brands 1995]. To participate, the Internet user is provided with a tamper-resistant device by the bank, which is typically a PCMCIA card and must be interfaced to the user's computer. This tamper-resistant device keeps track of the cash balance held by the user, by means of a counter, and can perform computations. One main advantage of the use of a tamper-resistant device is that it can guarantee prior restraint of double-spending. Besides, a mechanism based on a "one-show blind signature protocol" (based on the same idea as proposed by [Chaum/Fiat/Naor 1988]) is used to ensure that the contents of a compromised tamper-resistant device cannot be double spent without the owner being traced afterwards by the bank.

4.2.5 Protecting User Identities in Audit Data through Pseudonymous Auditing

Pseudonymous Auditing is a privacy-enhancing security auditing technique where user identifying audit data is pseudonymised [Sobirey/Fischer-Hübner 1996] [Sobirey/Fischer-Hübner/Rannenberg 1997]. Pseudonymous auditing can be enforced by a system installation where the identity protector is placed between the service provider representation and audit file (see Figure 4.10).

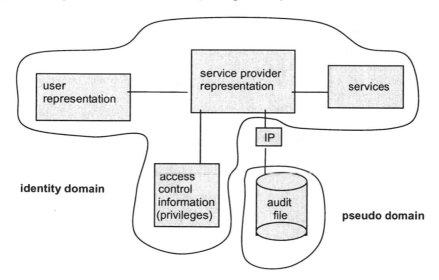

Fig. 4.10: Installation of the Identity Protector (IP) for enforcing pseudonymous auditing

As discussed in Chapter 3, there is a conflict where security mechanisms can both help to protect privacy of the data subjects and can at the same time be used to invade the privacy of the users and data subjects. Auditing provides the recording, analysis and review of data related to security relevant events. It aims at deterring and detecting penetrations of computer systems and forms a last line of defence against many kinds of security violations, which cannot be prevented by authentication and access control. However, auditing generates personal data about the activities and behaviour of users. This data provides detailed information about: *Who* has accessed *when*, *where* and *how*, *what* and *whose* resource.

Privacy is especially threatened by the increasing use of intrusion detection systems as powerful audit analysis tools. Intrusion detection systems are capable of detecting intrusive behaviour by monitoring the system usage for subversive, suspicious or anomalous, possibly security violating activities. Anomaly detection methods are using statistics about the users´ behaviour that could be misused e.g. for employee performance control.

Pseudonymous auditing can balance the conflict between accountability and privacy. Intrusion detection systems which operate with pseudonymised audit data offer a more socially and legally acceptable approach.

Pseudonymous auditing was first suggested in [Fischer-Hübner/Brunnstein 1990], and was first implemented in the IDA (Intrusion Detection and Avoidance) prototype at Hamburg University (see [Fischer-Hübner 1992]). The concept of pseudonymous auditing was then refined and implemented in the AID system (Adaptive Intrusion Detection system) at the Brandenburg University of Technology at Cottbus (see [Sobirey et al. 1996b]), which provides pseudonymous network monitoring. Pseudonymous auditing is discussed in [Sobirey/Fischer-Hübner 1996] and [Sobirey/Fischer-Hübner/Rannenberg 1997].

4.2.5.1 Functionality of Pseudonymous Auditing

Pseudonymous auditing is a special security auditing technique, where subject identifiers and further user identifying data in audit records are pseudonymised right after creation and where audit records are analysed in this representation, e.g. by an intrusion detection system (see Figure 4.11).

When analysing the audit data, the security officer does not have to know the real user identities of the monitored users. It is sufficient if his real identity can be determined, if suspicious or obvious intrusive behaviour of a user acting under a certain pseudonym is detected. Ideally, the security administrator should re-identify a user in order to unmask him as an intruder only in cooperation with a data protection officer.

Thus, pseudonymous auditing can provide both user accountability as well as pseudonymity. Figure 4.11 shows the functionality of pseudonymous operating system auditing. In principle, pseudonymous auditing is also applicable to other forms of auditing, e.g., application auditing.

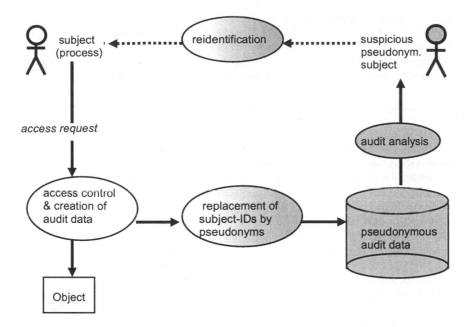

Fig. 4.11: Functionality of pseudonymous operating system auditing [Sobirey/Fischer-Hübner/Rannenberg 1997]

4.2.5.2 Pseudonymisation of User Identifying Data in Audit Records

Various fields in audit records contain data that is re-identifying a user or can be used to re-identify a user. The following example of a Solaris 2.4 audit record is given to explain the structure and content of audit data (see also [Sobirey/Fischer-Hübner 1996], [Sobirey/Fischer-Hübner/Rannenberg 1997]).

The record consists of several tokens (data lines) beginning with a token identifier. The *header* token contains general information, such as the seize of the record, the audit event and the time stamp. The *path* and *attribute* tokens provide object related information, e.g. the object name, the corresponding access rights, owner and owner group. The subject token that follows contains detailed information about the initiator of the recorded action, especially the audit ID, the effective user ID, the effective group ID, the real user ID, the real group ID and the hostname. The last token contains the status of the audit event and a return value.

```
header,113,2,open(2)-read,,Mon Jan 22 09:34:32 1996,+650002 msec
path, /home/richter/lib/libintl.so.1
attribute,100755,richter,rnks,8388638,29586,0
subject,richter,richter,rnks,richter,rkns, 854, 639,0 0 romeo
return,success,0
```

This record can be interpreted as follows:

On *22nd January 1996, 9.34:32,650002* user *"richter"* (see audit ID) acted on his own account (audit ID and the real user ID are identical) from the host system *"romeo"* and opened the file *libintl.so.1* successfully *(success,0)* for *reading (open(2) - read)*. Owner and owner group of the program are *"richter"* and *"rnks"*.

We distinguish directly user-identifying attributes, which are directly naming the user, and indirectly user identifying attributes, which together with supplementary knowledge can be used for re-identification.

Directly user-identifying data is contained in the subject token and in the attribute token (user, group and owner of the object).

Indirectly user identifying data is contained in the path token if a subject accesses own files or files owned by other users unlike system standard users such as *daemon*, *bin* or *sys*. In this case the name of the home directory often corresponds with the user name and is part of the recorded access path. Often the names and structure of subdirectories and the names of files/programs that are owned by regular users can be used to re-identify a user.

Besides, the following data can be used for unwanted re-identification:
− Host identifier, host name or host type (e.g., if a small number of users regularly work only on certain hosts or if users have their own workstations)
− Date and time stamp (e.g., if a small number of users work at certain hours or during week ends).
− Action and access rights in combination with final action status (e.g., if a file can be write-accessed only by its owner and a pseudonymous user has opened this file successfully for writing, then only the object owner or root can be the initiator of this action).

Pseudonymisation of user identifying data in audit records should ensure privacy protection for the user. However, pseudonymous audit records have still to be useful for audit trail analysis to achieve significant analysis results. Analysis problems will be caused, if the action field, date/time, access rights and action status are pseudonymised. If all directly and indirectly user identifying data in the audit record listed above were pseudonymised, the result would be a pseudonymous audit record, which only allows the following interpretation:

A *certain user* acted on his own account (pseudonyms of audit ID and real user ID are identical) and referred *somewhere, sometime, somehow* an *own file* (subject ID´s and object owner ID are identical).

Thus, extensively pseudonymised audit records provide no significant analysis results.

An effective pseudonymisation of audit records should replace the following fields by pseudonyms:
− All user IDs
− Location IDs
− Subdirectories and object names referring to user names (that are not system standard users).

4.2.5.3 Pseudonymisation Techniques

The analysis of pseudonymous audit data requires the ability to link the pseudonyms (to each other) that represent identical user identifying data. Thus, personal pseudonyms, which are aliases for the subject or object names, have to be used. However, the longer the period for that personal pseudonyms are used, the more amount of information about the persons acting under the pseudonyms can be accumulated, which can be used for re-identification purposes. Thus, it is necessary to change the personal pseudonyms after a period of time to protect against re-identification.

To minimise performance losses and especially to support real time intrusion detection, a fast technology for pseudonymisation is needed.

Pseudonymisation of audit data could be implemented through reference pseudonyms or cryptographic pseudonyms. For the implementation of reference pseudonyms, a pseudonym database has to be kept and administrated, which can cause considerable overhead. Cryptographic pseudonyms could for instance be generated by symmetric key encryption of user identifying data in audit records. Operational separation of duty could be enforced by a two- key encryption scheme. The decryption key is divided into two halves, where one half is kept by the security officer and the other half is kept by a person that is protecting the privacy interest of the users (This person could, for example, be the data protection officer or the works council in an organisation). Thus, re-identification of users should only be possible, if the two persons are willing to collaborate.

In the IDA system and in the AID system, cryptographic pseudonyms are used, which are created by secret key encryption (see [Sobirey/Fischer-Hübner 1996]).

4.2.6 Protecting User Identities from other Users and Services

If identity protectors are placed between the services and the other system elements, services will be located in the pseudo domain, while other system elements remain in the identity domain. This means that the user can use services anonymously, not only increasing privacy in terms of those particular services, but also in relation to other users [Registratiekamer 1995].

In this installation, however, the user´s real identity is still known by the service provider. Besides, the user´s privileges and actions are registered in the access control database and audit trail under his real user identity.

The functionality of the Calling Line Identification can be compared to the functionality of an identity protector, which is located between the service provider (i.e., the telephone company) and the receiving parties (callees) [Registratiekamer 1995]. The functionality of the Calling Line Identification in a digital telephone network allows the caller to decide whether his telephone number is to be revealed to the receiving party.

Another situation in which services are cordoned off is created when an Internet service provider is acting as a representative of its users by giving temporary pseudo-identities, with which its users can access Internet services.

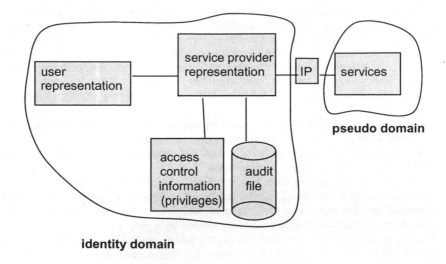

identity domain

Fig. 4.12: Installation of the Identity Protector (IP) cordoning off areas of services and other users

4.2.7 The Need for Anonymity and the Problem of its Potential Misuse

In this Chapter, we discuss privacy-enhancing technologies for protecting the user identities that can provide anonymity or unobservability.

As pointed out by Goldberg et al. [Goldberg/Wagner/Brewer 1997], outside of the Internet, anonymity is widely accepted and recognised as valuable in today's society. Anonymity is, for example, provided and regarded as important for the many social interactions: HIV lab testing should be done anonymously, social centres provide anonymous telephone hot-lines, it is possible to make anonymous telephone calls by stepping into a payphone box, and ordinary cash allows to purchase merchandise anonymously. Besides, it is possible to publish books or articles under pseudonyms. Elections are usually done anonymously. Thus, anonymous social interaction is both commonplace and culturally accepted in our society and should be preserved in the networked society.

On the other side, anonymity can also be misused to commit criminal activities without leaving any traces. For example, anonymous remailers can be misused to forward, for instance, copyright-protected material or espionage information, or to distribute illegal material, junk mail or logic bombs. Besides, with anonymous communication systems hackers could anonymously launch denial of service attacks. Onion routing may permit hackers to misuse privileges without leaving any traces. Furthermore, blind signatures can potentially be misused to commit perfect crime (see 4.2.4.2). Hence, with systems that are providing anonymity, it is no longer possible to track certain computer crimes to the person responsible and computer criminal law will thus lose its power of deterrence.

However, the ban of privacy technologies or restrictions to use them is not the right solution for this problem, because it would severely restrict the users´ possibilities to protect their privacy. Criminals, however, would still find other means or could set up their own technologies to commit crimes without leaving relevant traces.

IT-lawyers have for a long time already pointed out that computer criminal law should only be the last line of defence. "The criminal law is the strongest sanction available to the state, and it carries considering stigmatising effect. We must be careful not to extend this powerful tool to cases where its use is unnecessary or inappropriate, lest this devalues the impact of the law generally" [Wasik 1994]. Besides, also in non-anonymous information and communication systems, tracking computer criminals has always been a problem (e.g., there have been only two publicised cases of virus authors being convicted for virus writing).

Thus, instead of overestimating the role of computer criminal law, more effort should be put on crime prevention and user education. Some examples of technical means to prevent the abuse of anonymous remailers are for instance given in [Goldberg/Wagner/Brewer 1997]. For example, small anonymous payments for anonymous services would reduce spam, harassment, and denial of service attacks by making it too expensive to send a large volume of data. Besides, remailers often include alarms when they encounter a large volume of mail in a short time. The remailer operators can then delete the spammed messages and try to source block the spammer (i.e. blacklist the sender). Furthermore, harassment can be counteracted, if targeted individuals install mail filtering software.

Still, "abuse management and prevention is likely to remain a central challenge for future anonymity technologies" [Goldberg/Wagner/Brewer 1997].

4.3 System Concepts for Protecting Usee Identities - Inference Controls for Statistical Database Systems

According to the privacy principle of necessity of personal data collecting and processing, personal data should be depersonalised as soon as the purposes, for which the data were collected, permit this. In particular, it is usually not necessary to store, process or evaluate personal data collected for research purposes in non-anonymous form.

Personal data records can be depersonalised by deleting identity data and / or by reducing the number of demographic data attributes and number of possible values of each attribute (i.e., choosing a lower granularity) appropriately. In chapter 4.1.2.2 we have shown how the re-identification risk that is depending on the entropy of the demographic data attributes can be estimated.

As discussed above, in general-purpose database systems (e.g., medical databases), some users (e.g., physicians) need to access personal data attributes, while other user (e.g., researchers) only need to access a personal database by statistical queries. Thus, access control mechanisms should allow certain users to access data in anonymous form by performing statistical queries. However, by correlating different statistics, a user may succeed to deduce confidential information about some individual.

In the following section, we briefly discuss inference controls for statistical databases that shall ensure that the statistics released by the database do not lead to the disclosure of any confidential data. A good survey of statistical database security is given in [Denning 1982]).

Statistical Database Model:

A statistical database contains information about the attributes of N individuals, where each attribute has several different (numeric or non-numeric) values. Statistics are computed for subgroups of records having common attributes. A subgroup is specified by a characteristic formula C, which is defined as any logical formula over the values of attributes using the operators OR, AND, and NOT [Denning 1982].

For instance, a university could have a database with confidential student records. An example of a characteristic formula is
(SEX = FEMALE) AND ((MAJOR = CS) OR (MAJOR = BIO)),
which specifies all female students majoring either in computer science or biology.

The set of records whose values match a characteristic formula C is called the query set of C. In the following sections, "C" is used to denote both a formula and its query set, and |C| is used to denote the number of records in C (query set seize).

Statistics have the form: q(C, U) (or simply q(C)), where C is a characteristic formula specifying a query set, U is a set of attributes, and q is a statistical function. Statistics are calculated over the values (of the attributes in U) associated with the query set C. Examples of types of statistics are *counts*, *sums*, *relative frequencies* and *averages*, the *mean* and variance of an attribute, or correlation coefficient of two attributes.

For example, the statistic COUNT((SEX = MALE) AND (MAJOR = CS)) gives the number of female students majoring in computer science.

The statistic SUM(((SEX = MALE) AND (MAJOR = CS), GP) give the sum of the grade points (GP) of the group.

Methods of attacks:

A statistic is *sensitive* if confidential data could be deduced. If a statistic is either sensitive or its release could lead to the disclosure of a sensitive statistic, it is defined as *critical* [Denning 1982].
The following statistics for instance are sensitive:
Suppose a user knows that Smith is a female computer science student and is represented in the student record database.
The statistic COUNT ((SEX = FEMALE) AND (MAJOR = CS)) = 1
reveals that Smith is the only female computer science student.
The statistic SUM ((SEX = FEMALE) AND (MAJOR = CS), GP) reveals her exact GP.

The problem is to isolate all critical statistics, because many statistics are not critical by themselves, but may become critical when correlated with other statistics.

For example, the statistic COUNT (NOT ((SEX = FEMALE) AND (MAJOR = CS))) is not sensitive, but it is critical, because the sensitive statistic COUNT ((SEX = FEMALE) AND (MAJOR = CS)) can be computed from:
COUNT (ALL) - COUNT (NOT ((SEX = FEMALE) AND (MAJOR = CS))).

Such trivial compromises can be prevented by a *query-set-seize restriction*, which permits a statistic if and only if its query set seize is within the range [n, N-n], where N is the seize of the database and n ≤ 0 is a parameter.

Nevertheless, a query-set-seize restriction is not adequate by itself, because the database is still vulnerable to so-called *tracker attacks*, which were first detected by J.Schlörer [Schlörer 1975]. The basic idea of a tracker is to pad small query sets with enough extra records to put them in the allowable range, and then to subtract the effect of the padding. There are different types of trackers: individual trackers, general trackers, double trackers and union trackers (see [Denning 1982]).

An example of a general tracker attack follows:
A general tracker is any characteristic formula T such that $2*n \le |T| \le N-2*n$.

Suppose that for the student record database a query set seize control is implemented. We shall use the tracker T = (Sex = Male) to deduce the GP of the female computer science student Smith. The restricted statistic COUNT ((SEX = FEMALE) AND (MAJOR = CS)) can be computed with the following queries:

COUNT (ALL) = COUNT (SEX = MALE) + COUNT (NOT (SEX = MALE))

COUNT ((SEX = FEMALE) AND (MAJOR = CS)) =
COUNT (((SEX = FEMALE) AND (MAJOR = CS)) OR (SEX = MALE)) +
COUNT (((SEX = FEMALE) AND (MAJOR = CS)) OR (NOT (SEX = MALE))) -
COUNT (ALL).

Similarly, the restricted statistic SUM ((SEX = FEMALE) AND (MAJOR = CS), GP) can be computed:
SUM (ALL, GP) = SUM (SEX = MALE, GP) + SUM (NOT (SEX = MALE), GP)

SUM ((SEX = FEMALE) AND (MAJOR = CS), GP) =
SUM ((SEX = FEMALE) AND (MAJOR = CS)) OR (SEX = MALE), GP) +
SUM (((SEX = FEMALE) AND (MAJOR = CS)) OR (NOT (SEX = MALE)), GP) -
SUM (ALL, GP).

Controls for Statistical Inference Attacks:

Inference controls for statistical databases can be implemented by *data perturbation* or by *output controls*.

Data perturbation adds noise to the data values, either by permanently modifying the data stored in the database, or by temporarily modifying data when they are used to calculate some statistics. The first approach, however, cannot be used in general-purpose databases where data have to be accurate for non-statistical purposes.

Output controls can be divided into *output selection* mechanisms that restrict sensitive or critical statistics, and *output modification* mechanisms that add noise to the statistics.

With output selection techniques, correct results are provided. However, many results must be withheld in order to maintain security.

With output modification mechanisms, the output provided is close to but not exactly the actual value. They benefit from the difference between absolute and relative errors. If for instance the output 1003 instead of the true value 1000 is provided, the absolute error is 3, but the relative error is only 0.003. Such small relative error does not disturb the validity of the statistic. However, an absolute error of 3 is already helpful to protect against tracker attacks. Output modification mechanisms are generally more efficient to apply, and allow the release of more non-sensitive statistics.

Examples of output selection and output modification mechanisms follow (a more complete survey is given in [Denning 1982], [Schlörer 1982], [Fischer-Hübner 1987], [Castano et al. 1995]):

Output selection:

A *query-set-seize control* is a trivial output selection mechanism, which is simple to implement and valuable in combination with other controls, but not sufficient by itself.

Another possibility is a *maximum-order control*, which restricts statistics that employ too many attribute values. This control is aiming at preventing compromises that require a large number of attributes to identify a particular individual. However, it can be too restrictive, because many of the higher-order statistics may be safe [Denning 1982].

Another output selection technique is the so-called S_m/N-*criterion*, which was proposed by J.Schlörer [Schlörer 1976], [Schlörer 1982]. It restricts query sets over attributes $A_1,...,A_m$ that decompose the database into too many sets relative to the seize N of the database.

$$S_m = \prod_{i=1}^{m} |A_i|.$$

A statistic q(C) is restricted if $S_m/N > t$ for some threshold t (e.g., t = 0.1).

The S_m/N-criterion is efficient, easy to implement and less restrictive than a maximum order control. It can (and should) be combined with output modification mechanisms in such a way that the extent of modification increases as S_m/N increases.

The S_m/N-criterion can be used to estimate the identification risk. However, the S_m/N-criterion does neither consider dependencies between attributes nor frequency distributions of attribute values. The function RR defined in chapter 4.1.2.2 (see definition 4.4) provides a more precise measure for the average identification risk.

In [Fischer-Hübner 1987] a so-called *re-identification risk control* was suggested, which restricts a statistic q(C), where C is a query set over attributes $A_1,...,A_m$, if

$RR(A_1,...,A_m) > t$ for some threshold t.

The re-identification risk control is more costly to implement than the S_m/N-criterion. On the other hand, it is more precise and thus allows the release of more non-sensitive statistics.

Output modification:

With *rounding* the response q of a statistic q(C) is rounded up or down to the nearest multiple of some base b.

Systematic rounding always rounds q either up or down according to the following rule. Let $b' = \lfloor (b+1)/2 \rfloor$ and $d = q \bmod b$. Then

$$r(q) = \begin{cases} q & \text{if } d = 0 \\ q\text{-}d & \text{if } d < b' \text{ (round down)} \\ q + (b\text{-}d) & \text{if } d \geq b' \text{ (round up)}. \end{cases}$$

Under certain circumstances, it is however possible to recover the exact statistics from their rounded values by comparing the interval estimates for rounded values [Denning 1982]. Besides, systematic rounding is vulnerable to certain tracker attacks [Schlörer 1982].

Random rounding rounds a statistic q according to the following rule:

$$r(q) = \begin{cases} q & \text{if } d = 0 \\ q\text{-}d & \text{with probability } 1 - p \text{ (round down)} \\ q + (b\text{-}d) & \text{with probability } p \text{ (round up)}, \end{cases}$$

where $d = q \bmod b$ and $p = d/b$.

With random rounding, the bias (systematic error = difference between the expected rounded value E(r(q)) and the true value q) is zero, since $E(r(q)) = (1 - p) * (q - d) + (q + b - d) * p = q - d + b * p = f - d + b * (d/b) = f$.

Attacks based on comparison of interval estimates as well as tracker attacks are still possible, though more difficult to be performed. Besides, random rounding is vulnerable to another kind of attack: if a query is repeated many times, its true value can be deduced by averaging the rounded values [Denning 1982].

With a *Random-Sample Queries* (RSQ) control, which was introduced by D.Denning [Denning 1980], a result of a statistic q(C) is not derived from the whole query set C; instead the result is computed on a random sample C' of the query set. With RSQ the sample chosen is large enough (80-90%) to be valid. Besides, it uses a different sample to compute each statistic.

The RSQ control is defined as follows [Denning 1980]: As the query system locates records satisfying a given characteristic formula C, it applies a selection function f(C,i) to each record i satisfying C; f determines whether i is kept for the sample. The set of selected records forms a sampled query set $C^* = \{i \in C | f(C,i) = 1\}$. The statistic returned to the user is calculated from C^*. A parameter p specifies the sampling probability that a record is selected.

RSQ introduces enough uncertainty that users cannot control the composition of each query set. Thus, an intruder cannot isolate a single record or value by intersecting query sets, so that tracker attacks are no longer a useful tool for compromise.

Since the same query always returns the same response, no direct attacks based on error removal by averaging are possible. However, sampling errors could be removed by posing different but "equivalent" queries. One method, which involves averaging the responses of equivalent queries that use different formulas to specify the same query set, could be prevented if the selection function is a function of the query set C rather than the characteristic formula. Averaging that uses disjoint subsets of query sets to calculate statistics over a query set, however, is still possible, but requires a number of queries to obtain reliable estimates, which is too large for manual attacks. Systematic attacks, on the other hand, which automatically generate necessary queries, could be detected by auditing and intrusion detection methods.

In conclusion, inference controls for general-purpose databases should consist of a combination of output-selection and modification mechanisms. Random sample query control is an example of a very effective output-modification mechanism. It could augment simple selection techniques such as a query set seize control, the S_m/N-criterion or the re-identification risk control.

4.4 System Concepts and Mechanisms for Protecting Personal Data

Most Data Protection legislation requires security safeguards to protect the confidentiality, integrity and availability of personal data. For example, according to the EU Data Protection Directive, the data processing agency must implement appropriate technical and organisational measures to protect personal data against accidental or unlawful destruction or accidental loss, alteration, unauthorised disclosure or access, in particular where the processing involves the transmission of data over a network, and against all other unlawful forms of processing.

In Chapter 3.6, we point out that on one side security mechanisms can help to protect personal data. On the other side, however, they can also affect the user´s privacy. Nevertheless, it is possible to distinguish between "beneficial" security mechanisms that do not afford the storage of user-related personal data, and security mechanisms that are problematic with respect to the user´s privacy. Encryption mechanisms, for example, can be classified as the kind of "beneficial" security mechanisms (unless they require the storage of user-related data in certificates) that can protect the confidentiality and integrity of personal data, especially when transmitted. Encryption mechanisms were discussed in Chapter 3.3.7. Encryption mechanisms, however, do not prevent others from observing that encryption was applied to messages that are transmitted over a network. Steganographic encryption schemes can be used to hide the very existence of encrypted messages. Steganography will be briefly discussed in the next Section (4.4.1).

Furthermore, Access Control is an important security mechanism to protect personal data. Especially the legal privacy requirements of purpose binding and necessity of data processing can be technically enforced through appropriate security policies and access control mechanisms. In Section 4.4.2, privacy criteria for security models are defined and well-known security models, which were presented in Chapter 3, are evaluated according to these criteria. Unfortunately, today's security models are mostly not appropriate to enforce such basic privacy requirements. For this reason, a formal task-based privacy model has been developed and will be presented in the following chapters.

4.4.1 Steganographic Systems

Steganography literally means "covert writing" and is the art and science of transmitting secret messages through innocuous carriers in such a way that the very existence of the embedded message is undetectable. Possible cover carriers can be any innocent looking carriers such as images, text, audio or video data [Johnson/Jajodia 1998].

In contrast to cryptography, where the goal is to hide the content of a message and an attacker is nevertheless allowed to detect, intercept and modify a message, the goal of steganography is to hide the very existence of a message. With steganography, a message is the information that is hidden and may be encrypted or not.

It is possible to distinguish between two variants of steganographic systems with different intentions:

- Digital steganography is used to conceal a message in a cover where that hidden message is the object of communication.

- Digital watermarking is used to embed copyright, ownership and license information in a cover, where that cover is the object of communication.

In this Section, the emphasis will be on digital steganography. In areas where (strong) encryption is being outlawed, steganography can be used by citizens to circumvent such crypto policies and to transmit messages covertly.

The model of a steganographic system is illustrated in Figure 4.13 (see also Zöllner at al. 1997]). A steganographic embedding function E with a secret key (*stego-key*) is used to hide a message in a cover medium. The *result E(cover-medium, embedded-message, stegokey)* is a called a *stego-medium*. E^{-1} is the inverse operation to the embedding function E, and is used to extract *embedded-message** $= E^{-1}$ *(stego-medium, stego-key)*, where embedded-message* should be equal to embedded message.

In Figure 4.13 the same key is used for the function E and E^{-1} to mode a symmetric steganographic system, because so far no secure asymmetric steganographic systems are known.

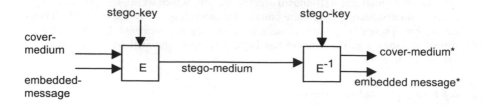

Fig. 4.13: Model of a steganographic system (see also [Zöllner et al. 1997], [Federrath/Pfitzmann 1997])

If steganography is combined with (either symmetric or asymmetric) cryptography, the message is encrypted before the embedding function E is applied. After execution of the extracting function E^{-1}, the embedded-message* has to be decrypted.

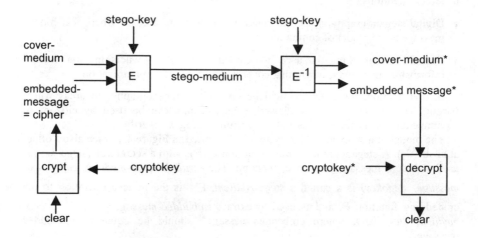

Fig. 4.14: Model of a steganographic system with encryption (see also [Zöllner et al. 1997])

Most available steganographic tools use images as carriers for hidden information. Simple steganographic systems can be categorised as *Image Domain* tools that hide information in the least significant bits (LSB) of an image. Examples of such steganographic tools are StegoDos, S-Tools, Hide and Seek. The image format typically used in such steganographic tools are lossless (such as GIF images that use lossless compression) and the data can be directly manipulated or recovered. Thus, most of these tools do not support the use of JPG images, which have lossy compression. An exception is the tool Jpeg-Jsteg that hides information by manipulating the rounding values of the JPEG DCT (Discrete Cosine Transform)

155

coefficients and that can thus be categorised as a *Transform Domain* tool. Information is hidden in the JPEG image by modulating the rounding choices either up or down in the DCT coefficients [Johnson], [Johnson/Jajodia 1998].

The primary aspect of attacks on digital steganography is the detection of the embedded message, whereas the main goal of attacks on digital watermarking is the destruction of the embedded message.

Techniques used for attacks on digital steganography (steganalysis techniques) correspond to known cryptanalysis techniques. Basic attacks are for instance *stego-only, chosen message, known cover attacks* [Johnson/Jajodia 1998]. A *stego-only attack* correspond to the ciphertext-only attack where only the stego-medium is available for analysis. With a *chosen message attack*, which is similar to a chosen plaintext attack, the steganalyst generates stego-media from some steganographic tool or algorithm from a known message. The attacker thereby tries to determine corresponding patterns in stego-media that may point to the use of specific steganographic tool or algorithm. A *known-cover (or cover-stego) attack* is one where both the "original" cover-media and the stego-media are available for an attacker.

If an attacker knows both the cover medium and the stego-medium, he can easily determine that steganography is used by looking for differences between both media. Hence, no secure steganographic system can be realised if cover-media and stego-media are both available to an attacker. However, a cover medium is normally created out of a source medium (i.e., the "original cover medium") by a random indeterministic process and can be kept confidential [Zöllner et al. 1997]. For example, a source-medium can be a picture in analogue form that is transferred by a scanning process into a digital image, which can serve as a cover-medium. Scanning is an indeterministic process, which will create different digital forms (image files) of the same picture if it is applied several times in a row. Thus, the scanning process usually creates enough uncertainty over the cover-medium even if the source-medium is known to an attacker. Thus, if a secure steganographic system can be achieved, if only the source medium (i.e., the "original cover medium") and not the "used" cover medium is known to an attacker [Zöllner et al. 1997].

Empirical research has been conducted to find criteria to assess digital images with relation to steganography and to decide whether a digital image includes steganographically embedded data (see [Franz/Pfitzmann 1998]). Differences between image files resulting from repeated scanning of the same picture were compared with differences between image files caused by steganographic programs. The comparisons showed that scanning causes greater differences than stegoprograms (especially at the picture's contours) and that the characteristics of the differences are not the same. A new stegoparadigm derived from these results states requires that a steganographic process should simulate "normal" indeterministic processes such as scanning. Such a stegonographic system could guarantee that even if an attacker could monitor input and output to a steganographic system, he would not be able to decide whether in- and output are cover- and stego-medium or two different images files created by another indeterministic process (such as scanning) [Franz/Pfitzmann 1998].

4.4.2 Access Control Models for Personal Data Protection

In Chapter 3, the most well known security models for access control have been presented. Unfortunately, they are more or less inappropriate for enforcing basic legal privacy requirements. In the next sections, we will set up privacy criteria for assessing security models and we will assess well-known security models according to those criteria and thereby show their limitations.

4.4.2.1 Privacy Criteria for Security Models

As mentioned above, most data protection legislation requires security mechanisms to protect the confidentiality, integrity and availability of personal data. According to § 9 BDSG (German Federal Data Protection Act), the data processing agency has to take "technical and organisational measures necessary to ensure the implementation of the provisions of this act" (i.e., BDSG). According to the EU Data Protection Directive, data processing agency must implement appropriate technical and organisational measures to protect personal data against accidental or unlawful destruction or accidental loss, alteration, unauthorised disclosure or access and against all other unlawful forms of processing.

Access control mechanisms for protecting confidentiality and integrity can be used to implement data protection provisions. In particular, they can enforce the privacy provisions for necessity of data processing and purpose binding, and can thus protect personal data against unlawful forms of processing violating these provisions.

Thus, security models for controlling access to personal data should in particular address confidentiality and integrity of personal data, esp. by enforcing the privacy provisions of necessity of data processing and purpose binding and disallowing unauthorised disclosure or modifications. Furthermore, additional confidentiality and integrity aspects should be addressed. In particular, security models should protect against accidental or unauthorised modifications by enforcing integrity principles such as separation of duty and the principle of well-formed transactions. Availability of personal data, i.e. prevention of unauthorised withholding of personal data, is a minor important privacy aspect and is thus not specifically addressed in the following considerations.

Hence, security models used for personal data protection should address the following privacy aspects:

- **protection of confidentiality of personal data**
- **protection of integrity of personal data**
- **purpose binding of accesses to personal data** *(the purpose of the user's current task must be contained in the set of purposes for which the personal data was obtained or there has to be a consent by the data subjects)*
- *necessity of personal data processing (a user may access personal data only if the access is necessary to perform his current task)*

The last two aspects (purpose binding, necessity of data processing) are part of the first two aspects (protection of confidentiality and integrity). Protection of confidentiality as well as of integrity, however, also consists of other measures in addition to controlling the necessity of data processing and purpose binding.

Another aspect for assessing the adequacy of a security model for privacy protection is the *ability to enable anonymous or pseudonymous system use*. System concepts allowing a user to use a system anonymously or pseudonymously (e.g. through authorisation certificates) have been discussed in 4.2.3. The focus of anonymous or pseudonymous system use, however, is on protecting user identities, whilst the other four privacy aspects listed above aim at personal data protection.

Besides, if personal data is related to the system users (i.e., the data subjects are also system users), another privacy aim could be **the implementation of the right of informational self-determination**, meaning the individual's right to determine the disclosure and use of his personal data on principle at his discretion (see Chapter 2.1). Allowing users to administrate accesses to their own personal data could help to enforce this basic right.

4.4.2.2 Privacy Evaluation of Security Models

In this section, we will evaluate how far well-known security models are capable to enforcing the privacy aspects protection of confidentiality of personal data, protection of integrity of personal data, purpose binding of accesses to personal data, necessity of personal data processing as well as anonymous or pseudonymous system use. The results are summarised in Table 4.1.

Bell LaPadula Model:

The Bell LaPadula model (see Chapter 3.2.1) was designed to protect confidentiality of classified information, which is the main security aim for military or governmental applications. Integrity and other confidentiality aspects are, however, not addressed. Even though Lipner has shown how security levels could be defined to enforce separation of duty in the commercial sector, its emphasis is on protecting secrecy of sensitive information and it is not appropriate to enforce essential integrity goals.

Besides, the Bell LaPadula policy does not seem to be adequate to protect the confidentiality of personal data:

Its Mandatory Access Control (MAC) policy (*simple security property* and **-property*) restricts the access to objects based on the sensitivity of the information contained in the objects and the clearance of the subjects. However, personal data cannot be classified accurately by its sensitivity *per se*, because the sensitivity of personal data is related to the purpose and context of its use. As already mentioned above, in its Census Decision the *German Constitutional Court* proclaimed that there is no non-sensitive personal data, as dependent on the purpose and context of use, all kinds of personal data can become sensitive.

The Bell LaPadula's Discretionary Access Control (DAC) policy (*ds-property*) restricts access to objects based on the identity of subjects and/or subject groups. DAC permits the granting and revoking of access privileges to data to be left to the discretion of a user with a certain access permission that has control over the data. If the personal data is related to the system users, DAC can enforce the user's right of informational self-determination. However, in practice the data subjects (e.g., patients or bank customers) are normally not users of the information systems at the same time. Under privacy aspects, personal data about a data subject should not be "owned" or "controlled" by another person.

Moreover, the Bell LaPadula model cannot enforce the privacy requirement of purpose binding. One might think that purpose binding could be enforced if the category sets of the sensitivity levels were used to model purposes. Each subject could be assigned a set consisting of a single purpose, and each personal data object could be assigned a set of purposes corresponding to the purposes for which the data was obtained. The Bell LaPadula policy, however, with its "no-read-up" and "no write down" restrictions only allows information flow in one (upward) direction and is thus too restrictive. The simple security property allows a subject to read-access an object only if the set of purposes of the subject's security level contains the set of purposes of the object's security level. According to the purpose binding principle, however, a subject is allowed to write- or read-access an object if the purpose of its task is contained in the set of purposes for which the personal data was obtained. If personal data is obtained for several different purposes, it means that it is allowed to use the data for each of these purposes.

The set of categories of the security levels can help to enforce need-to-know restrictions so that users can obtain access only to data that is relevant to their jobs. However, due to the "duality" of the simple security- and the *-property, the use of categories is not an appropriate means for expressing both necessary read- and necessary write-accesses for a subject.

A system enforcing Bell LaPadula's DAC policy cannot provide anonymous or pseudonymous system use, because discretionary access control decisions are based on the user's identity.

Lattice Model of Information Flow:

The Lattice Model of Information Flow (3.2.5) is an extension of the Bell LaPadula model and shares many of the Bell LaPadula model drawbacks. Like the Bell LaPadula model it addresses only some confidentiality aspects. The reasons why the Bell LaPadula model is not appropriate for enforcing purpose binding and necessity of data processing also apply to the lattice model.

Biba Model:

The Biba Model (3.2.3) addresses specific integrity goals, but ignores other security aspects.

Since Biba's strict integrity policy is dual to the Bell LaPadula policy, it is inappropriate for enforcing purpose binding and necessity of data processing for similar reasons.

Anonymous or pseudonymous system use can only be provided with the mandatory integrity policy, which is based on integrity levels. Biba's discretionary integrity policy is based on user identities and can thus not be used in combination with anonymous system accounts.

Clark Wilson Model:

The Clark Wilson Model effectively addresses all essential integrity aspects. Security concepts such as well-formed transactions and access triples are also effective means to prevent unauthorised disclosure of information and can therefore be used to protect the confidentiality of personal data.

By defining adequate access triples, granting users only accesses to CDIs by the execution of TPs that are necessary for the performance of their tasks, the privacy principle of necessity of personal data processing can be supported. The Clark Wilson access triples can specify accesses needed by users rather than accesses needed by tasks. However, the needed accesses of a user normally vary depending on his current tasks.

The Clark Wilson model was not designed to model purposes for data items or processes and is not capable of enforcing purpose binding.

Pseudonymous system accounts can be realised with access triples for pseudonymous user IDs. Anonymous systems use, however, cannot be supported satisfactorily, since access triples are defined with user IDs. Nevertheless, it is possible to define an access triple that relate an anonymous user, a TP, and the CDIs that the TP may reference on behalf of an anonymous user. This, however, means that all anonymous users are restricted to the same kind of privileges defined by the access triples for anonymous users.

Chinese Wall Model:

The Chinese Wall Model aims at protecting the confidentiality of sensitive information about competing companies to avoid conflict of interests, which could arise for consultants in the financial segment of the commercial sector. Besides "commercial" confidentiality aspects, it can also enforce the integrity principle of separation of duty.

As Ravi Sandhu has shown, the Chinese Wall policy is an interpretation of the Lattice-based information-flow policy, and thus it is also inappropriate for the implementation of the basic principles of purpose binding and necessity of data processing.

According to the refined Chinese Wall policy, a user can only access an object, if he is authorised to perform a certain named process and if this process may access the object. The Chinese Wall model could be enforced for anonymous users who could, for instance, prove to possess authorisation certificates with the permissions to execute certain named processes.

Role-Based Access Control (RBAC) Model:

RBAC is policy neutral and can be used to articulate different kinds of security policies. According to RBAC, a subject can only access an object, if it is performing a role for which it is authorised, and if the role is allowed to perform an operation and the operation is authorised to access the object. By carefully defining authorisations for roles and role privileges (authorised operations for a role), RBAC can be used to protect personal data against unauthorised disclosure or modifications. Such operations could, for instance, be well-formed certified transactions that allow users to manipulate data only in constrained ways and thereby ensure internal consistency. Besides, RBAC directly supports static and dynamic separation of duty. Thus, RBAC can be used to protect confidentiality and integrity of personal data.

The principle of necessity of personal data processing can be supported by RBAC if roles are defined for certain tasks and if each task is only assigned the minimum set of privileges required to perform this task. If, however, a user is able to activate multiple roles at the same time, he could be authorised for more privileges than required to perform his current task. Thus, the ability to activate multiple roles is in conflict with the principle of necessity of personal data processing. Consequently, necessity of personal data processing can only be enforced if users are allowed to perform one current role at the same time.

Since with RBAC, access control decisions are dependent on the current roles of a user and not on the identity of the user, RBAC could also be enforced for pseudonymous or anonymous users.

Nevertheless, one main disadvantage of RBAC is that it was not designed to model purposes, consents of data subjects and thus cannot enforce purpose binding.

Task-Based Authorisation Models

Task-based Authorisation Models such as the Workflow Authorisation Model (WAM) are focussed on secure workflow-management and capable to protect confidentiality and integrity of data. In particular, they are effective in enforcing necessity of data processing, because they ensure that authorisations for a task are granted only when a task starts and are revoked as soon as the task finishes. Besides, they support the integrity principle of separation of duty and allow the use of well-formed transactions as operations.

With WAM, the privilege to perform a task can be assigned to an organisational role rather than a human user. This means that WAM also enables pseudonymous or anonymous system use.

However, like most other security models Task-based Authorisation Models for secure workflow management were not designed to model purposes, consents of data subjects and cannot be used to enforce purpose binding.

Object-Oriented Security Models:

Object-oriented security model can be used to protect confidentiality and integrity of personal data in object-oriented systems.

However, inherited or implicit authorisations can be in conflict with the principle of necessity of personal data processing, because it could be possible that more implicit access rights can be derived than truly necessary. To deal with this problem, weak authorisations in combination with positive and negative authorisations can be used to model exceptions, but this way of modelling is not straightforward and quite cumbersome for modelling necessary accesses precisely.

Mandatory object oriented models enforcing the Bell LaPadula principles share most of the disadvantages of the Bell LaPadula model.

Discretionary object-oriented models that make access decisions dependent on user IDs cannot support anonymous or pseudonymous system accounts.

Besides, the known object-oriented security models are not directly addressing the privacy aspect of purpose binding.

The DORIS Personal Model of Data is useful to technically enforce the right of informational self-determination, because users can only send messages to their "acquaintances" querying about their knowledge or asking them to perform operations to modify their knowledge. Nevertheless, it does not address purpose binding either.

Conclusions:

A summary of privacy aspects that are supported or not supported in well-known security models for access control is given in Table 4.1. In this Table, mandatory object-oriented models stand for object-oriented models enforcing the Bell-LaPadula principles.

The evaluation has shown that the models are more or less inappropriate for personal data protection. The Bell LaPadula model is even only insufficiently addressing some privacy aspects. Only few models can effectively support the privacy principle of necessity of personal data processing. None of the models is capable of technically enforcing purpose binding.

For this reason, a formal Task-based Privacy Model has been proposed [Fischer-Hübner 1994a], [Fischer-Hübner 1994b], [Fischer-Hübner 1995], [Fischer-Hübner 1997c], [Fischer-Hübner et al. 1998], which is a formal state machine model designed to technically enforce and support all major privacy aspects. The formal privacy model enforces purpose binding and necessity of personal data processing. Besides, it enforces the concept of well-formed transactions and supports separation of duty. The privacy model has been implemented according to the Generalised Framework for Access Control in combination with other security models in the Linux operating system.

The formal task-based privacy model and the top-level specification of its implementation will be presented in the following chapters.

A similar approach to model the privacy aspects of purpose binding and necessity of data processing was taken in the project "Data protection as a requirement to system design" ("Datenschutz als Anforderung an die Systemgestaltung"), that was sponsored by the government of the German state North Rhine-Westphalia (see [Bräutigam/Höller/Scholz 1990]).

In this project, formal requirements for purpose binding and necessity of data processing were formulated. Besides, it was shown how these requirements could be technically enforced in a relational database system by storing security attributes in data dictionaries and by using query modifications. However, they have not defined a formal security model to state and prove privacy requirements in contrast to our approach, which includes a formal state machine model with formal proofs that all state transition functions preserve all defined privacy properties.

Table 4.1: Summary of Privacy Evaluation of well-known Security Models

	Bell LaPadula Model	Lattice Model	Biba Model	Clark Wilson Model	Chinese Wall Model	RBAC Model	WAM	Discretionary Object-Oriented Models	Mandatory Object-Oriented Models
Protection of confidentiality of personal data	(yes)	(yes)	no	yes	(yes)	yes	yes	yes	(yes)
Protection of integrity of personal data	no	no	(yes)	yes	(yes)	yes	yes	yes	no
necessity of personal data processing	no	no	no	(yes)	no	(yes)	yes	(yes)	no
Purpose binding of accesses to personal data	no	no	no	no	no	no	no	no	no
Ability to provide pseudonymity or anonymity	(yes)	yes	(yes)	(yes)	yes	yes	yes	no	yes

yes: privacy aspect can be enforced

no: privacy aspect cannot or hardly be enforced

(yes): enforcement of privacy aspect is not straightforward or only partly possible or only possible with restrictions

Besides, there are considerable functional differences between their approach and the approach of the formal privacy model. First of all, the approach by [Bräutigam/Höller/Scholz 1990] allows data to be obtained for only one single purpose although the German Federal Data Protection and other data protection legislations consider purposes for which data is collected.

Besides, no rules for information flow controls are formulated (which are in particular necessary to prevent illegal information flow from personal to non-personal data). Furthermore, no consents by data subjects are modelled and the integrity principle of well-formed transactions is not directly supported. In addition, the privacy model that will be presented in the next Chapter also contains several additional features such as a joint action scheme based on so-called one-time tickets for the execution of privileged functions (see 5.4.2), which can enforce operational separation of duty.

4.5 Privacy Evaluation of IT Security Evaluation Criteria

Analysis of early IT Security Evaluation Criteria has shown that none of the early IT Security Evaluation criteria such as TCSEC, ITSEC, CTCPEC really covers user and privacy friendly functionality, as they are focussed on the protection of system owners and operators rather than the protection of users and usees [Pfitzmann/Rannenberg 1993], [Rannenberg 1994].

The U.S. American TCSEC is mainly addressing military security needs and is focused on the security aspect "confidentiality" while neglecting "integrity" (the only integrity aspect that is directly addressed is label integrity) and ignoring "availability".

TCSEC uses the Bell LaPadula model as its reference security model, which is more or less inappropriate to protect the confidentiality of personal data. Techniques protecting user or usee identities cannot be described with TCSEC.

The European IT Security Evaluation Criteria (ITSEC) addresses the IT-Security aspects "confidentiality", "integrity" and "availability". Since ITSEC is independent of a specific security policy, it allows the specification of security policies that are appropriate for personal data protection. ITSEC, however, does not address security functionalities for protecting user identities. The eight "Generic Headings" defined by ITSEC (see 3.4.2.3), which are recommended for specification of security enforcing functions, do not consider privacy friendly functions for protecting user identities. It was suggested that this functionality could be integrated by the introduction of duals "anonymity", "pseudonymity" and "unlinkability" to the generic heading "identification and authentication" and "unobservability" to the generic heading "audit". However, these suggestions have not been followed [Pfitzmann/Rannenberg 1993].

The Canadian Trusted Computer Evaluation Criteria (CTCPEC) consists of confidentiality, integrity, availability and accountability criteria. Like ITSEC and other more recent security criteria, CTCPEC is policy neutral and allows specifying appropriate data protection policies. Though CTCPEC does not define security services for protecting user identities, its fourfold structure is at least extendible to cover privacy-friendly functionalities (see [Rannenberg 1994]). Since the confidentiality criteria do not contain the security service "audit", the confidentiality criteria could be extended by the security services "anonymity", "unobservability" and "unlinkability", and the accountability criteria could be extended by the security service "pseudonymity". This was one reason why the CTCPEC´s structure of functional criteria formed the basis for the functionality part of the ISO/IEC-ECITS part 2, which was extended for the security services "anonymity", "unlinkability" (to the security facet "confidentiality") and "pseudonymity" (to the security facet "accountability").

The Common Criteria (CC) contain a "Privacy Class" with the four families "anonymity", "pseudonymity", "unlinkability" and "unobservability". The privacy class is, however, focused on user protection against discovery and misuse of his identity by other users and does not address other privacy-enhancing security aspects. Nevertheless, the protection profiles and security targets of the CC allow the specification of other privacy-enhancing security requirements either from the CC, or stated explicitly.

Compared to other classes, the privacy class is quite concisely formulated. The privacy class of the CC Version 1.0 was under harsh criticism for several reasons. A major criticism was that the privacy class contained a number of provisions for privileged administrators, who could for instance be excluded from the unobservability protection of other users. It was pointed out that a partial protection only against users excluding administrator would be misleading. The concept of an authorised administrator, who overlooks the activities in the system, actually prevents unobservability, because unobservability can only be reached, if no data can be gained that an event has taken place [Rannenberg 1996].

Another limitation was that pseudonymous auditing was not covered by the CC Version 1.0, because it only covered auditing based on "classical" user identities. Although the term "identity" was not defined in the CC Version 1.0, the way in which it was used let no place for the interpretation that pseudonyms were covered [Sobirey/Fischer-Hübner/Rannenberg 1997].

The CC Versions 2.0 and 2.1 do not include the concept of authorised administrators any longer, who could be excluded from the set of users that cannot discover or misuse the identities of other users. Besides, from CC Version 2.0 onward "identity" is defined as "a representation uniquely identifying an authorised user, which can either be the full or abbreviated name of that user or a pseudonym". Thus, the CC Versions 2.0 and 2.1 also cover pseudonymous auditing.

4.6 Conclusions

In this Chapter, we have given a classification, overview and analysis to privacy enhancing technologies. We have classified privacy-enhancing security aspects into three categories: security aspects for protecting user identities, security aspects for protection usee identities and security aspects for protecting the confidentiality and integrity of personal data.

Access control models and mechanisms are necessary technical means for protecting the confidentiality and integrity of personal data. However, an analysis of today´s well-known security models has shown that they are more or less inappropriate for privacy protection.

For this reason, a formal task-based privacy model has been developed, which can technically enforce legal privacy requirements. The privacy model will be introduced in the next Chapter, whereas appendix A contains the formal mathematical model description and proofs. In Chapter 6, we present a top-level specification of the model implementation according to the Generalised Framework for Access Control approach in a Unix system.

5 A Task-Based Privacy Model

5.1 Introduction

This Chapter presents the concept of a formal security model that enforces basic legal privacy requirements, such as *purpose binding* or *necessity of data processing*. Besides, the model is based on the integrity concepts of well-formed transactions and separation of duty. The formal mathematical model is presented in Appendix A.

The **privacy policy,** which is to be enforced by the privacy model, can be informally described as follows:

A subject may only have access to personal data, if this access is necessary to perform its current task and only, if the subject is authorised to perform this task. The subject may only access data in a controlled manner by performing a (well-formed and certified) transformation procedure, for which the subject's current task is authorised. Besides, the purpose of its current task must correspond to the purposes for which the personal data was obtained or there has to be consent by the data subjects.

This privacy policy could for instance be used to implement § 14 BDSG (German Federal Data Protection Act), which regulates the storage, modification and use of personal data by public bodies (see 2.6.1). According to § 14 BDSG the storage, modification and use of personal data shall be admissible where it is necessary for the performance of the tasks of the controller of the data file and if it serves the purposes for which the data were collected. The storage, modification and use for other purposes shall be admissible if the data subject has consented.

5.2 Model Description

The **formal task-based privacy model** is defined as a state machine model. It contains the following model elements (state variables), invariants, constraints (privacy properties) and state transition functions (model rules):

5.2.1 Model Elements (State Variables)

First, the security-relevant (or more precisely: privacy-relevant) model elements (state variables) are defined. They are needed to formally define the privacy policy and the system states.

Subjects S: Subjects are the active entities of the system (e.g., processes).
S = set of current subjects = $\{S_1, S_2,...\}$

Subj is the identity of the subject that is currently active and is invoking the state transition function.

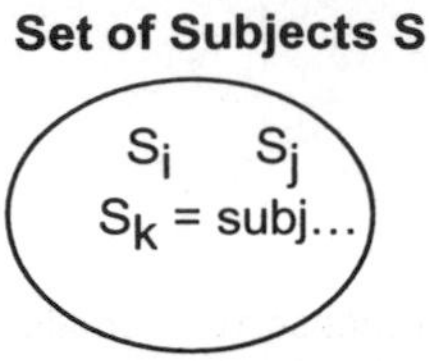

Set of Subjects S

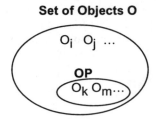

Fig. 5.1: Set S of current subjects including an active subject

Objects O: Objects are passive entities (e.g., files, records, sockets).
O = set of current objects = {O_1, O_2,....}.

Personal data objects are objects containing personal data.
OP = set of current objects O_i ∈ O containing personal data.

Personal data is data about an identified or identifiable person. The question whether a person can be identified depends on the supplementary knowledge of a potential attacker. Since it is often unknown, how much and what supplementary knowledge potential attackers have, all data is considered as personal data, if the possibility of re-identification cannot be excluded in practice.

Set of Objects O

Fig. 5.2: Set of current objects O including the set of personal data objects OP.

Object-classes O-class: A personal data object can normally be classified by a certain class, e.g. patient record in a hospital information system or accounting data.

The requirements of purpose binding and of necessity of data processing are checked for accesses to objects of specific object-classes. Objects are classified, because it is much easier to define and administrate necessary accesses and purposes for object classes instead of defining them for each single object. All non-personal data objects are classified by the predefined object class "none".
O-class = set of the different object-classes = {none, o-class$_1$, o-class$_2$,...}

Object-class function Class: Each object is classified by an object-class.
A function

Class: O -> O-class
is defined, where Class(O_j) is the object class of the object O_j.
$\forall$ O_j $\in$ O \ OP: Class(O_j) = none.

Figure 5.3 illustrates the relationship between objects and object classes. The single-headed arrow indicates a one to one relationship, whilst double-headed arrows (used in the following figures) indicate a one-to-many relationship. Thus, the single-headed arrow standing for the function "Class" indicates that this function assigns one object class to each object.

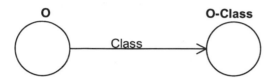

Fig. 5.3: Relationship between objects and object classes. Each object is classified by one object class.

Tasks T: A subject may access a personal data object only by performing a task. The tasks have to be defined for each application.
T = set of tasks = {T_1, T_2,....}.
Examples of tasks in a hospital information system are the tasks "diagnosing", "operation" or "therapy".

Current Task CT: The task that is currently performed by a subject is called its current task. If a subject is not currently performing a certain task, its current task is defined to have the standard value Nil. A function
CT: S -> T $\cup$ {Nil}
is defined, where CT(S_i) is the current task of subject S_i.

Authorised Tasks AT: A subject may be authorised to perform tasks. AT is a function that defines a set of tasks for a subject that this subject is authorised to perform.
AT: S -> $2^{T \cup \{Nil\}}$ \ $\emptyset$,
where AT(S_i) is the set of tasks that S_i is authorised to perform and
$\forall$ S_i $\in$ S: Nil $\in$ AT(S_i).

The relationship between subjects and tasks is depicted in Figure 5.4. The Double-headed arrow from the set S to the set T $\cup$ {Nil} standing for the function AT indicates that each subject can be authorised for several tasks. The set of authorised tasks AT(S_i) for a subject S_i is a subset of T $\cup$ {Nil}. The figure also illustrates one important security properties that will be stated below: A subject has to be authorised for its current task, that is, $CT(S_i) \in AT(S_i)$ for each subject S_i.

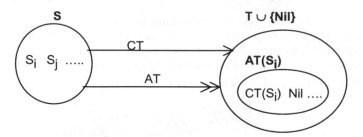

Fig. 5.4: Relationships between subjects and tasks

For an easier administration, an alternative approach could be to define authorised tasks for user-roles instead of defining authorised tasks for individual users.

User Roles: Subjects can be categorised by certain security-relevant roles that they can perform. As shown in Figure 5.5, each subject performs one user-role.

Role: S -> user-roles, where
user-roles = {user, sec-officer, data-protection-officer, tp-manager,...}.

These different user roles allow applying the principle of separation of duty for the administration of access control information:

The TP-manager is responsible for defining (and certifying) transformation procedures (see below). The data protection officer is a role for a person that was appointed as a data protection officer in an organisation according to § 36 BDSG (Federal German Data Protection Act). The data protection officer's duty is to define how to implement the privacy policy by specifying the needed access control information. The security officer should be responsible for enforcing these requirements. Further user roles could be defined.

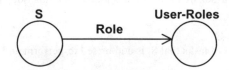

Fig. 5.5: Relationship between subjects and user roles.

Users who are defined as "responsible" for a task may request the delegation of this task. Therefore, a function "responsible" is defined:

Responsible Users: Each task can have responsible users, who can request sec-officer to define this task as an authorised task to other users.

Responsible: T -> 2^S,
where Responsible(T$_i$) is the set of subjects, who can request to delegate the task T$_i$.

Purposes P: Every task serves a certain purpose. Moreover, personal data is collected for certain purposes. For each application, it is necessary to determine purposes of tasks, as well as, purposes for that personal data is obtained. Usually, legislation allowing personal data processing should specify the purposes of personal data processing. Purposes are modelled by a set P of purposes:
P = set of purposes = {p$_1$, p$_2$,...}.

Purposes and tasks can be hierarchically structured (see [Bräutigam/Höller/Scholz 90, p.47], [Podlech 1988]). Purposes, for example, can be divided into different sub-purposes or combined into (in the hierarchy higher) "super" purposes. Analogously, tasks can be hierarchically structured. For example, the purpose "medical treatment" can be divided into sub-purposes "treatment of infections", "cancer treatment", etc. Similarly, the task "diagnosing" can be divided in the sub-tasks "diagnosing of infections", "diagnosing of cancer", etc.

Privacy aspects and practical reasons have to be considered when choosing an adequate level in this hierarchy for defining purposes and tasks. A low level in the hierarchy, where purposes are specified in more detail, provides better privacy protection, but might be less practical. For example, if the purpose "medical treatment" is divided into sub-purposes, it could mean that patients have to provide their personal identity and demographic data for each kind of medical treatment once again. The purposes of the chosen level within the hierarchy are used to define the elements of P. Consequently, only purposes of this level in the hierarchy and of higher levels can be modelled by elements and non-empty subsets of P.

Given the set P of purposes, a subset lattice can be derived from the set inclusion ordering ⊆ on the set of all subsets of P (see Figure 5.6).

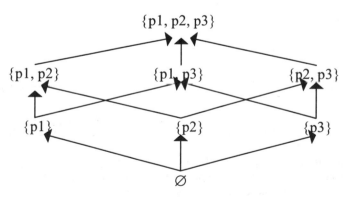

Fig. 5.6: Example: A subset lattice for P = {p1, p2, p3}

The elements of T have to be defined according to the purposes of P.

If for instance instead of the purpose "medical treatment" the sub-purposes "treatment of infections", "cancer treatment" are defined as elements of the set P, then instead of the task "diagnosing", which is serving the purpose medical treatment, the sub-tasks "diagnosing of infections" (serving the purpose "treatment of infections) , "diagnosing of cancer" (serving the purpose "cancer treatment"), etc. are defined to be elements of T.

Each task of T has to serve exactly one purpose, but each purpose can be achieved by the performance of different tasks. Different purposes are, however, achieved by disjunctive sets of tasks.

Purpose function for tasks T-Purpose: Every task serves exactly one purpose.
A function
T-Purpose: T -> P
is defined, where T-Purpose(T_i) is the purpose of task T_i.

Purpose function for object class O-Purposes: Each object-class has to have specified purposes for which personal data of this class is collected. Non-empty subsets of P define the purposes for each object-class.
A function

O-Purposes: O-class -> $2^P \setminus \emptyset$

is defined, where O-Purposes(O-class$_i$) are the purposes for which the objects of class O-class$_i$ are obtained.

Since in practice non-personal data is normally collected and used for all possible purposes, the set of purposes of the object class "none" (standing for the class of non personal data) is defined by the set P of all defined purposes:
O-purpose(none) = P.

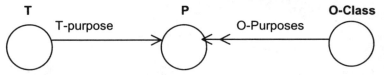

Fig. 5.7: Relationship between tasks and purposes and between object classes and purposes.

As shown in Figure 5.7, the function T-purpose assigns one purpose to each task, whereas the function O-purposes assigns one or more purposes to each object class.

Transformation Procedures TRANS: A subject is not allowed to access a personal data object arbitrarily. If it performs a task, it may execute certain transformation procedures that are accessing objects in a controlled manner. Transformation procedures are defined (and should be certified) by the TP-manager.
TRANS = {transp$_1$, transp$_2$,...}

A transaction is normally defined as a transformation procedure, plus a set of data items, which can be accessed by executing the transformation procedure. In this case, access control does not require any checks on the user's or transformation procedure's rights to access an object, since the accesses are built into the transactions. However, to enforce higher confidentiality requirements, it is also possible to redefine the meaning of "transactions" to refer only to transformation procedures, without including a binding to objects. This requires further checks to enforce control over the modes in which subjects can access objects through transaction programs.

Current Transformation Procedure CTP: The transformation procedure that is currently executed by a subject is called its current transformation procedure. If a subject is currently not executing any transformation procedure, its current transformation procedure is defined by the standard value Nil.
CTP: S -> Trans ∪ {Nil}

Authorised Transformation Procedures ATP: While performing a task, a subject is authorised to run certain transformation procedures.
ATP: T -> 2$^{\text{Trans} \cup \{Nil\}}$ \ ∅.
$\forall\, T_i \in T: Nil \in ATP(T_i)$.
Figure 5.8 illustrates these relationships between subjects, transactions and tasks.

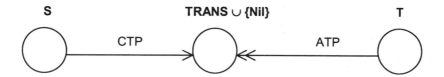

S   TRANS ∪ {Nil}   T

CTP   ATP

Fig. 5.8: Relationships between subjects, transformation procedures and tasks

Access rights A: The access rights that a subject can have to a personal data object are defined by access attributes A = {**read, write, append, delete, create**}.

Necessary accesses NA: For any task, it has to be defined in advance which accesses to which object-classes by executing which transformation procedure are needed to perform this task. This is done by defining the set **NA**, which consists of tuples of the form (**T$_i$, o-class$_j$, transp$_k$, x**), where o-class$_j$ ≠ none and transp$_k$ ≠ Nil.
(T_i, o-class$_j$, transp$_k$, x) ∈ NA means that it is necessary for a subject with a current task T_i to access a personal data object (∈ OP) of the class o-class$_j$ in mode x through the transformation procedure transp$_k$ (≠ Nil).

Note that the Clark Wilson access triples could be implemented by letting the modes x be the access modes required by transaction t, and having one-to-one relationships between subjects and tasks and between objects and object classes.

Current access set CA: A current x-access (with $x \in \{$read, write, append$\}$) of a subject S_i to an object O_j in the current state is represented by a triple (S_i, O_j, x). The current access set CA is a set of all such triples representing all current accesses.

Consent C: According to most national privacy laws, the processing and use of personal data shall also be admissible, if the data subject has consented. A set **C** is defined as a set of tuples (p_i, O_j). The tuple (p_i, O_j) means that the data subjects have consented that their personal data contained in the personal data object O_j are processed for the purpose p_i.

5.2.2 Model Invariants and Constraints (Privacy Properties)

In this Chapter, privacy properties of system states and state sequences are defined. The following invariants (privacy properties) define (necessary, but not sufficient) conditions for a system state to meet specific privacy principles. They formally define the privacy policy stated above. To enforce this privacy policy, it has to be guaranteed that these invariants are satisfied in each system state.

5.2.2.1 Privacy Invariants

Privacy invariant-1:
A subject's current task has to be authorised for the subject (task authorisation property):
$\forall S_i \in S$: $CT(S_i) \in AT(S_i)$.

Privacy invariant-2:
A subject's current transformation procedure has to be authorised for the subject's current task (TP authorisation property):
$\forall S_i \in S$: $CTP(S_i) \in ATP(CT(S_i))$.

Privacy invariant-3:
A subject may only have current access to a personal data object, if the access by executing a transformation procedure to personal data objects of this class is needed to perform the current task (property of necessity of data processing):
$\forall S_i \in S, O_j \in OP$: $(S_i, O_j, x) \in CA \implies (CT(S_i), Class(O_j), CTP(S_i), x) \in NA$

Privacy invariant-4:
A subject may only have current access to a personal data object, if the purpose of its current task corresponds to the purposes for that personal data objects of this class are obtained, or if there is a consent by the data subjects (property of purpose binding of personal data processing):
$\forall S_i \in S, O_j \in OP$: $(S_i, O_j, x) \in CA$
$\implies$ T-Purpose $(CT(S_i)) \in$ O-Purposes $(Class(O_j)) \lor$ (T-Purpose$(CT(S_i)), O_j) \in C$

5.2.2.2 Privacy Constraints

The privacy principles of necessity of data processing and purpose binding should also be checked, if personal data is created or deleted since also the integrity and availability of personal data have to be protected. For the creation or deletion of personal data, these principles can be formulated by adding constraints, which are properties of sequences of states. An invariant defines relationships between variables within individual states. A constraint differs from an invariant, because it takes into account the relationships between values in two successive states - before and after each state transition function.

In the following notation the convention of placing the symbol * behind a state variable is used to refer to the new state.

Privacy constraint-1:
A subject may create a personal data object, only if it is necessary for its current task (property of necessity of data creation):
$(CT(subj), o\text{-}class_k, CTP(subj), create) \notin NA \land O_j \notin OP$
$$\Rightarrow O_j \notin OP^* \lor class^*(O_j) \neq o\text{-}class_k$$

Privacy constraint-2:
A subject may delete a personal data object, only if it is necessary for its current task (property of necessity of data deletion):
$(CT(subj), Class(O_j), CTP(subj), delete) \notin NA \land O_j \in OP \Rightarrow O_j \in OP^*$

Privacy constraint-3:
A subject may create a personal data object, only if the purpose of its current task corresponds to the purposes of the object's class o-class$_k$ (property of purpose binding of data creation):
$T\text{-}Purpose\ (CT\ (S_i)) \notin O\text{-}Purposes\ (o\text{-}class_k) \land O_j \notin OP$
$$\Rightarrow O_j \notin OP^* \lor class^*(O_j) \neq o\text{-}class_k$$

Privacy constraint-4:
A subject may delete a personal data object, only if the purpose of its current task corresponds to the Purposes of the object's class, or if there is a consent from the data subjects (property of purpose binding of data deletion):
$T\text{-}Purpose\ (CT\ (S_i)) \notin O\text{-}Purposes\ (Class(O_j)) \land (T\text{-}Purpose(\ CT(S_i)),O_j\ ) \notin C$
$\land O_j \in OP \Rightarrow O_j \in OP^*.$

5.2.3 Model Rules (State Transition Functions)

In this Section, state transition functions, which are describing changes of state variables that may take place, are defined. They are divided into general transition functions for accessing objects and executing transformation procedures and privileged transition functions to administrate and define access control information.

5.2.3.1 General Transition Functions

General transition functions are defined for actions such as get access, release access, create object, delete object, change current task, execute transformation procedure, exit transformation procedure.

The sign "=" in a function should be read as a statement of mathematical equality. The functions do not imply any specific ordering of statements for an operation and are atomic.

get-access (S_i, O_j, x)
(Semantics: Subject S_i requests that access personal data object O_j in usage mode x be enabled, $x \in \{read, write, append\}$)

If $(CT (S_i), Class (O_j), CTP(S_i), x) \in NA$

$\wedge$

$[\text{ T-Purpose } (CT (S_i)) \in \text{O-Purposes } (Class (O_j))$

$\vee$

$(\text{T-Purpose } (CT (S_i)), O_j) \in C]$

then

$CA^* = CA \cup \{(S_i, O_j, x)\}$

release-access (S_i, O_j, x)
(Semantics: Subject S_i requests that access to personal data object O_j in usage mode x be disabled, $x \in \{read, write, append\}$)

$CA^* = CA - \{(S_i, O_j, x)\}$

Execute-TP $(S_i, transp_j)$:
(Semantics: Subject S_i requests to execute transformation procedure $transp_j$)

If $transp_j \in ATP (CT(S_i)) \wedge CTP (S_i) = NIL$

then

$CA^* = CA - (CA \cap (\{S_i \} \times O \times A))$

$CTP^* (S_i) = transp_j$

Exit-TP (S_i):
(Semantics: Subject S_i requests to exit processing its current TP)

$$CA^* = CA - (CA \cap (\{S_i\} \times O \times A))$$
$$CTP^*(S_i) = Nil$$

Change-current-task (S_i, T_j)
(Semantics: Subject S_i requests that its current task be changed to T_j)

If $T_j \in AT(S_i) \wedge CTP(S_i) = Nil$
then
$$CT^* (S_i) = T_j$$

create-subject (S_i)
(Semantics: Subject S_i requests to create a new subject, denoted S_{new})

If $CTP(S_i) = NIL$
then
$$S^* = S \cup \{S_{new}\}$$
$$CTP^*(S_{new}) = NIL$$
$$AT^*(S_{new}) = AT(S_i)$$
$$CT^*(S_{new}) = CT(S_i)$$
$$role^*(S_{new}) = role(S_i)$$

create-object $(S_i, \text{o-class}_k)$
(Semantics: Subject S_i requests to create of a personal data object, denoted O_{new}, of a class o-class$_k$)

If $(CT (S_i), \text{o-class}_k, CTP(S_i), create) \in NA$

$\wedge$

$T\text{-Purpose} (CT (S_i)) \in O\text{-Purposes} (\text{o-class}_k)$
then
$$OP^* = OP \cup \{O_{new}\}$$
$$O^* = O \cup \{O_{new}\}$$
$$Class^* (O_{new}) = \text{o-class}_k$$

delete-object (S_i, O_j)
(Semantics: Subject S_i requests to delete a personal data object O_j)

If $(CT (S_i), Class (O_j), CTP(S_i), delete) \in NA$

$$\wedge$$
$$[\text{ T-Purpose (CT } (S_i)) \in \text{O-Purposes (class } (O_j))$$
$$\vee$$
$$(\text{ T-Purpose (CT } (S_i)), O_j) \in C]$$

then

$$OP^* = OP - \{O_j\}$$
$$O^* = O - \{O_j\}$$
$$CA^* = CA - (CA \cap (S \times \{O_j\} \times A))$$
$$C^* = C - (C \cap (P \times \{O_j\}))$$

5.2.3.2 Privileged Transition Functions

A subject is only allowed to perform a privileged transition function, if its user role is authorised to perform this function (one exception is the function create-ticket that under certain circumstances can also be executed by responsible users).

Privileged functions are needed to define and change access control information, such as tasks, purposes, authorised tasks for a subject, authorised transformation procedures for a task, object classes and their purposes, necessary accesses and consents. We require that these privileged functions can only be executed by the security officer. However, in order to support the principle of operational separation of duty (so-called "4-eyes principle" or "2-person-control"), administration of access control information should be done in co-operation with another person, who cares for the privacy interests of the data subjects. This person could for instance be the data protection officer in an organisation or the works council. According to the German data protection act, each organisation engaged in the processing of personal data, has to appoint a data protection officer. In the EU directive, a similar role of a "data protection official" is defined.

The data protection officer, who is responsible for enforcing privacy regulations in an organisation and for setting up a privacy policy, should first define all required access control information. The security officer, who is responsible for enforcing security policies, should then set the access control information according to these requirements.

In order to define and implement such a joint action scheme, another system variable for a so-called "one-time" ticket is introduced:

A Ticket **TKT(S_i ,function-type, parameter-list):** is issued (or signed) by a subject S_i and sent to the security officer (user in the role "sec-officer"). The ticket means that S_i requests the security officer to perform a certain function with certain parameters. The issuer of a ticket is normally a user in the role of "data protection officer" or a responsible user of a task, if authorisation to this task shall be granted to or revoked from another subject. TKT is defined as the set of all issued tickets.

A ticket is created by performing the following privileged function:

create-ticket (S_i, function-type, parameter-list)
(Semantics: S_i requests to create a ticket TKT(S_i,function-type, parameter-list))

    If role (S_i) = data-protection-officer $\vee$
    [(function-type = add-auth-Task) $\vee$ (function-type = delete-auth-Task))
    $\wedge$ (parameter-list = (S_m, T_n))$\wedge$ ($S_i \in$ responsible (T_n))]
    then
        TKT* =TKT $\cup$ {TKT(S_i function-type, parameter-list)}

With an appropriate ticket the security officer can execute a corresponding privileged function (see Figure 5.9).

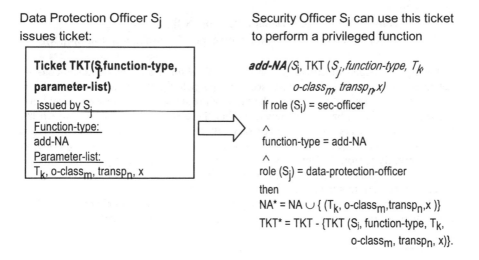

Data Protection Officer S_j issues ticket:

    Ticket TKT($S_j$function-type, parameter-list)
    issued by S_j
    Function-type:
    add-NA
    Parameter-list:
    T_k, o-class$_m$, transp$_n$, x

Security Officer S_i can use this ticket to perform a privileged function

add-NA *(S_i, TKT (S_j,function-type, T_k*
    o-class$_m$, transp$_n$,x)
    If role (S_i) = sec-officer
    $\wedge$
    function-type = add-NA
    $\wedge$
    role (S_j) = data-protection-officer
    then
    NA* = NA $\cup$ { (T_k, o-class$_m$,transp$_n$,x)}
    TKT* = TKT - {TKT (S_i, function-type, T_k,
        o-class$_m$, transp$_n$, x)}.

Fig. 5.9: Joint action scheme for the execution of privileged functions

Thus, privileged functions have the following form:

add-NA (S_i, TKT(S_j function-type, T_k, o-class$_m$, transp$_n$, x))
(Semantics: S_i requests to add the tuple (T_k, o-class$_m$, transp$_n$, x) to NA. S_i provides a corresponding ticket issued by S_j)

    If role (S_i) = sec-officer $\wedge$
    function-type = add-NA $\wedge$
    role(S_j) = data-protection-officer

then
$$NA^* = NA \cup \{(T_k, \text{o-class}_m, \text{transp}_n, x) \}$$
$$TKT^* = TKT - \{TKT(S_j, \text{function-type}, T_k, \text{o-class}_m, \text{transp}_n, x)\}$$

delete-NA $(S_i, TKT(S_j, \text{function-type}, T_k, \text{o-class}_m, \text{transp}_n, x))$
(Semantics: S_i requests to delete the tuple $(T_k, \text{o-class}_m, \text{transp}_n, x)$ from NA. S_i provides a corresponding ticket issued (or signed) by S_j)

If role (S_i) = sec-officer $\wedge$

function-type = delete-NA $\wedge$

role(S_j) = data-protection-officer $\wedge$

$[\forall S_p \in S, O_q \in OP, r \in A:$

IF $(S_p, O_q, r) \in CA$ then

$(CT (S_p), \text{class} (O_q), CTP (S_p), r) \neq (T_k, \text{o-class}_m, \text{transp}_n, x)]$

then
$$NA^* = NA - \{(T_k, \text{o-class}_m, \text{transp}_n, x)\}$$
$$TKT^* = TKT - \{TKT(S_j, \text{function-type}, T_k, \text{o-class}_m, \text{transp}_n, x)\}$$

For the privileged function delete-NA as well as for the functions delete-consent, delete-authorised-task, delete-authorised-TP (see below), the restrictions printed in italic letters are defined to preserve the privacy properties: If a necessary access or a consent is deleted, it has to be guaranteed that there is no current access, which has been granted because of this necessary access or consent. Similarly, if the authorisation of a subject for a task is revoked, it has to be guaranteed that the subject is not currently performing this task. If the authorisation of a task for a transformation procedure is revoked, there should not be a subject that is currently performing this task and executing this transformation procedure at the same time.

Alternative definitions of those privileged functions are given in chapter 5.4, where the problem of revocation of authorisations is discussed in more detail.

add-task $(S_i, TKT(S_j, \text{function-type}, p_m))$
(Semantics: S_i requests to define the task T_{new}, which shall serve the purpose p_m. S_i provides a corresponding ticket issued (or signed) by S_j)

If role (S_i) = sec-officer $\wedge$

function-type = add-task $\wedge$

role(S_j) = data-protection-officer

then
$$T^* = T \cup \{T_{new}\}$$
$$\text{T-Purpose}^*(T_{new}) = p_m$$
$$ATP^*(T_{new}) = \{Nil\}$$
$$\text{responsible}^* (T_{new}) = \varnothing$$
$$TKT^* = TKT - \{TKT(S_j, \text{function-type}, p_m)\}$$

delete-task (S_i, TKT (S_j, function-type, T_k))

(Semantics: S_i requests to delete the task T_k from T. S_i provides a corresponding ticket issued (or signed) by S_j)

> If role (S_i) = sec-officer ∧
> function-type = delete-task ∧
> role(S_j) = data-protection-officer ∧
> [∀ S_q ∈ S: CT (S_q) ≠ T_k]
> then
>> $T^* = T - \{T_k\}$
>> $NA^* = NA - (NA \cap (\{T_k\} \times \text{O-Class} \times \text{TRANS} \times A))$
>> $TKT^* = TKT - \{TKT(S_j, \text{function-type}, T_k)\}$

add-object-class (S_i, TKT(S_j, function-type, P_m))

(Semantics: S_i requests to define the object class o-class$_{new}$, which shall serve the purposes of set P_m. S_i provides a corresponding ticket issued (or signed) by S_j)

> If role (S_i) = sec-officer ∧
> function-type = add-o-class ∧
> role(S_j) = data-protection-officer
> then
>> $\text{O-class}^* = \text{O-class} \cup \{\text{o-class}_{new}\}$
>> $\text{O-Purpose}^* (\text{o-class}_{new}) = P_m$
>> $TKT^* = TKT - \{TKT(S_j, \text{function-type}, P_m)\}$

delete-object-class (S_i, TKT(S_j, function-type, o-class$_k$))

(Semantics: S_i requests to delete the object-class o-class$_k$ from O-class. S_i provides a corresponding ticket issued (or signed) by S_j)

> If role (S_i) = sec-officer ∧
> function-type = delete-o-class ∧
> role(S_j) = data-protection-officer ∧
> [∀ O_q ∈ O: class (O_q) ≠ o-class$_k$]
> then
>> $\text{O-class}^* = \text{O-class} - \{\text{o-class}_k\}$
>> $NA^* = NA - (NA \cap (T \times \{\text{o-class}_k\} \times \text{TRANS} \times A))$
>> $TKT^* = TKT - \{TKT(S_j, \text{function-type}, \text{o-class}_k)\}$

add-authorised-TP $(S_i, TKT(S_j, \text{function-type}, T_k, \text{transp}_m))$

(Semantics: S_i requests to authorise task T_k for transformation procedure transp$_m$. S_i provides a corresponding ticket issued (or signed) by S_j)

> If role (S_i) = sec-officer $\wedge$
>
> function-type = add-auth-TP $\wedge$
> role(S_j) = data-protection-officer
> then
>> $ATP^*(T_k) = ATP(T_k) \cup \{\text{transp}_m\}$
>> $TKT^* = TKT - \{TKT(S_j, \text{function-type}, T_k, \text{transp}_m)\}$

delete-authorised-TP $(S_i, TKT(S_j, \text{function-type}, T_k, \text{transp}_m.))$

(Semantics: S_i requests to revoke the authorisation for transformation procedure transp$_m$ from the task T_k. S_i provides a corresponding ticket issued (or signed) by S_j)

> If role (S_i) = sec-officer $\wedge$
>
> function-type = delete-auth-TP $\wedge$
> role(S_j) = data-protection-officer $\wedge$
> $[\ \forall S_p \in S: CTP(S_p) \neq \text{transp}_k \vee CT(S_p) \neq T_k\ ]$
> then
>> $ATP^*(T_k) = ATP(T_k) - \{\text{transp}_m\}$
>> $TKT^* = TKT - \{TKT(S_j, \text{function-type}, T_k, \text{transp}_m)\}$

add-consent $(S_i, TKT(S_j, \text{function-type}, O_k, p_m))$

(Semantics: S_i requests to add the tuple (O_k, p_m) to C. S_i provides a corresponding ticket issued (or signed) by S_j)

> If role (S_i) = sec-officer $\wedge$
>
> function-type = add-consent $\wedge$
> role(S_j) = data-protection-officer
> then
>> $C^* = C \cup \{(O_k, p_m)\}$
>> $TKT^* = TKT - \{TKT(S_j, \text{function-type}, O_k, p_m)\}$

delete-consent $(S_i, TKT(S_j, \text{function-type}, O_k, p_m))$

(Semantics: S_i requests to delete the tuple (O_k, p_m) from C. S_i provides a corresponding ticket issued (or signed) by S_j)

If role (S_i) = sec-officer $\wedge$

function-type = delete-consent $\wedge$
role(S_j) = data-protection-officer $\wedge$

$[\forall S_p \in S, r \in A:$
IF $(S_p, O_k, r) \in CA$ then
(T-Purpose $(CT(S_p)) \neq p_m$) $\vee$
(T-Purpose$(CT(S_p)) \in$ O-Purposes(class $(O_k))]$
then

$\qquad C^* = C - \{(O_k, p_m)\}$
$\qquad TKT^* = TKT - \{TKT(S_j, \text{function-type}, O_k, p_m)\}$

add-purpose $(S_i, TKT(S_j, \text{function-type}))$

(Semantics: S_i requests to add the purpose p_{new} to P. S_i provides a corresponding ticket issued (or signed) by S_j)

If role (S_i) = sec-officer $\wedge$

function-type = add-consent $\wedge$
role(S_j) = data-protection-officer
then

$\qquad P^* = P \cup \{p_{new}\}$
$\qquad TKT^* = TKT - \{TKT(S_j, \text{function-type})\}$

delete-purpose $(S_i, TKT(S_j, \text{function-type}, p_k))$

(Semantics: S_i requests to delete the purpose p_k from P. S_i provides a corresponding ticket issued (or signed) by S_j)

If role (S_i) = sec-officer $\wedge$

function-type = delete-consent $\wedge$
role(S_j) = data-protection-officer $\wedge$

$[(\forall O_q \in O: p_k \notin$ O-Purposes (class $(O_q)) \wedge$
$(\forall \text{o-class}_t \in$ O-class: O-Purposes(o-class$_t$) $\neq \{p_k\}) \wedge$
$(\forall T_p \in T:$ T-Purpose $(T_p) \neq p_k)]$
then

$\qquad P^* = P - \{p_k\}$
$\qquad TKT^* = TKT - \{TKT(S_j, \text{function-type}, p_k)\}$
$\qquad \forall \text{o-class}_t \in$ O-class: O-Purposes*(o-class$_t$) =
$\qquad$ O-Purposes(o-class$_t$) - (O-Purpose(o-class$_t$) $\cap \{p_k\}$)

184

set-role $(S_i, TKT(S_j, \text{function-type}, S_k, \text{user-role}_m))$
(Semantics: S_i requests to assign user-role$_m$ to subject S_k. S_i provides a corresponding ticket issued (or signed) by S_j)

> If role (S_i) = sec-officer $\wedge$
> function-type = set-role $\wedge$
> role(S_j) = data-protection-officer $\wedge$
> then
>> role* (S_k) = user-role$_m$
>> TKT* = TKT - {TKT$(S_j$, function-type, S_k, user-role$_m)$}

add-responsible-users $(S_i, TKT(S_j, \text{function-type}, S_k, T_m))$
(Semantics: S_i requests to define the subject S_k as responsible for T_m. S_i provides a corresponding ticket issued by S_j)

> If role (S_i) = sec-officer $\wedge$
> function-type = add-resp $\wedge$
> role(S_j) = data-protection-officer
> then
>> responsible* (T_m) = responsible $(T_m) \cup \{S_k\}$
>> TKT* = TKT - {TKT$(S_j$, function-type, S_k, $T_m)$}

delete-responsible-users $(S_i, TKT(S_j, \text{function-type}, S_k, T_m))$
(Semantics: S_i requests to define the subject S_k as not being responsible for T_m anymore. S_i provides a corresponding ticket issued by S_j)

> If role (S_i) = sec-officer $\wedge$
> function-type = delete-resp $\wedge$
> role(S_j) = data-protection-officer
> then
>> responsible* (T_m) = responsible $(T_m) - \{S_k\}$
>> TKT* = TKT - {TKT$(S_j$, function-type, S_k, $T_m)$}

For some applications, it might be necessary to permit users to delegate tasks to other users. However, we do not allow users to delegate tasks directly, because a discretionary access control scheme by which a user can grant access rights to other users is vulnerable to trojan horse attacks. Moreover, it is more secure, if the delegation of tasks is also subject to a 2-person-control, i.e. it is permitted and controlled by the security officer.

Thus, if a user wants to delegate a task, he has to be responsible for this task and has to issue a corresponding ticket to sec-officer, thereby requesting the delegation. The sec-officer can use this ticket to delegate this task to other users.

A privileged function to define authorised tasks for users is defined as follows:

add-authorised-task $(S_i, TKT(S_j, \text{function-type}, S_m, T_n))$
(Semantics: S_i requests to authorise S_m for T_n. S_i provides a corresponding ticket issued by S_j)

> If role (S_i) = sec-officer $\wedge$
>
> function-type = add-auth-Task $\wedge$
> (role(S_j)) = data-protection-officer
>
> $\vee$ $S_j \in$ responsible (T_n))
>
> then
>> $AT^*(S_m) = AT(S_m) \cup \{T_n\}$
>> $TKT^* = TKT - \{TKT(S_j, \text{function-type}, S_m, T_n)\}$

Users can also request revocation of authorisations for tasks for which they are responsible from other users.

delete-authorised-task $(S_i, TKT(S_j, \text{function-type}, S_k, T_m))$
(Semantics: S_i requests to revoke the authorisation for the task T_m from S_k. S_i provides a corresponding ticket issued by S_j)

> If role (S_i) = sec-officer $\wedge$
>
> function-type = delete-auth-Task $\wedge$
> (role(S_j) = data-protection-officer $\vee$ responsible(T_m)) $\wedge$
> $[CT(S_k) \neq T_m]$
>
> then
>> $AT^*(S_k) = AT(S_k) - \{T_m\}$
>> $TKT^* = TKT - \{TKT(S_j, \text{function-type}, S_k, T_m)\}$

The security officer, in cooperation with the data protection officer or other responsible persons, is thus responsible for enforcing the privacy policy. The privacy policy is non-discretionary, as users cannot pass directly access rights on to other users at their discretion. The privacy model enforces a form of mandatory control that is not based on multilevel security requirements and is therefore different from MAC as defined in the TCSEC.

Only users in the role TP-manager may define transformation procedures by using the following privileged functions:

create-TP (S_i)

(Sematics: Subject S_i requests to create a new transformation procedure)

    If role(S_i) = tp-manager
    then
            TRANS* = TRANS ∪ {transp$_{new}$}

delete-TP (S_i, transp$_j$)

(Semantics: Subject S_i requests to delete a transformation procedure transp$_j$ shall from TRANS)

    If role(S_i) = tp-manager ∧
    [∀ S_k ∈ S: CTP(S_k) ≠ transp$_j$]
    then
            TRANS* = TRANS - {transp$_j$};
            NA* = NA - (NA ∩ (T × O- Class × {transp$_j$} × A))
            ∀ T_m ∈ T: ATP(T_m) = ATP(T_m) - (ATP(T_m) ∩ {transp$_j$}).

Consequently, the principle of separation of duties is enforced for the administration of TPs. The TP-manager is authorised to define TPs, but only the security officer in cooperation with the data protection officer is allowed to authorise users for the execution of TPs.

5.3 Information Flow Control

According to the principle of purpose binding, a subject may access an object, if the purpose of its current task is contained in the set of purposes for which data of the object-class is obtained.

However, the following attack-scenario (in a hospital environment), shown in Figure 5.10, may allow illegal information flow.

In this scenario, a subject while performing task T_1 could read object O_1 and write sensitive data from O_1 to object O_2. Consequently, another subject that is performing T_2 (with T-Purpose AD) could read data from O_1 (with O-Purposes (class(O_1) = {MT}), which was written to O_2. Hence, the principle of purpose binding could be violated !

In particular, it has to be prevented that a subject can read from a personal data object O_1 (with O-Purposes(class(O_1)) ⊂ P) and write the information obtained from O_1 to a non-personal data object O_2 (with O-Purposes(Class(O_2)) = O-Purposes(none) = P).

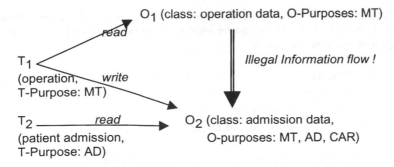

MT: medical treatment, AD: administration, CAR: intensive care

Fig. 5.10: Illegal Information Flow

Such illegal information flow can be prevented, if the following security invariant is guaranteed:

Invariant (A):

In any state, if a subject S_i has simultaneous current read-access to object O_1 and current write- or append-access to object O_2, then:

O-Purposes (class (O_1)) $\supseteq$ O-Purposes (class (O_2)).

Information flow control mechanisms by access control or by program certification of the transformation procedures could be used to satisfy this condition.

Certification mechanisms:

A subject can access an object only by executing a certified transformation procedure (transaction program) that is authorised for its current task. A program certification mechanism could check that each statement in the transformation procedure, if executed, would not cause an information flow violation. Certification mechanisms could be integrated into a compiler or flow proofs could be combined with correctness proofs to achieve a more precise certification mechanism.

However, in order to check and certify the information flow, the certifier has to have information about object classes of objects and their purposes.

Illegal information flow could thus be prevented by a careful design of (certified) transformation procedures, as well as, by an appropriate definition of necessary accesses.

Flow-secure Access Control:

A simple flow control can be integrated into the access control mechanism of the operating system. Information flow control enforced by the system can increase the system's overhead at run-time, but on the other hand, provides higher assurance.

Note that a subject can access personal data, only if it is executing a transformation procedure. Thus, it is sufficient to control information flow for subjects, which are executing transformation procedures.

An information flow access control mechanism guaranteeing *invariant (A)* has to check for each get-read request to an object O_1 if

O-Purposes (class (O_1)) $\supseteq$ O-Purposes (class (O_2))

for each object O_2 to which the requesting process has currently write or append access.

Similarly, it has to be checked for each get-write request to an object O_2 if

O-Purposes (class (O_1)) $\supseteq$ O-Purposes (class (O_2))

for each object O_1 to which the requesting process has currently read access. This, however, can be a time-consuming and complicated task.

Thus, we use a more restricted security invariant for secure information flow. To formally model the access control of information flow, the privacy model is extended. A new state variable *Input-Purposes* is introduced:

For each subject, the intersection of O-Purposes sets of the object classes of the objects to which the subject has had read-access, is recorded.

A function **Input-Purposes: S -> 2^P** is defined, were Input-Purposes(S_i) is the intersection set of purpose sets of object classes of data that S_i has read. It defines the set of purposes that all objects, which S_i has read, have in common. Initially (after process creation and when starting the execution of a transformation procedure) Input-Purposes (S_i) is set to P. If S_i gets read-access to an object O_j, Input-Purposes(S_i) in the new system state is set to Input-Purposes (S_i) $\cap$ O-Purposes (class (O_j)).

Illegal information flow can be prevented, if it is guaranteed that S_i may not write to an object which was obtained for purposes not contained in Input-Purposes (S_i). Therefore, the following security invariant should be guaranteed:

Invariant (B):
$\forall\ S_i \in S, O_j \in O, x \in \{write, append\}$:
$(S_i, O_j, x) \in CA => $ O-Purposes (class (O_j)) $\subseteq$ Input-Purposes (S_i).

In order to guarantee this security invariant, the state transition functions have to be extended appropriately. The state transition function get-access is replaced by the two functions get-write and get-read:

get-write (S_i, O_j, x)
(Semantics: Subject S_i requests that access to object O_j in usage mode x be enabled, $x \in \{append, write\}$)
    If [$(O_j \in OP)$

$\wedge$
(CT (S_i), Class (O_j), CTP(S_i), x) $\in$ NA

$\wedge$
[T-Purpose (CT (S_i)) $\in$ O-Purposes (Class (O_j))

$\vee$
(T-Purpose (CT (S_i)), O_j) $\in$ C]

$\wedge$
O-Purposes (class (O_j)) $\subseteq$ Input-Purposes (S_i)]
or
[($O_j \notin$ OP)

$\wedge$
Input-Purposes (S_i) = P]
(* in this case: O-Purposes (class (O_j)) = O-Purposes(none) = P $\subseteq$
Input-Purposes (S_i) *)
then
   CA* = CA $\cup$ {(S_i, O_j, x)}

get-read (S_i, O_j)
(Semantics: Subject S_i requests that access to object O_j in usage mode read be enabled)
     If ($O_j \notin$ OP)

$\vee$
[$(O_j \in$ OP)

$\wedge$
(CT (S_i), Class (O_j), CTP(S_i), read) $\in$ NA

$\wedge$
(T-Purpose (CT (S_i)) $\in$ O-Purposes (Class (O_j))

$\vee$
(T-Purpose (CT (S_i)), O_j) $\in$ C)

$\wedge$
($\forall O_k$:$(S_i, O_k, r) \in$ CA , r $\in$ {write, append}:
O-Purposes(class(O_k)) $\subseteq$ O-Purposes(class(O_j)))]
then
          CA* = CA $\cup$ {$(S_i, O_j, read)$}
          Input-Purposes *(S_i) =
          Input-Purposes $(S_i) \cap$ O-Purposes (class (O_j))

Example 5.1:

If a subject S_i with input-purposes(S_i) = P is performing a current task T_1 and gets current write access to a personal data object O_1 of the class operation with O-Purposes(operation) = {MT} (see Figure 5.10), input-purposes(S_i) is set to {MT}. Now, S_i can only get write-access to personal data objects of classes which are collected exclusively for the purpose MT.

Another possibility is that a subject S_i with input-purposes(S_i) = P while performing the current task T_1 first gets current write access to object O_2 with O-Purposes(class(O_2)) = {MT, AD, CAR}. Subsequently, S_i will only be able to read personal data objects O_j with O-Purposes(class(O_j)) ⊇ {MT, AD, CAR}, unless it releases the current write access to O_2.

Thus, S_i cannot have current read access to O_1 and current write access to O_2 at the same time. Consequently, illegal information flow as shown in Figure 5.10 is prevented.

An access control mechanism which is implementing the state transition function get-read still has to check every time that a subject requests read-access to a personal data object, if this read-access is in conflict with any of the subject´s current write accesses. However, as already pointed out above, the checking of all current write-accesses could be quite a time-consuming and complicated task.

Therefore, the access control checks should be further simplified:

A new state variable **Output-Purposes: S -> 2^P** is defined. The Output-Purposes of a subject is the union set of O-Purposes of the object classes of objects to which the subject has been granted write- or append-access. Thus Output-Purposes(S_i) defines all possible purposes for that data to which S_i has current write-access can be used. Initially (after creation of S_i), Output-Purposes(S_i) is defined by the empty set ∅.

If S_i gets current write- or append-access to an object O_j, Output-Purposes(S_i) in the new system state is set to Output-Purposes (S_i) ∪ O-Purposes (class (O_j)).

Illegal information flow can be prevented, if it is guaranteed that Output-Purposes(S_i) is contained in Input-Purposes(S_i). Therefore, the following information flow control invariant should be guaranteed:

Information flow invariant:
∀ S_i∈ S : Output-Purposes (S_i) ⊆ Input-Purposes (S_i).

It can be easily shown that if the information flow invariant is satisfied then invariant (A) is satisfied as well:
Suppose that the information flow invariant is satisfied and let S_i be an arbitrary subject.
Then Output-Purposes (S_i) ⊆ Input-Purposes (S_i). Suppose S_i has current read-access to object O_1 and current write- or append access to object O_2.

Since S_i has current read-access to object O_1, Input-Purposes(S_i) has been set to
Input-Purposes(S_i) $\cap$ O-Purposes(class(O_1)) =>
Input-Purposes(S_i) $\subseteq$ O-Purposes (class(O_1))

Since S_i has current write- or append-access to object O_2, Output-Purposes(S_i) has
been set to Output-Purposes(S_i) $\cup$ O-Purposes(class(O_2))
=> O-Purposes (class(O_2)) $\subseteq$ Output-Purposes(S_i).

Hence: O-Purposes(class(O_2)) $\subseteq$ Output-Purposes (S_i) $\subseteq$ Input-Purposes (S_i)
  $\subseteq$ O-Purposes (class(O_1)).
Thus, information flow invariant A is satisfied as well.

To enforce the information flow invariant, the state transition functions get-write,
get-access, execute-TP, exit-TP, create-subject are once again redefined:

get-write (S_i, O_j, x)
*(Semantics: Subject S_i requests that access to object O_j in usage mode x be
enabled, x $\in$ {append, write})*
    If [($O_j \in$ OP)

    $\wedge$
    (CT (S_i), Class (O_j), CTP(S_i), x) $\in$ NA

    $\wedge$
    [T-Purpose (CT (S_i)) $\in$ O-Purposes (Class (O_j))

    $\vee$
    (T-Purpose (CT (S_i)), O_j) $\in$ C]

    $\wedge$
    Output-Purposes (S_i) $\cup$ O-Purposes (class (O_j))
    $\subseteq$ Input-Purposes (S_i)]

    $\vee$
    [($O_j \notin$ OP)

    $\wedge$
    Input-Purposes(S_i) = P
    (* in this case: Output-Purposes (S_i) $\cup$ O-Purposes (class (O_j)) $\subseteq$
                Input-Purposes (S_i) *)]
    then
       CA* = CA $\cup$ {(S_i, O_j, x)}
       Output-Purposes*(S_i) = Output-Purposes (S_i) $\cup$
                   O-Purposes (class (O_j))

get-read (S_i, O_j)

(Semantics: Subject S_i requests that access to object O_j in usage mode read be enabled)

$\quad$ If $(O_j \notin OP)$

$\qquad \vee$

$\qquad [(O_j \in OP)$

$\qquad \wedge$

$\qquad (CT (S_i),\ Class (O_j),\ CTP(S_i),\ read) \in NA$

$\qquad \wedge$

$\qquad (((\ T\text{-Purpose } (CT (S_i)) \in O\text{-Purposes } (Class (O_j))$

$\qquad \vee$

$\qquad (\ T\text{-Purpose } (\ CT (S_i)),\ O_j) \in C\ )\ )$

$\qquad \wedge$

$\qquad$ Output-Purposes $(S_i) \subseteq$

$\qquad$ Input-Purposes $(S_i)\ \cap\ O\text{-Purposes}(class(O_j))\ \ ]$

$\quad$ then

$\qquad CA^* = CA\ \cup \{(S_i, O_j, read)\}$

$\qquad$ Input-Purposes $^*(S_i) =$

$\qquad$ Input-Purposes $(S_i) \cap O\text{-Purposes } (class (O_j))$

Execute-TP $(S_i,\ transp_j\ )$:

(Semantics: Subject S_i requests to execute transformation procedure $transp_j$)

$\quad$ If $transp_j \in ATP (CT(S_i))$

$\quad$ then

$\qquad CA^* = CA - (CA \cap (\{S_i\} \times O \times A))$

$\qquad CTP^* (S_i) = transp_j$

$\qquad$ Input-Purposes$^* (S_i) = P$

$\qquad$ Output-Purposes$^* (S_i) = \varnothing.$

Exit-TP (S_i):

(Semantics: Subject S_i requests to exit processing its current TP)

$\qquad CA^* = CA - (CA \cap (\{S_i\} \times O \times A))$

$\qquad CTP^*(S_i) = Nil$

$\qquad$ Input-Purposes$^* (S_i) = P$

$\qquad$ Output-Purposes$^* (S_i) = \varnothing.$

create-subject (S_i)

(Semantics: Subject S_i requests to create of a new subject, denoted S_{new})

     If $CTP(S_i) = NIL$

     then

         $S^* = S \cup \{S_{new}\}$

         $CTP^*(S_{new}) = NIL$

         $AT^*(S_{new}) = AT(S_i)$

         $CT^*(S_{new}) = CT(S_i)$

         $Role^*(S_{new}) = role(S_i)$

         Input-Purposes$^* (S_{new}) = P$

         Output-Purposes$^* (S_{new}) = \varnothing$.

In the specification and implementation of the privacy policy, the information flow invariant defined above was enforced. The information flow invariant is more restrictive than the two other security invariants for information flow control (*invariant A* and *invariant B*) which we have discussed above. The Output-Purposes of a subject depend on all write-accesses which the subject has gained while executing a transformation procedure, even those write-accesses that the subject has already released. Thus, the information flow invariant might be more restrictive than necessary. However, in practice, a process is normally not closing write-opened files before exiting a transformation procedure.

Example 5.2:

If a subject S_i with output-purposes$(S_i) = \varnothing$ performing a current task T_1 gets current write access to a personal data object O_2 of the class administration data with O-Purposes(administration data) = {MT, AD, CAR}, output-purposes(S_i) is set to {MT, AD, CAR}. Subsequently, even if S_i releases the current write access to O_2, S_i will only be able to get current read-access to a personal data object O_j with O-Purposes(class(O_j)) $\supseteq$ {MT, AD, CAR}.

In Appendix A, a "privacy-oriented state" is defined as a system state that satisfies the four privacy invariants-1-4 as well as the information flow invariant. A state sequence is defined as a "privacy-oriented state sequence", if each state of the state sequence is privacy-oriented and all successive states of the sequence satisfy the four privacy-constraints-1-4. It is formally proven that all state transition functions preserve the four privacy invariants-1-4, the information flow invariant as well as the four privacy-constraints-1-4. Hence, if a system that implements the privacy model starts in a privacy-oriented state, all possible state sequences will be privacy-oriented.

5.4 Revocation of Authorisations

In this section, three different approaches to deal with the problem of revocation of authorisations are discussed. The privacy model as defined above is based on the first approach.

1. Approach: Additional security conditions:

As described in 5.2.3.2, for the privileged functions *delete-NA, delete-authorised tasks, delete-authorised-TP, delete-consent* certain conditions have to be fulfilled to preserve the privacy properties: If a necessary access or a consent is deleted, it has to be guaranteed that there is no current access which has been granted because of this necessary access or consent. Similarly, if the authorisation of a subject for a task is revoked, it has to be guaranteed that the subject is not currently performing this task. If the authorisation of a task to execute a transformation procedure is revoked, there should not be a subject that is currently performing this task and executing this transformation procedure at the same time.

The enforcement of those conditions is, however, problematic. In particular it has to be prevented that at the time that one of those privileged functions shall be executed, there is a process that is in conflict with the conditions of that function and is executing infinitely. Besides, it has to be prevented that permanently new processes start that are in conflict with the conditions. Otherwise the privileged function could never be executed. This problem is avoided if the privileged functions *delete-NA, delete-authorised tasks, delete-authorised-TP, delete-consent* are only executed while no other user is currently performing a task. Thus, to successfully execute those privileged functions (which is probably not required very often), the security officer must first force all users to finish their tasks within some time limits before he can execute those privileged functions.

2. Approach: Release of current accesses and current executions:

Another possibility is to define privileged functions which release current accesses, stop the execution of transformation procedures or stop the performance of tasks.

For example, another definition of the function delete-NA could be:

delete-NA $(S_i, TKT(S_j, \text{function-type}, T_k, \text{o-class}_m, \text{transp}_n, x))$
(Semantics: S_i requests to delete the tuple $(T_k, \text{o-class}_m, \text{transp}_n, x)$ from NA. S_i provides a corresponding ticket issued (or signed) by S_j)

  If role (S_i) = sec-officer $\wedge$
  function-type = delete-NA $\wedge$
  role(S_j) = data-protection-officer $\wedge$
  then
    $NA^* = NA - \{(T_k, \text{o-class}_m, \text{transp}_n, x)\}$
    $CA^* = CA - \{(S_p, O_q, r) | (CT(S_p), \text{class}(O_q), CTP(S_p), r) =$

$(T_k,$ o-class$_m$, transp$_n$, x) }

TKT* =TKT- {TKT(S$_j$, function-type, T$_k$, o-class$_m$, transp$_n$, x)}

However, it is normally required that transactions (i.e., transformation procedures) are atomic to preserve consistency. If a transformation procedure is stopped before normal termination or if a current access to personal data is revoked from a transformation procedure, the transformation procedure can leave the modified personal data in an inconsistent state. Consequently, this approach will also require the implementation of appropriate recovery mechanisms. For this reason, we are not following this approach.

(Note that in [Bell LaPadula 1976] in the formal definition of the function rescind-access, a current access that was granted because of a revoked access right is released. However, probably due to such consistency problems, the current access is not released in the specification of the Multics kernel-function rescind-access also specified in Bell LaPadula 1976]).

3. Keeping revoked authorisations valid for current accesses and executions

Another possibility is to take the viewpoint that the time when a subject requests a permission should be relevant: If a subject received the right to access an object or to perform a TP (or task), it should be allowed to keep this right until it completes its TP (or current task). For example, if a subject receives the permission to access an object because of a necessary access and if this necessary access is later revoked, the subject should still keep the access right, because it was necessary when requested. Thus, even if a necessary access is deleted, it remains valid for those subjects that have received a current access because of that necessary access. For new get-access requests, however, a deleted necessary access has to be regarded as invalid.

To formally define this approach, new state variables have to be defined and further constraints have to be fulfilled. Besides, some state transition functions have to be redefined.

The set NA of necessary accesses is divided into the sets NA_{def} and NA_{del};

that is $NA = NA_{def} \cup NA_{del}$.

NA_{def} is the set of all necessary accesses that have been defined and have since then not been deleted (the so-called set of "defined necessary accesses"). NA_{del} is the set of necessary accesses with access modes from the set {read, write, append} that have been deleted from NA_{def}.

Analogously, the set C of consents is divided into the sets C_{def} and C_{del};

that is $C = C_{def} \cup C_{del}$.

C_{def} is the set of all consents that have been defined and have since then not been deleted (set of "defined consents"). C_{del} is the set of consents that have been deleted from C_{def}.

Similarly, the function AT of authorised tasks for subjects is defined by the two functions AT_{def} ("defined authorised tasks) and AT_{del}.

$\forall\ S_i \in S: AT(S_i) = AT_{del}\ (S_i) \cup AT_{def}(S_i)$ and $Nil \in AT_{def}\ (S_i)$.

The function ATP is defined by the two functions ATP_{def} ("defined authorised TPs") and ATP_{del}.

$\forall\ T_i \in T: ATP(T_i) = ATP_{del}\ (T_i) \cup ATP_{def}(T_i)$ and $Nil \in ATP_{def}\ (T_i)$.

If a subject requests to get current access to an object, it has to be checked whether this access is necessary according to the "defined" necessary accesses NA_{def}. Besides, only consents contained in the set C_{def} should be regarded as valid when checking access requests. Similarly, a subject is allowed to change its current task only if the new task is a "defined authorised task" for the subject, and a subject may start the execution of a new current transformation procedure only if this transformation procedures is a "defined authorised TP" for the subject´s current task.

Thus subsequent states have to fulfil the following additional constraints:

Constraint-5:
$T_j \notin AT_{def}(subj) \wedge CT(subj) \neq T_j => CT^*(subj) \neq T_j$

Constraint-6:
$transp_j \notin ATP_{def}(CT(subj)) \wedge CTP(subj) \neq transp_j => CTP^*(subj) \neq transp_j$

Constraint-7:
$(CT(subj), class(O_j), CTP(subj), x) \notin NA_{def} \wedge (subj, O_j, x) \notin CA =>$
$(subj, O_j, x) \notin CA^*$

Constraint-8:
$T\text{-}Purpose(CT(subj)) \notin O\text{-}Purposes\ (class(O_j)) \wedge (T\text{-}Purpose(CT(subj)), O_j) \notin C_{def}$
$\wedge\ (subj, O_j, x) \notin CA => (subj, O_j, x) \notin CA^*$

The privileged state transition functions *delete-NA, delete-authorised-task, delete-authorised-TP, delete-consent, add-NA, add-authorised-tasks, add-authorised-TP, add-consent, add-task, delete-TP* as well as the state transition functions *get-read, get-write, create-object, delete-object, execute-TP* and *change-current-task* are slightly modified:
In the state transition function *add-NA* the variable NA is replaced by NA_{def}, whilst in *add-authorised-task* the function AT is replaced by AT_{def}, in *add-authorised-TP* the function ATP is replaced by ATP_{def}, and in *add-consent* the

variable C is replaced by C_{def}. Similarly, in the state transition functions *get-read*, *get-write, create-object, delete-object*, the variable NA is replaced by NA_{def} and C is replaced by C_{def}. In *change-current-task* the function AT is replaced by AT_{def} and in *execute-TP, delete-TP, add-task* the function ATP is replaced by ATP_{def}. Besides, $ATP_{del}(T_{new})$ in the next state is set to $\emptyset$ in the statement part of the state transition function *add-task*.

The state transition functions delete-NA, delete-authorised-task, delete-authorised-TP and delete-consent are redefined as follows:

delete-NA $(S_i, TKT(S_j, \text{function-type}, T_k, \text{o-class}_m, \text{transp}_n, x))$
    If role (S_i) = sec-officer $\wedge$
    function-type = delete-NA $\wedge$
    role(S_j) = data-protection-officer $\wedge$
    then
        $NA_{def}{}^* = NA_{def} - (NA_{def} \cap \{(T_k, \text{o-class}_m, \text{transp}_n, x)\})$
        $TKT^* = TKT - \{TKT(S_j, \text{function-type}, T_k, \text{o-class}_m, \text{transp}_n, x)\}$
        If $x \in \{\text{read, write, append}\}$
        then
            $NA_{del}{}^* = NA_{del} \cup (NA_{def} \cap \{(T_k, \text{o-class}_m, \text{transp}_n, x)\})$

delete-authorised-TP $(S_i, TKT(S_j, \text{function-type}, T_k, \text{transp}_m))$
    If role (S_i) = sec-officer $\wedge$
    function-type = delete-auth-TP $\wedge$
    role(S_j) = data-protection-officer $\wedge$
    then
        $ATP_{def}{}^*(T_k) = ATP_{def}(T_k) - (ATP_{def}(Tk) \cap \{\text{transp}_m\})$
        $ATP_{del}{}^*(T_k) = ATP_{del}(T_k) \cup (ATP_{def}(Tk) \cap \{\text{transp}_m\})$
        $TKT^* = TKT - \{TKT(S_j, \text{function-type}, T_k, \text{transp}_m)\}$

delete-consent $(S_i, TKT(S_j, \text{function-type}, O_k, p_m))$
    If role (S_i) = sec-officer $\wedge$
    function-type = delete-consent $\wedge$
    role(S_j) = data-protection-officer $\wedge$
    then
        $C_{def}{}^* = C_{def} - (C_{def} \cap \{(O_k, p_m)\})$
        $C_{del}{}^* = C_{del} \cup (C_{def} \cap \{(O_k, p_m)\})$
        $TKT^* = TKT - \{TKT(S_j, \text{function-type}, O_k, p_m)\}$

delete-authorised-task *(S$_i$, TKT(S$_j$, function-type, S$_k$, T$_m$))*

　　If role (S$_i$) = sec-officer ∧
　　function-type = delete-auth-Task ∧
　　(role(S$_j$) = data-protection-officer ∨ responsible(T$_m$))
　　then
$$AT_{def}^*(S_k) = AT_{def}(S_k) - (AT_{def}(S_k) \cap \{T_m\})$$
$$AT_{del}^*(S_k) = AT_{del}(S_k) \cup (AT_{def}(S_k) \cap \{T_m\})$$
$$TKT^* = TKT - \{TKT(S_j, \text{function-type}, S_k, T_m)\}$$

The formal mathematical privacy model presented in Appendix A is based on the first approach. However, in order to follow the third approach the formal definitions of state variables and state transition functions can easily be modified as described above. It can then be easily proven that the modified state transition functions still preserve the four privacy invariants 1.-4., the information flow invariant as well as the four privacy constraints 1.-4. Besides, it is easily shown that all state transition functions preserve the four additional constraints 5.-8.

5.5　Example: Application of the Privacy Model in a Hospital Information System

Hans-Jürgen Seelos presented a privacy policy for the protection of personal patient data in a distributed hospital information system [Seelos 1991]. He used an access matrix to specify the types of accesses that certain tasks, which are performed within the areas of medical treatment, care, and administration, should have on information variables referring to personal patient data. Thus, the privacy model can easily be used to enforce the privacy policy specified by Seelos.

　　The following example shall demonstrate how the privacy model can be applied in a hospital environment.

　　The organisation of a hospital is typically divided in the areas, medical treatment, care, research and administration. Some hospitals, especially university hospitals, are also doing medical research. Consequently, appropriate purposes for separating the main areas in a hospital could be: MT (medical treatment), AD (administration), CAR (care) and RE (research).

　　Within each area, different tasks (with a task-purpose that is corresponding to the area) can be defined. Examples of possible tasks (with T-purposes in parentheses) are: diagnosing (MT), operation (MT), therapy (MT), intensive care (CAR), patient-admission (AD), billing(AD), statistical analysis (RE),....

Examples for possible object classes of personal patient data are (with O-Purposes in parentheses): admission data (AD, MT, CAR), billing data (AD), diagnosis (MT, CAR), treatment data - e.g. operational treatment data, mental treatment data, etc.- (MT), treatment request (MT, CAR), treatment protocol (AD, MT), statistics (RE),...

Transformation procedures (TRANS) could be: accounting procedures, statistical procedures, editors, append-only-editors, display-program, create-personal-data program, archive program,...

Necessary Accesses (NA) could be defined as follows:
(diagnosing, diagnosis, editor, read/write/create/append)
(diagnosing, treatment-protocol, append-only-editor, append)
(diagnosing, treatment-request, create-personal-data program, create)
.....
(statistical analysis, diagnosis, statistical procedures, read)
......

Furthermore, users (or user roles) have to be authorised for their tasks: For example, a surgeon is authorised for the operation task (among others), an internist is authorised for diagnosis and therapy, a therapist is authorised for therapy, the registration staff is authorised for the task patient-admission, the billing staff is authorised for accounting, a researcher is authorised for statistical analysis,...

This example demonstrates the differences between the concept of necessity of data processing and the concept of purpose binding: For a researcher it might be necessary to do a statistical analysis by running a statistical program with read-access on diagnosis data. However, diagnosis data is collected exclusively for the purpose MT (medical treatment) and the purpose of the task statistical analysis is RE (research). Consequently, the principle of purpose binding can allow an access to diagnosis data of a patient for research purposes only, if the patient has consented to it.

We have elaborated an imaginary hospital scenario and have implemented it as a demonstration example using our GFAC (Generalized Framework for Access Control) system implementation of the privacy model. The scenario is described in Appendix B.

5.6 Analysis of the Privacy Model

The formal task-based privacy model was designed to enforce legal privacy requirements, such as necessity of data processing or purpose binding.

Besides, it is based on the concept of well-formed transformation procedures that allows users to manipulate data only in constrained ways and thereby help to protect the integrity of personal data. By defining adequate tuples of necessary accesses, the integrity principle of separation of duty can be enforced. As pointed out above in Section 5.2, the Clark Wilson access triples could be implemented with the set NA of necessary accesses. In fact, the Clark Wilson policy could be implemented by the privacy model.

As a further advantage, the privacy model also enables the control of pseudonymous or anonymous system access control. Anonymous system access control can, for instance, be implemented by authorisation certificates that are expressing the users´ authorisations for certain tasks.

The privacy model, however, is focussed only on personal data processing and enforces basic privacy principles. Hence, the privacy model policy should be implemented in combination with other security policies addressing additional security goals. Particularly non-personal sensitive data (e.g., business related data) and security-relevant system data should be protected by additional security models.

For this reason, we have implemented the privacy model policy in combination with the Bell LaPadula policy, FC (Functional Control) policy and SIM (Security Information Modification) policy following the GFAC (Generalized Framework for Access Control) approach (see next Chapter). The FC and the SIM policies (see 3.2.13.1) could be used to restrict access to and modification of security relevant system files. A further advantage of following the GFAC approach is that more specific, application-dependent privacy rules could additionally be implemented and could be given higher priority than the general privacy rules.

6 Specification and Implementation of the Privacy Policy Following the Generalised Framework for Access Control-Approach

6.1 Introduction

In this Chapter, it is specified how the privacy policy can be enforced according to the Generalised Framework for Access Control (GFAC) Approach in Unix System V. GFAC (see [Abrams et al. 1990], [LaPadula 1995] and Chapter 3.2.13.1) is a framework for expressing and integrating multiple policy components. It makes it feasible to configure a system with security policies chosen from a vendor provided set of options, with confidence, that the resulting system's security policies will be properly enforced.

A draft top-level specification, which specifies how the GFAC approach enforcing the Bell LaPadula policy, the Clark Wilson policy and two supporting policies (Functional Control (FC) policy and Security Information Modification (SIM) policy) can be implemented in Unix System V, was published in [LaPadula 1995]. This top-level specification was further elaborated and extended with the policy rules of the privacy model. It was then used and adapted for the implementation and integration of the privacy policy according to the GFAC-approach together with other security policies (Bell LaPadula, FC, SIM) in the Linux operating system (see [Ott 1997]). Hence, the privacy model has been implemented in one of the first complete GFAC-implementations.

Linux, although it is not designed for security, was chosen as a demonstration system, because it is a robust system, its source code is available and because it has functionalities of System V. Furthermore, it keeps most important Unix standards (Linux 2.2 is in most parts conforming to the Posix standard). The results of the project (in particular, the privacy policy-specific Access Decision Facility- and Access Control Information modules) can be easily transferred to more secure Unix versions.

The GFAC approach was chosen, because it makes it easily possible to combine the privacy policy that enforces general privacy rules (as for instance required by the German Federal Data Protection Act) together with other more specific privacy regulations (e.g., privacy provisions of a hospital information law), which can be granted a higher priority. This is important, because in Germany according to the Federal data protection act and according to the data protection laws of the states, in so far as other legal provisions are applicable to personal data, such provisions shall take precedence.

According to the GFAC approach, the Trusted Computing Base (TCB) consists of an access control enforcement facility (AEF) and an access control decision facility (ADF). ADF implements the system's mandatory security policies and a metapolicy

202

to decide whether processes' requests satisfy these security policies. AEF uses the ADF-decisions to implement the access operations.

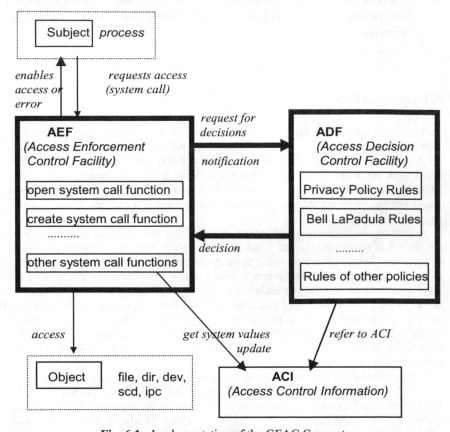

Fig. 6.1: Implementation of the GFAC Concept

In our GFAC system, the access control system of the Linux system kernel is divided into the AEF and ADF components and the ACI-module, which administrates Access Control Information (ACI, e.g. security attributes). Figure 6.1 shows the interactions between the system components. For each security-relevant system call, e.g. if a process requests to access an object (file, directory (dir), device (dev), security control data (scd) or interprocess communication data (ipc)), or if a process wants to clone itself or to send a signal, AEF sends a decision request to ADF. Parameters of the decision request are the request type, describing the desired type of functionality, the identification of the calling process and possibly the identifications of one or more targets of access. A target can be a subject or an object. ADF evaluates its privacy policy and its additional security policies by using the policy rules for the request type and the ACI needed for these rules. It then evaluates its metapolicy, which uses the decisions of the different security policies to finally decide about the process's request. AEF then enforces the decision, by either performing the system call functionality and setting the attributes accordingly, or returning an error to the calling process. Finally, control is returned to the process.

The GFAC project directed by Abrams motivated the Rule-Set Modelling approach, which is a new approach to formal modelling of a trusted computer system. In traditional security modelling approaches, the security model rules describe both access policy and system behaviour. For example, the get-access rule of the privacy model uses built-in criteria to decide whether to permit the request (Is the requested current access satisfying the privacy and information flow properties ?), and the rules describe the behaviour of the modelled system as a state transition (grant current access or return an error). The rule set modelling approach separates the decision criteria from the state transition. A rule set embodies the security policies of the modelled system, while a finite-state machine describes its behaviour.

Rule-Set Modelling is used in [LaPadula 1995] to model a trusted computer system designed according to the GFAC concept: AEF corresponds to a state machine model that targets the class of Unix System V systems. The state machine has a state transition rule for each Unix System V system call, which is an abstraction of the corresponding system call. ADF corresponds to the rule-set model and expresses the security policies of the modelled system in its rules of access.

6.2 The Specification of the Privacy Policy Rules Component

In [LaPadula 95], a state machine model and a rule set model expressing the Bell LaPadula-, the Clark Wilson as well as the FC- and SIM -policies were presented. These model specifications serve as top-level specifications of the corresponding AEF and ADF components that are both constituting a security kernel for a Unix System V system designed according to the GFAC-Approach. For the implementation of the privacy policy rules component it was necessary to extend and to further elaborate the draft specifications of the AEF and ADF components.

In order to integrate the privacy model to this system specification, the main tasks were

1. to specify the Access Control Information needed for the privacy model

2. to extend the AEF-specification with a specification of system operation functions for new system calls (*pm_change-current-task*, *pm_create_file* as well as all *pm_privileged_function* for all privileged functions) that are exclusively needed for the privacy model

3. to extend the definition of the interface between AEF and ADF to cover requests that relate to the functionality of the privacy model specific system calls

4. to add the specification of the privacy rules to the ADF-specification.

Furthermore, for the implementation in Linux it was necessary to extend the AEF-specification as well as the interface between AEF and ADF to cover Linux-specific security relevant system calls and requests that relate to their functionality.

6.2.1 Access Control Information (ACI)

The administration of Access Control Information (ACI) is implemented as an independent module (the so-called ACI module). A process and the user who is the owner of the process correspond to a subject in the security models. Files, directories, devices, system control data and interprocess communication objects, such as message queues, shared memory or sockets, correspond to objects. The ACI module is thus responsible for a reliable administration of security attributes of processes (process-ACI), of users (user-ACI) and of all resources that are needed and controlled by the security policies (object-ACI). Besides, it administrates other security relevant access control information, such as the lists of necessary accesses or of defined tasks and their security attributes.

In [Abrams et al. 90], ACI and ACC (access control context) information is differentiated by its associations with subjects and objects. ACI are characteristics or properties of subjects or objects. ACC is additional information, such as time of day, used in access control decisions, which is not directly associated to subjects or objects. However, ACC can be regarded as another kind of access control information. Thus, we use the term ACI (instead of ACC) also for access control context information.

Access to ACI is only possible by defined function calls. User-, process-, file-, device- and ipc-object-ACI can be stored in lists that are kept in main memory. Lists of user- and file- and device-ACI have to be kept on secondary storage memory at the same time. Storage format of user and file ACI on secondary storage is independent of the used file system.

Most of the ACI used by ADF to make access decisions correspond to the state variables of the privacy model. The Tables below list the access control information needed for the system specification and implementation of the privacy model, the corresponding variables of the privacy model and their value domains. Predefined values are printed in bold letters. ID is the abbreviation for identifier.

The ACI attributes that correspond to state variables of the privacy model can be explained by the meaning of their corresponding state variables. Additional ACI attributes with no direct correspondence in the privacy model are explained below.

Table 6.1: Access Control Information of users

User-ACI	Model variable	Values
authorised-tasks	AT	a list of task-IDs including **NIL**
role	role	**sec-officer, user, data-protection-officer, tp-manager, system-admin**

Table 6.2: Access Control Information of processes

Process-ACI	Model variable	Values
owner (pointer to user)		
transformation-procedure	CTP	a transformation-procedure-ID or **NIL**
current-task	CT	a task-ID or **NIL**
process-type		**NIL, TP**
Input-Purposes	Input-Purposes	a list of purpose-IDs
Output-Purposes	Output-Purposes	a list of purpose-IDs

Each Unix process points to a user who is the owner of the process. A process that is executing a transformation procedure is of the type TP. All other processes are of the type NIL.

Table 6.3: Access Control Information of objects

Object-ACI	Model variable	Values
class	class	an object-class-ID or **none**
transformation-procedure		a transformation-procedure-ID or **NIL**
object-type		**file, dir, ipc, scd, dev**
data-type		**NIL, TP, personal data, non-personal-data**

The object-type values defined for the specification of the privacy model are **file**, **dir** (directory), **dev** (device) **ipc** and **scd**. **file, dir** and **device** have their obvious Unix meanings. **ipc** means "inter process communication": message queues or shared memory in Unix System V or sockets in BSD Unix map to this type. **scd** means "system control data" (e.g., system time).

For objects of the type **file**, the data-type attribute is defined. The data-type value for a file containing personal data (which has a class value unequal to none) is **personal-data**. The data-type value for a file containing non-personal data (which has the class none) is **non-personal-data**. The data-type containing the executable code of a (certified) transformation procedure is **TP**. All other files (e.g., other executable programs) have the data-type **NIL**.

Table 6.4: Access Control Information of object classes

Object-class-ACI	Model variable	Values
purposes	O-Purpose	a list of purpose-IDs

Table 6.5: Further Access Control Information (not directly associated with other system elements)

Further ACI	Model variable	Values
Necessary-Accesses	NA	list with entries of the form (task-ID, class-ID, transformation-procedure-ID, access-right)
Consents	C	list with entries of the form (purpose-ID, object-ID)
Purpose-list	P	list of purpose-IDs
Task-list	T	list of task-Ids
Tickets	TKT	set of records of the form (ticket-ID, issuer, function-type, parameter-list, timestamp)
Object-Class-list	O-Class	list of object-class-Ids
Transformation-procedure-list	TRANS	list of transformation-procedure-IDs

The parameter list of tickets consists of components in dependence of the ticket's function-type.

Table 6.6: Access Control Information of tasks

Task-ACI	Model variable	Values
purpose	T-Purpose	a purpose-ID
authorised-TP	ATP	list of transformation-procedure-IDs including **NIL**
responsible	responsible	list of user-IDs

Table 6.7: Access Control Information of tickets

Ticket-ACI	Values
ticket-issuer	a user-ID
function-type	**add_authorised_tasks, delete_authorised_tasks, add_task, delete_task, add_NA, delete_NA add_purpose, delete_purpose, add_object-class, delete_object_class , add_authorised-TP, delete_authorised_TP, add_consent, delete_consent, add_responsible_user, delete_responsible_user, set-role, set-object-class, set-device-object-class**
parameter-list	(depending on the function-type)
timestamp	system time value (end of validity)

In addition to the ACI listed above, an **Open-Objects Table** with entries of the form (process-ID, object-ID, mode), can be defined as further access control context information needed to specify the privacy policy. This table shows, by process, the objects the process currently has open and the mode of the open (read, write, append, or read&write). This open-objects table corresponds to the set CA of current accesses in the privacy model. A data structure for the open-objects table as part of the ACI-module has not been implemented, since information about current accesses of processes to objects is stored and available in various data structures of the Unix system:

The information that a process has opened a file for a certain access mode is contained in an entry of the user file descriptor table in the u-area of a process and an entry in the global file table to which the user file descriptor table entry is pointing to. If a process opens a (personal data-) file, the kernel allocates an entry in the user file descriptor table (the private table of open files) in the u- area of a process and an entry in the global file table. The file descriptor that is returned to the user after the open-operation can be used as an index for the respective entry of the user file descriptor table, which points to the entry in the global file table. The global file table entry contains a pointer to the inode of the open file and a field that indicates the byte offset in the file where the kernel expects the next *read* or *write* operation to begin (see Figure 6.2). If the file is opened in *write-append* mode, the kernel initialises the offset to the size of the file and the offset cannot be changed to a lower value by the process.

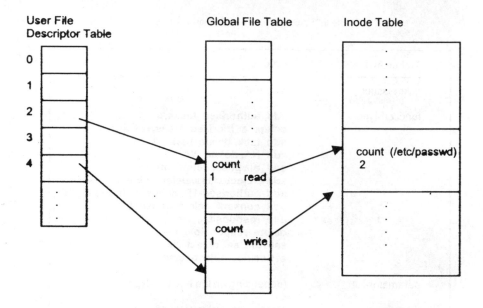

Fig. 6.2: Data Structures after Open system call indicating that a process has current read and current write access to /etc/passwd (see also [Bach 1986])

Information about current accesses to sockets can be obtained similarly. The socket system call creates a socket and returns a socket descriptor to the user, which is in the same name space as file desriptors. A socket descriptor indexes the array of open "files" in the u area of the process, and has a global file entry allocated for it. The global file entry points to a socket structure instead of an inode, which has a state field telling whether the socket is connected or unconnected. The chief difference between file descriptors and socket descriptors is that the operating system binds a file descriptor to a specific file or device with the open system call, but it can create sockets without binding them to specific destination addresses. Sockets used with connectionless datagram services need not be connected before they are used.

If a process has current access to a shared memory region (i.e. the region is attached to the virtual address space of the process), the private per process region table will have an entry with a pointer to the global region table entry of the shared memory region. The global region table entry contains the physical location of the region and information that the region type is shared memory. The per process region table entry contains the starting virtual address of the region in the process and also a permission field that indicates the type of access allowed to the process (read-only, read-write) (see Figure 6.3).

A current write (read) access to message queues means that a process is currently sending (receiving) a message by executing the msgsnd (msgrcv) system call. This information is contained in the kernel stack of the process. Since there is no system call for message queues that is roughly analogous to the open system call for files, there are no other data structures indicating that a process has current access to a message queue.

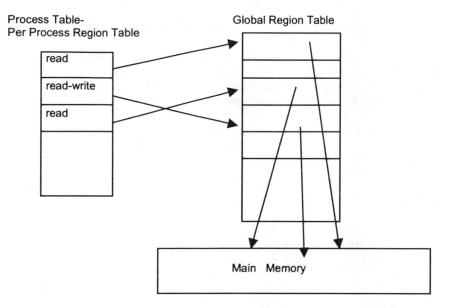

Fig. 6.3: Data Structures for Shared Memory after shmat system call indicating that a process has current accesses to shared memory regions

6.2.2 Access Control Enforcement Facility (AEF) and Its Interface to ADF

AEF is implemented by extending all security-relevant system call functions with ADF-requests. As described in [LaPadula 1995], the interface between AEF and ADF is defined by the desired action of the process and a set of relevant attributes (access control information).

The requests have the form: request "(" process [,target] {/target} {,argument} ")".

The *request* usually identifies the action that the process wants to do, but it can also identify a notification message from AEF to ADF. The argument *target* specifies the target which the requesting process wants to access and its associated attributes (access control information). A target of a request can be a process or a file, directory, device, interprocess communication (ipc) object and/or system control data (scd). Some requests are using further arguments (e.g., attribute values).

Table 6.8 that follows below lists requests that AEF can send to ADF, as well as Unix System V system calls that are using these requests. Linux-specific system calls (and particularly socket-specific system calls) are written in brackets in italic letters. This table is an extension and modification of lists of requests presented in [LaPadula 1995] and [Ott 1997]. For each security-relevant Unix System V or Linux system call, there is at least one ADF-request that relates to its functionality, but also further requests might be necessary. For example, the open system call has to be extended with ADF-requests for reading a directory, creating a directory/file, truncating a file and for append-/read-/write/read-write-opening a file.

Furthermore, AEF was extended with system calls that are exclusively needed for the privacy model (*pm_change_current_task*, *pm_create_file* as well as *pm_privileged_function* for all privileged privacy model functions) or for other security models. Consequently, some requests have no counterparts in the set of Unix system calls.

The system calls *pm_change_current_task* and *pm_create_file* realise the state transition functions change-current-task and create-object of the privacy model. The *pm_privileged_function* system call realises all privileged privacy model functions. The system call *pm_privileged_function* has the desired privileged function, a list of parameters needed for this function and, if necessary, a ticket identifier as parameters.

For all privacy model specific system calls, the rules of operations are specified as a part of the AEF kernel and the rules of access are specified as a part of the ADF kernel. One might argue that an AEF-ADF partitioning of the privacy model specific system calls is not necessary, because these system calls are exclusively needed for the privacy model (consider that the AEF-ADF partitioning of system calls shall make the configuration of different security policies feasible). Therefore, in another approach the privacy model-specific system calls could be implemented by functions that are a part of ADF and are enforcing both the access policy as well as the system behaviour as a part of ADF. However, our approach is consistent with the GFAC view and supports a subsequent integration of other models that are enforcing further privacy rules.

Table 6.9 lists all requests from AEF to ADF that are needed for the privacy model specific system calls. In Table 6.9 and in the following sections, the arguments or parameters task, class, purpose, transformation-procedure, user-id and role specify identifiers for a task, an object-class, a purpose, a transformation procedure, a user and a user-role.

Table 6.8: List of requests from AEF to ADF

Request:	Description of requested action:	Unix System system calls:
ADD-TO-KERNEL (process, file)	add a kernel module to the kernel	*(Linux-specific)*
ALTER (process, ipc)	modify control data of an ipc-type object	msgctl(), shmctl(),
APPEND-OPEN (process, file/ ipc)	open a file/ ipc-object to append data	msgsnd(), open(), *(sendto (), sendmsg())*
CHANGE-GROUP (process, process / file/ ipc/ dir)	change the group of a file, directory, ipc-object or process	setgid(), setpgrp(), shmctl(), msgctl()
CHANGE-OWNER (process, process/ file/ dir /ipc)	change the owner or group of a file or directory or change the owner of a process or ipc-object	chown(), setuid(), shmctl(), msgctl()
CHDIR (process, directory)	change current directory	chdir()
CLONE (process1, process2)	process1 wants to create a clone of itself. (process2)	fork()
CLOSE (process, file/ directory/ ipc)	object was closed (notification message from AEF to ADF)	close(), shmdt(), msgrcv(), msgsnd(), *(sentto (), recvfrom(), shutdown())*
CREATE (process, file/ dir/ scd/ ipc)	create a new object	creat(), mknod(), open(), shmget(), msgget(), *(socket(), accept())*
DELETE (process, file/ directory/ scd/ipc)	delete the indicated object	unlink(), msgctl(), shmctl(), *(close())*
EXECUTE (process, file)	execute the file	exec()
GET-PERMISSION-DATA (process, file/ directory / scd/ ipc)	read discretionary access permissions for the indicated object	access()
GET-STATUS-DATA (process, file/ directory/ scd/ ipc)	read status data about the indicated object	stat(), fstat(), ustat(), msgctl(), shmctl()
LINK-HARD (process, file)	create a hard link (alias) for the file	link()
MODIFY-ACCESS-DATA (process, file/ directory)	modify access information for the object	utime()
MODIFY-ATTRIBUTE (process, user/ process/ file/ directory/ ipc, attribute, value)	modify an attribute of the user, the process or an object	*(specific request needed for various security models)*
MODIFY-PERMISSION-DATA (process, scd)	change discrete access rights	chmod()
MODIFY-SYSTEM-DATA(process, scd)	modify system data, e.g. time	stime()
MOUNT(process, dev/ directory)	mount file system to a specified directory	mount()
READ (process, directory)	read data from the indicated directory	read()

READ-ATTRIBUTE (process, user/ process/ file/ directory/ ipc, attribute)	read an attribute of the user, the process or an object	*(GFAC internal)*
READ&WRITE-OPEN (process, file/ipc/dev)	open the object for reading or writing	open(), shmat(), mount(), *(connect(), listen())*
READ-OPEN (process, file/ipc/directory/dev)	open the object for reading	open(), shmat(), msgrcv(), mount(), *(recvfrom, recvmsg())*
REMOVE-FROM-KERNEL (process)	remove kernel module	*(Linux-specific)*
RENAME (process, file/ directory)	rename a file or directory	*(rename())*
SEARCH (process, directory)	read the directory requested by AEF	*(internal kernel request)*
SEND-SIGNAL (process1, process2)	send signal to process2	kill()
SHUTDOWN (process)	shutdown of the system	*reboot()*
SWITCH-LOG (process)	switch logging for ADF module on or off	*(GFAC internal)*
SWITCH-MODULE (process)	switch ADF module on or off	*(GFAC internal)*
TERMINATE (process)	inform ADF that the system has terminated the process	exit()
TRACE (process1, process2)	process1 wants to trace process2	ptrace()
TRUNCATE (process, file)	delete all data in the file	open()
UMOUNT (process, dir/dev)	unmount the filesystem	umount()
WRITE (process, dir)	write data to the directory	creat()
WRITE-OPEN (process, file/dev)	open the file or device for writing	open()

A distinction is made between *read* and *read-open* and between *write* and *write-open*. Read-open (write-open) enables the process to *read* (*write*) the object, whereas *read* (*write*) actually transfers data from (to) the open object into (from) the memory space of the process. The privacy policy for controlling read (write) access (like the Bell-LaPadula-, FC-and SIM-Policy specified in [LaPadula 95]) applies at the read-open (write-open). However, no operations of the ipc mechanisms for message queues and shared memory are equivalent to the file open and close system calls. The *msgget* and *shmget* system calls are similar to the *creat* and *open* system call, because they return a kernel-chosen descriptor for use in other system calls. Nevertheless, even if a process never did a "get" call, it can access an ipc message mechanism, if it guesses the correct ID and if access permissions are suitable.

For consistency, we extend the *msgsnd* system call with an append-open and a close ADF-request, although *msgsnd* is actually more analogous to the actual write operation. Similarly, *msgrev* system call is extended with a read-open and a close ADF request.

Also socket system calls do not strictly follow the traditional Unix open-read-write-close paradigm. The *connect* system call, which binds a permanent destination to a socket, and the *listen* system call correspond to the open system call. However, sockets used with connectionless datagram services need not be connected before they are used, if a destination is specified for each data transfer. Thus, for consistency the system calls *sendto* and *sendmsg*, which both allow the caller to send a message through an unconnected socket, are extended with append-open and close ADF-requests. Similarly, the system calls *recvfrom* and *recvmsg* are extended with read-open and close ADF-requests.

The *shmat* and *shmdt* system calls for attaching and detaching of shared memory to the virtual address space of a process are in a way analogous to the file *open* and *close* system calls. The shmat system call has to be called before a process can access shared memory, much as the *open* system call has to be executed before a process has access to a file. After attaching a shared memory, it becomes part of the virtual address space of the process and can be accessed. Note that, however, in contrast to the *open* system call for files, after the *shmat* system call, no system calls are needed to access data in shared memory, which are accessible in the same way as other virtual addresses are.

Table 6.9: List of requests from AEF to ADF for Privacy Policy specific system calls

Request:	Description of requested action:	privacy model specific system call:
CHANGE-TASK (process, task)	change the current task of the owner of the process	pm_change_current_task()
CREATE-PERS-DATA (process, file, class)	create personal data of a certain class	pm_create_file()
CREATE-TICKET (process, function-type, parameter-list)	create a ticket for a privileged function with specified parameters	pm_privileged_function
ADD-NA (process, task, class, transformation-procedure, access-right, ticket-ID)	add a necessary access entry to the list of necessary accesses	pm_privileged_function
DELETE-NA (process, task, class, transformation-procedure, access-right, ticket-ID)	delete a necessary access entry from the list of necessary accesses	pm_privileged_function
ADD-TASK (process, task, purpose, ticket-ID)	add task with the specified purpose to the list of tasks	pm_privileged_function
DELETE-TASK (process, task, ticket-ID)	delete task from the list of tasks	pm_privileged_function
ADD-OBJECT-CLASS (process, class, purpose-set, ticket-ID)	add class with purposes purpose-set to the list of object-classes	pm_privileged_function
DELETE-OBJECT-CLASS (process, class, ticket-ID	delete class from the list of object classes	pm_privileged_function

ADD-AUTH-TP (process, task, transformation-procedure, ticket-ID)	add transformation-procedure to the list of authorised TPs of task	pm_privileged_function
DELETE-AUTH-TP (process, task, transformation-procedure, ticket-ID)	delete transformation-procedure from the list of authorised TPs of task	pm_privileged_function
ADD-CONSENT (process, file-name, purpose, ticket-ID)	add the entry (file-name, purpose) to the list of consents	pm_privileged_function
DELETE-CONSENT (process, file-name, purpose, ticket-ID)	delete entry (file-name, purpose) from the list of consents	pm_privileged_function
ADD-PURPOSE (process, purpose, ticket-ID)	add purpose to the list of purposes	pm_privileged_function
ADD-RESP-USERS (process, user-id, task, ticket-ID)	add user-id to the list of responsible users for task	pm_privileged_function
DELETE-RESP-USERS (process, user-id, task, ticket-ID)	delete user-id from the list of responsible users for task	pm_privileged_function
SET-ROLE (process, user-id, role, ticket-ID)	define the role of a user	pm_privileged_function
ADD-AUTH-TASK (process, user-id, task, ticket-ID)	authorise a user for a task	pm_privileged_function
DELETE-AUTH-TASK (process, user-id, task, ticket-ID)	revoke authorisation of a user for a task	pm_privileged_function
SET-OBJECT-CLASS (process, file, class, ticket-ID)	change object class of an object	pm_privileged_function
SET-DEV-OBJECT-CLASS (process, dev, class, ticket_ID)	change/define object class of a device	pm_privileged_function
CREATE-TP (process, transformation-procedure)	define an identifier for a transformation procedure	pm_privileged_function
DELETE-TP (process, transformation-procedure)	delete an identifier for a transformation procedure	pm_privileged_function
SET-TP (process, file, transformation-procedure)	define an executable file as a transformation procedure	pm_privileged_function

AEF consists of all security-relevant Unix system call functions and all privacy model-specific system call functions that are extended with ADF-requests. In each security relevant system call of the AEF-kernel, the ADF-kernel is requested, usually after the discretionary access control conditions have been checked. If the decision of the ADF-kernel is negative, the operation of the system call will not be performed.

The Unix System V system calls were defined by Bach [Bach 86]. In [LaPadula 95], a draft state machine model specification was given, that served as a top level specification of the corresponding AEF-kernel.

For our implementation, this specification was extended and slightly modified. The reader, who is interested in the specification of Unix system calls, should refer to [LaPadula 95]. In this Chapter, it is only specified how the privacy model can be implemented according to the GFAC-approach. Therefore, in the following Section the AEF specification of the privacy policy-specific system calls will be presented.

In the top-level specification that follows, we use a specification language and model constructs, which are defined in the Appendix A of [LaPadula 1995]. The specification language uses a mixture of programming language statements and limited mathematical notation and is supposed to be intuitively understandable to a broad audience. Please refer to [LaPadula 1995] for a definition and description of the specification language.

For the specification of decision parts the privacy model specific system calls, an additional construct for a boolean expression was defined:

> **FOR-ALL** variable: type:
> [boolean-expression]

This construct has the value TRUE if the inner boolean expression is true for all entities of the specified type.

The brackets ⌈ and ⌋ are used to define begin and end of a block statement.

AEF specification of the privacy policy-specific system call functions:

- **pm_change_current_task**(task). The pm_change_current_task system call is used to change the current task of a process.

  IF Access-Rules(change-task, current_process, task)
  (* check if the owner of the current process is authorised for the task and if the current process is not performing a TP *)
  THEN
        (* set current_task (current_process) = task *)
        set-attributes;
        normal-exit;
  ELSE
        error-exit;

- **pm_create_file**(file_name, class). The pm_create_file system call is used to create a personal data file of a specified class.

  IF NOT(STATUS(class == "exist")
  THEN
        error-exit;
  IF STATUS(file_name) == "unused" (* the directory search was valid and the file does not exist *)
  THEN
        save; (* save the attribute values of current-process, file-name and directory *)
        IF Access-Rules (create, current_process, file_name) (*check if the process may create a new file in the system *)
        THEN
              set-attributes;
              IF Access-Rules (create-pers-data, current_process, file_name, class)
              (* check if the process may create a personal data file of the specified class *)
              THEN
                    set-attributes;
                    IF Access-Rules (write, current_process, directory)
                    (* check if it is permissible to write to the relevant directory - directory is found by the namei kernel subroutine in Unix *)
                    THEN
                        set-attributes;
                        IF Access-Rules (write-open, current-process, file-name) (* check if it is allowed

                                                                    to write open the file *)
THEN

                                        set-attributes;
                                        [* create the file with appropriate
                                            directory entry and write-open it *];
ELSE

                                        restore (*restore the attribute values
                                                of current_process,
                                                file_name, and directory *)
                                        error-exit;
            ELSE

                                restore;
                                error-exit;
        ELSE

                        restore;
                        error-exit;
    ELSE

                error-exit;
ELSE

        error-exit;

* **pm_privileged_function** (function, parameters, ticket-id). The system call pm_privileged_function is used to implement all privileged functions of the privacy model. It has the desired function, a list of parameters needed for this function and, if necessary, a ticket identifier as parameters. The AEF part checks if the specified parameters are referring to existing objects or ACI items. Furthermore, if a ticket is used, it will be checked whether the specified privileged function type corresponds to the ticket-function type, and whether the parameters of the privileged function corresponds to the ticket parameters.

SELECT CASE   function
    CASE create-ticket   (* parameters are: function-type, parameter-list, ticket-id *)
                IF (STATUS (ticket-id) =="exist")
                THEN
                        error-exit;
                IF Access-Rules (create-ticket, current_process, function-type,
                                        parameter-list)
                THEN
                        [* create ticket with ticket-id and components:
                            issuer = currrent_process, function-type, parameter-list *];
                        normal-exit;
                ELSE
                        error exit;
    CASE add-NA (*parameters are: task, class, transformation-procedure,
                        access-right, ticket-id *)
                IF NOT(STATUS (task) == "exist" **AND**
                                STATUS (class) == "exist" **AND**

                STATUS (transformation-procedure) == "exist" **AND**
                STATUS (ticket-id) == "exist")

THEN
      error-exit;
IF NOT (ticket.function-type is add-NA **AND**
      Task == ticket.task **AND**
      Class == ticket.class **AND**
      transformation-procedure == ticket.transformation-procedure
      AND access-right== ticket.access-right)
THEN
      error-exit;
IF Access-Rules (add-NA, current_process, task, class,
                transformation-procedure, access-right, ticket-id)
THEN
      [* add (task, class, transformation-procedure, access-right)
      to Necessary-Accesses; delete ticket *]
      normal-exit;
ELSE
      error-exit;
CASE delete-NA (*parameters are: task, class, transformation-procedure,
                access-right, ticket-id*)
    IF NOT(STATUS (task) == "exist" **AND**
                STATUS (class) == "exist" **AND**
                STATUS (transformation-procedure) == "exist" **AND**
                STATUS (ticket-id) == "exist")
THEN
      error-exit;
IF NOT (ticket.function-type is delete-NA **AND**
      task == ticket.task **AND**
      class == ticket.class **AND**
      transformation-procedure == ticket.transformation-procedure
      AND access-right == ticket.access-right)
THEN
      error-exit;
IF Access-Rules (delete-NA, current_process, task, class,
                transformation-procedure, access-right, ticket-id)
THEN
      [* delete (task, class, transformation-procedure, access-right)
      from Necessary-Accesses; delete ticket *];
      normal-exit;
ELSE
      error-exit;
CASE add-task (* parameters are: task, purpose, ticket-id *)
    IF NOT(STATUS(task) =="unused" **AND**
                STATUS (purpose) == "exist" **AND**
                STATUS (ticket-id) == "exist")
THEN

```
                    error-exit;
        IF NOT(ticket.function-type is add-task AND
                task == ticket.task AND
                purpose == ticket.purpose)
        THEN
                error-exit;
        IF Access-Rules (add-task, current_process, task, purpose, ticket-id)
        THEN
                        [* add task with the task-ACI purpose(task) = purpose to the
                list of  task-IDs;  delete ticket *];
                normal-exit;
        ELSE
                error-exit;
CASE delete-task  (* parameters are:  task, ticket-id *)
        IF NOT( STATUS (task) == "exist" AND
                        STATUS (ticket-id) == "exist")
        THEN
                error-exit;
        IF NOT(ticket.function-type is delete-task AND
                task == ticket.task)
        THEN
                error-exit;
        IF Access-Rules (delete-task, current_process, task, ticket-id)
        THEN
                        [* delete task-ID from the list of task-IDs*];
                FOR-EACH necessary-accesses-entry
                        IF task is component of necessary-accesses-entry
                        THEN
                                [* delete necessary-accesses-entry *]
                END-FOR-EACH;
                [* delete ticket *];
                normal-exit;
        ELSE
                error-exit;
CASE add-object-class  (* parameters are: class, purpose, ticket-id *)
        IF NOT( STATUS (class) == "unused" AND
                        STATUS (purpose) == "exist" AND
                        STATUS (ticket-id) == "exist")
        THEN
                error-exit;
        IF NOT( ticket.function-type is add-object-class AND
                class == ticket.class AND
                purpose == ticket.purpose)
        THEN
                error-exit;
          IF Access-Rules (add-object-class, current_process, class,
                                    purpose, ticket-id)
```

THEN

      [* add class with the object-class-ACI
      purposes(class) = purpose to the list of object-class-IDs;
      delete ticket *];
      normal-exit;

ELSE

      error-exit;

CASE delete-object-class (* parameters are: class, ticket-id *)
    IF NOT(STATUS (class) == "exist" **AND**
           STATUS (ticket-id) == "exist")

THEN

      error-exit;

    IF NOT(ticket.function-type is delete-object-class **AND**
        class == ticket.class **AND**

THEN

      error-exit;

     IF Access-Rules (delete-object-class, current_process, class,
                 ticket-id)

THEN

      [* delete class-ID from the list of object-class-IDs *]
      FOR-EACHnecessary-access-entry
         IF object-class is component of necessary-access-entry
         THEN
              [* delete necessary-accesses-entry *]
      END-FOR-EACH
      [* delete ticket *];
      normal-exit;

ELSE

      error-exit;

CASE add-authorised-TP (* parameters are: task, transformation-procedure,
                 ticket-id *)
    IF NOT(STATUS (task) == "exist" **AND**
           STATUS(transformation-procedure) == "exist" **AND**
           STATUS (ticket-id) == "exist")

THEN

      error-exit;

    IF NOT(ticket.function-type is add-authorised-TP **AND**
        task == ticket.task **AND**
        transformation-procedure == ticket.transformation-procedure)

THEN

      error-exit;

     IF Access-Rules (add-authorised-TP, current_process, task,
                 transformation-procedure, ticket-id)

THEN

      [* add ticket.transformation-procedure to the task-ACI
       authorised-TP of ticket.task; delete ticket *];
      normal-exit;

ELSE
  error-exit;
CASE delete-authorised-TP (* parameters are: task, transformation-procedure,
               ticket-id *)
  IF NOT(STATUS (task) == "exist" **AND**
        STATUS(transformation-procedure) == "exist" **AND**
        STATUS (ticket-id) == "exist")
  THEN
    error-exit;
  IF NOT(ticket.function-type is delete-authorised-TP **AND**
    task == ticket.task **AND**
    transformation-procedure == ticket.transformation-procedure)
  THEN
    error-exit;
  IF Access-Rules (delete-authorised-TP, current_process, task,
         transformation-procedure, ticket-id)
  THEN
    [* delete transformation-procedure from the task-ACI
     authorised-TP of ticket.task; delete ticket *];
    normal-exit;
  ELSE
    error-exit;
CASE add-consent (* parameters are: file-name, purpose, ticket-id *)
  IF NOT(STATUS (file-name) == "exist" **AND**
       STATUS(purpose) == "exist" **AND**
       STATUS (ticket-id) == "exist")
  THEN
    error-exit;
   IF NOT(ticket.function-type is add-consent **AND**
    file(identified by file-name) == file (identified by ticket.file-name)
    AND purpose == ticket.purpose)
  THEN
    error-exit;
   IF Access-Rules (add-consent, current_process, file-name, purpose,
        ticket-id)
  THEN
    [* add (purpose, file-name) to the consents-list;
     delete ticket *];
    normal-exit;
  ELSE
    error-exit;
CASE delete-consent (file-name, purpose, ticket-id)
  IF NOT(STATUS (file-name) == "exist" **AND**
       STATUS(purpose) == "exist" **AND**
       STATUS (ticket-id) == "exist")
  THEN
    error-exit;

```
         IF NOT (ticket.function-type is delete-consent AND
                    file (identified by file-name)  == file (identified by ticket.file-name)
                    AND purpose  == ticket.purpose)
         THEN
                    error-exit;
            IF Access-Rules (delete-consent, current_process, file-name, purpose,
                        ticket-id)
         THEN
                    [* delete (purpose, file-name) from the consents-list;
                        delete ticket *];
                    normal-exit;
         ELSE
                    error-exit;
    CASE add-purpose  (* parameters are: purpose, ticket-id *)
         IF NOT ( STATUS(purpose) =="unused" AND
                            STATUS (ticket-id) == "exist")
         THEN
                    error-exit;
         IF NOT (ticket.function-type is add-purpose AND
                    purpose  == ticket.purpose)
         THEN
                    error-exit;
            IF Access-Rules (add-purpose, current_process, purpose, ticket-id)
         THEN
                    [* add purpose-ID to the list of purpose-IDs;
                        add default_class(purpose) to Object-Class-list;
                        delete ticket *];
                    (* default-class is defined below *)
                    normal-exit;
         ELSE
                    error-exit;
    CASE delete-purpose  (* parameters are: purpose, ticket-id *)
         IF NOT ( STATUS(purpose) == "exist" AND
                            STATUS (ticket-id) == "exist")
         THEN
                    error-exit;
         IF NOT (ticket.function-type is delete-purpose AND
                    purpose  == ticket.purpose)
         THEN
                    error-exit;

            IF Access-Rules (delete-purpose, current_process, purpose, ticket-id)
         THEN
                    [* delete purpose-ID from the list of purpose-IDs;
                        delete default-class(purpose) from the list of object-class-IDs;
                        delete ticket *];
                    normal-exit;
```

ELSE
      error-exit;
CASE add-responsible-users (* parameters are: user-id, task, ticket-id *)
    IF NOT(STATUS(task) == "exist" **AND**
                 STATUS (ticket-id) == "exist")
    THEN
      error-exit;
    IF NOT(ticket.function-type is add-responsible-users **AND**
        user-id == ticket.user-id **AND**
        (task == ticket.task)
    THEN
      error-exit;
      IF Access-Rules (add-responsible-users, current_process, user-id, task,
                    ticket-id)
    THEN
         [* add responsible(task) = user-id to the task-ACI
        responsible(task);   delete ticket *];
        normal-exit;
    ELSE
      error-exit;
CASE delete-responsible-users (* parameters are: user-id, task, ticket-id *)
    IF NOT(STATUS(task) == "exist" **AND**
                 STATUS (ticket-id) == "exist")
    THEN
      error-exit;
    IF NOT(ticket.function-type is delete-responsible-users **AND**
        user-id == ticket.user-id **AND**
        task == ticket.task)
    THEN
      error-exit;
      IF Access-Rules (delete-responsible-users, current_process, user-id,
                task, ticket-id)
    THEN
         [* delete user-id from the task-ACI responsible(task);
          delete ticket *];
         normal-exit;
    ELSE
      error-exit;
CASE set-role (* parameters are: user-id, role, ticket-id *)
    IF NOT(STATUS (role) == "exist" **AND**
                 STATUS (ticket-id) == "exist")
    THEN
      error-exit;
    IF NOT(ticket.function-type is set-role **AND**
        user-id == ticket.user-id **AND**
        role == ticket.role)
    THEN

```
                    error-exit;
          IF Access-Rules (set-role, current_process, user-id, role, ticket-id)
          THEN
                         [* set role(user-id) = role;  delete ticket *];
                         normal-exit;
          ELSE
                         error-exit;
   CASE add-authorised-task  (* parameters are: task, user-id, ticket-id *)
          IF NOT( STATUS (task) == "exist" AND
                         STATUS (ticket-id) == "exist")
          THEN
                         error-exit;
          IF NOT  (ticket.function-type is add-authorised-task AND
                   task  == ticket.task AND
                   user-id  == ticket.user-id
          THEN
                         error-exit;
            IF Access-Rules (add-authorised-task, current_process, task, user-id,
                            ticket-id)
          THEN
                         [* add task to the list of authorised-tasks of
                            user-id;  delete ticket *];
                         normal-exit;
          ELSE
                         error-exit;
   CASE delete-authorised-task  (* parameters are: task, user-id, ticket-id *)
          IF NOT( STATUS (task) == "exist" AND
                         STATUS (ticket-id) == "exist")
          THEN
                         error-exit;
          IF NOT(ticket.function-type is add-authorised-task AND
                  task  == ticket.task AND
                  user-id  == ticket.user-id
          THEN
                         error-exit;
            IF Access-Rules (delete-authorised-task, current_process, task, user-id,
                            ticket-id)
          THEN
                         [* delete task from the list of authorised-tasks of
                            user-id; delete ticket *];
                         normal-exit;
          ELSE
                         error-exit;
   CASE set-object-class (* parameters are: file-name, class, ticket-id *)
          IF NOT( STATUS (file-name) == "exist" AND
                   STATUS (class) = "exist" AND
                      STATUS (ticket-id) == "exist")
```

225

THEN
　　　　error-exit;
IF NOT(ticket.function-type is set-object-class **AND**
　　　　file(identified by file-name) == ticket.file(identified by file-name)
AND

　　　　class == ticket.class)
THEN
　　　　error-exit;

　　　IF Access-Rules (set-object-class, current_process, file-name, class,
　　　　　　ticket-id)
THEN
　　　　set-attributes;
　　　　[* delete ticket *];
　　　　normal-exit;
ELSE
　　　　error-exit;
CASE set-dev-object-class (* parameters are: device-name, class, ticket-id *)
　　　IF NOT　　(STATUS (device-name) == "exist" **AND**
　　　　　　STATUS (class) = "exist" **AND**
　　　　　　STATUS (ticket-id) == "exist")
THEN
　　　　error-exit;
IF NOT(ticket.function-type is set-dev-object-class **AND**
　　　　device(identified by device-name) ==
　　　　ticket.device(identified by device-name) **AND**
　　　　class == ticket.class)
THEN
　　　　error-exit;
　　　IF Access-Rules (set-dev-object-class, current_process, device-name,
class, ticket-id)
THEN
　　　　set-attributes;
　　　　[* delete ticket *];
　　　　normal-exit;
ELSE
　　　　error-exit;
CASE create-TP-ID (* parameter: transformation-procedure *);
　　　IF NOT　　(STATUS (transformation-procedure) == "unused"
THEN
　　　　error-exit;
　　　IF Access-Rules (create-TP-ID, current_process,
　　　transformation-procedure)
THEN
　　　　[* add transformation-procedure-id to the list TRANS *];
　　　　normal-exit;
ELSE

```
                            error-exit;
CASE delete-TP-ID (* parameter: transformation-procedure*);
        IF NOT( STATUS (transformation-procedure) == "exist")
        THEN
                            error-exit;
            IF Access-Rules (delete-TP-ID, current_process, transformation-
                            procedure)
        THEN
                    [* delete transformation-procedure-id from the list TRANS *]
                    FOR-EACHfile:
                            IF transformation-procedure(file) ==
                            transformation-procedure
                            THEN
                                    [* set transformation-procedure(file) = NIL;
                                    set data-type (file) = NIL *]
                    END-FOR-EACH
                    FOR-EACHNecessary-Accesses entry:
                            IF transformation-procedure is component of the
                                    Necessary-Accesses entry
                            THEN
                                    [* delete Neccessary accesses entry, *]
                    END-FOR-EACH
                        FOR-EACHtask
                            IF transformation-procedure is element of the list
                                    authorised-TP(task)
                            THEN
                                    [* delete transformation-procedure-id from
                                    the list   authorised-TP(task) *]
                        END-FOR-EACH;
                    normal-exit;
        ELSE
                    error-exit;
CASE set-TP (* parameters are: file-name, transformation-procedure *);
        IF NOT(STATUS(transformation-procedure =="exist" AND
                    STATUS (file-name) == "exist")
        THEN
                    error-exit;
        IF Access-Rules(set-TP, file-name, transformation-procedure *)
        THEN
                    [* set transformation-procedure(file) to transformation-procedure*]
                    normal-exit;
        ELSE
                    error-exit;

END-SELECT
```

6.2.3 Access Control Decision Facility (ADF)

The ADF component is implemented as an independent module and receives access requests from AEF. The access requests are evaluated by the rules of the different policies (privacy policy, Bell-LaPadula policy, FC- and SIM policy among others). Each policy is implemented as one or more rules. A metarule is using the policy decisions to evaluate the overall access decision.

Following LaPadula's approach, each rule is an expression having one of four values (see [LaPadula 95, p.219]):

- **YES.** This value means the request has been evaluated by the rule and the result is that the request may be granted according to the rule's policy.

- **NO.** This value means the request has been evaluated by the rule and the result is that the request may not be granted according to the rule's policy.

- **DC.** This value means that the request has been recognised by the rule. The rule's policy is tolerant to the request in the sense that the policy "does not care" (DC).

- **UNDEFINED.** This value means that the request has been recognised by the rule, but the rule-set model is not cognisant of the request. This return value can help to detect improper configurations of the system.

In addition, a rule may specify an effect that will occur if the request of the process is ultimately acted on by the AEF kernel. Since all effects are changes to attribute values, an effect is specified in the form

   set-attribute(attribute name, attribute value).

In our system specification, we use a metarule defined in [LaPadula 95,p.220], which evaluates the overall access decision by combining the results of the policy rules with the binary operator (+) (pronounced "and plus") defined in Table 6.10.

Table 6.10: Definition of the binary operator (+) [LaPadula 95, p. 220]

A	B	A (+) B
YES	YES	YES
YES	NO	NO
YES	DC	YES
YES	UNDEFINED	UNDEFINED
NO	YES	NO
NO	NO	NO
NO	DC	NO
NO	UNDEFINED	UNDEFINED
DC	YES	YES
DC	NO	NO
DC	DC	DC

DC	UNDEFINED	UNDEFINED
UNDEFINED	YES	UNDEFINED
UNDEFINED	NO	UNDEFINED
UNDEFINED	DC	UNDEFINED
UNDEFINED	UNDEFINED	UNDEFINED

The Access-Rules function of ADF, which enforces the metarule, is defined as

Access-Rules (request[input argument], process/object[input argument], ...,
process/object[input argument]):
function-value= PM (+) BLP (+) FC (+) SIM;
IF function-value= UNDEFINED
THEN
    record('undefined request:', request[input argument],
process/object[input argument], ..., process/object[input argument])
return(NOT_GRANTED)
ELSE
return (**function-value**);

where PM, BLP, FC, SIM stand for the return values of the rules of the privacy-, Bell
LaPadula-, FC-, and the SIM-policy.

A policy rule can be specified with a Case-statement.

SELECT CASE request
  CASE request, request,.., request
    statement block
      *
      *
  CASE request, request,.., request
    statement block
END-SELECT

where requests stand for the different access-requests that are sent by AEF .

In [LaPadula 95], representative CASEs for the Bell LaPadula-, Clark Wilson-,
FC-, SIM-policies are given to illustrate the modelling approach.
In the following Section, a complete rule set implementing the privacy model
policy is presented.

Specification of the Privacy Policy Rules:

The specification that follows below is defining the decision criteria of the privacy policy for a Unix system environment. For each privacy model-relevant request it is checked if this request is in accordance with the privacy policy.

Besides, for most requests (also for those not relevant for the privacy model), it is checked if a proper target has been specified. If this is not the case, the return value UNDEFINED can indicate an improper system configuration.

Access restrictions also have to be defined for some requests that do not have any counterpart in the set of state transition functions of the privacy model. For example, for a reliable support and administration of the privacy policy it is necessary to restrict the execution of some actions (modify-system-data, mount, umount, add-to-kernel, remove-from-kernel, shutdown) to the system administrator.

Furthermore, the following additional constraints are needed to support the intent of the privacy policy in a Unix environment (note that similar restrictions are defined by [LaPadula 95] to support the Clark Wilson model) :

- Changing ownership of TPs and personal data is not allowed.

- Aliasing (via the *link* system call in Unix) of TPs and personal data is not allowed, because by aliasing, the attempt to remove the object from the system could be defeated.

- Tracing (via the *ptrace* system call in Unix) of TPs is not allowed, since tracing would enable modification of a TP during its execution.

- Only a user in the role TP-manager may modify status information about TPs.

- A TP-type process is not allowed to clone (Unix fork). Allowing a TP-type process to spawn another TP-type process would require unwarranted complex coordination between parent and child to preserve integrity and would mean a more complex certification of the original TP code, but would not add functional capability. However, for concurrent processing user-level threads could be used within TP-type processes.

- A TP-type process is allowed to receive a signal from a non-TP-type process. Allowing signalling preserves functionality, but could enable that the TP-type process could be killed at such a time that the personal data on which it was operating would be left in an invalid state. TPs should therefore be designed to take appropriate action on the personal data before exiting. Besides, we further restrict the ability to kill TP-type processes by demanding that only processes running on behalf of the TP-manager may send kill-signals to TP-processes.

In order to implement the state transition function *create-object* defined as part of the privacy model, the *pm_create_file* system call can be used to create personal data files. The class of the new file has to be specified as a parameter.

In order to preserve functionality with the Unix system, it should be allowed for a TP-type process to create an object also by using the ordinary Unix *creat* (create) system call. If a TP-type process creates a file or an ipc-object, these objects have to be treated as personal data to prevent illegal information flow. However, if the ordinary *creat* system call is invoked, no object class for the new file or ipc-type object can be specified as a parameter.

Therefore, for each purpose p_j a unique default-class with the purpose p_j is defined, with: purposes(default-class(p_j)) = p_j.

If a TP-type process is creating a file or ipc-type object by using the ordinary *creat* system call, the object-class of the new object will be set to the default-class of the purpose of the processes' current task. Consequently, the new object can later only be used for the purpose for that it was created. However, the privileged *pm_privileged_function*system call with the function set-object-class can later be used to change the object class, for example, in case the object should also be used for other purposes.

For ipc-type objects, consents by data subjects cannot be defined and consequently, consents are not checked for ipc-type objects.

Analogously, consents are not defined and not checked for devices. The privacy properties of necessity of data processing, purpose binding and the information flow control property is only checked for block devices and character devices such as tapes. Character devices such as terminals, sound cards or printers have by default the object-class "dev-trusted", which means that the privacy policy will grant access to them. Access to block devices (and to tapes), however, has to be controlled, because it has to be prevented that a user can directly read- or write-access personal data on unmounted devices. Devices with a class unequal to "dev-trusted" should contain only objects of that class. This principle has to be enforced also by organisational measures.

In the specification, the following predicates mean:

Necessary (task, class, transformation-procedure, right) <=> (task, class, transformation-procedure, right) is element of the list of Necessary-Accesses.
Purpose-binding(task, class) <=> Purpose(task) is element of Purposes(class).
Consent(task, object) <=> (purpose(task), object-id) is element of the consents list.

The Privacy Rules:

SELECT CASE request:

    CASE add-to-kernel
        SELECT CASE target[input-argument]
           CASE file
               IF role (user pointed to by owner(process)) is
               system-admin
               AND
               data-type(object) is NIL **OR** non-personal-data
               THEN
                    return(YES);
               ELSE
                    return(NO);
           CASE ELSE
               return(UNDEFINED);

    CASE alter
        SELECT CASE target[input-argument]
           CASE ipc
               return(DC);
           CASE ELSE
               return(UNDEFINED);

    CASE append-open
        SELECT CASE target[input-argument]
           CASE file
               SELECT CASE data-type(object)
                   CASE personal-data
                      IF Necessary (current-task
                      (process), class (object),
                      transformation-procedure (process),
                      append)
                      AND
                      [Purpose-binding (current-task
                      (process), class (object))
                      OR
                      CONSENT (current-task (process),
                      object)]
                      AND
                      UNION (Output-Purposes(process),
                      purposes(class(object))) in
                      Input-Purposes(process)

232

        THEN

            return(set-attribute(Output-Purposes (process), UNION (Output-Purposes(process), purposes(class(object)))); YES);

        ELSE

            return(NO);

      CASE TP

        return (NO)

        (* it is not allowed to modify TPs directly*)

      CASE non-personal-data

        IF Input-Purposes(process) is P

        (* P: value for the set of all possible purposes *)

        THEN

            return(set-attribute(Output-Purposes(process),P); YES);

        ELSE

            return(NO);

      CASE ELSE

        return(NO);

CASE ipc

    IF class(object) is none

    (*object contains non-personal-data*)

    THEN

        ⌈ **IF** Input-Purposes(process) is P

        THEN

            return(set-attribute(Output-Purposes (process), P);YES);

        ELSE

            return(NO);⌋

    ELSE   (* object contains personal data *)

        IF Necessary (current-task(process), class(object), transformation-procedure (process), append)

        AND

        Purpose-binding (current-task (process), class(object))

        AND

        UNION (Output-Purposes(process), purposes(class(object))) in Input-Purposes(process)

        THEN

```
                                (* consents are not defined for ipc-objects *)
                                        return(set-attribute(Output-
                                        Purposes(process),
                                        UNION (Output-Purposes(process),
                                         purposes(class(object))));YES);
                    ELSE
                                        return (NO);
            CASE ELSE
                        return (UNDEFINED);


    CASE change-group
            SELECT CASE  target[input-argument]
                    CASE  file, dir, ipc
                            return(DC);
                    CASE ELSE
                            return(UNDEFINED);


    CASE  change-owner (* arguments: process, target, new-owner *)
            SELECT CASE  target[input-argument]
                    CASE process
                    (* change of the attribute owner of a process requested *)
                            IF current-task (process) in authorised-task (new-owner)
                            AND ( (NOT role(owner(process)) is sec-officer,
                                    data-protection-officer, tp-manager,
                                    system-admin)
                                    AND(NOT role(new-owner) is sec-officer,
                                    data-protection-officer, tp-manager,
                                    system-admin))
                    THEN
                                    return(YES);
                    ELSE
                                    return(NO);
                    CASE file  (* change of owner or group of a file *)
                            IF data-type(object) is TP OR personal data
                            THEN
                                    return(NO);
                            ELSE
                                    return(YES);
                    CASE dir, ipc
                            return(DC);

            CASE ELSE
                        return(UNDEFINED);

    CASE  clone
            SELECT CASE  target[input-argument]
                    CASE process
```

```
                              IF process-type (process) is NIL
                              THEN
                                          return (set-attribute (process-type(process-2),
                                          NIL)
                                          set-attribute(transformation-procedure
                                          (process-2) , NIL)
                                          set-attribute (owner(process-2),
                                          owner(process))
                                          set-attribute(Input-Purposes(process-2), P)
                                          set-attribute(Output-Purposes(process-2, NIL)
                                          (* NIL: empty list of purposes *)
                                          set-attribute (current-task(process-2),
                                          current-task(process)); YES)
                  ELSE
                                          return (NO);
                                          (* a TP-type process is not allowed to clone *)
            CASE ELSE
                        return(UNDEFINED);

CASE   create  (* normal create system call *)
      SELECT CASE   target[input-argument]
            CASE file
                        IF process-type(process) is TP
                        THEN
                                ⌈IF Necessary ( current-task(process),
                                 default-class [purpose(current-
                                 task(process))],
                                 transformation-procedure(process), create)
                                 THEN
                                              return (set-attribute
                                              data-type(object), personal-data),
                                              set-attribute (object-type(object),
                                              file),
                                              set-attribute (class(object),
                                              default-class[purpose(current-
                                              task(process))]);YES);
                                 ELSE
                                              return(NO);⌋
                  ELSE
                                  return (set-attribute( data-type(object),
                                  non-personal-data),
                                  set-attribute (class(object), none),
                                    set-attribute (object-type(object), file)) ;YES);
            CASE ipc
                        IF process-type(process) is TP
                        THEN
                                  ⌈IF Necessary (current-task (process),
```

235

                                        default-class [purpose(current-
                                        task(process))],
                                        transformation-procedure (process), create)
                                    THEN
                                                return (set-attribute (class(object),
                                                default-class (purpose(current-
                                                task(process))))),
                                                set-attribute (object-type(object),
                                                ipc)); YES)
                                    ELSE
                                                return(NO);⌋
                            ELSE
                                        return (set-attribute(class(object), none)
                                            set-attribute (object-type(object), ipc); YES);
                    CASE dir
                                return(set-attribute (object-type(object), dir); DC)
                    CASE ELSE
                                return(UNDEFINED);

    CASE delete
            SELECT CASE target[input-argument]
                    CASE file
                            SELECT CASE data-type(object)
                                    CASE personal-data
                                            IF Necessary (current-task
                                                (process), class (object),
                                                transformation-procedure
                                                (process), delete)
                                            AND
                                            Purpose-binding (current-task
                                              (process), class (object))
                                            OR
                                            CONSENT (current-task
                                            (process),object)
                                            THEN
                                                        return(YES);
                                            ELSE
                                                        return(NO);
                                    CASE TP
                                            IF role (user identified by
                                                owner(process)) is tp-manager
                                            THEN
                                                        return(YES);
                                            ELSE
                                                        return(NO);
                                    CASE ELSE
                                                return (DC);

CASE ipc
    IF class (object) is NOT none
    THEN
       ⌈**IF** Necessary (current-task(process),
       class(object), transformation-procedure
       (process), delete)
       AND
         Purpose-binding (current-task (process),
                   class (object))
       THEN
         return (YES);
       ELSE
         return (NO);⌋
    ELSE
      return (DC);
  CASE dir
    return(DC);
  CASE ELSE
    return(UNDEFINED);

CASE execute
  SELECT CASE target[input-argument]
    CASE file
      IF data-type (object) is TP
      THEN
        ⌈**IF** transformation-procedure(object) IN
        authorised-TP (current-task (process))
        AND
        process-type (process) = NIL
        THEN
          return (set-attribute
          (transformation-procedure(process),
          transformation-procedure (object));
          set-attribute(process-type
          (process),TP);
          set-attribute(Input-purposes
          (process), P);
          set-attribute(Output-Purposes
          (process), NIL); YES);
        ELSE
          return (NO);⌋
      ELSE
        return(DC);
    CASE ELSE
      return(UNDEFINED);

CASE get-permission-data, get-status-data

```
        SELECT CASE  target[input-argument]
              CASE file, dir, ipc, scd
                    return(DC);
              CASE ELSE
                    return(UNDEFINED);

CASE link-hard
        SELECT CASE  target[input-argument]
              CASE file
                    SELECT CASE  data-type(object)
                          CASE TP, personal data
                                return(NO);
                                (* aliasing could defeat attempts to
                                remove a TP or personal data from
                                the system *)
                          CASE ELSE
                                return(DC);
              CASE ELSE
                    return(UNDEFINED);

CASE modify-access-data, rename
        SELECT CASE  target[input-argument]
              CASE file
                    SELECT CASE  data-type(object)
                          CASE TP
                                IF role (user identified by
                                    owner(process) is TP-manager)
                                THEN
                                        return(YES);
                                (* Only TP-managers may modify
                                administrative information about TPs*)
                                ELSE
                                        return(NO);
                          CASE ELSE
                                return(DC);
              CASE dir
                    return(DC);
              CASE ELSE
                    return(UNDEFINED);

CASE modify_attribute (* only modification of attributes that are not Privacy Model-
                        relevant is allowed *)
        SELECT CASE  target[input argument]
              CASE user
                    IF (attribute[input argument] is authorised-tasks
                        OR role)
                    THEN
```

```
                        return (NO);
             ELSE
                        return(DC);
CASE process
        IF (attribute[input argument] is transformation procedure
             OR current_task OR process-type OR owner OR
             input-purposes OR output-purposes
        THEN
                    return (NO);
             ELSE
                        return(DC);
CASE file, dir, ipc
        IF (attribute[input argument] is class OR transformation-
             procedure OR object-type OR data-type)
        THEN
                    return (NO);
             ELSE
                        return(DC);
CASE ELSE
        return(DC);


CASE modify-permission data
        SELECT CASE   target[input argument]
             CASE  file
                    SELECT CASE  data-type(object)
                             CASE TP
                                    IF role (user pointed to by
                                        owner(process)) is tp-manager
                                    THEN
                                            return(YES);
                                    ELSE
                                            return(NO);


                             CASE ELSE
                                    return(DC);
             CASE scd, dir, ipc
                    return(DC);
        CASE ELSE
                return(UNDEFINED);


CASE modify-system-data
             SELECT CASE  target[input-argument]
                    CASE scd
                            IF role(user pointed to by owner(process)) is
                            system-admin
                            THEN
                                    return(YES);
```

```
                                        ELSE
                                                    return(NO);
                              CASE ELSE
                                        return(UNDEFINED);


CASE mount
                    SELECT CASE  target[input-argument-1]
                              CASE dev, dir
                                        IF role(user pointed to by owner(process)) is
                                        system-admin
                                        THEN
                                                    return(YES);
                                        ELSE
                                                    return(NO);
                              CASE ELSE
                                        return(UNDEFINED);


          CASE read, search
                    SELECT CASE  target[input-argument]
                              CASE dir
                                        return(DC);
                              CASE ELSE
                                        return(UNDEFINED);


CASE read-attribute
          IF (attribute[input argument] in (authorised-tasks, role,
                    transformation-procedure, current-task, process-type, class,
                    object-type, purpose, data-type, owner)
          THEN
                    IF role(user pointed to by owner(process)) is sec-officer
                    OR
                    role (user pointed to by owner(process)) is data-protection-officer
                    THEN
                              return(YES);
                    ELSE
                              return(NO);


CASE read-open
          SELECT  target[input-argument]
                    CASE file
                              SELECT CASE  data-type(object)
                                        CASE personal-data
                                                  IF  Necessary (current-task
                                                  (process),  class (object),
                                                  transformation-procedure(process),
                                                  read )
                                                  AND
```

[Purpose-binding (current-task
(process), class (object))
OR
CONSENT (current-task (process),
object)]
AND
Output-Purposes(process) in
INTERSECTION(Input-
Purposes(process),
purposes(class(object)))
THEN

return(set-attribute
(Input-Purposes(process),
INTERSECTION(Input-
Purposes (process),
purposes(class(object))));
YES);
ELSE
return(NO);
CASE TP
return (NO);
CASE ELSE
return (YES);
CASE ipc
IF class(object) is NOT none
THEN
⌈**IF** Necessary (current-task(process),
class(object), transformation-procedure
(process), read)
AND
Purpose-binding (current-task (process),
class(object))
AND
Output-Purposes(process) in
INTERSECTION(Input-
Purposes(process),
purposes(class(object)))
THEN
return(set-attribute (Input-
Purposes(process),
INTERSECTION(Input-Purposes
(process),
purposes(class(object)))); YES);
ELSE
return (NO);⌋
ELSE
return (YES);

```
                CASE dev
                    IF NOT((class(object) is none) OR
                    (class(object) is dev-trusted))
                    THEN
                            ⌈IF Necessary (current-task(process),
                             class(object), transformation-procedure
                             (process), read)
                             AND
                             Purpose-binding (current-task (process),
                                            class(object))
                        AND
                                Output-Purposes(process) in
                                INTERSECTION(Input-
                                Purposes(process),
                                purposes(class(object)))
                        THEN
                                return(set-attribute (Input-
                                Purposes(process),
                                INTERSECTION(Input-Purposes
                                (process),
                                purposes(class(object))))); YES);
                        ELSE
                                return (NO);⌋
                ELSE
                        return (YES);
            CASE dir
                    return(DC);
            CASE ELSE
                    return(UNDEFINED);


    CASE read&write-open
        SELECT CASE  target[input-argument]
            CASE file
                    SELECT CASE  data-type(object)
                        CASE personal-data
                                IF Necessary (current-task
                                (process),  class (object),
                                transformation-procedure
                                (process),  read&write )
                                 AND
                                [Purpose-binding (current-task
                                (process), class (object))
                                OR
                                CONSENT ( current-task (process),
                                object)]
                                AND
                                UNION(Output-Purposes(process),
```

purposes(class(object))) in INTERSECTION (Input-Purposes(process), purposes(class(object)))
THEN

return(set-attribute (Input-Purposes(process), INTERSECTION (Input-Purposes (process), purposes(class(object)))) (set-attribute (Output-Purposes (process), UNION(Output-Purposes(process), purposes (class(object)))); YES);

ELSE

return(NO);

CASE TP

return (NO);

CASE non-personal-data

IF Input-Purposes(process) is P
THEN

return(set-attribute(Output-Purposes(process), P);YES);

ELSE

return(NO);

CASE ELSE

return (DC);

CASE ipc

IF class(object) is none
THEN

⌈ **IF** Input-Purposes(process) is P
THEN

return(set-attribute(Output-Purposes (process), P);YES);

ELSE

return(NO);⌋

ELSE (* class(object) is NOT none *)

⌈**IF** Necessary (current-task(process), class(object), transformation-procedure (process), read&write)

AND

Purpose-binding (current-task (process), class (object))

```
                            AND
                            UNION(Output-Purposes(process),
                            purposes(class(object))) in
                            INTERSECTION (Input-Purposes(process),
                            purposes(class(object)))
                            THEN
                                    return(set-attribute (Input-
                                    Purposes(process),
                                    INTERSECTION (Input-Purposes
                                    (process), purposes(class(object))))
                                    (set-attribute (Output-Purposes
                                    (process),
                                    UNION(Output-Purposes(process),
                                    purposes (class(object)))); YES);
                            ELSE
                                    return (NO);⌋
CASE dev
        SELECT CASE  class(object)
                    CASE dev-trusted
                            return(YES);
                    CASE none
                            IF Input-Purposes(process) is P
                            THEN
                                    return(set-attribute(Output-
                                    Purposes (process),
                                    P);YES);
                            ELSE
                                    return(NO);
                    CASE ELSE
                    (* object contains personal data*)
                            IF Necessary (current-task(process),
                            class(object), transformation-
                            procedure (process), read&write)
                            AND
                            Purpose-binding (current-task
                            (process), class (object))
                            AND
                            UNION(Output-Purposes(process),
                            purposes(class(object))) in
                            INTERSECTION (Input-
                            Purposes(process),
                            purposes(class(object)))
                            THEN
                                    return(set-attribute (Input-
                                    Purposes(process),
                                    INTERSECTION (Input-
                                    Purposes (process),
```

purposes(class(object))))
(set-attribute (Output-
Purposes (process),
UNION(Output-
Purposes(process),
purposes   (class(object)));
YES);
                        ELSE
                            return (NO);
            CASE ELSE
                return(UNDEFINED);

    CASE remove-from-kernel, shutdown
                SELECT CASE target[input argument]
                        CASE none
                            IF role(user pointed to by owner(process)) is
                            system-admin
                            THEN
                            return(YES);
                            ELSE
                                return(NO);
                        CASE ELSE
                            return(UNDEFINED);

    (* **CASE** rename: see modify access data *)

    (***CASE** search: see read *)

    CASE send-signal
                SELECT CASE target[input-argument]
                        CASE process
                            IF process-type(process-1) is NIL
                            THEN
                                ⌈**IF** signal =hard-kill (*SIGKILL*)
                            THEN
                                    ⌈**IF** process-type(process-2) is TP
                                THEN
                                        ⌈**IF** role(user pointed to by
                                        owner(process-1)) is
                                        TP-manager
                                        THEN
                                            return(YES);
                                        (* TP has to be designed
                                        to take appropriate actions
                                        before exiting *)
                                        ELSE
                                            return(NO);⌋

ELSE
                                    return (DC);⌋
                    ELSE
                        return(YES);⌋
            ELSE
                return(NO);
        CASE ELSE
            return(UNDEFINED);

CASE switch-log, switch-module
        SELECT CASE target[input-argument]
                CASE none
                    IF role(user pointed to by owner(process)) is sec-officer
                    THEN
                            return(YES);
                    ELSE
                            return(NO);
                CASE ELSE
                    return(UNDEFINED);

CASE terminate
        SELECT CASE target[input-argument]
                CASE process
                        return(DC);
                ELSE
                        return(UNDEFINED);

CASE trace
        SELECT CASE target[input-argument]
                CASE process
                        IF process-type(process-1) =NIL
                        AND process-type(process-2) = NIL
                        THEN
                            return(YES);
                        ELSE
                            return(NO);
                            (* tracing would enable modification of a TP
                            during its execution *)
                CASE ELSE
                    return(UNDEFINED);

CASE truncate (*delete data*)
        SELECT CASE target[input-argument]
                CASE file
                        SELECT CASE data-type(object)
                                CASE personal-data
                                        IF Necessary (current-task

```
                              (process), class (object),
                                transformation-procedure (process),
                                write)
                              AND
                              [Purpose-binding (current-task
                                (process), class (object))
                              OR
                              CONSENT ( current-task
                                (process),object)]
                              THEN
                                          return(YES);
                              ELSE
                                      return(NO);
                        CASE TP
                            return(NO);
                        CASE ELSE
                            return (DC);
                CASE ELSE
                    return (UNDEFINED);

CASE umount
        SELECT CASE  target[input-argument]
                CASE dir, dev, none
                        IF role(user pointed to by owner(process)) is
                            system-admin
                        THEN
                                return(YES);
                        ELSE
                                return(NO);
                CASE ELSE
                    return(UNDEFINED);

CASE write
        SELECT CASE  target[input-argument]
                CASE dir
                    return(DC);
                CASE ELSE
                    return(UNDEFINED);

CASE write-open
        SELECT CASE  target[input-argument]
                CASE file
                        SELECT CASE  data-type(object)
                        CASE personal-data
                                IF Necessary (current-task
                                (process), class (object),
                                transformation-procedure (process),
```

```
                    write)
                    AND
                    [Purpose-binding (current-task
                    (process),  class (object))
                    OR
                    CONSENT ( current-task
                    (process),object)]
                    AND
                    UNION (Output-Purposes(process),
                    purposes(class(object))) in
                    Input-Purposes(process)
                    THEN
                            return(set-attribute(Output-
                            Purposes, UNION (Output-
                            Purposes(process),
                            purposes(class(object)))));
                            YES);
               ELSE
                            return(NO);
        CASE TP
                    return(NO);
        CASE non-personal-data
                    IF Input-Purposes(process) is P
                    THEN
                            return(set-attribute(Output-
                            Purposes (process), P);
                            YES);
               ELSE
                            return(NO);
        CASE ELSE
                    return (NO);
CASE dev
        SELECT CASE  class(object)
               CASE dev-trusted
                    return(YES);
               CASE none
               (*object contains non-personal-data*)
                      ⌈ IF Input-Purposes(process) is P
                       THEN
                            return(set-attribute(Output-
                            Purposes (process),
                            P);YES);
               ELSE
                            return(NO)⌋
        CASE ELSE
        (* object contains personal data *)
```

248

```
                                        IF Necessary (current-task(process),
                                        class(object), transformation-
                                        procedure (process), write)
                                        AND
                                        Purpose-binding (current-task
                                        (process), class(object))
                                        AND
                                        UNION (Output-Purposes(process),
                                        purposes(class(object))) in
                                        Input-Purposes(process)
                                        THEN
                                                return(set-attribute(Output-
                                                Purposes(process),
                                                UNION (Output-
                                                Purposes(process),
                                                purposes(class(object)))));
                                                YES);
                                        ELSE
                                                return (NO);
                        CASE ELSE
                                return (UNDEFINED);


(************************ Privacy Model specific requests ****************************************)

        CASE change_current_task  (*argument: task *)
                SELECT CASE  target[input-argument]
                        CASE process
                                IF task in authorised-tasks (user identified by
                                                owner (process))
                                        AND
                                        process-type (process) is NIL
                                        THEN
                                                return (set-attribute (current-task (process),
                                                        task); YES);
                                        ELSE
                                                return (NO);
                        CASE ELSE
                                return(UNDEFINED);

        CASE create-pers-data
                SELECT CASE  target[input-argument]
                        CASE file
                                IF  Necessary (current-task (process), class[input
                                        argument], transformation-procedure (process),
                                        create)
                                        AND
```

Purpose-binding (current-task (process),
class [input-argument])
THEN
return(set-attribute(object-type(object), file);
set-attribute(data-type(object),
personal-data);
set-attribute(class(object), class); YES);
ELSE
return(NO);
CASE ELSE
return(UNDEFINED);

CASE create-ticket
IF role(user pointed to by owner(process)) is sec-officer
OR
(function-type is add-auth-Task **OR** delete-auth-task
AND
process in responsible(parameter-list.task))
THEN
return(YES);
ELSE
return(NO);

CASE add-NA, add-task, add-object-class, add-authorised-TP, add-consent,
add-purpose, add-responsible-users, delete-responsible-users, set-role,
add-authorised-task
IF (role(user pointed to by owner(process)) is sec-officer) **AND**
(role(ticket.issuer) is data-protection-officer)
THEN
return(YES);
ELSE
return(NO);

CASE delete-NA (* arguments: task, class, transformation-procedure,
access-right *)
IF role(user pointed to by owner(process)) is sec-officer
AND
role(ticket.issuer) is data-protection-officer
AND
(FOR-ALL(proc, obj, right): open-objects-table entry:*
[NOT (current-task(proc), class(obj), transformation-procedure(proc),
*right) == (task, class, transformation-procedure, access-right))] *)*
THEN
return(YES);
ELSE
return(NO);

```
CASE delete-task (* argument: task *)
        IF role(user pointed to by owner(process)) is sec-officer
        AND
        role(ticket.issuer) is data-protection-officer
        AND
        FOR-ALLp: process:
                [NOT (current-task(p) is task)]
        THEN
                return(YES);
        ELSE
                return(NO);


CASE delete-object-class (* arguments are: class, ticket *)
        IF role(user pointed to by owner(process)) is sec-officer
        AND
        role(ticket.issuer) is data-protection-officer
        AND
        FOR-ALLobj:object:
                [NOT (class(obj) is class)]
        THEN
                return(YES);
        ELSE
                return(NO);


CASE delete-authorised-TP (* arguments are: task, transformation-procedure*)
        IF role(user pointed to by owner(process)) is sec-officer
        AND
        role(ticket.issuer) is data-protection-officer
        AND
        (* FOR-ALLp:process:
                [NOT((transformation-procedure(p) is transformation-procedure)
                        AND (current-task(p) is task))]   *)
        THEN
                return(YES);
        ELSE
                return(NO);


CASE delete-consent (* arguments are: object, purpose*)
        IF role(user pointed to by owner(process)) is sec-officer
        AND
        role(ticket.issuer) is data-protection-officer
        AND
        (* FOR-ALL(proc, obj, r): open-objects-table-entry:
                [NOT (object == obj)
                OR
                (NOT (purpose(current-task(proc)) == purpose) OR
```

*purpose-binding (current-task(proc), obj))]   *)*
THEN
    return(YES);
ELSE
    return(NO);

CASE delete-purpose (* arguments are: purpose, ticket *)
    IF role(user pointed to by owner(process)) is sec-officer
    AND
    role(ticket.issuer) is data-protection-officer
    AND
    FOR-ALLobj: object:
        [NOT(purpose in purposes(class(obj)))]
    FOR-ALLt: task:
        [NOT (purpose == purpose(t))]
    FOR-ALLobj-cl : object-class:
        [NOT (purpose in purposes(obj-cl))]
    THEN
        return(YES);
    ELSE
        return(NO);

CASE delete-authorised-Task (* arguments are: task, user *)
    IF role(user pointed to by owner(process)) is sec-officer
    AND
    role(ticket.issuer) is data-protection-officer
(*   **AND**
    *NOT (current-task(user) == task)) *)*
    THEN
        return(YES);
    ELSE
        return(NO);

CASE set-object-class (* arguments are: object, class, ticket *)
    SELECT CASE   target[input-argument-1]
        CASE file
            IF role(user pointed to by owner(process)) is sec-officer
            AND
            role(ticket.issuer) is data-protection-officer
            AND
            data-type(object) is NIL **OR** personal-data **OR**
            non-personal-data
            THEN
                ⌈**IF** class == NONE
                THEN

```
                                                return (set-attribute
                                                (data-type(object)),
                                                non-personal-data);
                                                set-attribute(class(object), class);
                                                YES);
                                    ELSE
                                                return(set-attribute(object)),
                                                personal-data);
                                                set-attribute(class(object), class),
                                                YES);⌋
                        ELSE
                                    return(NO);
                    CASE ELSE
                                return(UNDEFINED);

    CASE set-dev-object-class (* arguments are: object, class, ticket *)
            SELECT CASE  target[input-argument-1]
                        CASE dev
                                    IF role(user pointed to by owner(process)) is sec-officer
                                    AND
                                    role(ticket.issuer) is data-protection-officer
                                    THEN
                                                return(set-attribute(class(object), class), YES);
                                    ELSE
                                                return(NO);
                        CASE ELSE
                                    return(UNDEFINED);


    CASE create-TP-ID, set-TP;
            IF role(user pointed to by owner(process)) is TP-manager
            THEN
                        return(YES);
            ELSE
                        return(NO);


    CASE delete-TP-ID; (*argument: transformation-procedure *)
            IF role(user pointed to by owner(process)) is TP-manager
            AND
            FOR-ALLproc: process:
                        [NOT (transformation-procedure(proc) == transformation-
                        procedure)]
            THEN
                        return(YES);
            ELSE
                        return(NO);

CASE ELSE
```

```
        return (UNDEFINED);

END SELECT  (*** Privacy Rules ***)
```

In the specification of the ADF-rules for the privacy model specific requests *delete-NA, delete-authorised-TP, delete-consent, delete-authorised-task*, there are some conditions printed in italic letters in commentary brackets. These conditions are used to specify a scheme of authorisation revocations following the first approach described in chapter 5.3.

We have written these conditions in commentary brackets, because they have not been implemented in our GFAC-implementation. By omitting these conditions we have actually followed the third approach described in chapter 5.3. In this case the ACI Necessary-Accesses corresponds to the model element NA_{def}, Consents corresponds to C_{def}, the User-ACI authorised-tasks corresponds to AT_{def}, and the task-ACI authorised-TP corresponds to ATP_{def}. It can in fact be shown that in this case the system specification corresponds to the modified privacy model as defined in 5.3.

6.3 Implementation

In a project, which started as a Diploma thesis project, the GFAC-approach enforcing the privacy-, Bell LaPadula-, FC- and SIM policies, was implemented for the Linux operating system. Initially Linux Version 2.0.3.0 was taken, but the GFAC implementation has continuously been transferred to later Linux versions. Linux, although it was not designed for security, was chosen as a demonstration system, because it is a robust system, its source code is freely available and because it has functionalities of LaPadula´s reference system Unix System V. Furthermore, it keeps most important Unix standards (Linux 2.2 is to a large extent Posix compatible). Nevertheless, the results of the project (in particular, the privacy policy-specific Access Control Decision Facility- and Access Control Information components) can be easily transferred to more secure Unix versions. The program package was named "Rule Set Based Access Control" (RSBAC).

The results of the diploma project were published in [Ott 1997]. Updated project reports as well as the RSBAC source code are published in [Ott].

6.3.1 RSBAC Implementation

The main goal of the RSBAC project was the implementation of the GFAC-approach enforcing the privacy policy specification. Besides, further (partly system specific) design criteria were enforced:

- The rules of each security policy were encapsulated into independent modules (the rule sets). Each rule set module can be configured independently or switched on or off at runtime under its own control (i.e. if permitted by its security policy). New rule set modules can easily be added to the system configuration.

- ADF and the ACI component are encapsulated into independent modules, which can only be accessed by the use of well-defined functions.

- All policy-dependent functionalities are implemented by ADF and ACI. AEF is designed as a policy-independent component.

- In LaPadula's specification, which was used and extended in this thesis, security attributes were updated by AEF. Before, AEF received information through the decision message from ADF, about how security attributes had to be set. In the RSBAC implementation, security attributes are set by ADF. After successful execution of a system call, ADF is notified by AEF, so that all decision modules can adjust their attributes accordingly.

- All mechanisms are independent of the used file systems. This aspect is realised by the use of the Linux Virtual Filesystem Switch. The storage format of file ACI on secondary storage is independent of the used file systems.

- Reliable and efficient administration of ACI: All user and file ACI are kept in parallel in main memory and on secondary storage (so that they can be easily recovered after each system start) and are especially protected from unauthorised accesses. All accesses to ACI are synchronised. File and directory ACI are stored in double-linked lists, which are kept for each device. A hash search algorithm, which is using the inode number as an index, is used for an efficient access to file and directory ACI within each of those lists.

- Pseudonymous auditing is implemented: All security relevant system calls are recorded in a log file. Before the audit data is written to the log file, all directly user identifying data is replaced by pseudonyms.

Besides, administration tools for viewing and defining security attributes and for the back-up of security attributes have been implemented within the RSBAC project.

6.3.2 Integration of Heuristic Policy Rules

In our networked society, malicious code (malware) is a serious threat to system integrity, security and privacy. The major threats are viruses, which can import malicious code into local workstations from the Internet, Trojan horses, which can exploit features or weaknesses of Internet services. Macro viruses (viruses written in interpreted code hosted by applications) are a significant risk because they are platform independent, easier to write than "traditional" file viruses and reside in what one usually considers "data files", which get exchanged far more frequently than executable files. Besides, the user's privacy is especially endangered by technology that uses downloaded code, such as ActiveX controls or Java. Malicious downloaded programs can scan the end user's hard disk or network through security holes for important information and then smuggle the data to the outside world using the computer's network connection. Special security mechanisms are needed to deal with malicious code threats, and are also required by legislation: Art. 17 of the EU-

Directive on Data Protection, for example, requires the implementation of security measures to protect personal data against accidental or unlawful destruction or accidental loss, alteration, unauthorised disclosure or access.

In [Ott/Fischer-Hübner/Swimmer 1998] , we showed how we have implemented an on-access malware protection policy within the Generalised Framework for Access Control. We have implemented an On-Access Scanner using the GFAC concept by integrating a scanner policy rules component to ADF and adding further access control information to the ACI administration module. Although GFAC was originally designed as a framework for expressing and integrating policy components of formal security models (usually, state machine-type models), we showed that it could also be used to integrate heuristic policies. Virus scanners are inherently heuristic, as there is no known method for always determining the presence of a virus in a file. Currently, all known antiviruses are only able to detect previously known viruses reliably. Additional ACI and policy rules needed for the integration and implementation of the scanner policy component, are described in the following sections.

Access control information:

For each file, a new security attribute MS-scan-result is used. Possible values of the scan-result attribute are a version number, "rejected" or "unscanned". The scan-result attribute of a file will have the value of a version number of a scanner, if the file is scanned with this scanner version and no infection is found. If the file was scanned and a virus infection was detected, the file attribute is set to "rejected". The file attribute is set to "unscanned," if the file has not been scanned so far, or if the file has been modified by the last access to it. A new attribute MS-trusted is introduced. The attribute MS-trusted is set for the antivirus or backup programs and processes that are executing those programs. Furthermore, the ACI-module administrates a database of virus patterns/signatures, which also has a version number attached to it.

On-access scanner policy rules:

The scanner policy rules are invoked at each execute or open decision request sent to ADF by AEF. Infections by file viruses are caused by the execution of an infected file, whereas reading an infected document causes infections by macro viruses. Thus, each request from AEF to ADF to execute or to read a file should only be positively decided by ADF, if the file has first been scanned with the latest scanner version and if no infections were found.

Hence, if the access request type is execute, read-open or read-write-open, then the decision rule will be as follows:

If the file has not been scanned so far with the latest scanner version (i.e., the scan-attribute value is "unscanned" or is a version number that is less than the version number of the virus pattern database), then the file will be scanned for possible infections. In this case, the access decision will only be positive, if no infection is found. The MS-scan-result attribute will then be set to the current version number if the access decision is positive, or else to "rejected".

If the MS-scan-result attribute value is equal to the current version number, the access decision is positive.

If the MS-scan-result attribute value is "rejected", the access decision is only positive, if the current process has the attribute MS-trusted set. Thus, only trusted programs (e.g. antivirus tools) can be used to access "rejected" files.

For the modifying access request types write-open, append-open and truncate, no decision rules are defined. However, for these and for read-write-open, the scan-attribute value is reset to "unscanned", because it might have been infected or disinfected.

The integration of the scanner policy rules to the access decision facility (ADF) has some impact on the overall system performance. If a file is to be read, the scanner policy rules are only invoked on the read- (or read-write) open request, and then do not have to be invoked for each single read access. Moreover, upon execute-, read-open and read-write open requests, files have only to be scanned, if they were modified or if a new scanner version was installed (that is, if the virus pattern database was extended and has received a new version number).

This on-access malware scanner policy provides a reliable and tamper-proof protection against known malware in executable files. Increasingly however, malware is brought into the system by a network connection, often executed without ever being saved to a file. Therefore, we extended our approach to include scanning and denying access to data, if appropriate, from a given origin of network connections by controlling UNIX-type sockets (see [Ott/Fischer-Hübner/Swimmer 1998]).

Additional scanner policy rules, that are also part of the ADF component of the GFAC-system, control all read accesses to network connection sockets. If malware is detected in the data stream further read access is denied and a new error code "malware-detected" is returned. Depending on the configuration, the connection can be closed by the kernel, or a trusted process can allow the whole stream to be delivered anyway.

A major limitation of the socket-level malware scanner approach is that it cannot detect application-level encrypted malware. Thus, another approach is to incorporate more knowledge of the application environment into the access control, which is discussed in [Ott/Fischer-Hübner/Swimmer 1998] in more detail.

6.4 Outlook

RSBAC in Linux is an ongoing project (see [Ott] for more details).

Within the project one interest is to analyse how easy it is to transfer the ADF- and ACI-modules (that are more or less platform independent) to other system platforms. Particularly the transfer of RSBAC to other Unix platforms should be straightforward: The major work is to implement AEF by adding ADF-requests to all security relevant system calls, while ADF and ACI should be transferable without major modifications.

Another interesting approach could be the definition and use of rules for metapolicies to describe new security policies. A metapolicy could be a set of rules about a single policy, specifying what kind of policy it is, what elements make up the policy, the domain to which the policy applies and the informal and formal statement of the policy [Hosmer 1992]. Metapolicies could help to formulate and add new ADF-policy components for new security policies.

Furthermore, additional enhancements of the privacy model and its specification and implementation could be added:

One major improvement could be a signing function that can be used to digitally sign an object with a digital signature indicating its object class. This would enable to transfer (e.g., by network communication or disk transfer) a personal data object together with its object class (as indicated by the signature) to other system domains which do not belong to system domain, where the object's access control data is administrated. The functionality of the privileged function "set-object-class" should then be extended to allow to set the object class of a signed object to the class defined by its signature.

Moreover, a further interesting enhancement could be the implementation of distributed anonymous access control for the privacy model with the help of SPKI certificates (see also 4.2.3.2). A user could also be allowed to perform a task, if he proves to be in the possession of the private key belonging to a SPKI certificate that authorises him to perform this task in that system domain. This SPKI certificate must be the last certificate in a SPKI certificate sequence chain. The first certificate within that sequence must be issued by the verifier of the sequence (i.e., the security officer of the GFAC system). Thus, with a SPKI certificate an anonymous user could be authorised for a task and by performing this task receive privileges as defined for that task.

So far the emphasis of the RSBAC project has been on enhancing the security functionality. Nevertheless, currently more work and efforts are invested in security testing and documentation to raise assurance.

7 Concluding Remarks

On the way to the Global Information Society privacy is increasingly at risk and cannot be effectively protected solely by privacy legislation. Thus, in addition to privacy protection by data protection legislation, privacy should also be technically enforced and should be a design criterion for information and communication systems.

This thesis discusses privacy, IT security and its relationship to privacy, as well as privacy-enhancing technologies. Recent reports on privacy-enhancing technologies discuss technologies that protect user identities enforcing anonymity, pseudonymity, unobservability or unlinkability. Such technologies are important means to protect users from traffic analysis and the creation of communication and user profiles.

Nevertheless, there is also a need for privacy technologies, such as encryption and access control mechanisms, to protect personal data that has to be collected, processed or transmitted. As stated by Ravi Sandhu [Sandhu 1996a], access control is an indispensable security technology that, however, has been relatively neglected by the research community in the last decade. In this thesis we have evaluated today's most well-known security models for access control according to basic privacy criteria, which are namely their capability to enforce necessity of data processing and purpose binding, their capability to protect the confidentiality and integrity of personal data as well as the criterion whether they can be used to implement anonymous or pseudonymous access control. The result of the privacy evaluation is that none of them is capable to meet all of those basic privacy requirements.

A second problem concerning the relationship between security and privacy is that there is a conflict between security and privacy, because most security mechanisms collect and use personal control data.

In order to address the first problem, we have developed a formal task-based privacy model that can be used to technically enforce all privacy criteria stated above. A top-level specification of a Unix System V kernel designed according to the GFAC approach implementing the privacy model policy has been given. In the RSBAC (Rule Set Based Access Control) project, this specification was used and adapted for the implementation of the privacy policy in combination with further security policies in the Linux operating system. The resulting Linux GFAC-system implementation is called RSBAC-system ("Rule-Set Based Access Control") and is one of the (worldwide) first complete GFAC-implementations.

Linux, although it is not designed for security, was chosen as a demonstration system, because it is a robust system, its source code is available and because it has functionalities of Unix System V. One goal within the RSBAC project is to develop a security-enhanced Linux version that meets at least the functionality requirements of the Orange Book Class B1. Nevertheless, since the privacy policy-specific Access Control Decision Facility- and Access Control Information modules are more or less system-independent, they can be easily transferred and integrated to more secure Unix versions or even to other system platforms. The transfer or integration of the RSBAC system to other system platforms is one future project task of special interest.

The formal task-based privacy model has been defined as a state machine model that is proven consistent with its axioms. Hence, it could be used for the development of systems with an (Common Criteria) Assurance Level EAL5 or higher.

As we have shown, the privacy policy could also be used for anonymous access control. Hence a further interesting project task could be the enhancement of the RSBAC system to enforce distributed anonymous access control with the help of SPKI certificates. This enhancement following the privacy principle of avoidance of personal (user related) data, allows a user to access and use a system anonymously.

In conclusion, the privacy model can be used to implement a privacy-enhancing access control, which enforces basic legal privacy requirements. Besides, access control systems enforcing the privacy model policy can enable anonymous system use, which operates with non-personal control data. Moreover, the privacy model can particularly be used to protect personal control data (e.g., audit data) from illegal and unnecessary accesses. Thus, the privacy model can contribute to a privacy-enhancing design and use of access control systems, which in turn can enforce a privacy enhancing use IT-security mechanisms. Hence, it can also be an effective technical means to address the conflict between security and privacy.

Appendix A: Formal Mathematical Privacy Model

In this Appendix, the formal mathematical privacy model is presented. A definition of a privacy-oriented system will be given, which is partly analogous to the defintion of a secure system given in [Bell LaPadula 76]. It will be formally proven that the system defined by the formal privacy model is privacy-oriented.

1. Model Components

The following elements (state variables) of the mathematical model were already defined in Chapter 5:
Subjects **S**, the active subject **subj**, objects **O**, personal data objects **OP**, object-classes **O-class**, object-class function **class**, tasks **T**, current task function **CT**, authorised tasks function **AT**, function for responsible users of tasks **responsible**, user role function **role**, purposes **P**, purpose function for tasks **T-Purpose**, purpose function for object classes **O-Purposes**, transformation procedures **TRANS**, current transformation procedure function **CTP**, authorised transformation procedure function **ATP**, access rights **A**, necessary accesses **NA**, current access set **CA**, Consent **C**, a function **Input-Purposes** and a function **Output-Purposes**.

In order to formally define tickets, further system elements are introduced:

$\text{TKT} \subseteq$

$\quad$ S × {add-NA} × T × O-Class × TRANS × A ∪

$\quad$ S × {delete-NA} × T × O-Class × TRANS × A ∪

$\quad$ S × {add-task} × P ∪

$\quad$ S × {delete-task} × T ∪

$\quad$ S × {add-o-class} × 2^P ∪

$\quad$ S × {delete-o-class} × O-Class ∪

$\quad$ S × {add-auth-TP} × T × TRANS ∪

$\quad$ S × {delete-auth-TP} × T × TRANS ∪

$\quad$ S × {add-consent} × OP × P ∪

$\quad$ S × {delete-consent} × OP × P ∪

$\quad$ S × {add-purpose} ∪

$\quad$ S × {delete-purpose} × P ∪

$\quad$ S × {set-role} × S × role ∪

$\quad$ S × {add-resp-users} × S × T ∪

$\quad$ S × {delete-resp-users} × S × T ∪

$\quad$ S × {add-auth-task} × S × T ∪

$\quad$ S × {delete-auth-task} × S × T

Ticket templates arc used in requests to create tickets:

TKT-template = {add-NA} × T × O-Class × TRANS × A ∪

{delete-NA} × T × O-Class × TRANS × A ∪

{add-task} × P) ∪ {delete-task} × T ∪ {add-o-class} × 2^P ∪
{delete-o-class} × O-Class ∪
{add-auth-TP} × T × TRANS ∪ {delete-auth-TP} × T × TRANS ∪
{add-consent} × OP × P ∪ {delete-consent} × OP × P ∪ {(add-purpose)} ∪
{delete-purpose} × P ∪ {set-role} × S × role ∪ {add-resp-users} × S × T ∪
{delete-resp-users} × S × T ∪ {add-auth-task} × S × T ∪
{delete-auth-task} × S × T

In order to formally define and prove a privacy-oriented system, the following elements are defined as well:

Requests R: ∪ $R^{(i)}$, where
$$1 \le i \le 29$$

$R^{(1)}$ = {get-read}× S × O × {read} :   requests to get read-access

$R^{(2)}$ = {get-write}× S × O × {write, append} :   requests to get write -access

$R^{(3)}$ = {release} × S × O × {read, write, append} :   requests to release access

$R^{(4)}$ = {execute-tp} × S × TRANS: requests to execute a transformation procedure

$R^{(5)}$ = {exit-tp} × S: requests to exit to process a transformation procedure

$R^{(6)}$ = {change-CT} × S × T: requests to change the current task of a subject

$R^{(7)}$ = {create-subject} × S :   requests to create a new subject

$R^{(8)}$ = {create-object} × S × O-class: requests to create a personal data object of a specific object-class

$R^{(9)}$ = {delete} × S × OP: requests to delete a personal data object

$R^{(10)}$ = {create-ticket} × S × TKT-template: requests to create a ticket

$R^{(11)}$ = {add-NA} × S × TKT: requests to add a necessary access to NA

$R^{(12)}$ = {delete-NA} × S × TKT: requests to delete a necessary

	access from NA
$R^{(13)} = \{\text{add-task}\} \times S \times TKT:$	requests to define a new task
$R^{(14)} = \{\text{delete-task}\} \times S \times TKT:$	requests to delete a task
$R^{(15)} = \{\text{add-o-class}\} \times S \times TKT:$	requests to define an object class
$R^{(16)} = \{\text{delete-o-class}\} \times S \times TKT:$	requests to delete an object class
$R^{(17)} = \{\text{add-auth-TP}\} \times S \times TKT:$	requests to authorise a task to execute a transformation procedure
$R^{(18)} = \{\text{delete-auth-TP}\} \times S \times TKT:$	requests to revoke authorisation from a task to execute a transformation procedure.
$R^{(19)} = \{\text{add-consent}\} \times S \times TKT:$	requests to add a consent
$R^{(20)} = \{\text{delete-consent}\} \times S \times TKT:$	requests to delete a consent
$R^{(21)} = \{\text{add-purpose}\} \times S \times TKT:$	requests to define a purpose
$R^{(22)} = \{\text{delete-purpose}\} \times S \times TKT:$	requests to delete a purpose
$R^{(23)} = \{\text{set-role}\} \times S \times TKT:$	requests to set a user role
$R^{(24)} = \{\text{add-resp-users}\} \times S \times TKT:$	requests to define a subject as responsible for a task
$R^{(25)} = \{\text{delete-resp-users}\} \times S \times TKT:$	requests to define a subject as not being responsible for a task
$R^{(26)} = \{\text{add-auth-task}\} \times S \times TKT:$	requests to authorise a subject for a task
$R^{(27)} = \{\text{delete-auth-task}\} \times S \times TKT:$	requests to revoke authorisation for a task from a subject
$R^{(28)} = \{\text{create-TP}\} \times S:$	requests to define a new transformation procedure
$R^{(29)} = \{\text{delete-TP}\} \times S \times TRANS:$	requests to delete a transformation procedure.

Decisions D: $\{\underline{\text{yes}}, \underline{\text{no}}, \underline{\text{error}}, \underline{?}\}$: decisions of requests; an arbitrary element of D is written D_m.

Time set T: $\{0, 1, 2, ..., t, ...\}$: indices for identification of discrete moments; an element t is an index to request, decision and state sequences as well as to state elements.

Request sequences X: R^T; an arbitrary element of X is written x.

(The notation A^B denotes the set of all functions from B to A).

Decision sequences Y: D^T; an arbitrary element of Y is written y.

States V: system states are defined by the state variables S, CA, NA, CT, AT, CTP, ATP, class, T-Purpose, O-Purposes, C, O, OP, O-Class, T, P, TRANS, TKT, role, responsible, Input-Purposes, Output-Purposes.
An arbitrary element v of V, a state of the model, is defined by the tuple (S, CA, NA, CT, AT, CTP, ATP, class, T-Purpose, O-Purposes, C, O, OP O-Class, T, P, TRANS, TKT, role, responsible, Input-Purposes, Output-Purposes).

We have defined the variables TKT, role, responsible as state variables, although they are not directly mentioned in the privacy invariants and constraints. We might consider them as not being relevant for the privacy invariants and constraints and hence not relevant for defining the system state. However, we include them to define the results of the privileged functions.

State sequences Z: V^T; an arbitrary element of Z is written z; z_t in z is the t-th state in the state sequence z.

2. Privacy-Oriented System

System:
A system is defined as follows:

Suppose that $W \subset R \times D \times V \times V$.
The system $\Sigma (R, D, W, z_0) \subset X \times Y \times Z$ is defined by
$(x, y, z) \in \Sigma (R, D, W, z_0)$ iff $(x_t, y_t, z_t, z_{t-1}) \in W$ for each t in T,
where z_0 is the initial state of the system.
z_0 is usually of the form (S, CA, NA, CT, AT, CTP, ATP, class, T-Purpose, O-Purposes, C, O, OP, T, P, TRANS, TKT, role, responsible, Input-Purposes, Output-Purposes),
with $\forall S_i \in S$: CTP (S_i) = Nil, CT (S_i) = Nil, Input-Purposes(S_i) =P,
Output-Purposes(S_i) = $\varnothing$,
and with $\forall (S_i, O_j, r) \in$ CA: $O_j \notin$ OP.

Privacy invariants and Information flow invariant:
Privacy invariants and the information flow invariant, as already introduced in Chapter 5, are defined in terms of the members of a state sequence. The system satisfies a specified invariant if each state of every state sequence of the system satisfies the invariant.

Given a system state
v = (S, CA, NA, CT, AT, CTP, ATP, class, T-Purpose, O-Purposes, C, O, OP, O-Class, T, P, TRANS, TKT, role, responsible, Input-Purposes, Output-Purposes).

Privacy invariant-1:
A state v satisfies the privacy invariant-1, iff
$\forall\, S_i \in S : CT(S_i) \in AT(S_i)$.

Privacy invariant-2:
A state v satisfies the privacy invariant-2, iff
$\forall\, S_i \in S : CTP(S_i) \in ATP(CT(S_i))$.

Privacy invariant-3:
A state v satisfies the privacy invariant-3, iff
$\forall\, S_i \in S,\, O_j \in OP$:
$(S_i, O_j, x) \in CA \;\Rightarrow\; (CT(S_i), Class(O_j), CTP(S_i), x) \in NA$.

Privacy invariant-4:
A state v satisfies the privacy invariant-4, iff
$\forall\, S_i \in S,\, O_j \in OP$:
$(S_i, O_j, x) \in CA \;\Rightarrow$
T-Purpose $(CT(S_i)) \in$ O-Purposes $(Class(O_j))\; \vee\;$ (T-Purpose$(CT(S_i)), O_j) \in C$.

Information flow invariant:
A state v satisfies the information flow invariant, iff
$\forall\, S_i \in S$: Output-Purposes $(S_i) \subseteq$ Input-Purposes (S_i)

Privacy Constraints:
Privacy constraints (as already introduced in Chapter 5) are defined for two arbitrary successive states of a state sequence:

Given two successive states z_{t-1}, z_t of a state sequence z, where
z_{t-1}= (S, CA, NA, CT, AT, CTP, ATP, class, T-Purpose, O-Purposes, C, O, OP, O-Class, T, P, TRANS, TKT, role, responsible, Input-Purposes, Output-Purposes) and
z_t = (S*, CA*, NA*, CT*, AT*, CTP*, ATP*, class*, T-Purpose*, O-Purposes*, C*, O*, OP*, O-Class*, T*, P*, TRANS*, TKT*, role*, responsible*, Input-Purposes*, Output-Purposes*) and subj is the active subject in state z_{t-1}.

Privacy constraint-1:

(z_{t-1}, z_t) satisfies the privacy constraint-1, iff

(CT(subj), o-class$_k$, CTP(subj), create) $\notin$ NA $\land$ O$_j \notin$ OP

$\Rightarrow$ O$_j \notin$ OP* $\lor$ class*(O$_j$) $\neq$ o-class$_k$.

Privacy constraint-2:

(z_{t-1}, z_t) satisfies the privacy constraint-2, iff

(CT(subj), Class(O$_j$), CTP(subj), delete) $\notin$ NA $\land$ O$_j \in$ OP

$\Rightarrow$ O$_j \in$ OP*.

Privacy constraint-3:

(z_{t-1}, z_t) satisfies the privacy constraint-3, iff

T-Purpose (CT (subj)) $\notin$ O-Purposes (o-class$_k$) $\land$ O$_j \notin$ OP

$\Rightarrow$ O$_j \notin$ OP* $\lor$ class*(O$_j$) $\neq$ o-class$_k$.

Privacy constraint-4:

(z_{t-1}, z_t) satisfies the privacy constraint-4, iff

T-Purpose (CT (subj)) $\notin$ O-Purposes (Class(O$_j$)) $\land$ (T-Purpose(CT(subj)),O$_j$) $\notin$ C

$\land$ O$_j \in$ OP $\Rightarrow$ O$_j \in$ OP*.

Privacy-oriented system:

A state v is a privacy-oriented state iff v satisfies the privacy invariants-1-4 and the information flow invariant.

A state sequence z is a privacy-oriented state sequence iff z_t is a privacy-oriented state for each t $\in$ T and all successive states (z_t, z_{t+1}) satisfy the privacy constraints-1-4.

Call (x, y, z) $\in \Sigma$ (R, D, W, z$_0$) an appearance of the system.

(x, y, z) $\in \Sigma$ (R, D, W, z$_0$) is a privacy-oriented appearance iff z is a privacy-oriented state sequence.

Σ (R, D, W, z$_0$) is a privacy-oriented system iff every appearance of Σ (R, D, W, z$_0$) is a privacy-oriented appearance.

Similar definitions pertain for the notions:

(i) the system Σ (R, D, W, z$_0$) satisfies the privacy invariants-1-4, information flow invariant.

(ii) the system Σ (R, D, W, z$_0$) satisfies the privacy constraints-1-4.

Definition of Rule:

A <u>rule</u> is a function $\varphi: R \times V \rightarrow D \times V$.

1.) A rule φ is privacy invariant-1 preserving iff
   whenever $\varphi(R_k, v) = (D_m, v^*)$

   v^* satisfies privacy invariant-1, if v satisfies privacy invariant-1.
   Similar definitions pertain for the notions:
2.) φ is privacy invariant-2 preserving.
3.) φ is privacy invariant-3 preserving.
4.) φ is privacy invariant-4 preserving.
5.) φ is information flow invariant preserving.

6.) A rule φ is privacy constraint-1 preserving iff
   whenever $\varphi(R_k, v) = (D_m, v^*)$

   the tuple of the successive states (v, v^*) satisfies the privacy constraint-1.
Similar definitions pertain for the notions:
7.) φ is privacy constraint-2 preserving.
8.) φ is privacy constraint-3 preserving.
9.) φ is privacy constraint-4 preserving.

10.) A rule φ is privacy-oriented state sequence preserving iff
   whenever $\varphi(R_k, v) = (D_m, v^*)$

(i) v^* is a privacy-oriented state, if v is a privacy-oriented state.
   (φ is privacy invariants -1-4 preserving[*] and information flow
   invariant preserving).

(ii) the tuple of the successive states (v, v^*) satisfies the privacy constraint-1, privacy
   constraint-2, privacy constraint-3 and privacy constraint-4.
   (φ is privacy constraints-1-4 preserving).

Suppose $\omega = \{\varphi_1, ..., \varphi_s\}$ is a set of rules.
The relation $W(\omega)$ is defined by

$(R_k, D_m, v^*, v) \in W(\omega)$ iff $D_m \neq \underline{?}$ and

$(D_m, v^*) = \varphi_i(R_k, v)$ for unique i, $1 \leq i \leq s$.

---

[*] We write that a rule is privacy invariants-1-4 preserving if it is privacy invariant-1
preserving and privacy invariant-2 preserving and privacy invariant-3 preserving and
privacy invariant-4 preserving.

3. Theorems

Theorem 1:

Suppose ω is a set of privacy invariant-1 preserving rules and z_0 is an initial state which satisfies the privacy invariant-1.

Then the system $\Sigma (R, D, W(\omega), z_0)$ satisfies privacy invariant-1.

Argument:

It has to be shown that every appearance $(x,y,z) \in \Sigma (R, D, W(\omega), z_0)$ satisfies privacy invariant-1, i.e. each state of the state sequence z satisfies privacy invariant-1, $z = \{z_0, z_1,..., z_n, z_{n+1},....\}$.

Proof by induction:

$\underline{n= 0:}$ z_0 satisfies privacy invariant-1 by definition.

$\underline{n -> n+1:}$ Suppose z_n satisfies privacy invariant-1.

By definition of $\Sigma (R, D, W(\omega), z_0)$:

$(R_k, D_m, z_n, z_{n+1}) \in W (\omega)$.

Then, by definition of $W (\omega)$, there is a $\varphi_i \in \omega$ such that:

$(D_m, z_n) = \varphi_i (R_k, z_{n+1})$.

Since φ_i is privacy invariant-1 preserving, z_{n+1} satisfies privacy invariant-1 according to definition 6.1.).

q.e.d.

Theorem 2:

Suppose ω is a set of privacy invariant-2 preserving rules and z_0 is an initial state which satisfies the privacy invariant-2.

Then the system $\Sigma (R, D, W(\omega), z_0)$ satisfies privacy invariant-2.

Argument: The argument is that of theorem 1 with the substitution of privacy invariant-2 for privacy invariant-1.

Theorem 3:

Suppose ω is a set of privacy invariant-3 preserving rules and z_0 is an initial state which satisfies the privacy invariant-3.

Then the system $\Sigma (R, D, W(\omega), z_0)$ satisfies privacy invariant-3.

Theorem 4:
Suppose ω is a set of privacy invariant-4 preserving rules and z_0 is an initial state which satisfies the privacy invariant-4.
Then the system Σ (R, D, W(ω), z_0) satisfies privacy invariant-4.

Theorem 5:
Suppose ω is a set of information flow invariant preserving rules and z_0 is an initial state which satisfies the information flow invariant.
Then the system Σ (R, D, W(ω), z_0) satisfies the information flow invariant.

Theorem 6:
Suppose ω is a set of privacy constraint-1 preserving rules.
Then the system Σ (R, D, W(ω), z_0) satisfies privacy constraint-1.

Argument (by contradiction):
Suppose Σ (R, D, W(ω), z_0) does not satisfy privacy constraint-1.
Then there is an appearance $(x,y,z) \in \Sigma$ (R, D, W(ω), z_0) which does not satisfy privacy constraint-1.
This means that there are two successive states z_t, z_{t+1} of the state sequence z with (z_t, z_{t+1}) does not satisfy privacy constraint-1.

Since $(D_m, z_{t+1}) = \varphi_i (R_k, z_t)$, $\varphi_i \in \omega$ is a privacy constraint-1 preserving rule, (z_t, z_{t+1}) satisfies privacy constraint-1 according to definition 6.

This contradiction shows that Σ (R, D, W(ω), z_0) satisfies privacy constraint-1.

Theorem 7:
Suppose ω is a set of privacy constraint-2 preserving rules.
Then the system Σ (R, D, W(ω), z_0) satisfies privacy constraint-2.

Argument: The argument is that of theorem 5 with the substitution of privacy constraint-2 for privacy constraint-1.

Theorem 8:
Suppose ω is a set of privacy constraint-3 preserving rules.
Then the system Σ (R, D, W(ω), z_0) satisfies privacy constraint-3.

Theorem 9:
Suppose ω is a set of privacy constraint-4 preserving rules.
Then the system Σ (R, D, W(ω), z_0) satisfies privacy constraint-4.

Corollary 1:
Suppose ω is a set of privacy-oriented state sequence preserving rules and z_0 is an initial privacy-oriented state. Then Σ (R, D, W(ω), z_0) is a privacy-oriented system.

In the following sections, the symbol "\" will be used in expressions of the form "A \ B" to mean "proposition A except as modified by proposition B."

Theorem 10:

Let φ be a rule and $\varphi(R_k, v) = (D_m, v^*)$, where

v = (S, CA, NA, CT, AT, CTP, ATP, class, T-Purpose, O-Purposes, C, O, OP, O-Class, T, P, TRANS, TKT, role, responsible, Input-Purposes, Output-Purposes) and
v^* = (S*, CA*, NA*, CT*, AT*, CTP*, ATP*, class*, T-Purpose*, O-Purposes*, C*, O*, OP*, O-Class*, T*, P*, TRANS*, TKT*, role*, responsible*, Input-Purposes*, Output-Purposes*).

If
(i) $CT^* = CT$ and $\forall\, S_i \in S$: $AT^*(S_i) \supseteq AT(S_i)$, $S^* = S$

  or

(ii) $CT^* = CT \setminus CT(S_j) <\!\!- T_k \wedge\ T_k \in AT^*(S_j)$, $S_j \in S^* \wedge$
   $\forall\, S_i \in S^*,\ S_i \neq S_j$: $AT^*(S_i) = AT(S_i)$

  or

(iii) $CT = CT^*$, $\forall\, S_i \in S$: $CT(S_i) \neq T_m$, $S^* = S$ and
   $AT^* = AT \setminus AT(S_i) <\!\!- AT(S_i) - (AT(S_i) \cap \{T_m\})$

$=>$

φ is privacy invariant-1 preserving.

Argument:
(i) If v satisfies privacy invariant-1, then
$\forall\, S_i \in S$: $CT(S_i) \in AT(S_i)$.
Since $CT^* = CT$ and $\forall\, S_i \in S$: $AT^*(S_i) \supseteq AT(S_i)$, $S^* = S\ =>$
$\forall\, S_i \in S$: $CT^*(S_i) = CT(S_i) \in AT(S_i) \subseteq AT^*(S_i)$.
$=> v^*$ satistfies the privacy invariant-1

(ii) Suppose v satisfies the privacy invariant-1.
   $\forall\, S_l \in S^*$:

$$CT^*(S_l) = \begin{cases} CT(S_l) & \text{for } S_l \neq S_j \\ \\ T_k \in AT^*(S_j) & \text{for } S_l = S_j. \end{cases}$$

For $S_l \neq S_j$:
According to the assumptions and since v satisfies privacy invariant-1:
$CT^*(S_l) = CT(S_l) \in AT(S_l) = AT^*(S_l) => v^*$ satisfies the privacy invariant-1.

For $S_l = S_j$:
$CT^*(S_l) = T_k, T_k \in AT^*(S_l) => v^*$ satisfies the privacy invariant-1.

$=> v^*$ satisfies privacy invariant-1.

(iii) Suppose v satisfies privacy invariant-1:
$\forall S_i \in S = S^*$:

$CT^*(S_i) = CT(S_i) \in AT(S_i)$.

$$AT^*(S_i) = \begin{cases} AT(S_i) - \{T_m\} & \text{if } T_m \in AT(S_i) \\ \\ AT(S_i) & \text{else} \end{cases}$$

If $T_m \notin AT(S_i) \Rightarrow CT^*(S_i) = CT(S_i) \in AT(S_i) = AT^*(S_i)$

If $T_m \in AT(S_i)$:

    Since $CT(S_i) \neq T_m \Rightarrow$

    If $CT(S_i) \in AT(S_i) \Rightarrow CT^*(S_i) = CT(S_i) \in AT(S_i) - \{T_m\} = AT^*(S_i)$.

$\Rightarrow$ v* satisfies privacy invariant-1.

$\Rightarrow \varphi$ is privacy invariant-1 preserving.

Theorem 11:
Let φ be a rule and φ $(R_k, v) = (D_m, v^*)$, where
v = (S, CA, NA, CT, AT, CTP, ATP, class, T-Purpose, O-Purposes, C, O, OP, O-Class, T, P, TRANS, TKT, role, responsible, Input-Purposes, Output-Purposes) and
v* = (S*, CA*, NA*, CT*, AT*, CTP*, ATP*, class*, T-Purpose*, O-Purposes*, C*, O*, OP*, O-Class*, T*, P*, TRANS*, TKT*, role*, responsible*, Input-Purposes*, Output-Purposes*).

If
(i) CTP* = CTP, CT* = CT, $\forall S_i \in S$: ATP* $(CT(S_i)) \supseteq ATP(CT(S_i))$, S* = S
or
(ii) CTP* = CTP \ CTP $(S_j) <- \beta$, β= Nil $\vee$ β = transp$_k$ $\in$ ATP (CT (S_j)) ,
    $\wedge$ ATP* = ATP $\wedge$ CT * =CT
or
(iii) For a $S_j \in$ S*: CT* $(S_j) = T_k$ and CTP*(S_j) = Nil,
    $\forall S_i \in$ S*, $S_i \neq S_j$: CTP*(S_j) = CTP(S_j) and CT*(S_i) = CT(S_i),
    ATP* =ATP
or
(iv) CTP* = CTP, CT* = CT,

$\forall T_k \in T$: $ATP^* = ATP \setminus ATP(T_k) <- ATP(T_k) - (ATP(T_k) \cap \{transp_m\})$
and $\forall S_i \in S$: $CTP(S_i) \neq transp_m \vee CT(S_i) \neq T_k$, $S^* = S$.

=>

φ is privacy invariant-2 preserving.

Argument:
(i) If v satisfies privacy invariant 2, then
$\forall S_i \in S$: $CTP(S_i) \in ATP(CT(S_i))$.
Since $CTP^* = CTP$, $CT^* = CT$, $\forall S_i \in S$: $ATP^* (CT(S_i)) \supseteq ATP(CT(S_i))$, $S^* = S$ =>
$\forall S_i \in S^*$: $CTP^*(S_i) = CTP(S_i) \in ATP(CT(S_i)) \subseteq ATP^*(CT^*(S_i))$.
=> v^* satisfies the privacy invariant-2.

(ii) Suppose v satisfies the privacy invariant 2.
$\forall S_l \in S^*$:

$$CTP^* (S_l) = \begin{cases} CTP(S_l) & \text{for } S_l \neq S_j \\ Nil \vee transp_k \in ATP(CT(S_j)) & \text{for } S_l = S_j. \end{cases}$$

For $S_l \neq S_j$:
According to the assumptions and since v satisfies the privacy invariant-2:
$CTP^*(S_l) = CTP(S_l) \in ATP(CT(S_l)) = ATP^*(CT^*(S_l))$
=> v^* satisfies the privacy invariant-2.

For $S_l = S_j$:
If $CTP^*(S_l) = Nil$:

Since $\forall T_m \in T^*$: $Nil \in ATP^*(T_m)$ according to the definition of the
state element ATP^*:
=> $CTP^*(S_l) \in ATP^*(CT^*(S_l))$ => v^* satisfies the privacy invariant-2
Else:

$CTP^*(S_l) = transp_k$, $transp_k \in ATP(CT(S_l)) = ATP^*(CT^*(S_l))$
=> v^* satisfies the privacy invariant-2.

(iii) Suppose v satisfies the privacy invariant-2.

$\forall S_l \in S^*$:
If $S_l \neq S_j$:

$CTP^*(S_l) = CTP(S_l) \in ATP(CT(S_l)) = ATP^*(CT^*(S_l))$ according to the assumptions and since v satisfies privacy invariant-2.
=> v* satisfies privacy invariant-2.

If $S_l = S_j$:

$CTP^*(S_l) = Nil \in ATP^*(CT^*(S_l))$ according to the assumptions and definition of the element ATP*.
=> v* satisfies privacy invariant-2.

(iv) According to the assumptions:
$\forall S_i \in S: CTP(S_i) \neq transp_m \vee CT(S_i) \neq T_k$.

If $CTP(S_i) \neq transp_m$:
     Since $\forall T_k \in T$: $ATP^* = ATP \setminus ATP(T_k)$ <-
                $ATP(T_k) - (ATP(T_k) \cap \{transp_m\})$:
     and
     $CTP(S_i) \in ATP(CT(S_i))$ (as v satisfies the privacy invariant-2)
     =>
     $CTP^*(S_i) = CTP(S_i) \in ATP^*(CT(S_i))$ (as $CTP(S_i) \neq transp_m$).
     $= ATP^*(CT^*(S_i))$.

If $CT(S_i) \neq T_k$:
     $ATP(CT(S_i)) = ATP^*(CT(S_i)) = ATP^*(CT^*(S_i))$ according to the assumptions.
     Since v satisfies privacy invariant-2:
     $CTP^*(S_i) = CTP(S_i) \in ATP(CT(S_i)) = ATP^*(CT^*(S_i))$.

=> v* satisfies privacy invariant-2.

=> φ is privacy invariant-2 preserving.

Theorem 12:
Let φ be a rule and $\varphi(R_k, v) = (D_m, v^*)$, where

v = (S, CA, NA, CT, AT, CTP, ATP, class, T-Purpose, O-Purposes, C, O, OP, O-Class, T, P, TRANS, TKT, role, responsible, Input-Purposes, Output-Purposes) and
v* = (S*, CA*, NA*, CT*, AT*, CTP*, ATP*, class*, T-Purpose*, O-Purposes*, C*, O*, OP*, O-Class*, T*, P*, TRANS*, TKT*, role*, responsible*, Input-Purposes*, Output-Purposes*).

If
(i) $(S_i, O_j, x) \notin CA$, $CA^* = CA \cup \{(S_i, O_j, x)\}$ $\wedge$

    $[(O_j \in OP \wedge (CT(S_i), Class(O_j), CTP(S_i), x) \in NA) \vee (O_j \notin OP)]$ $\wedge$

    $CT^* = CT$, $Class^* = Class$, $CTP^* = CTP$, $NA^* = NA$

or
(ii) $CA^* \subseteq CA$, $\forall S_i \in S$: $CT^*(S_i) = CT(S_i)$, $CTP^*(S_i) = CTP(S_i)$, $NA^* \supseteq NA$,

    $\forall O_j \in OP$: $Class^* (O_j) = Class (O_j)$

or
(iii) $CA^* \subseteq CA$,

    $CTP^* = CTP \setminus CTP(S_i)$ <- β, $\beta = Nil \vee \beta = transp_j$,

    and $\forall O_k \in OP$, $x \in A$: $(S_i, O_k, x) \notin CA^*$,

    and $CT^* = CT$, $Class^* = Class$, $NA^* = NA$

or
(iv) $CA^* \subseteq CA$,

    $CT^* = CT \setminus CT(S_i)$ <- T_j $\wedge$ $\forall O_k \in OP$, $x \in A$: $(S_i, O_k, x) \notin CA^*$,

    $CTP^* = CTP$, $Class^* = Class$, $NA^* = NA$

or
(v) $CA^* = CA$, $CT^* = CT$, $Class^* = Class$, $CTP^* = CTP$,

    $NA^* = NA - NA^+$, $NA^+ \subseteq NA$ and

    $\forall (S_i, O_j, x) \in CA \Rightarrow (CT(S_i), Class(O_j), CTP(S_i), x) \notin NA^+$

$\Rightarrow$

φ is privacy invariant-3 preserving.

Argument:
(i) Suppose v satisfies the privacy invariant-3 and
    (S_l, O_k, y) is an arbitrary element of CA^*, $O_k \in OP$:

$(S_l, O_k, y) \in CA^* \Rightarrow$
$(S_l, O_k, y) \in [CA \cup \{(S_i, O_j, x)\}]$

If $(S_l, O_k, y) \in CA \Rightarrow$ $(CT^*(S_l), Class^*(O_k), CTP^*(S_l), y) =$
                                        $(CT(S_l), Class(O_k), CTP(S_l), y) \in NA = NA^*$
                                        according to the assumptions and since v satisfies the
                                        privacy invariant-3.

If $(S_l, O_k, y) = (S_i, O_j, x) \Rightarrow$

If $O_j \notin OP$: privacy invariant-3 is satisfied.

If $O_j \in OP$:

$$(CT^*(S_l), Class^*(O_k), CTP^*(S_l), y) = (CT^*(S_i), Class^* (O_j), CTP^*(S_i), x) =$$
$$(CT(S_i), Class(O_j), CTP(S_i), x) \in NA = NA^*.$$

$\Rightarrow v^*$ satisfies privacy invariant-3.

(ii) Suppose v satisfies the privacy invariant-3 and
  (S_l, O_k, y) is an arbitrary element of CA^*, $O_k \in OP^*$:

$(S_l, O_k, y) \in CA^* \Rightarrow (S_l, O_k, y) \in CA \Rightarrow (CT (S_l), Class (O_k), CTP (S_l), y) \in NA.$
$\Rightarrow (CT^*(S_l), Class^* (O_k), CTP^*(S_l), y) \in NA \subseteq NA^*,$
  since $\forall S_i \in S: CT^*(S_i) = CT(S_i), CTP^*(S_i) = CTP(S_i), NA \subseteq NA^*,$
    $\forall O_j \in OP: Class^* (O_j) = Class (O_j).$

$\Rightarrow v^*$ satisfies the privacy invariant-3.

(iii) Suppose v satisfies the privacy invariant-3 and
  (S_l, O_k, y) is an arbitrary element of CA^*, $O_k \in OP^*$:

$(S_l, O_k, y) \in CA^* \Rightarrow (S_l, O_k, y) \in CA$
$\qquad\qquad\qquad \Rightarrow (CT (S_l), Class (O_k), CTP (S_l), y) \in NA.$

By the assumptions, it is:

$$CTP^* (S_l) = \begin{cases} CTP(S_l) & \text{if } S_l \neq S_i \\ \\ transp_j \vee Nil & \text{if } S_l = S_i. \end{cases}$$

If $S_l \neq S_i \Rightarrow (CT^*(S_l), Class^*(O_k), CTP^*(S_l), y) =$
$\qquad\qquad\qquad (CT(S_l), Class(O_k), CTP(S_l), y) \in NA = NA^*.$

If $S_l = S_i \Rightarrow (S_l, O_k, y) \notin CA^*$ by assumption.

Hence, for all $(S_l, O_k, y) \in CA^*$
$\Rightarrow (CT^*(S_l), Class^*(O_k), CTP^*(S_l), y) \in NA^*$

$\Rightarrow v^*$ satisfies privacy invariant-3.

(iv) Suppose v satisfies the privacy invariant-3 and
  (S_l, O_k, y) is an arbitrary element of CA^*, $O_k \in OP^*$:

$(S_l, O_k, y) \in CA^* \Rightarrow (S_l, O_k, y) \in CA$
$$\Rightarrow (CT(S_l), Class(O_k), CTP(S_l), y) \in NA.$$

By the assumptions, it is:

$$CT^*(S_l) = \begin{cases} CT(S_l) & \text{if } S_l \neq S_i \\ T_j & \text{if } S_l = S_i. \end{cases}$$

If $S_l \neq S_i \Rightarrow (CT^*(S_l), Class^*(O_k), CTP^*(S_l), y) =$
$$(CT(S_l), Class(O_k), CTP(S_l), y) \in NA = NA^*.$$

If $S_l = S_i \Rightarrow (S_l, O_k, y) \notin CA^*$ by assumption.

Hence, for all $(S_l, O_k, y) \in CA^*$
$\Rightarrow (CT^*(S_l), Class^*(O_k), CTP^*(S_l), y) \in NA^*$

$\Rightarrow v^*$ satisfies privacy invariant-3.

(v) Suppose v satisfies the privacy invariant-3 and
   (S_l, O_k, y) is an arbitrary element of CA^*, $O_k \in OP^*$:

$(S_l, O_k, y) \in CA^* \Rightarrow (S_l, O_k, y) \in CA$
$$\Rightarrow (CT(S_l), Class(O_k), CTP(S_l), y) \in NA$$
   Since $NA^* = NA - NA^+$ and
   $(CT(S_l), Class(O_k), CTP(S_l), y) \notin NA^+ \Rightarrow$
   $(CT(S_l), Class(O_k), CTP(S_l), y) = (CT^*(S_l), Class^*(O_k), CTP^*(S_l), y) \in NA^*.$

$\Rightarrow v^*$ satisfies privacy invariant-3.

$\Rightarrow \varphi$ is privacy invariant-3 preserving.

Theorem 13:
Let φ be a rule and $\varphi(R_k, v) = (D_m, v^*)$, where
v = (S, CA, NA, CT, AT, CTP, ATP, class, T-Purpose, O-Purposes, C, O, OP, O-Class, T, P, TRANS, TKT, role, responsible, Input-Purposes, Output-Purposes) and

$v^* = (S^*, CA^*, NA^*, CT^*, AT^*, CTP^*, ATP^*, class^*, T\text{-}Purpose^*, O\text{-}Purposes^*, C^*,$
$O^*, OP^*, O\text{-}Class^*, T^*, P^*, TRANS^*, TKT^*, role^*, responsible^*, Input\text{-}Purposes^*,$
$Output\text{-}Purposes^*).$

If

(i) $(S_i, O_j, x) \notin CA, CA^* = CA \cup \{(S_i, O_j, x)\}$ $\wedge$

$[(O_j \in OP \wedge ((T\text{-}Purpose (CT(S_i)) \in O\text{-}Purposes (Class (O_j)) \vee$

$(T\text{-}Purpose (CT(S_i)), O_j) \in C)) \vee (O_j \notin OP)]$ $\wedge$

$O\text{-}Purposes^* = O\text{-}Purposes, T\text{-}Purpose^* = T\text{-}Purpose, Class^* = Class, CT^* = CT,$
$C^* = C, O^* = O.$

or

(ii) $CA^* \subseteq CA,$

$CT^* = CT, \forall O_j \in OP: O\text{-}Purposes^* (Class(O_j)) = O\text{-}Purposes(Class(O_j)),$

$\forall T_k \in T: T\text{-}Purpose^*(T_k) = T\text{-}Purpose(T_k), (C^* \supseteq C$

or $C^* = C - (C \cap (P \times \{O_j\}))$ with $(S \times \{O_j\} \times A) \not\subset CA^*))$

$\forall O_j \in O: Class^* (O_j) = Class (O_j)$

or

(iii) $CA^* \subseteq CA,$

$CT^* = CT \setminus CT^* (S_i) = T_j$ and

$\forall O_k \in OP, x \in A: (S_i, O_k, x) \notin CA,$

$O\text{-}Purposes^* = O\text{-}Purposes, T\text{-}Purpose^* = T\text{-}Purpose, Class^* = Class, C^* = C.$

or

(iv) $CA^* = CA, CT^* = CT,$

$\forall O_j \in O: O\text{-}Purposes^* (Class^*(O_j)) = O\text{-}Purposes(Class(O_j)),$

$Class^* = Class, T\text{-}Purpose^* = T\text{-}Purpose, C^* = C - (C \cap \{(p_m \times O^-)\})$

for a subset $O^- \subseteq O$ and $\forall (S_i, O_j, x) \in CA =>$

$T\text{-}Purpose(CT(S_i)) \neq p_m \vee T\text{-}Purpose(CT(S_i)) \in O\text{-}Purposes(Class(O_j)).$

$=> \varphi$ is privacy invariant-4 preserving.

Argument:
(i) Suppose v satisfies privacy invariant-4 and (S_l, O_k, y) is an arbitrary element of CA^*:

$(S_l, O_k, y) \in CA^* => (S_l, O_k, y) \in [CA \cup \{(S_i, O_j, x)\}]$

If $(S_l, O_k, y) \in CA, O_k \in OP$

$=> T\text{-}Purpose (CT(S_l)) \in O\text{-}Purposes (Class (O_k)) \vee$

$(T\text{-}Purpose (CT(S_l)), O_k) \in C,$

since v satisfies privacy invariant-4.

Then according to the assumptions:

$$\Rightarrow \; \text{T-Purpose*} (CT^*(S_l)) \in \text{O-Purposes*} (\text{Class *}(O_k)) \lor$$
$$(\text{T-Purpose*} (CT^*(S_l)), O_k) \in C^*)$$

$\Rightarrow v^*$ satisfies privacy invariant-4.

If $(S_l, O_k, y) = (S_i, O_j, x)$:

If $O_j \notin OP$: privacy invariant-4 is satisfied.

If $O_j \in OP$:

Then, by the assumptions:
$\Rightarrow$
T-Purpose $(CT(S_l)) \in$ O-Purposes $(\text{Class } (O_k)) \lor$
(T-Purpose $(CT(S_l)), O_k) \in C$
$\Rightarrow$
T-Purpose*$(CT^*(S_l)) \in$ O-Purposes*$(\text{Class*}(O_k)) \lor$
(T-Purpose*$(CT^*(S_l)), O_k) \in C^*$

Hence: $\forall S_l \in S^*, O_k \in OP^* \; (S_l, O_k, y) \in CA^* \Rightarrow$
T-Purpose*$(CT^*(S_l)) \in$ O-Purposes*$(\text{Class*}(O_k)) \lor$
(T-Purpose*$(CT^*(S_l)), O_k) \in C^*$

$\Rightarrow v^*$ satisfies privacy invariant-4.

(ii) Suppose v satisfies privacy invariant-4 and (S_l, O_k, y) is an arbitrary element
   of $CA^*, O_k \in OP^*$:

$(S_l, O_k, y) \in CA^* \Rightarrow (S_l, O_k, y) \in CA$
$\Rightarrow$ 　　　　　　　　T-Purpose $(CT(S_l)) \in$ O-Purposes $(\text{Class } (O_k)) \lor$
　　　　　　　　(T-Purpose $(CT(S_l)), O_k) \in C,$
　　　　　　　　since v satisfies privacy invariant-4.

Since $(C^* \supseteq C$ or $C^* = C - (C \cap (P \times \{O_j\}))$ with $(S \times \{O_j\} \times A) \not\subset CA^*))$:
(T-Purpose $(CT(S_l)), O_k) \in C^*$

Since according to the assumptions:

T-Purpose(CT(S_l)) = T-Purpose*(CT*(S_l)) and

O-Purposes (Class (O_k)) = O-Purposes* (Class *(O_k)) and $C \subseteq C^*$:

=> T-Purpose* (CT*(S_l)) $\in$ O-Purposes* (Class *(O_k)) $\vee$

(T-Purpose* (CT*(S_l)), O_k) $\in$ C^*

=> v^* satisfies the privacy invariant-4.

(iii) Suppose v satisfies privacy invariant-4 and (S_l, O_k, y) is an arbitrary element of CA^* , O_k $\in$ OP^* :

(S_l, O_k, y) $\in$ CA^* => (S_l, O_k, y) $\in$ CA =>

T-Purpose (CT(S_l)) $\in$ O-Purposes (Class (O_k)) $\vee$

(T-Purpose (CT(S_l)), O_k) $\in$ C,

since v satisfies privacy invariant-4.

By the assumptions:

$$CT^* (S_l) = \begin{cases} CT(S_l) & \text{if } S_l \neq S_i \\ T_j & \text{if } S_l = S_i. \end{cases}$$

If $S_l \neq S_i$:

T-Purpose (CT(S_l)) $\in$ O-Purposes (Class (O_k)) $\vee$

T-Purpose (CT(S_l)), O_k $\in$ C =>

T-Purpose* (CT*(S_l)) $\in$ O-Purposes* (Class* (O_k)) $\vee$

(T-Purpose* (CT*(S_l)), O_k) $\in$ C^*

If $S_l = S_i$:   (S_l, O_k, x) $\notin$ CA => (S_l, O_k, y) $\notin$ CA^*.

Hence, for all (S_l, O_k, y) $\in$ CA^* =>

T-Purpose* (CT*(S_l)) $\in$ O-Purposes* (Class* (O_k)) $\vee$

(T-Purpose* (CT*(S_l)), O_k) $\in$ C^*

(iv) Suppose v satisfies privacy invariant-4 and (S_l, O_k, y) is an arbitrary element of CA^*, O_k $\in$ OP^* :

(S_l, O_k, y) $\in$ CA^* => (S_l, O_k, y) $\in$ CA =>

$$\text{T-Purpose } (CT(S_l)) \in \text{O-Purposes (Class } (O_k)) \vee$$
$$(\text{T-Purpose } (CT(S_l)), O_k) \in C.$$

According to the assumptions:

(*) $\text{T-Purpose}(CT(S_l)) \neq p_m \vee \text{T-Purpose}(CT(S_l)) \in \text{O-Purposes}(\text{Class}(O_k))$.

If $\text{T-Purpose}(CT(S_l)) \in \text{O-Purposes}(\text{Class}(O_k))$:

$\Rightarrow \text{T-Purpose}*(CT*(S_l)) \in \text{O-Purposes}*(\text{Class}*(O_k))$.

If not $[\text{T-Purpose}(CT(S_l)) \in \text{O-Purposes}(\text{Class}(O_k))]$:

$\Rightarrow \text{T-Purpose}(CT(S_l)) \neq p_m$ according to (*)

and $(\text{T-Purpose } (CT(S_l)), O_k) \in C$ since v satisfies the privacy invariant-4.

$\Rightarrow \text{T-Purpose}*(CT* (S_l)) \neq p_m$ and $(\text{T-Purpose}* (CT*(S_l)), O_k) \in C$.

Since $C* = C - (C \cap \{(p_m \times \bar{O})\})$ for a subset $\bar{O} \subseteq OP \Rightarrow$
$(\text{T-Purpose}* (CT*(S_l), O_k) \in C*$.

Hence: $(S_l, O_k, y) \in CA* \Rightarrow \text{T-Purpose}* (CT*(S_l)) \in \text{O-Purposes}* (\text{Class}* (O_k)) \vee$
$(\text{T-Purpose}* (CT*(S_l)), O_k) \in C*$.

$\Rightarrow$v* satisfies privacy invariant-4.

$\Rightarrow \varphi$ is privacy invariant-4-preserving.

Theorem 14:

Let φ be a rule and $\varphi (R_k, v) = (D_m, v*)$, where

$v = $ (S, CA, NA, CT, AT, CTP, ATP, class, T-Purpose, O-Purposes, C, O, OP, O-Class, T, P, TRANS, TKT, role, responsible, Input-Purposes, Output-Purposes) and
$v* = $ (S*, CA*, NA*, CT*, AT*, CTP*, ATP*, class*, T-Purpose*, O-Purposes*, C*, O*, OP*, O-Class*, T*, P*, TRANS*, TKT*, role*, responsible*, Input-Purposes*, Output-Purposes*).

If

(i) $(S_i, O_j, x) \notin CA, CA* = CA \cup \{(S_i, O_j, x)\}, x \in \{\text{write, append}\} \wedge$

$[(O_j \in OP \wedge \text{Output-Purposes } (S_i) \cup \text{O-Purpose } (\text{class}(O_j)) \subseteq \text{Input-Purposes}(S_i))$

$\vee (O_j \notin OP \wedge \text{Input-Purposes}(S_i) = P)] \wedge$

$\text{O-Purposes}* = \text{O-Purposes} \setminus \text{O-Purposes } (S_i) \leftarrow \text{Output-Purposes } (S_i) \cup$
$\text{O-Purposes } (\text{class } (O_j))$,

$\text{Input-Purposes}* = \text{Input-Purposes}.$

or

(ii) $(S_i, O_j, \text{read}) \notin CA$, $CA^* = CA \cup \{(S_i, O_j, \text{read})\} \wedge$

   $[(O_j \in OP \wedge \text{Output-Purposes}(S_i) \subseteq$

    $\text{Input-Purposes}(S_i) \cap \text{O-Purposes}(\text{class}(O_j)))$

    $\vee (O_j \notin OP)] \wedge$

    $\text{Input-Purposes}^* = \text{Input-Purposes} \setminus \text{Input-Purposes}(S_i) \leftarrow \text{Input-Purposes}(S_i) \cap$

                         $\text{O-Purposes}(\text{class}(O_j)),$

    $\text{Output-Purposes}^* = \text{Output-Purposes}.$

or

(iii) $\forall S_i \in S \cap S^*$: $\text{Input-Purposes}^*(S_i) \supseteq \text{Input-Purposes}(S_i)$ and

                $\text{Output-Purposes}^*(S_i) \subseteq \text{Output-Purposes } (S_i),$

   $\forall S_i \in S^* - S$: $\text{Input-Purposes}^*(S_i) = P$, $\text{Output-Purposes}^*(S_i) = \emptyset$.

$\Rightarrow$

φ is information flow invariant preserving.

Argument:

(i) Suppose v satisfies the information flow invariant and S_l is an arbitrary
   element of S^*.
   If $S_l \neq S_i$:

        $\text{Output-Purposes}(S_l) \subseteq \text{Input-Purposes } (S_l)$

              since v satisfies the information flow invariant.
   Then, according to the assumptions:
   $\text{Output-Purposes}^* (S_l) \subseteq \text{Input-Purposes }^*(S_l).$

   If $S_l = S_i$:

        $\text{Output-Purposes}^* (S_l) = \text{Output-Purposes } (S_l) \cup \text{O-Purposes } (\text{class } O_j))$

                $\subseteq \text{Input-Purposes } (S_l) = \text{Input-Purposes}^* (S_l).$

              according to the assumptions.

$\Rightarrow v^*$ satisfies the information flow invariant.

(ii) Suppose v satisfies the information flow control invariant and S_l is an arbitrary
    element of S^*.

   If $S_l \neq S_i$ $\Rightarrow$ $\text{Output-Purposes}(S_l) \subseteq \text{Input-Purposes } (S_l)$

              since v satisfies the information flow invariant.
   Then, according to the assumptions:
    $\text{Output-Purposes}^* (S_l) \subseteq \text{Input-Purposes }^*(S_l).$

If $S_l = S_i$:

      Output-Purposes* (S_l) = Output-Purposes (S_l)

        If $O_j \in$ OP: Output-Purposes (S_l)

               $\subseteq$ Input-Purposes $(S_l) \cap$ O-Purposes (class O_j))

               = Input-Purposes* (S_l).

          according to the assumptions.

        If $O_j \notin$ OP: Output-Purposes $(S_l) \subseteq$ Input-Purposes (S_l)

                      since v satisfies the information flow invariant

              = Input-Purposes $(S_l) \cap$ O-Purposes (class O_j))

                  since O-Purposes (class (O_j)) = O-Purposes(none) = P

              = Input-Purposes* (S_l).

    => Output-Purposes* $(S_l) \subseteq$ Input-Purposes *(S_l).

=> v* satisfies the information flow invariant.

(iii) Suppose v satisfies the information flow invariant and S_i is an arbitrary
     element of S*.

  If $S_i \in$ S : Output-Purposes$(S_i) \subseteq$ Input-Purposes (S_i)

              since v satisfies the information flow invariant.

       According to the assumptions:
       Output-Purposes*$(S_i) \subseteq$ Output-Purposes $(S_i) \subseteq$ Input-Purposes $(S_i) \subseteq$
       Input-Purposes* (S_i)

  If $S_i \notin$ S : Output-Purposes*$(S_i) = \varnothing \subseteq$ Input-Purposes*$(S_i) = P$
                 according to the assumptions

=> v* satisfies the information flow invariant.

=> φ is information flow invariant preserving.

Theorem 15:

Let φ be a rule and $\varphi\,(R_k, v) = (D_m, v^*)$, where

$v = $ (S, CA, NA, CT, AT, CTP, ATP, class, T-Purpose, O-Purposes, C, O, OP, O-Class, T, P, TRANS, TKT, role, responsible, Input-Purposes, Output-Purposes) and
$v^* = $ (S*, CA*, NA*, CT*, AT*, CTP*, ATP*, class*, T-Purpose*, O-Purposes*, C*, O*, OP*, O-Class*, T*, P*, TRANS*, TKT*, role*, responsible*, Input-Purposes*, Output-Purposes*).

If
(i) $OP^* \subseteq OP$
or
(ii) $OP^* = OP \cup \{O_j\}$, $(CT(subj), \text{o-class}_k, CTP\,(subj), create) \in NA$,
    $Class^* = Class \setminus Class(O_j) \leftarrow \text{o-class}_k$.
$\Rightarrow \varphi$ is privacy constraint-1 preserving.

<u>Argument:</u>
(i) Since $OP^* \subseteq OP$:
    If $O_j \notin OP \Rightarrow O_j \notin OP^*$

According to logical rules the following implication holds for propositions p, q, r, s:
$(p \Rightarrow q) \Rightarrow (p \wedge r \Rightarrow q \vee s)$.

Hence, the following implication holds as well:
 $(CT(subj), \text{o-class}_k, CTP\,(subj), create) \notin NA \wedge O_j \notin OP \Rightarrow$
  $O_j \notin OP^* \vee class^*(O_j) \neq \text{o-class}_k$.

$\Rightarrow (v, v^*)$ satisfies privacy constraint-1.

(ii) Privacy constraint-1 is satisfied, iff for arbitrary O_1:
   (*) $O_1 \in OP^* \wedge class^*(O_j) = \text{o-class}_k \Rightarrow$
        $O_1 \in OP \vee (CT(subj), \text{o-class}_k, CTP\,(subj), create) \in NA$
Since $OP^* = OP \cup \{O_j\}$:
   $O_1 \in OP^* \Rightarrow O_1 \in OP \vee O_1 = O_j$.

If $O_1 \in OP$:
Since $O_1 \in OP^* \Rightarrow O_1 \in OP$, the implication (*) holds according to rules of logic.

If $O_1 = O_j$:
According to the assumptions: $(CT(subj), \text{o-class}_k, CTP\,(subj), create) \in NA$ and
  $class^*(O_j) = \text{o-class}_k$.

$=>$ (Class*(O_l) = o-class$_k$)$=>$ (CT(subj), o-class$_k$, CTP (subj), create) $\in$ NA
and the implication (*) holds according to rules of logic.

q.e.d.

$=>$ (v, v*) satisfies privacy constraint-1.

Theorem 16:

Let φ be a rule and φ (R_k, v) = (D_m, v*), where

v = (S, CA, NA, CT, AT, CTP, ATP, class, T-Purpose, O-Purposes, C, O, OP,
O-Class, T, P, TRANS, TKT, role, responsible, Input-Purposes, Output-Purposes) and
v* = (S*, CA*, NA*, CT*, AT*, CTP*, ATP*, class*, T-Purpose*, O-Purposes*, C*,
O*, OP*, O-Class*, T*, P*, TRANS*, TKT*, role*, responsible*, Input-Purposes*,
Output-Purposes*).

If
(i) OP* $\supseteq$ OP
or
(ii) OP* = OP - {O_j}, (CT(subj), Class(O_j), CTP (subj), delete) $\in$ NA
$=>$ φ is privacy constraint-2 preserving.

Argument:

(i) Since OP* $\supseteq$ OP:

$O_j \in$ OP $=>$ $O_j \in$ OP*
$=>$
If (CT(subj), Class(O_j), CTP (subj), delete) $\in$ NA $\wedge$ $O_j \in$ O $=>$ $O_j \in$ O*.

$=>$ (v, v*) satisfies privacy constraint-2.

(ii) Privacy constraint-2 is satisfied, iff
$O_1 \notin$ OP* $=>$ $O_1 \notin$ OP $\vee$ (CT(subj), Class(O_1), CTP (subj), delete) $\in$ NA.

$O_1 \notin$ OP* $=>$ $O_1 \notin$ OP $\vee$ $O_1 = O_j$.

Since (CT(subj), Class(O_j), CTP (subj), delete) $\in$ NA by assumption:

$=>$ If $O_1 = O_j$ $=>$ (CT(subj), Class(O_1), CTP (subj), create) $\in$ NA .

=> $O_1 \notin OP^*$ => $O_1 \notin OP \vee$ (CT(subj), Class(O_1), CTP (subj), delete) $\in$ NA.

=> (v, v^*) satisfies privacy constraint-2.

q.e.d.

Theorem 17:
Let φ be a rule and $\varphi (R_k, v) = (D_m, v^*)$, where

$v =$ (S, CA, NA, CT, AT, CTP, ATP, class, T-Purpose, O-Purposes, C, O, OP, O-Class, T, P, TRANS, TKT, role, responsible, Input-Purposes, Output-Purposes) and
$v^* =$ (S*, CA*, NA*, CT*, AT*, CTP*, ATP*, class*, T-Purpose*, O-Purposes*, C*, O*, OP*, O-Class*, T*, P*, TRANS*, TKT*, role*, responsible*, Input-Purposes*, Output-Purposes*).

If
(i) $OP^* \subseteq OP$
or
(ii) $OP^* = OP \cup \{O_j\}$, T-Purpose(CT(subj)) $\in$ O-Purposes (o-class$_k$),
    Class* = Class \ Class(O_j) <- o-class$_k$.

=> φ is privacy constraint-3 preserving.

Argument:

(i) Since $OP^* \subseteq OP$:

 If $O_j \notin OP$ => $O_j \notin OP^*$
  =>
T-Purpose(CT(subj)) $\notin$ O-Purposes (o-class$_k$) $\wedge O_j \notin OP$ =>
$O_j \notin OP^* \vee$ Class*(O_1) $\neq$ o-class$_k$.

=> (v, v^*) satisfies privacy constraint-3.

(ii) Privacy constraint-3 is satisfied, iff
    (*) $O_1 \in OP^* \wedge$ Class*(O_1) = o-class$_k$ =>
        $O_1 \in OP \vee$ T-Purpose(CT(subj)) $\in$ O-Purposes (o-class$_k$),

Since $OP^* = OP \cup \{O_j\}$:
  $O_1 \in OP^*$ => $O_1 \in OP \vee O_1 = O_j$.

If $O_1 \in OP$:

Since $O_1 \in OP^* \Rightarrow O_1 \in OP$, the implication (*) is implied by rules of logic.

If $O_1 = O_j$:

According to the assumptions: T-Purpose(CT(subj)) $\in$ O-Purposes (o-class$_k$) and
Class*(O_j) = o-class$_k$.

=>

(Class*(O_1) = o-class$_k$) => (T-Purpose(CT(subj)) $\in$ O-Purposes (o-class$_k$))
and the implication (*) holds according to rules of logic.

=> (v, v*) satisfies privacy constraint-3.

q.e.d.

Theorem 18:
Let φ be a rule and $\varphi (R_k, v) = (D_m, v^*)$, where

v = (S, CA, NA, CT, AT, CTP, ATP, class, T-Purpose, O-Purposes, C, O, OP,
O-Class, T, P, TRANS, TKT, role, responsible, Input-Purposes, Output-Purposes) and
v* = (S*, CA*, NA*, CT*, AT*, CTP*, ATP*, class*, T-Purpose*, O-Purposes*, C*,
O*, OP*, O-Class*, T*, P*, TRANS*, TKT*, role*, responsible*, Input-Purposes*,
Output-Purposes*).

If
(i) OP* $\supseteq$ OP
or
(ii) OP* = OP - $\{O_j\}$, T-Purpose(CT(subj)) $\in$ O-Purposes (Class(O_j)) $\lor$
$\qquad\qquad\qquad$ (T-Purpose(CT(subj), O_j) $\in$ C.

=> φ is privacy constraint-4 preserving.

Argument:

(i) Since OP* $\supseteq$ OP:

If $O_j \in OP \Rightarrow O_j \in OP^*$
$\quad$ =>
$\quad$ T-Purpose(CT(subj)) $\notin$ O-Purposes (Class(O_j)) $\land$ (T-Purpose(CT(subj), O_j) $\notin$ C
$\quad \land O_j \in OP \Rightarrow O_j \in OP^*$

=> (v, v*) satisfies privacy constraint-4.

(ii) Privacy constraint-3 is satisfied, iff for an arbitrary O_l:

$$O_l \notin OP^* \Rightarrow O_l \notin OP \vee \text{T-Purpose}(CT(subj)) \in \text{O-Purposes (Class}(O_l)) \vee$$
$$(\text{T-Purpose}(CT(subj)), O_l) \in C$$

$$O_l \notin OP^* \Rightarrow O_l \notin OP \vee O_l = O_j.$$

Since
$$\text{T-Purpose}(CT(subj)) \in \text{O-Purposes (Class}(O_j)) \vee (\text{T-Purpose}(CT(subj)), O_j) \in C$$
by assumption:
$$\Rightarrow \text{If } O_l = O_j \Rightarrow \text{T-Purpose}(CT(subj)) \in \text{O-Purposes (Class}(O_l))$$
$$\vee (\text{T-Purpose}(CT(subj)), O_l) \in C.$$
$$\Rightarrow$$
$$O_l \notin OP^* \Rightarrow O_l \notin OP \vee \text{T-Purpose}(CT(subj)) \in \text{O-Purposes (Class}(O_l))$$
$$\vee (\text{T-Purpose}(CT(subj)), O_l) \in C.$$

$\Rightarrow (v, v^*)$ satisfies privacy constraint-4.

q.e.d.

Corollary 2:
Let φ be a rule and $\varphi (R_k, v) = (D_m, v^*)$, where

v = (S, CA, NA, CT, AT, CTP, ATP, class, T-Purpose, O-Purposes, C, O, OP, O-Class, T, P, TRANS, TKT, role, responsible, Input-Purposes, Output-Purposes) and
v* = (S*, CA*, NA*, CT*, AT*, CTP*, ATP*, class*, T-Purpose*, O-Purposes*, C*, O*, OP*, O-Class*, T*, P*, TRANS*, TKT*, role*, responsible*, Input-Purposes*, Output-Purposes*).

If OP* = OP $\Rightarrow$
(v, v^*) satisfies privacy contraints -1-4.

4. Formal Definition of the Model Rules

The state transition functions of the privacy model that informally define the rules of the model, were presented in Chapter 6.4.

Formal definitions of the rules of the privacy model are given in this Chapter in order to prove that the rules are privacy-oriented state sequence preserving.

Rule 1 (R1): get-read-access:

Domain of R1: all R_k = (get-read, S_i, O_j, read) in $R^{(1)}$. (Denote domain of R_i by $dom(R_i)$):

$$R1(R_k, v) = \begin{cases} (?, v) & \text{if } R_k \notin \text{dom (R1)} \\ \\ (\underline{yes}, (S, CA \cup \{(S_i, O_j, \text{read})\}, NA, CT, AT, CTP, ATP, \\ \quad \text{class, T-Purpose, O-Purposes, C, O, OP, Class, T, P,} \\ \quad \text{TRANS, TKT, role, responsible,} \\ \quad \text{Input-Purposes} \setminus \text{Input-Purposes}(S_i) <\text{- Input-Purposes}(S_i) \\ \quad \cap \text{O-Purposes(class}(O_j)), \text{Output-Purposes)}) \\ \qquad \text{if } [R_k \in \text{dom (R1)}] \wedge \\ \qquad [O_j \in OP \wedge \\ \qquad ((CT (S_i), \text{Class}(O_j), CTP (S_i), \text{read}) \in NA) \\ \qquad \wedge ((\text{T-Purpose}(CT(S_i) \in \text{O-Purposes (Class}(O_j)) \\ \qquad \vee (\text{T-Purpose}(CT(S_i), O_j) \in C)) \wedge \\ \qquad (\text{Output-Purposes}(S_i) \subseteq \text{Input-Purposes}(S_i) \\ \qquad \cap \text{O-Purposes(class}(O_j)))] \\ \qquad \vee [O_j \notin OP] \\ \\ (\underline{no}, v) & \text{otherwise} \end{cases}$$

Rule 2 (R2): get-write-access:

Domain of R2: all R_k = (get-write, S_i, O_j, r) in $R^{(2)}$. (Denote domain of R_i by dom(R_i)):

$$R2(R_k, v) = \begin{cases}
(\underline{?}, v) & \text{if } R_k \notin \text{dom (R2)} \\
\\
(\underline{yes}, (S, CA \cup \{(S_i, O_j, r) \mid r \in \{write, append\}\}, NA, CT, \\
\quad AT, CTP, \ ATP, class, T\text{-Purpose, O-Purposes, C, O, OP,} \\
\quad Class, T, P, TRANS, TKT, role, responsible, \\
\quad Input\text{-Purposes,} \\
\quad Output\text{-Purposes} \setminus Output\text{-Purposes}(S_i) \\
\quad\quad <\text{-- } Output\text{-Purposes}(S_i) \cup O\text{-Purposes}(class(O_j)))) \\
\quad\quad\quad \text{if } [R_k \in \text{dom (R2)}] \wedge \\
\quad\quad\quad [(O_j \in OP) \wedge \\
\quad\quad\quad ((CT (S_i), Class(O_j), CTP (S_i), r) \in NA) \\
\quad\quad\quad \wedge ((T\text{-Purpose}(CT(S_i) \in O\text{-Purposes }(Class(O_j)) \\
\quad\quad\quad\quad \vee (T\text{-Purpose}(CT(S_i), O_j) \in C)) \wedge \\
\quad\quad\quad\quad (Output\text{-Purposes}(S_i) \cup O\text{-Purposes}(class(O_j) \subseteq \\
\quad\quad\quad\quad Input\text{-Purposes}(S_i))] \\
\quad\quad\quad\quad \vee [(O_j \notin OP) \wedge (Input\text{-Purposes}(S_i) = P)] \\
\\
(\underline{no}, v) & \text{otherwise}
\end{cases}$$

Rule 3 (R3): release access:

Domain of R3: all R_k = (release, S_i, O_j, r) $\in R^{(3)}$.

$$R3(R_k, v) = \begin{cases}
(\underline{yes}, (S, CA - \{(S_i, O_j, r) \mid r \in \{read, write, append\}\}, NA, \\
\quad CT, AT, CTP, ATP, class, T\text{-Purpose, O-Purposes,} \\
\quad C, O, OP, O\text{-Class, T, P, TRANS, TKT, role, responsible,} \\
\quad Input\text{-Purposes, Output-Purposes})) \\
\quad\quad\quad\quad \text{if } R_k \in \text{dom (R3)} \\
\\
(\underline{?}, v) & \text{otherwise.}
\end{cases}$$

Rule 4 (R4): execute-TP:

Domain of R4: all R_k = (execute-TP, S_i, $transp_j$) in $R^{(4)}$:

$$R4(R_k, v) = \begin{cases}
(\underline{?}, v) & \text{if } R_k \notin \text{dom (R4)} \\[2ex]
(\underline{yes}, (S, CA - (CA \cap (\{S_i\} \times O \times A)), NA, CT, AT, \\
\quad CTP\backslash CTP(S_i) \text{ <- } transp_j, ATP, class, \\
\quad \text{T-Purpose, O-Purposes, C, O, OP, O-Class, T, P, TRANS,} \\
\quad \text{TKT, role, responsible,} \\
\quad \text{Input-Purposes} \backslash \text{Input-Purposes}(S_i) \text{<- P,} \\
\quad \text{Output-Purposes} \backslash \text{Output-Purposes}(S_i) \text{ <- } \varnothing \,)) \\
\qquad \text{if } [R_k \in \text{dom (R4)}] \wedge \\
\qquad\quad [\, (transp_j \in ATP (CT(S_i)) \wedge (CTP(S_i) = Nil) \,] \\[2ex]
(\underline{no}, v) & \text{otherwise.}
\end{cases}$$

Rule 5 (R5): exit-TP:

Domain of R5: all R_k = (exit-tp, S_i, $transp_j$) $\in R^{(5)}$.

$$R5(R_k, v) = \begin{cases}
(\underline{yes}, (S, CA - (CA \cap (\{S_i\} \times O \times A)), \\
\quad \text{NA, T, AT, CTP} \backslash CTP(S_i) \text{ <- Nil, ATP, class, T-Purpose,} \\
\quad \text{O-Purposes, C, O, OP, O-Class, T, P, TRANS, TKT, role,} \\
\quad \text{responsible, Input-Purposes} \backslash \text{Input-Purposes}(S_i)\text{<- P,} \\
\quad \text{Output-Purposes} \backslash \text{Output-Purposes}(S_i) \text{ <- } \varnothing \,)) \\
\qquad \text{if } R_k \in \text{dom (R5)} \\[2ex]
(\underline{?}, v) & \text{otherwise.}
\end{cases}$$

Rule 6 (R6): change-CT:

Domain of R6: all R_k = (change-CT, S_i, T_j) in $R^{(6)}$:

$$R6(R_k, v) = \begin{cases}
(\underline{?}, v) & \text{if } R_k \notin \text{dom (R6)} \\
\\
(\underline{\text{yes}}, (S, CA, NA, CT \setminus CT(S_i) <\text{-} T_j, AT, CTP, ATP, \text{class}, \\
\quad \text{T-Purpose, O-Purposes, C, O, OP, O-Class, T, P,} \\
\quad \text{TRANS, TKT, role, responsible, Input-Purposes,} \\
\quad \text{Output-Purposes)}) \\
\qquad\qquad \text{if } [R_k \in \text{dom (R6)}] \wedge \\
\qquad\qquad [\,(T_j \in AT(S_i) \wedge (CTP(S_i) = \text{Nil})\,] \\
\\
(\underline{\text{no}}, v) & \text{otherwise.}
\end{cases}$$

Rule 7 (R7): create-subject:

Domain of R7: all R_k = (create-subject, S_i) in $R^{(7)}$:

$$R7(R_k, v) = \begin{cases}
(\underline{?}, v) & \text{if } R_k \notin \text{dom (R7)} \\
\\
(\underline{\text{yes}}, (S \cup \{S_{new}\}, CA, NA, CT \cup (S_{new}, CT(S_i)), \\
\quad AT \cup (S_{new}, AT(S_i)), CTP \cup (S_{new}, \text{Nil}), \\
\quad \text{ATP, class, T-Purpose, O-Purposes, C,} \\
\quad \text{O, OP, O-Class, T, P, TRANS, TKT,} \\
\quad \text{role} \cup (S_{new}, \text{role}(S_i)), \\
\quad \text{responsible, Input-Purposes} \cup (S_{new}, P), \\
\quad \text{Output-Purposes} \cup (S_{new}, \varnothing))) \\
\qquad\qquad \text{if } [R_k \in \text{dom (R7)}] \wedge \\
\qquad\qquad [\,(CTP(S_i) = \text{Nil})\,] \\
\\
(\underline{\text{no}}, v) & \text{otherwise.}
\end{cases}$$

Rule 8 (R8): create-object:

Domain of R8: all R_k = (create-object, S_i, o-class$_n$) in $R^{(8)}$:

$$R8(R_k, v) = \begin{cases}
(\underline{?}, v) \quad \text{if } R_k \notin \text{dom (R8)} \\[1em]
(\underline{yes}, (S, CA, NA, CT, AT, CTP, ATP, \\
\quad \text{Class} \cup (O_{new}, \text{o-class}_n), \text{T-Purpose}, \\
\quad \text{O-Purposes}, C, O \cup \{O_{new}\}, OP \cup \{O_{new}\}, \\
\quad \text{O-Class, T, P, TRANS, TKT, role, responsible.} \\
\quad \text{Input-Purposes, Output-Purposes)}) \\[0.5em]
\qquad \text{if } [R_k \in \text{dom (R8)}] \wedge \\
\qquad\quad [(CT (S_i), \text{o-class}_n, CTP (S_i), \text{create}) \in NA] \wedge \\
\qquad\quad [\text{T-Purpose}(CT(S_i)) \in \text{O-Purposes (o-class}_n)] \\[1em]
(\underline{no}, v) \quad \text{otherwise}
\end{cases}$$

Rule 9 (R9): delete-object:

Domain of R9: all R_k = (delete, S_i, O_j) in $R^{(9)}$:

$$R9(R_k, v) = \begin{cases}
(\underline{?}, v) \quad \text{if } R_k \notin \text{dom (R9)} \\[1em]
(\underline{yes}, (S, CA - (CA \cap (S \times \{O_j\} \times A)), NA, CT, AT, CTP, \\
\quad \text{ATP, Class, T-Purpose, O-Purposes,} \\
\quad C - (C \cap (P \times \{O_j\})), \\
\quad O - \{O_j\}, OP - \{O_j\}, \\
\quad \text{O-Class, T, P, TRANS, TKT, role, responsible,} \\
\quad \text{Input-Purposes, Output-Purposes)}) \\[0.5em]
\qquad \text{if } [R_k \in \text{dom (R9)}] \wedge \\
\qquad\quad [(CT (S_i), \text{Class}(O_j), CTP (S_i), \text{delete}) \in NA] \wedge \\
\qquad\quad [(\text{T-Purpose}(CT(S_i)) \in \text{O-Purposes (Class}(O_j)) \vee \\
\qquad\quad (\text{T-Purpose}(CT(S_i)), O_j) \in C)] \\[1em]
(\underline{no}, v) \quad \text{otherwise}
\end{cases}$$

Rule (R10): create-ticket:

Domain of R10: all R_k = (create-ticket, S_i, template$_a$) in $R^{(10)}$.

$$R10\ (R_k, v) = \begin{cases} (\underline{?}, v) & \text{if } R_k \notin \text{dom (R10)} \\[2ex] \begin{array}{l} (\underline{\text{yes}}, (\text{S, CA , NA, CT, AT, CTP, ATP, class, T-Purpose,} \\ \text{O-Purposes, C, O, OP, O-Class, T, P, TRANS,} \\ \text{TKT} \cup (S_i, \text{template}_a), \text{role,} \\ \quad \text{responsible, Input-Purposes, Output-Purposes))} \\ \qquad \text{if } [R_k \in \text{dom (R10)}] \wedge \\ \qquad\quad [\text{ role } (S_i) = \text{data-protection-officer}] \vee \\ \qquad\quad [[\text{template}_a = (\text{add-auth-task, } S_m, T_n) \vee \\ \qquad\qquad\quad \text{template}_a = (\text{delete-auth-task, } S_m, T_n)] \\ \qquad\qquad\quad \wedge (S_i \in \text{responsible}(T_n))] \end{array} \\[2ex] (\underline{\text{no}}, v) & \text{otherwise.} \end{cases}$$

Rule 11 (R11): add-NA:

Domain of R11: all R_k = (add-NA, S_i, TKT$_a$) in $R^{(11)}$, where
$$TKT_a = (S_j, \text{add-NA}, T_l, \text{o-class}_p, \text{transp}_n, r).$$

$$R11\ (R_k, v) = \begin{cases} (\underline{?}, v) & \text{if } R_k \notin \text{dom (R11)} \\[2ex] \begin{array}{l} (\underline{\text{yes}}, (\text{S, CA , NA} \cup \{(T_l, \text{o-class}_p, \text{transp}_n, r)\}, \\ \text{CT, AT, CTP, ATP, class, T-Purpose, O-Purposes, C, O,} \\ \text{OP, O-Class, T, P, TRANS, TKT - } \{TKT_a\}, \\ \text{role, responsible, Input-Purposes, Output-Purposes))} \\ \qquad \text{if } [R_k \in \text{dom (R11)}] \wedge \\ \qquad\quad [\text{role } (S_i) = \text{sec-officer}] \wedge \\ \qquad\quad [\text{ role } (S_j) = \text{data-protection-officer}] \end{array} \\[2ex] (\underline{\text{no}}, v) & \text{otherwise.} \end{cases}$$

Rule 12 (R12): delete-NA:

Domain of R12: all R_k = (delete-NA, S_i, TKT_a) in $R^{(12)}$, where

$$TKT_a = (S_j, \text{delete-NA}, T_l, \text{o-class}_p, \text{transp}_n, r).$$

$$R12 (R_k, v) = \begin{cases}
(\underline{?}, v) & \text{if } R_k \notin \text{dom (R12)} \\[2ex]
(\underline{yes}, (S, CA, NA - \{(T_l, \text{o-class}_p, \text{transp}_n, r)\}, \\
\quad CT, AT, CTP, ATP, \text{class}, \text{T-Purpose}, \text{O-Purposes}, \\
\quad C, O, OP, \text{O-Class}, T, P, TRANS, TKT - \{TKT_a\}, \\
\quad \text{role, responsible, Input-Purposes, Output-Purposes})) \\
\qquad \text{if } [R_k \in \text{dom (R12)}] \wedge \\
\qquad\quad [\text{role } (S_i) = \text{sec-officer}] \wedge \\
\qquad\qquad [\text{ role } (S_j) = \text{data-protection-officer}] \wedge \\
\qquad\qquad\quad [\forall\ S_p \in S, O_q \in OP, x: A: \\
\qquad\qquad\qquad (S_w, O_q, x) \in CA => \\
\qquad\qquad\qquad (CT(S_w), \text{class}(O_q), CTP(S_w), x) \\
\qquad\qquad\qquad \neq (T_l, \text{o-class}_p, \text{transp}_n, r)] \\[2ex]
(\underline{no}, v) & \text{otherwise.}
\end{cases}$$

Rule 13 (R13): add-task:

Domain of R13: all R_k = (add-task, S_i, TKT_a) in $R^{(13)}$, where

$$TKT_a = (S_j, \text{add-task}, p_w).$$

$$R13 (R_k, v) = \begin{cases}
(\underline{?}, v) & \text{if } R_k \notin \text{dom (R13)} \\[2ex]
(\underline{yes}, (S, CA, NA, CT, AT, CTP, ATP \cup (T_{new}, \{Nil\})), \\
\quad \text{class}, \text{T-Purpose} \cup (T_{new}, p_w), \text{O-Purposes}, C, O, \quad OP, \\
\quad \text{O-Class}, T \cup \{T_{new}\}, P, TRANS, \\
\quad TKT - \{TKT_a\}, \text{role, responsible}, \\
\quad \text{Input-Purposes, Output-Purposes})) \\
\qquad \text{if } [R_k \in \text{dom (R13)}] \wedge \\
\qquad\quad [\text{role } (S_i) = \text{sec-officer}] \wedge \\
\qquad\qquad [\text{ role } (S_j) = \text{data-protection-officer}] \\[2ex]
(\underline{no}, v) & \text{otherwise.}
\end{cases}$$

Rule 14 (R14): delete-task:

Domain of R12: all $R_k = $ (delete-task, S_i, TKT_a) in $R^{(14)}$, where
$$TKT_a = (S_j, \text{delete-task}, T_p).$$

$$
R14\,(R_k, v) = \begin{cases}
(\underline{?}, v) & \text{if } R_k \notin \text{dom (R14)} \\[2ex]
\begin{array}{l}
(\underline{yes}, (S, CA, \\
NA - (NA \cap (\{T_p\} \times O\text{-class} \times TRANS \times A)), CT, \\
AT \setminus AT(S_l) <- AT(S_l) - (AT(S_l) \cap \{T_p\}): \forall\, S_l \in S, \\
CTP, ATP, \text{class}, T\text{-Purpose}, O\text{-Purposes}, C, O, OP, \\
O\text{-Class}, T - \{T_p\}, P, TRANS, TKT\text{-} \{TKT_a\}, \text{role}, \\
\text{responsible, Input-Purposes, Output-Purposes)}) \\
\qquad \text{if } [R_k \in \text{dom (R14)}] \wedge \\
\qquad\quad [\text{role } (S_i) = \text{sec-officer}] \wedge \\
\qquad\quad [\text{ role } (S_j) = \text{data-protection-officer}] \wedge \\
\qquad\quad [\forall\, S_l \in S: CT(S_l) \neq T_p]
\end{array} \\[2ex]
(\underline{no}, v) & \text{otherwise.}
\end{cases}
$$

Rule 15 (R15): add-o-class:

Domain of R15: all $R_k = $ (add-o-class, S_i, TKT_a) in $R^{(15)}$, where
$$TKT_a = (S_j, \text{add-o-class}, \text{p-set}_w).$$

$$
R15\,(R_k, v) = \begin{cases}
(\underline{?}, v) & \text{if } R_k \notin \text{dom (R15)} \\[2ex]
\begin{array}{l}
(\underline{yes}, (S, CA, NA, CT, AT, CTP, ATP, \text{class}, \\
T\text{-Purpose}, O\text{-Purposes} \cup (o\text{-class}_{new}, \text{p-set}_w), C, O, \; OP, \\
O\text{-Class} \cup \{o\text{-class}_{new}\}, T, P, TRANS, TKT\text{-} \{TKT_a\}, \\
\text{role, responsible, Input-Purposes, Output-Purposes)}) \\
\qquad\quad \text{if } [R_k \in \text{dom (R15)}] \wedge \\
\qquad\qquad [\text{role } (S_i) = \text{sec-officer}] \wedge \\
\qquad\qquad [\text{ role } (S_j) = \text{data-protection-officer}]
\end{array} \\[2ex]
(\underline{no}, v) & \text{otherwise.}
\end{cases}
$$

Rule 16 (R16): delete-o-class:

Domain of R14: all R_k = (delete-o-class, S_t, TKT_a) in $R^{(16)}$, where

$$TKT_a = (S_j, \text{delete-o-class}, \text{o-class}_p).$$

$$R16 \ (R_k, v) = \begin{cases} (\underline{?}, v) & \text{if } R_k \notin \text{dom (R16)} \\[1em] (\underline{yes}, (S, CA, \\ \quad NA - (NA \cap (T \times \{\text{o-class}_p\} \times TRANS \times A)), CT, \\ \quad AT, CTP, ATP, \text{class}, \\ \quad \text{T-Purpose, O-Purposes, C, O, OP,} \\ \quad \text{O-Class} - \{\text{o-class}_p\}, \ T, P, TRANS, TKT- \{TKT_a\}, \\ \quad \text{role, responsible, Input-Purposes, Output-Purposes)}) \\ \qquad \text{if } [R_k \in \text{dom (R16)}] \wedge \\ \qquad\quad [\text{role } (S_i) = \text{sec-officer}] \wedge \\ \qquad\quad [\text{ role } (S_j) = \text{data-protection-officer}] \wedge \\ \qquad\quad [\forall \ O_l \in O: \text{Class}(O_l) \neq \text{o-class}_p] \\[1em] (\underline{no}, v) & \text{otherwise.} \end{cases}$$

Rule 17 (R17): add-auth-TP:

Domain of R17: all R_k = (add-task, S_i, TKT_a) in $R^{(17)}$, where

$$TKT_a = (S_j, \text{add-auth-TP}, T_m, \text{transp}_n).$$

$$R17 \ (R_k, v) = \begin{cases} (\underline{?}, v) & \text{if } R_k \notin \text{dom (R17)} \\[1em] (\underline{yes}, (S, CA, NA, CT, AT, CTP, \\ \quad ATP \setminus ATP(T_m) <- ATP(T_m) \cup \{\text{transp}_n\}, \text{class}, \\ \quad \text{T-Purpose, O-Purposes, C, O, OP, O-Class, T, P,} \\ \quad TRANS, TKT- \{TKT_a\}, \text{role, responsible,} \\ \quad \text{Input-Purposes, Output-Purposes)}) \\ \qquad \text{if } [R_k \in \text{dom (R17)}] \wedge \\ \qquad\quad [\text{role } (S_i) = \text{sec-officer}] \wedge \\ \qquad\quad [\text{ role } (S_j) = \text{data-protection-officer}] \\[1em] (\underline{no}, v) & \text{otherwise.} \end{cases}$$

Rule 18 (R18): delete-auth-TP:

Domain of R18: all R_k = (delete-auth-TP, S_i, TKT_a) in $R^{(18)}$, where

$$TKT_a = (S_j, \text{delete-auth-TP}, T_m, transp_n).$$

$R18(R_k, v) =$

$(\underline{?}, v)$ if $R_k \notin \text{dom (R18)}$

$(\underline{yes}, (S, CA, NA, CT, AT, CTP,$
$ATP \setminus ATP(T_p) <- ATP(T_p) - \{transp_n\},$ class,
T-Purpose, O-Purposes, C, O, OP, O-Class, T, P,
TRANS, TKT- $\{TKT_a\}$, role, responsible,
Input-Purposes, Output-Purposes))
  if $[R_k \in \text{dom (R18)}] \wedge$
    $[\text{role } (S_i) = \text{sec-officer}] \wedge$
    $[\text{role } (S_j) = \text{data-protection-officer}] \wedge$
    $[\forall S_l \in S: CTP (S_l) \neq transp_n \vee CT(S_l) \neq T_p]$

$(\underline{no}, v)$ otherwise.

Rule 19 (R19): add-consent:

Domain of R19: all R_k = (add-consent, S_i, TKT_a) in $R^{(19)}$, where

$$TKT_a = (S_j, \text{add-consent}, O_p, p_n).$$

$R19(R_k, v) =$

$(\underline{?}, v)$ if $R_k \notin \text{dom (R19)}$

$(\underline{yes}, (S, CA, NA, CT, AT, CTP, ATP,$ class,
T-Purpose, O-Purposes, C $\cup \{(p_n, O_p)\}$, O, OP, O-Class,
T, P, TRANS, TKT- $\{TKT_a\}$, role, responsible,
Input-Purposes, Output-Purposes))
  if $[R_k \in \text{dom (R19)}] \wedge$
    $[\text{role } (S_i) = \text{sec-officer}] \wedge$
    $[\text{role } (S_j) = \text{data-protection-officer}]$

$(\underline{no}, v)$ otherwise.

Rule 20 (R20): delete-consent:

Domain of R20: all R_k = (delete-consent, S_i, TKT_a) in $R^{(20)}$, where
$$TKT_a = (S_j, \text{delete-consent}, O_p, p_n).$$

$R20\ (R_k, v) =$

$(\underline{?}, v)$ if $R_k \notin$ dom (R20)

(<u>yes</u>, (S, CA , NA, CT, AT, CTP, ATP , class,
T-Purpose, O-Purposes, C - {(p_n, O_p)}, O, OP, O-Class,
T, P, TRANS, TKT- {TKT_a}, role, responsible, Input-
Purposes, Output-Purposes))
  if [$R_k \in$ dom (R20)] ∧
    [role (S_i) = sec-officer] ∧
    [role (S_j) = data-protection-officer] ∧
    [∀ $S_l \in$ S, r ∈ A : (S_l, O_p, r) ∈ CA =>
      (T-Purpose(CT(S_l)) ≠ p_n ∨
        T-Purpose(CT(S_l)) ∈ O-Purposes(class(O_p)))
    ]

(<u>no</u>, v)   otherwise.

Rule 21 (R21): add-purpose:

Domain of R21 all R_k = (add-purpose, S_i, TKT_a) in $R^{(21)}$, where
$$TKT_a = (S_j, \text{add-purpose}).$$

$R21\ (R_k, v) =$

$(\underline{?}, v)$ if $R_k \notin$ dom (R21)

(<u>yes</u>, (S, CA , NA, CT, AT, CTP, ATP, class,
T-Purpose, O-Purposes, C , O, OP, O-Class, T,
P ∪ {p_{new}},
TRANS, TKT- {TKT_a}, role, responsible,
Input-Purposes, Output-Purposes))
  if [$R_k \in$ dom (R21)] ∧
    [role (S_i) = sec-officer] ∧
    [role (S_j) = data-protection-officer]

(<u>no</u>, v)   otherwise.

Rule 22 (R22): delete-purpose:

Domain of R22: all R_k = (delete-purpose, S_i, TKT_a) in $R^{(22)}$, where

$$TKT_a = (S_j, \text{delete-purpose}, p_w).$$

$$R21\,(R_k, v) = \begin{cases}
(\underline{?}, v) & \text{if } R_k \notin \text{dom (R22)} \\[2mm]
(\underline{yes}, (S, CA, NA, CT, AT, CTP, ATP, \text{class}, \text{T-Purpose}, \\
\text{O-Purposes} \backslash \text{O-Purposes}(\text{o-class}_n) <- \\
\text{O-Purposes}(\text{o-class}_n) - \\
(\text{O-Purposes}(\text{o-class}_n) \cap \{p_w\}) : \forall\, \text{o-class}_n \in \text{O-class}, \\
C - (C \cap (\{p_w\} \times OP)), O,\ OP,\ \text{O-Class}, \\
T, P - \{p_w\}, TRANS, TKT - \{TKT_a\}, \text{role, responsible})) \\
\qquad \text{if } [R_k \in \text{dom (R22)}] \wedge \\
\qquad\quad [\text{role } (S_i) = \text{sec-officer}] \wedge \\
\qquad\quad [\text{role } (S_j) = \text{data-protection-officer}] \wedge \\
\qquad\quad [\forall\, O_l \in OP: p_w \notin \text{O-Purposes}(\text{class}(O_l))] \wedge \\
\qquad\quad [\forall\, \text{o-class}_l \in \text{O-class}: \{p_w\} \neq \\
\qquad\qquad \text{O-Purposes}(\text{o-class}_l)] \wedge \\
\qquad\quad [\forall\, T_n \in T: \text{T-Purpose}(T_n) \neq p_w] \\[2mm]
(\underline{no}, v) & \text{otherwise.}
\end{cases}$$

Rule 23 (R23): set-role:

Domain of R23: all R_k = (set-role, S_i, TKT_a) in $R^{(23)}$, where

$$TKT_a = (S_j, \text{set-role}, S_m, \text{role}_n).$$

$$R21\,(R_k, v) = \begin{cases}
(\underline{?}, v) & \text{if } R_k \notin \text{dom (R23)} \\[2mm]
(\underline{yes}, (S, CA, NA, CT, AT, CTP, ATP, \text{class}, \\
\text{T-Purpose, O-Purposes}, C, O, OP, \text{O-Class}, T, P, TRANS, \\
TKT - \{TKT_a\}, \text{role} \backslash \text{role}(S_m) <- \text{role}_n, \\
\text{responsible, Input-Purposes, output-Purposes}) \\
\qquad \text{if } [R_k \in \text{dom (R23)}] \wedge \\
\qquad\quad [\text{role } (S_i) = \text{sec-officer}] \wedge \\
\qquad\quad [\text{role } (S_j) = \text{data-protection-officer}] \\[2mm]
(\underline{no}, v) & \text{otherwise.}
\end{cases}$$

Rule 24 (R24: add-resp-users:

Domain of R24 all R_k = (add-resp-users, S_i, TKT_a) in $R^{(24)}$, where

$\qquad TKT_a$= (S_j, add-resp-users, S_l, T_n).

$$R21\,(R_k, v) = \begin{cases} (\underline{?}, v) & \text{if } R_k \notin \text{dom (R24)} \\ \\ (\underline{yes},\ (S, CA, NA, CT,\ AT, CTP, ATP\ ,\ \text{class},\\ \text{T-Purpose, O-Purposes, C, O,OP, O-Class, T, P,}\\ \text{TRANS, TKT-}\{TKT_a\},\ \text{role,}\\ \text{responsible} \setminus \text{responsible}(T_n) \text{ <-}\\ \text{responsible}(T_n) \cup \{S_l\},\\ \text{Input-Purposes, Output-Purposes)}\\ \quad \text{if } [R_k \in \text{dom (R24)}] \wedge\\ \qquad [\text{role } (S_i) = \text{sec-officer}] \wedge\\ \qquad [\text{ role } (S_j) = \text{data-protection-officer}] \\ \\ (\underline{no}, v) & \text{otherwise.} \end{cases}$$

Rule 25 (R25): delete-resp-users:

Domain of R25: all R_k = (delete-resp-users, S_i, TKT_a) in $R^{(25)}$, where

$\qquad TKT_a$= (S_j, delete-resp-users, S_l, T_n).

$$R21\,(R_k, v) = \begin{cases} (\underline{?}, v) & \text{if } R_k \notin \text{dom (R25)} \\ \\ (\underline{yes},\ (S, CA\ , NA, CT,\ AT, CTP, ATP\ ,\ \text{class},\\ \text{T-Purpose, O-Purposes, C, O, OP, O-Class, T, P, TRANS,}\\ \text{TKT-}\{TKT_a\},\ \text{role,}\\ \text{responsible} \setminus \text{responsible}(T_n) \text{ <- responsible}(T_n) - \{S_l\},\\ \text{Input-Purposes, Output-Purposes)}\\ \quad \text{if } [R_k \in \text{dom (R25)}] \wedge\\ \qquad [\text{role } (S_i) = \text{sec-officer}] \wedge\\ \qquad [\text{ role } (S_j) = \text{data-protection-officer}] \\ \\ (\underline{no}, v) & \text{otherwise.} \end{cases}$$

Rule 26 (R26): add-auth-task:

Domain of R26: all R_k = (add-auth-task, S_i, TKT_a) in $R^{(26)}$, where

$\qquad TKT_a = (S_j$, add-auth-task, S_l, $T_n)$.

$R26 (R_k, v) =$ $\begin{cases} (\underline{?}, v) & \text{if } R_k \notin \text{dom (R26)} \\[2mm] (\underline{yes}, (S, CA, NA, CT, \ AT \setminus AT(S_l) <\text{-} AT(S_l) \cup \{T_n\}, \\ \quad CTP, ATP, class, \ T\text{-Purpose, O-Purposes, C, O, OP,} \\ \quad O\text{-Class, T, P, TRANS, } TKT\text{-}\{TKT_a\}, role, \\ \quad responsible, \ Input\text{-Purposes, Output-Purposes)} \\ \qquad \text{if } [R_k \in \text{dom (R26)}] \wedge \\ \qquad\quad [\text{role } (S_i) = \text{sec-officer}] \wedge \\ \qquad\quad [\text{ role } (S_j) = \text{data-protection-officer} \\ \qquad\qquad \vee S_j \in \text{responsible}(T_n) \,] \\[2mm] (\underline{no}, v) & \text{otherwise.} \end{cases}$

Rule 27 (R27): delete-auth-task:

Domain of R27: all R_k = (delete-auth-task, S_i, TKT_a) in $R^{(27)}$, where

$\qquad TKT_a = (S_j$, delete-auth-task, S_l, $T_n)$.

$R27 (R_k, v) =$ $\begin{cases} (\underline{?}, v) & \text{if } R_k \notin \text{dom (R27)} \\[2mm] (\underline{yes}, (S, CA, NA, CT, \ AT \setminus AT(Sl) <\text{-} AT(S_l) - \{T_n\}, \\ \quad CTP, ATP, class, T\text{-Purpose, O-Purposes, C, O, OP,} \\ \quad O\text{-Class, T, P, TRANS, } TKT\text{-}\{TKT_a\}, role, \\ \quad responsible, \ Input\text{-Purposes, Output-Purposes)} \\ \qquad \text{if } [R_k \in \text{dom (R27)}] \wedge \\ \qquad\quad [\text{role } (S_i) = \text{sec-officer}] \wedge \\ \qquad\quad [\text{ role } (S_j) = \text{data-protection-officer} \\ \qquad\qquad \vee S_j \in \text{responsible}(T_n) \,] \wedge \\ \qquad\quad [\ CT(S_l) \neq T_n \,] \\[2mm] (\underline{no}, v) & \text{otherwise.} \end{cases}$

Rule 28 (R28): create-TP:

Domain of R28: all R_k = (create-TP, S_i) in $R^{(28)}$.

$$R28 (R_k, v) = \begin{cases} (?, v) & \text{if } R_k \notin \text{dom (R28)} \\[1em] (\underline{\text{yes}}, (S, CA, NA, CT, AT, CTP, ATP, \text{class}, \\ \text{T-Purpose, O-Purposes, C, O, OP, O-Class, T, P,} \\ \text{TRANS} \cup \{\text{transp}_{\text{new}}\}, \text{TKT, role, responsible,} \\ \text{Input-Purposes, Output-Purposes)} \\ \qquad \text{if } [R_k \in \text{dom (R28)}] \wedge \\ \qquad\quad [\text{role } (S_i) = \text{tp-manager}] \\[1em] (\underline{\text{no}}, v) & \text{otherwise.} \end{cases}$$

Rule 29 (R29): delete-TP:

Domain of R29: all R_k = (create-TP, S_i, transp_n) in $R^{(29)}$.

$$R29 (R_k, v) = \begin{cases} (?, v) & \text{if } R_k \notin \text{dom (R29)} \\[1em] (\underline{\text{yes}}, (S, CA, NA - (NA \cap (T \times \text{O-class} \times \{\text{transp}_n\} \times A)), \\ \text{CT, AT, CTP, ATP} \backslash \text{ATP}(T_j) <\text{- ATP}(T_j) - \\ (\text{ATP}(T_j) \cap \{\text{transp}_n\}) \colon \forall T_j \in T, \text{class}, \\ \text{T-Purpose, O-Purposes, C, O, OP, O-Class, T, P,} \\ \text{TRANS} - \{\text{transp}_n\}, \text{TKT, role, responsible,} \\ \text{Input-Purposes, Output-Purposes)} \\ \qquad \text{if } [R_k \in \text{dom (R26)}] \wedge \\ \qquad\quad [\text{role } (S_i) = \text{tp-manager}] \wedge \\ \qquad\quad [\forall S_l \in S \colon \text{CTP}(S_l) \neq \text{transp}_n] \\[1em] (\underline{\text{no}}, v) & \text{otherwise.} \end{cases}$$

5. Proofs

In this Section, it will be formally proven that the rules R1,...,R29 of the privacy model are privacy-oriented state sequence preserving:

Rule R1: get-read- access:

Suppose v satisfies the privacy invariants-1-4, the information flow invariant and $R_k \in R$, $R1(R_k, v) = (D_m, v^*)$ with

(i) $v^* = v$

(ii) $v^* = (S, CA \cup \{(S_i, O_j, read)\}, NA, CT, AT, CTP, ATP, Class, T\text{-Purpose},$
O-Purposes, C, O, OP, O-Class, T, P, TRANS, TKT, role, responsible,
Input-Purposes \ Input-Purposes(S_i) <- Input-Purposes(S_i) $\cap$
O-Purposes(class (O_j)), Output-Purposes).

If $v^* = v$, then v^* satisfies privacy invariants-1-4 and the information flow invariant. Since $OP = OP^*$ => (v, v^*) satisfies privacy constraints-1-4 by corollary 2.

Suppose (ii). If $(S_i, O_j, read) \in CA$, then $v^* = v$.

Suppose $(S_i, O_j, read) \notin CA$.

Then , since according to R1

$[(O_j \in OP) \wedge$

$((CT (S_i), Class(O_j), CTP (S_i), read) \in NA) \wedge$

$(((T\text{-Purpose}(CT(S_i)) \in O\text{-Purposes} (Class(O_j))) \vee (T\text{-Purpose}(CT(S_i), O_j) \in C)) \wedge$

$(Output\text{-Purposes}(S_i) \subseteq Input\text{-Purposes}(S_i) \cap O\text{-Purposes}(class(O_j)))]$

$\vee [(O_j \notin OP)]$ and

$S = S^*, NA^* = NA, CT^* = CT, AT^* = AT, CTP^* = CTP, ATP^* = ATP, Class^* = Class,$
O-Purposes*=O-Purposes, T-Purpose*= T-Purpose, O*=O, OP=OP*, C* = C,
Input-Purposes* = Input-Purposes \ Input-Purposes(S_i) <- Input-Purposes(S_i) $\cap$
O-Purposes(class (O_j)), Output-Purposes* = Output-Purposes:

v^* satisfies privacy invariant-1 by theorem 10 (i).
v^* satisfies privacy invariant-2 by theorem 11 (i).
v^* satisfies privacy invariant-3 by theorem 12 (i).
v^* satisfies privacy invariant-4 by theorem 13 (i).
v^* satisfies the information flow invariant by theorem 14 (ii).

Since $OP^* = OP$ according to R1, (v, v^*) satisfies privacy constraints-1-4 by corollary 2.

=> R1 is privacy-oriented state sequence preserving.

Rule R2: get-write-access:

Suppose v satisfies the privacy invariants-1-4, the information flow invariant and $R_k \in R$, $R2(R_k, v) = (D_m, v^*)$ with

(i) $v^* = v$

(ii) $v^* = (S, CA \cup \{(S_i, O_j, r) | r \in \{write, append\}\}, NA, CT, AT, CTP, ATP,$
     Class, T-Purpose, O-Purposes, C, O, OP, O-Class, T, P, TRANS, TKT,
     role, responsible, Input-Purposes,
     Output-Purposes \ Output-Purposes(S_i) <- Output-Purposes(S_i) $\cup$
     O-Purposes(class(O_j)))

If $v^* = v$, then v^* satisfies privacy invariants-1-4 and the information flow invariant. Since $OP = OP^* \Rightarrow (v, v^*)$ satisfies privacy constraints-1-4 by corollary 2.

Suppose (ii). If $(S_i, O_j, r) \in CA$, then $v^* = v$.

Suppose $(S_i, O_j, r) \notin CA$.

Then , since according to R2

$[(O_j \in OP) \wedge$

$((CT (S_i), Class(O_j), CTP (S_i), r) \in NA) \wedge$

$(((T\text{-Purpose}(CT(S_i)) \in O\text{-Purposes } (Class(O_j))) \vee (T\text{-Purpose}(CT(S_i), O_j) \in C)) \wedge$

$(Output\text{-Purposes}(S_i) \cup O\text{-Purposes}(class(O_j)) \subseteq Input\text{-Purposes}(S_i))]$

$\vee [(O_j \notin OP) \wedge (Input\text{-Purposes}(S_i) = P)]$ and

$S = S^*$, $NA^* = NA$, $CT^*=CT$, $AT^*=AT$, $CTP^*=CTP$, $ATP^*=ATP$, Class*=Class,
O-Purposes*=O-Purposes, T-Purpose*= T-Purpose, O*=O, OP=OP*, C* = C,
Input-Purposes* = Input-Purposes, Output-Purposes* = Output-Purposes \
Output-Purposes(S_i) <- Output-Purposes(S_i) $\cup$ O-Purposes(class(O_j)):

v^* satisfies privacy invariant-1 by theorem 10 (i).
v^* satisfies privacy invariant-2 by theorem 11 (i).
v^* satisfies privacy invariant-3 by theorem 12 (i).
v^* satisfies privacy invariant-4 by theorem 13 (i).
v^* satisfies the information flow invariant by theorem 14 (i).

Since $OP^* = OP$ according to R2, (v, v^*) satisfies privacy constraints-1-4
by corollary 2.

$\Rightarrow$ R2 is privacy-oriented state sequence preserving.

Rule R3: release access:

Suppose v is a privacy-oriented state.

According to R3: $S^* = S$, $CA^* \subseteq CA$,
$NA^* = NA$, $CT^*=CT$, $AT^*=AT$, $CTP^*=CTP$, $ATP^*=ATP$, Class*=Class,
O-Purposes*=O-Purposes, T-Purpose*= T-Purpose, $O^*=O$, $OP^* = OP$, $C^* = C$,
Input-Purposes* = Input-Purposes, Output-Purposes* = Output-Purposes.

v^* satisfies privacy invariant-1 by theorem 10 (i).
v^* satisfies privacy invariant-2 by theorem 11 (i).
v^* satisfies privacy invariant-3 by theorem 12 (ii).
v^* satisfies privacy invariant-4 by theorem 13 (ii).
v^* satisfies the information flow invariant by theorem 14 (iii).

Since $OP^* = OP$ according to R3, (v, v^*) satisfies privacy constraints-1-4
by corollary 2.

=> R3 is privacy-oriented state sequence preserving.

Rule R4: execute-TP:

Suppose v satisfies the privacy invariants-1-4, the information flow invariant and
$R_k \in R$, $R4(R_k, v) = (D_m, v^*)$ with
(i) $v^* = v$
(ii) $v^* = (S, CA - (CA \cap (\{S_i\} \times O \times A)), NA, CT, AT, CTP \setminus CTP(S_i)$ <- $transp_j$,

      ATP, Class, T-Purpose, O-Purposes, C, O, OP, O-Class, T, P, TRANS, TKT,

      role, responsible, Input-Purposes \ Input-Purposes(S_i)<- P,

      Output-Purposes \ Output-Purposes(S_i) <- $\emptyset$).

If $v^* = v$, then v^* satisfies privacy invariants-1-4 and the information flow invariant.
Since $OP = OP^*$ => (v, v^*) satisfies privacy constraints -1-4 by corollary 2.

Suppose (ii).
According to R4:
$(transp_j \in ATP (CT(S_i)) \wedge (CTP(S_i) = Nil)$ and
$S^* = S$, $CA^* = CA - (CA \cap (\{S_i\} \times O \times A))$, $NA^* = NA$, $CT^*=CT$, $AT^*=AT$,
$CTP^* = CTP \setminus CTP(S_i)$ <- $transp_j$, $ATP^*=ATP$, Class*=Class,
O-Purposes*=O-Purposes, T-Purpose*= T-Purpose, $O^*=O$, $OP^* = OP$, $C^* = C$,
Input-Purposes* = Input-Purposes \ Input-Purposes(S_i)<- P,

Output-Purposes* = Output-Purposes \ Output-Purposes(S_i) <- $\emptyset$.

v* satisfies privacy invariant-1 by theorem 10 (i).
v* satisfies privacy invariant-2 by theorem 11 (ii).
v* satisfies privacy invariant-3 by theorem 12 (iii).
v* satisfies privacy invariant-4 by theorem 13 (ii).
v* satisfies the information flow invariant by theorem 14 (iii).

Since OP* = OP according to R4, (v, v*) satisfies privacy constraints-1-4 by corollary 2.

=> R4 is privacy-oriented state sequence preserving.

Rule R5: exit-TP:

Suppose v is a privacy-oriented state.

According to R5: $CA^* = CA - (CA \cap (\{S_i\} \times O \times A))$, $CTP^*(S_i) = Nil$,
$NA^* = NA$, $CT^* = CT$, $AT^* = AT$, $ATP^* = ATP$, Class*=Class,
O-Purposes*=O-Purposes, T-Purpose*= T-Purpose, $O^* = O$, $OP^* = OP$, $C^* = C$,
Input-Purposes*(S_i) = P, Output-Purposes*(S_i) = $\emptyset$.

v* satisfies privacy invariant-1 by theorem 10 (i).
v* satisfies privacy invariant-2 by theorem 11 (ii).
v* satisfies privacy invariant-3 by theorem 12 (iii).
v* satisfies privacy invariant-4 by theorem 13 (ii).
v* satisfies the information flow invariant by theorem 14 (iii).

Since OP* = OP according to R5, (v, v*) satisfies privacy constraints-1-4 by corollary 2.

=> R5 is privacy oriented state sequence preserving.

Rule R6: change-CT:

Suppose v satisfies the privacy invariants-1-4 and the information flow invariant, and $R_k \in R$, $R6(R_k, v) = (D_m, v^*)$ with
(i) $v^* = v$
(ii) $v^* = (S, CA, NA, CT \setminus CT(S_i) <- T_j, AT, CTP, ATP, Class, T-Purpose,$
        O-Purposes, C, O, OP, O-Class, T, P, TRANS, TKT, role, responsible,

Input-Purposes, Output-Purposes).

If $v^* = v$, then v^* satisfies privacy invariants-1-4 and the information flow invaraint. Since OP $=$ OP* => (v, v^*) satisfies privacy constraints-1-4 by corollary 2.

Suppose (ii).
According to R6:
$(T_j \in AT(S_i) \wedge CTP(S_i) = Nil)$ and
CA* = CA, NA* = NA, AT*=AT, CTP* = CTP, ATP*=ATP, Class*=Class, O-Purposes*=O-Purposes, T-Purpose*= T-Purpose, O*=O, OP*=OP, C* = C, Input-Purposes* = Input-Purposes, Output-Purposes* = Output-Purposes.

Since v satisfies privacy invariant-3 =>
$\forall O_t \in O, r \in A: (S_i, O_t, r) \in CA => (CT(S_i), class(O_t), CTP(S_i), r) \in NA$.
This is a contradiction to the definition of NA, because is defined by a set of tuples $(T_j, o\text{-}class_k, transp_l, r)$ with $transp_l \neq Nil$.
Hence: $CTP(S_i) = Nil => \forall O_t \in OP, r \in A: (S_i, O_t, r) \notin CA$.

v^* satisfies privacy invariant-1 by theorem 10 (ii).
v^* satisfies privacy invariant-2 by theorem 11 (iii).
v^* satisfies privacy invariant-3 by theorem 12 (iv).
v^* satisfies privacy invariant-4 by theorem 13 (iii).
v^* satisfies the information flow invariant by theorem 14 (iii).

Since OP* = OP according to R6, (v, v^*) satisfies privacy constraints-1-4 by corollary 2.

=> R6 is privacy-oriented state sequence preserving

Rule R7: create-subject:

Suppose v satisfies the privacy invariants-1-4 and the information flow invariant and $R_k \in R, R7(R_k, v) = (D_m, v^*)$ with
(i) $v^* = v$
(ii) $v^* = (S \cup \{S_{new}\}, CA, NA, CT \cup (S_{new}, CT(S_i)), AT \cup (S_{new}, AT(S_i)),$
    $CTP \cup (S_{new}, Nil), ATP, Class, T\text{-}Purpose, O\text{-}Purposes, C, O, OP,$
    $O\text{-}Class, T, P, TRANS, TKT, \quad role \cup (S_{new}, role(S_i)), responsible,$
    $Input\text{-}Purposes \cup (S_{new}, P), Output\text{-}Purposes \cup (S_i, \varnothing)).$

If $v^* = v$, then v^* satisfies privacy invariants-1.-4 and the information flow invariant. Since OP $=$ OP* => (v, v^*) satisfies privacy constraints-1-4 by corollary 2.

Suppose (ii).
According to R7:
$CTP(S_i) = Nil$ and

$S^* = S \cup \{S_{new}\}$, $CA^* = CA$, $NA^* = NA$, $CT^* = CT \cup (S_{new}, CT(S_i))$,

$AT^* = AT \cup (S_{new}, AT(S_i))$, $CTP^* = CTP \cup (S_{new}, Nil)$, $ATP^* = ATP$,

$Class^* = Class$, O-Purposes*=O-Purposes, T-Purpose* = T-Purpose, $O^* = O$,

$OP^* = OP.$, $C^* = C$, Input-Purposes* = Input-Purposes $\cup (S_{new}, P)$,

Output-Purposes* = Output-Purposes $\cup (S_i, \varnothing)$.

Since $CT^*(S_{new}) = CT(S_i) \in AT(S_i) = AT^*(S_{new}) =>$
v^* satisfies privacy invariant-1 by theorem 10 (ii).

v^* satisfies privacy invariant-2 by theorem 11 (iii).
v^* satisfies privacy invariant-3 by theorem 12 (ii).
v^* satisfies privacy invariant-4 by theorem 13 (iii).
V^* satisfies the information flow invariant by theorem 14 (iii).

Since $OP^* = OP$ according to R7, (v, v^*) satisfies privacy constraints-1-4
by corollary 2.

=> R7 is privacy-oriented state sequence preserving.

Rule R8: create-object:

Suppose v is a privacy-oriented state and $R_k \in R$, $R8(R_k, v) = (D_m, v^*)$ with
(i) $v^* = v$
(ii) $v^* = (S, CA, NA, CT, AT, CTP, ATP, Class \cup (O_{new}, \text{o-class}_n),$
     T-Purpose, O-Purposes, C, $O \cup \{O_{new}\}$, $OP \cup \{O_{new}\}$,
     O-Class, T, P, TRANS, TKT, role, responsible, Input-Purposes,
     Output-Purposes).

If $v^* = v$, then v^* satisfies privacy invariants-1.-4.
Since $OP = OP^* => (v, v^*)$ satisfies privacy constraints-1-4 by corollary 2.

Suppose (ii).
According to R8:
$(CT(S_i), \text{o-class}_n, CTP(S_i), \text{create}) \in NA \wedge$
$(\text{T-Purpose}(CT(S_i) \in \text{O-Purposes }(\text{o-class}_n))$ and
$S^* = S$, $CA^* = CA$, $NA^* = NA$, $CT^* = CT$, $AT^* = AT$, $CTP^* = CTP$, $ATP^* = ATP$,

O-Purposes*=O-Purposes, T-Purpose*= T-Purpose, C* = C, Input-Purposes* = Input-Purposes, Output-Purposes* = Output-Purposes,
$\forall\, O_j \in O: Class^*(O_j) = Class(O_j)$.

v* satisfies privacy invariant-1 by theorem 10 (i).
v* satisfies privacy invariant-2 by theorem 11 (i).
v* satisfies privacy invariant-3 by theorem 12 (ii).
v* satisfies privacy invariant-4 by theorem 13 (ii).
v* satisfies the information flow invariant by theorem 14 (iii).

(v, v*) satisfies privacy constraints-1 by theorem 15 (ii).
(v, v*) satisfies privacy constraints-2 by theorem 16 (i).
(v, v*) satisfies privacy constraints-3 by theorem 17 (ii).
(v, v*) satisfies privacy constraints-1 by theorem 18 (i).

=> R8 is privacy-oriented state sequence preserving.

Rule R9: delete-object:

Suppose v is a privacy-oriented state and $R_k \in R$, $R9(R_k, v) = (D_m, v^*)$ with
(i) v* = v
(ii) v* = (S, CA - (CA $\cap$ (S $\times$ {O_j } $\times$ A), NA, CT, AT, CTP, ATP, Class, T-Purpose,
     O-Purposes, C- (C $\cap$ (P $\times$ {O_j}))), O - {O_j}, OP - {O_j}, O-Class, T, P,
     TRANS, TKT, role, responsible, Input-Purposes, Output-Purposes).

If v* = v, then v* satisfies privacy invariants-1-4.
Since OP =OP* => (v, v*) satisfies privacy constraints-1-4 by corollary 2.

Suppose (ii).
According to R9:
 (CT (S_i),Class(O_j) , CTP (S_i), delete) $\in$ NA $\wedge$
 [(T-Purpose(CT(S_i)) $\in$ O-Purposes (Class(O_j)) $\vee$

(T-Purpose(CT(S_i), O_j) $\in$ C)] and
S* = S, CA* $\subseteq$ CA, NA* = NA, CT* =CT, AT*=AT, CTP* = CTP, ATP*=ATP,
O-Purposes*=O-Purposes, T-Purpose*= T-Purpose, Class* = Class, C* = C,
Input-Purposes* = Input-Purposes, Output-Purposes* = Output-Purposes

v* satisfies privacy invariant-1 by theorem 10 (i).

v* satisfies privacy invariant-2 by theorem 11 (i).
v* satisfies privacy invariant-3 by theorem 12 (ii).
v* satisfies privacy invariant-4 by theorem 13 (ii).
v* satisfies the information flow invariant by theorem 14 (iii).

(v, v*) satisfies privacy constraints-1 by theorem 15 (i).
(v, v*) satisfies privacy constraints-2 by theorem 16 (ii).
(v, v*) satisfies privacy constraints-3 by theorem 17 (i).
(v, v*) satisfies privacy constraints-1 by theorem 18 (ii).

=> R9 is privacy-oriented state sequence preserving.

Rule R10: create-ticket:

Suppose v is a privacy-oriented state and $R_k \in R$, $R10(R_k, v) = (D_m, v^*)$.

According to R10:
$S^* = S$, $CA^* = CA$, $NA^* = NA$, $CT^*=CT$, $AT^*=AT$, $CTP^*=CTP$, $ATP^*=ATP$, Class*=Class, O-Purposes*=O-Purposes, T-Purpose*= T-Purpose, $O^*=O$, $OP^* = OP$, $C^* = C$, Input-Purposes* = Input-Purposes, Output-Purposes* = Output-Purposes.

v* satisfies privacy invariant-1 by theorem 10 (i).
v* satisfies privacy invariant-2 by theorem 11 (i).
v* satisfies privacy invariant-3 by theorem 12 (ii).
v* satisfies privacy invariant-4 by theorem 13 (ii).
v* satisfies the information flow invariant by theorem 14 (iii).

Since $OP^* = OP$ according to R10, (v, v*) satisfies privacy constraints-1-4 by corollary 2.

=> R10 is privacy-oriented state sequence preserving.

Rule R11: add-NA:

Suppose v is a privacy-oriented state and $R_k \in R$, $R11(R_k, v) = (D_m, v^*)$ with
(i) $v^* = v$
(ii) $v^* = (S, CA, NA \cup \{(T_1, \text{o-class}_p, \text{transp}_n, r)\}, CT, AT, CTP, ATP, Class,$
    T-Purpose, O-Purposes, C, O, OP, O-Class, T, P, TRANS, TKT-$\{TKT_a\}$,
    role, responsible, Input-Purposes, Output-Purposes).

If $v^* = v$, then v* satisfies privacy invariants-1-4.
Since $OP =OP^* =>$ (v, v*) satisfies privacy constraints -1-4 by corollary 2.

Suppose (ii).
According to R11:
S* =S, CA* = CA, NA* $\supseteq$ NA, CT*=CT, AT*=AT, CTP* = CTP, ATP*=ATP, Class*=Class, O-Purposes*=O-Purposes, T-Purpose*= T-Purpose, O*=O, OP* = OP, C* = C, Input-Purposes* = Input-Purposes, Output-Purposes* = Output-Purposes.

v* satisfies privacy invariant-1 by theorem 10 (i).
v* satisfies privacy invariant-2 by theorem 11 (i).
v* satisfies privacy invariant-3 by theorem 12 (ii).
v* satisfies privacy invariant-4 by theorem 13 (ii).
v* satisfies the information flow invariant by theorem 14 (iii).

Since OP* = OP according to R11, (v, v*) satisfies privacy constraints-1-4 by corollary 2.

=> R11 is privacy-oriented state sequence preserving.

Rule R12: delete-NA:

Suppose v is a privacy-oriented state and $R_k \in R$, $R12(R_k, v) = (D_m, v^*)$ with
(i) v* = v
(ii) v* = (S, CA, NA - {$(T_l$, o-class$_p$, transp$_n$, r)}, CT, AT, CTP, ATP, Class,
        T-Purpose, O-Purposes, C, O, OP, O-Class, T, P, TRANS, TKT-{TKT_a},
        role, responsible, Input-Purposes, Output-Purposes).

If v* = v, then v* satisfies privacy invariants-1-4.
Since OP=OP* => (v, v*) satisfies privacy constraints -1-4 by corollary 2.

Suppose (ii).
According to R12:
S* = S, CA* = CA, NA* = NA-{$(T_l$, o-class$_p$, transp$_n$, r)}, CT*=CT, AT*=AT,
CTP* = CTP, ATP*=ATP, Class*=Class, O-Purposes*=O-Purposes,
T-Purpose*= T-Purpose, O*=O, OP* = OP, C* = C, Input-Purposes* = Input-Purposes,
Output-Purposes* = Output-Purposes,
$\forall$ (S_i, O_j, x) $\in$ CA => (CT(S_i), class(O_j), CTP(S_i), x) $\neq$ (T_l, o-class$_p$, transp$_n$, r).

v* satisfies privacy invariant-1 by theorem 10 (i).
v* satisfies privacy invariant-2 by theorem 11 (i).
v* satisfies privacy invariant-3 by theorem 12 (v).
v* satisfies privacy invariant-4 by theorem 13 (ii).

v* satisfies the information flow invariant by theorem 14 (iii).

Since OP* = OP according to R12, (v, v*) satisfies privacy constraints-1-4 by corollary 2.

=> R12 is privacy-oriented state sequence preserving.

Rule R13: add-task:

Suppose v is a privacy-oriented state and $R_k \in R$, $R13(R_k, v) = (D_m, v^*)$ with
(i) $v^* = v$
(ii) $v^* = $ (S, CA, NA, CT, AT, CTP, ATP $\cup$ (T_{new}, {Nil})), Class,

     T-Purpose $\cup$ (T_{new}, p_w), O-Purposes, C, O, OP, O-Class,

     $T \cup \{T_{new}\}$, P, TRANS, TKT-{TKT_a}, role, responsible $\cup$ (T_{new}, $\varnothing$),

     Input-Purposes, Output-Purposes).

If $v^* = v$, then v* satisfies privacy invariants-1-4.
Since OP =OP* => (v, v*) satisfies privacy constraints -1-4 by corollary 2.

Suppose (ii).
According to R13:
S* =S, CA* = CA, NA* = NA, CT*=CT, AT*=AT, CTP*=CTP,
ATP*=ATP $\cup$ (T_{new}, {Nil}), Class*=Class, O-Purposes*=O-Purposes,
T-Purpose*= T-Purpose $\cup$ (T_{new}, p_w), O*=O, OP* = OP, C* = C,
Input-Purpoese* = Input-Purposes, Output-Purposes* = Output-Purposes,
$T^* = T \cup \{T_{new}\}$, $\forall S_l \in S$: $T_{new} \notin CT(S_l)$ since $T_{new} \notin T$.

v* satisfies privacy invariant-1 by theorem 10 (i).
v* satisfies privacy invariant-2 by theorem 11 (i).
v* satisfies privacy invariant-3 by theorem 12 (ii).
v* satisfies privacy invariant-4 by theorem 13 (ii).
v* satisfies the information flow invariant by theorem 14 (iii).

Since OP* = OP according to R13, (v, v*) satisfies privacy constraints-1-4 by corollary 2.

=> R13 is privacy-oriented state sequence preserving.

Rule R14: delete-task:

Suppose v is a privacy-oriented state and $R_k \in R$, $R14(R_k, v) = (D_m, v^*)$ with
(i) $v^* = v$
(ii) $v^* = (S, CA, NA - (NA \cap (\{T_p\} \times O\text{-class} \times TRANS \times A)), CT,$

AT \ $AT(S_l)$<- $AT(S_l) - (AT(S_l) \cap \{T_p\})$: $\forall$ $S_l \in S$, CTP, ATP,

Class, T-Purpose, O-Purposes, C, O, OP, O-Class, T - $\{T_p\}$, P, TRANS,

TKT-$\{TKT_a\}$, role, responsible, Input-Purposes, Output-Purposes).

If $v^* = v$, then v^* satisfies privacy invariants-1-4.
Since OP =OP* => (v, v^*) satisfies privacy constraints -1-4 by corollary 2.

Suppose (ii).
According to R14:
$S^* = S$, $CA^* = CA$, $NA^* = NA- (NA \cap (\{T_p\} \times O\text{-class} \times TRANS \times A))$, $CT^*=CT$,

$AT^*=AT \setminus AT(S_l)$<- $AT(S_l) - (AT(Sl) \cap \{T_p\})$: $\forall$ $S_l \in S$, $ATP^*=ATP$, $CTP^* = CTP$,

Class*=Class, O-Purposes*=O-Purposes, T-Purpose*= T-Purpose, $O^*=O$, $OP^* = OP$,
$C^* = C$, Input-Purposes* = Input-Purposes, Output-Purposes* = Output-Purposes,
and $[\forall$ $S_l \in S$: $CT(S_l) \neq T_p]$.

v^* satisfies privacy invariant-1 by theorem 10 (iii).
v^* satisfies privacy invariant-2 by theorem 11 (i).
v^* satisfies privacy invariant-3 by theorem 12 (v).
v^* satisfies privacy invariant-4 by theorem 13 (ii).
v^* satisfies the information flow invariant by theorem 14 (iii).

Since $OP^* = OP$ according to R14, (v, v^*) satisfies privacy constraints-1-4 by corollary 2.

=> R14 is privacy-oriented state sequence preserving.

Rule R15: add-o-class:

Suppose v is a privacy-oriented state and $R_k \in R$, $R15(R_k, v) = (D_m, v^*)$ with
(i) $v^* = v$
(ii) $v^* = (S, CA, NA, CT, AT, CTP, ATP, Class, T\text{-Purpose},$

O-Purposes $\cup$ (o-class$_{new}$, p-set$_w$), C, O, OP, O-Class $\cup$

$\{$o-class$_{new}\}$, T, P, TRANS, TKT-$\{TKT_a\}$, role, responsible,

Input-Purposes, Output-Purposes).

If $v^* = v$, then v^* satisfies privacy invariants-1-4.
Since OP = OP* => (v, v*) satisfies privacy constraints -1-4 by corollary 2.

Suppose (ii).
According to R15:
$S^* = S$, $CA^* = CA$, $NA^* = NA$, $CT^*=CT$, $AT^*=AT$, $CTP^*=CTP$, $ATP^*=ATP$,
Class*=Class, O-Purposes*=O-Purposes\ O-Purposes(o-class$_{new}$) <- p-set$_w$,
T-Purpose*= T-Purpose, $O^*=O$, $OP^* = OP$, $C^* = C$,
Input-Purposes* = Input-Purposes, Output-Purposes* = Output-Purposes

v^* satisfies privacy invariant-1 by theorem 10 (i).
v^* satisfies privacy invariant-2 by theorem 11 (i).
v^* satisfies privacy invariant-3 by theorem 12 (ii).
v^* satisfies privacy invariant-4 by theorem 13 (ii).
v^* satisfies the information flow invariant by theorem 14 (iii).

Since OP* = OP according to R15, (v, v*) satisfies privacy constraints-1-4 by corollary 2.

=> R15 is privacy-oriented state sequence preserving.

Rule R16: delete-o-class:

Suppose v is a privacy-oriented state and $R_k \in R$, $R16(R_k, v) = (D_m, v^*)$ with
(i) $v^* = v$
(ii) $v^* =$ (S, CA, NA, CT, AT, CTP, ATP, Class, T-Purpose,
O-Purposes, C, O, OP, O-Class-{o-class$_p$}, T, P, TRANS, TKT-{TKT$_a$},
role, responsible, Input-Purposes, Output-Purposes).

If $v^* = v$, then v^* satisfies privacy invariants-1-4.
Since OP =OP* => (v, v*) satisfies privacy constraints -1-4 by corollary 2.

Suppose (ii).
According to R16:
$S^* = S$, $CA^* = CA$, $NA^* = NA$, $CT^*=CT$, $AT^*=AT$, $CTP^*=CTP$, $ATP^*=ATP$,
Class*=Class, O-Purposes*=O-Purposes, T-Purpose*= T-Purpose, $O^*=O$, $OP^* = OP$,
$C^* = C$, O-Class* = O-Class-{o-class$_p$}, Input-Purposes* = Input-Purposes,
Output-Purposes* = Output-Purposes.

v^* satisfies privacy invariant-1 by theorem 10 (i).
v^* satisfies privacy invariant-2 by theorem 11 (i).
v^* satisfies privacy invariant-3 by theorem 12 (ii).

v^* satisfies privacy invariant-4 by theorem 13 (ii).
v^* satisfies the information flow invariant by theorem 14 (iii).

Since $OP^* = OP$ according to R16, (v, v^*) satisfies privacy constraints-1-4 by corollary 2.

=> R16 is privacy-oriented state sequence preserving.

Rule R17: add-auth-TP:

Suppose v is a privacy-oriented state and $R_k \in R$, $R17(R_k, v) = (D_m, v^*)$ with
(i) $v^* = v$
(ii) $v^* = $ (S, CA, NA, CT, AT, CTP, ATP\ ATP(T_m) <- ATP(T_m) $\cup$ {transp$_n$}, Class,
   T-Purpose, O-Purposes, C, O, OP, O-Class, T, P, TRANS, TKT-{TKT$_a$},
   role, responsible, Input-Purposes, Output-Purposes).

If $v^* = v$, then v^* satisfies privacy invariants-1-4.
Since $OP = OP^*$ => (v, v^*) satisfies privacy constraints -1-4 by corollary 2.

Suppose (ii).
According to R17:
$S^* = S$, $CA^* = CA$, $NA^* = NA$, $CT^*=CT$, $AT^*=AT$, $CTP^*=CTP$,
$ATP^*=ATP \setminus ATP(T_m)$ <- $ATP(T_m) \cup$ {transp$_n$},
Class*=Class, O-Purposes*=O-Purposes, T-Purpose*= T-Purpose, $O^*=O$, $OP^* = OP$,
$C^* = C$, Input-Purposes* = Input-Purposes, Output-Purposes* = Output-Purposes.

v^* satisfies privacy invariant-1 by theorem 10 (i).
v^* satisfies privacy invariant-2 by theorem 11 (i).
v^* satisfies privacy invariant-3 by theorem 12 (ii).
v^* satisfies privacy invariant-4 by theorem 13 (ii).
v^* satisfies the information flow invariant by theorem 14 (iii).

Since $OP^* = OP$ according to R17, (v, v^*) satisfies privacy constraints-1-4 by corollary 2.

=> R17 is privacy-oriented state sequence preserving.

Rule R18: delete-auth-TP:

Suppose v is a privacy-oriented state and $R_k \in R$, $R18(R_k, v) = (D_m, v^*)$ with
(i) $v^* = v$

(ii) $v^* = (S, CA, NA, CT, AT, CTP, ATP \setminus ATP(T_p) <- ATP(T_p) - \{transp_{new}\}$,
Class, T-Purpose, O-Purposes, C, O, OP, O-Class, T, P, TRANS,
TKT-$\{TKT_a\}$, role, responsible, Input-Purposes, Output-Purposes).

If $v^* = v$, then v^* satisfies privacy invariants-1-4.
Since OP = OP* => (v, v*) satisfies privacy constraints -1-4 by corollary 2.

Suppose (ii).
According to R18:
$S^* = S$, $CA^* = CA$, $NA^* = NA$, $CT^*=CT$, $AT^*=AT$, $CTP^*=CTP$, $ATP^*=ATP -$
$\{transp_{new}\}$, Class*=Class, O-Purposes*=O-Purposes, T-Purpose*= T-Purpose,
$O^*=O$, $OP^* = OP$, $C^* = C$, Input-Purposes* = Input-Purposes, Output-Purposes* =
Output-Purposes and $\forall\ S_l \in S$: $CTP\ (S_l) \neq transp_n \lor CT(S_l) \neq T_p$.

v^* satisfies privacy invariant-1 by theorem 10 (i).
v^* satisfies privacy invariant-2 by theorem 11 (iv).
v^* satisfies privacy invariant-3 by theorem 12 (ii).
v^* satisfies privacy invariant-4 by theorem 13 (ii).
v^* satisfies the information flow invariant by theorem 14 (iii).

Since OP* = OP according to R18, (v, v*) satisfies privacy constraints-1-4
by corollary 2.

=> R18 is privacy-oriented state sequence preserving.

Rule R19: add-consent:

Suppose v is a privacy-oriented state and $R_k \in R$, $R19(R_k, v) = (D_m, v^*)$ with
(i) $v^* = v$
(ii) $v^* = (S, CA, NA, CT, AT, CTP, ATP, Class, T-Purpose, O-Purposes,$
$C \cup \{(p_n, O_p)\}, O, OP, O-Class, T, P, TRANS, TKT-\{TKT_a\}$, role,
responsible, Input-Purposes, Output-Purposes).

If $v^* = v$, then v^* satisfies privacy invariants-1-4.
Since OP = OP* => (v, v*) satisfies privacy constraints -1-4 by corollary 2.

Suppose (ii).
According to R19:
$S^* = S$, $CA^* = CA$, $NA^* = NA$, $CT^*=CT$, $AT^*=AT$, $CTP^*=CTP$, $ATP^*=ATP$,
Class*=Class, O-Purposes*=O-Purposes, T-Purpose*= T-Purpose, $O^*=O$, $OP^* = OP$,
$C^* = C \cup \{(p_n, O_p)\}$, Input-Purposes* = Input-Purposes,

Outpt-Purposes* = Output-Purposes.

v* satisfies privacy invariant-1 by theorem 10 (i).
v* satisfies privacy invariant-2 by theorem 11 (i).
v* satisfies privacy invariant-3 by theorem 12 (ii).
v* satisfies privacy invariant-4 by theorem 13 (ii).
v* satisfies the information flow invariant by theorem 14 (iii).

Since OP* = OP according to R19, (v, v*) satisfies privacy constraints-1-4 by corollary 2.

=> R19 is privacy-oriented state sequence preserving.

Rule R20: delete-consent:

Suppose v is a privacy-oriented state and $R_k \in R$, $R20(R_k, v) = (D_m, v^*)$ with
(i) $v^* = v$
(ii) $v^* = $ (S, CA, NA, CT, AT, CTP, ATP, Class, T-Purpose, O-Purposes,
$\quad\quad$ C - $\{(p_n, O_p)\}$, O, OP, O-Class, T, P, TRANS, TKT-$\{TKT_a\}$, role,
$\quad\quad$ responsible, Input-Purposes.Output-Purposes).

If $v^* = v$, then v* satisfies privacy invariants-1-4.
Since OP = OP* => (v, v*) satisfies privacy constraints -1-4 by corollary 2.

Suppose (ii).
According to R20:
S* = S, CA* = CA, NA* = NA, CT*=CT, AT*=AT, CTP*=CTP, ATP*=ATP, Class*=Class, O-Purposes*=O-Purposes, T-Purpose*= T-Purpose, O*=O, OP* = OP, C* = C - $\{(p_n, O_p)\}$, Input-Purposes* = Input-Purposes,
Output-Purposes* = Output-Purposes and
$[\forall S_1 \in S, r \in A : (S_1, O_p, r) \in CA => $ (T-Purpose(CT(S_1)) $\neq p_n \vee$
$\quad\quad\quad\quad\quad\quad\quad\quad\quad\quad\quad$ T-Purpose(CT(S_1)) $\in$ O-Purposes(class(O_p)))]

v* satisfies privacy invariant-1 by theorem 10 (i).
v* satisfies privacy invariant-2 by theorem 11 (i).
v* satisfies privacy invariant-3 by theorem 12 (ii).
v* satisfies privacy invariant-4 by theorem 13 (iv).
v* satisfies the information flow invariant by theorem 14 (iii).

Since OP* = OP according to R20, (v, v*) satisfies privacy constraints-1-4 by corollary 2.

=> R20 is privacy-oriented state sequence preserving.

Rule R21: add-purpose:
The argument is that of the proof of rule R10 with the substitution of R21 for R10.

Rule R22: delete-purpose:
Suppose v is a privacy-oriented state and $R_k \in R$, $R22(R_k, v) = (D_m, v^*)$ with

(i) $v^* = v$

(ii) $v^* = $ (S, CA, NA, CT, AT, CTP, ATP, Class, T-Purpose,

O-Purposes\ O-Purposes(o-class$_n$) <- O-Purposes(o-class$_n$) -

(O-Purposes(o-class$_n$)∩{p_w}) : ∀ o-class$_n$ ∈ O-class,

$C - (C \cap (\{p_w\} \times OP))$, O, OP, O-Class, T, P - {p_w},

TRANS, TKT-{TKT_a}, role,

responsible, Input-Purposes, Output-Purposes).

If $v^* = v$, then v^* satisfies privacy invariants-1-4.
Since OP = OP* => (v, v^*) satisfies privacy constraints -1-4 by corollary 2.

Suppose (ii).
According to R22:
$S^* = S$, $CA^* = CA$, $NA^* = NA$, $CT^*=CT$, $AT^*=AT$, $CTP^*=CTP$, $ATP^*=ATP$,
Class*=Class,
O-Purposes*= O-Purposes\ O-Purposes(o-class$_n$) <-

O-Purposes(o-class$_n$) - (O-Purposes(o-class$_n$)∩{p_w}) : ∀ o-class$_n$ ∈ O-class,

T-Purpose*= T-Purpose, $O^*=O$, $OP^* = OP$,

$C^* = C - (C \cap (\{p_w\} \times OP))$, Input-Purposes* = Input-Purposes,

Output-Purposes* = Output-Purposes and

[∀ O_1 ∈ O: O-Purposes(class(O_1)) ≠ p_w] ∧

[∀ o-class$_1$ ∈ O-class: {p_w} ≠ O-Purposes(o-class$_1$)] ∧

[∀ T_n ∈ T: T-Purpose(T_n) ≠ p_w].

=> ∀ S_q ∈ S: T-Purpose(CT(S_q)) ≠ p_w.

v^* satisfies privacy invariant-1 by theorem 10 (i).
v^* satisfies privacy invariant-2 by theorem 11 (i).
v^* satisfies privacy invariant-3 by theorem 12 (ii).
v^* satisfies privacy invariant-4 by theorem 13 (iv).
v^* satisfies the information flow invariant by theorem 14 (iii).

Since OP* = OP according to R22, (v, v^*) satisfies privacy constraints-1-4
by corollary 2.

=> R22 is privacy-oriented state sequence preserving.

Rule R23: set role:
The argument is that of the proof of rule R10 with the substitution of R23 for R10.

Rule R24: add-resp-users:
The argument is that of the proof of rule R10 with the substitution of R24 for R10.

Rule R25: delete-resp-users:
The argument is that of the proof of rule R10 with the substitution of R25 for R10.

Rule R26: add-auth-task:

Suppose v is a privacy-oriented state and $R_k \in R$, $R26(R_k, v) = (D_m, v^*)$ with
(i) $v^* = v$
(ii) $v^* = (S, CA, NA, CT, AT \setminus AT(S_l) <- AT(S_l) \cup \{T_n\}, CTP,$

$ATP, Class, T\text{-}Purpose, O\text{-}Purposes, C, O, OP, O\text{-}Class, T, P, TRANS,$
$TKT\text{-}\{TKT_a\}, role, responsible, Input\text{-}Purposes, Output\text{-}Purposes).$

If $v^* = v$, then v^* satisfies privacy invariants-1-4.
Since $OP = OP^* => (v, v^*)$ satisfies privacy constraints -1-4 by corollary 2.

Suppose (ii).
According to R26:
$S^* = S, CA^* = CA, NA^* = NA, CT^* = CT, AT^* = AT \setminus AT(S_l) <- AT(S_l) \cup \{T_n\},$
$CTP^* = CTP, ATP^* = ATP, Class^* = Class, O\text{-}Purposes^* = O\text{-}Purposes,$
$T\text{-}Purpose^* = T\text{-}Purpose, O^* = O, OP^* = OP, C^* = C,$
Input-Purposes* = Input-Purposes, Output-Purposes* = Output-Purposes.

v^* satisfies privacy invariant-1 by theorem 10 (i).
v^* satisfies privacy invariant-2 by theorem 11 (i).
v^* satisfies privacy invariant-3 by theorem 12 (ii).
v^* satisfies privacy invariant-4 by theorem 13 (ii).
v^* satisfies the information flow invariant by theorem 14 (iii).

Since $OP^* = OP$ according to R26, (v, v^*) satisfies privacy constraints-1-4 by corollary 2.

=> R26 is privacy-oriented state sequence preserving.

Rule R27: delete-auth-task:

Suppose v is a privacy-oriented state and $R_k \in R$, $R27(R_k, v) = (D_m, v^*)$ with

(i) $v^* = v$

(ii) $v^* = (S, CA, NA, CT, AT \setminus AT(S_l) <- AT(S_l) - \{T_n\}, CTP,$

ATP, Class, T-Purpose, O-Purposes, C, O, OP, O-Class, T, P, TRANS, TKT-$\{TKT_a\}$, role, responsible, Input-Purposes, Output-Purposes).

If $v^* = v$, then v^* satisfies privacy invariants-1-4.
Since $OP = OP^* => (v, v^*)$ satisfies privacy constraints -1-4 by corollary 2.

Suppose (ii).
According to R27:
$S^* = S$, $CA^* = CA$, $NA^* = NA$, $CT^*=CT$, $AT^*=AT \setminus AT(S_l) <- AT(S_l) - \{T_n\}$,

$CTP^*=CTP$, $ATP^*=ATP$, Class*=Class, O-Purposes*=O-Purposes,
T-Purpose*= T-Purpose, $O^*=O$, $OP^* = OP$, $C^* = C$, Input-Purposes* =
Input-Purposes, Output-Purposes* = Output-Purposes and $CT(S_l) \neq T_n$.

According to R27: $\forall S_q \in S$:

$$AT^*(S_q) = \begin{cases} AT^*(S_q) - \{T_n\} & \text{for } S_q = S_l \\ \\ AT(S_q) & \text{for } S_q \neq S_l. \end{cases}$$

If $S_q \neq S_l =>$ $\quad AT^*(S_q) = AT(S_q)$ and

$\quad\quad$ since $\quad CT^*(S_q) = CT(S_q) \in AT(S_q)$

$\quad\quad\quad\quad$ (as v satisfies privacy invariant-1)

$\quad\quad\quad => CT^*(S_q) \in AT^*(S_q)$

If $S_q = S_l =>$ $\quad AT^* (S_q) = AT (S_q) - \{T_n\}$

$\quad\quad\quad CT(S_q) = CT^*(S_q) \in AT(S_i)$ $\quad$ (as v satisfies privacy invariant-1)

$\quad\quad$ and $\quad CT^*(S_q) \neq T_n$ $\quad\quad\quad\quad\quad\quad\quad$ according to R27

$\quad\quad\quad => CT^*(S_q) \in AT^*(S_q)$.

$=> v^*$ satisfies privacy invariant-1.

v^* satisfies privacy invariant-2 by theorem 11 (i).
v^* satisfies privacy invariant-3 by theorem 12 (ii).
v^* satisfies privacy invariant-4 by theorem 13 (ii).
v^* satisfies the information flow invariant by theorem 14 (iii).

Since OP* = OP according to R27, (v, v*) satisfies privacy constraints-1-4 by corollary 2.

=> R27 is privacy-oriented state sequence preserving.

Rule R28: create-TP:
The argument is that of the proof of rule R10 with the substitution of R28 for R10.

Rule R29: delete-TP:
Suppose v is a privacy-oriented state and $R_k \in R$, R29(R_k, v) = (D_m, v*) with

(i) v* = v

(ii) v* = (S, CA, NA, CT, AT, CTP,

$\quad$ ATP\ ATP(T_j) <- ATP(T_j) - (ATP(T_j) $\cap${$transp_n$}): $\forall T_j \in$ T,

$\quad$ Class, T-Purpose, O-Purposes, C, O, OP, O-Class, T, P, TRANS - {$transp_n$},

$\quad$ TKT, role, responsible, Input-Purposes, Output-Purposes).

If v* = v, then v* satisfies privacy invariants-1-4.
Since OP = OP* => (v, v*) satisfies privacy constraints -1-4 by corollary 2.

Suppose (ii).
According to R29:
S* = S, CA* = CA, NA* = NA, CT*=CT, AT*=AT, CTP*=CTP,
ATP* =ATP\ ATP(T_j) <- ATP(T_j) - (ATP(T_j) $\cap${$transp_n$}): $\forall T_j \in$ T,
Class*=Class, O-Purposes*=O-Purposes, T-Purpose*= T-Purpose,
O*=O, OP* = OP, C* = C, Input-Purposes* = Input-Purposes,
Outpt-Purposes* = Output-Purposes and [$\forall S_l \in$ S: CTP(S_l) $\neq transp_n$].

v* satisfies privacy invariant-1 by theorem 10 (i).

According to R29 :
$\forall S_l \in$ S: ATP* (CT*(S_l)) = ATP(CT(S_l)) - (ATP(CT(S_l)) $\cap${$transp_n$}).
Since CTP*(S_l) = CTP(S_l) $\in$ ATP (CT*(S_l)) (as v satisfies privacy invariant-1)
and CTP*(S_l) = CTP(S_l) $\neq transp_n$ (according to R29) =>
CTP*(S_l) $\in$ ATP* (CT*(S_l)).
=> v* satisfies privacy invariant-2.

v* satisfies privacy invariant-3 by theorem 12 (ii).
v* satisfies privacy invariant-4 by theorem 13 (ii).
v* satisfies the information flow invariant by theorem 14 (iii).

Since OP* = OP according to R29, (v, v*) satisfies privacy constraints-1-4 by corollary 2.

=> R29 is privacy-oriented state sequence preserving.

Corollary 3:

Given the system Σ (R, D, W(ω), z_0), ω = {R1,...,R29 },

z_0 = (S, CA, NA, CT, AT, CTP, ATP, Class, T-Purpose, O-Purposes, C, O, OP, O-Class, T, P, TRANS, TKT, role, responsible, Input-Purposes, Output-Purposes) with $\forall$ S_i $\in$ S: CTP(S_i) = Nil, CT (S_i) = Nil, Input-Purposes(S_i) = P, Output-Purposes(S_i) = $\varnothing$,

and with $\forall$ (S_i, O_j, r)$\in$ CA: O_j $\notin$ OP.

Then Σ (R, D, W(ω), z_0) is a privacy-oriented system.

Appendix B: Implementation of a Hospital Scenario as a Demonstration Example

In Chapter 5.6, we outlined how the privacy model could be used to protect personal patient data in a hospital information system. We have used the GFAC-implementation of the privacy model to implement an imaginary hospital scenario. Though the scenario is quite simplified and only describes a part of personal data processing in a hospital environment, it demonstrates how the privacy model can be applied. Particularly, it shows how a privacy policy for hospital environments similar as defined by [Seelos 1991] could be enforced by the privacy model.

In the imaginary hospital scenario, the privacy model can protect personal patient data by enforcing the privacy principles of necessity of data processing and purpose binding. In particular, the personal data processing of patient related data in the areas medical treatment, administration and care should be separated as far as possible. For example, administration personnel should not have access to medical data and doctors (physicians) should not have access to billing data. Diagnosis data and treatment instructions may be transferred to another medical treatment centre or care ward. Researchers may use patient data for statistical (research) purposes, if the patients have given their consent. Besides, billing information is transferred to the patient´s insurance companies. Such data transfers require a secure network connection.

In this simplified scenario, we only consider the medical treatment in a surgical ward. Personal patient data is processed at each of the following subsequent steps:

1. Patient admission

2. Diagnosis and treatment instruction by an examination specialist

3. Operation by a surgeon, therapy or transfer to another medical treatment centre or care ward

4. Patient discharge

5. Transfer of billing information to the patient´s health insurance company

As stated in Chapter 5.6, the organisation of a hospital is typically divided into the areas medical treatment, care, administration and research. Consequently, appropriate purposes for separating the main areas in a hospital are:

Table B.1: Purposes for personal data processing in a hospital environment

Purposes:
MT (medical treatment)
AD (administration)
CAR (care)
RE (research)

Within each area, different tasks (with a purpose that is corresponding to the area) can be defined. Possible tasks for the purposes MT, AD, CAR, RE are:

Table B.2: Tasks and purposes of tasks in a hospital environment

MT	AD	CAR	RE
Diagnosing	Admission	Care-Transfer	Statistical analysis
Operation	Discharge		
Therapy	Billing		
Treatment-Transfer	Data-Transfer		

The following object classes of personal patient data are defined:

Table B.3: Object classes and their purposes

Object class:	Purposes:	Content:
Admission data	AD, MT, CAR	Administrative, social, demographic and insurance information about a patient
Billing data	AD	billing oriented (financial) information about a patient and his medical treatment
Diagnosis	MT, CAR	Diagnosis data
Treatment request	MT, CAR	Instructions for surgeons and therapists
Operational treatment data	MT	Operation protocol
Treatment protocol	AD, MT	Protocol of actions and treatments (needed for creating billing data and for control)
Statistics	RE	Statistical data (which can later be classified as non-personal data)

Next, users are authorised for their tasks:

Table B.4: Authorised tasks for users

User (Role):	Authorised Tasks:
Examination specialist	Diagnosing, Therapy, Treatment-Transfer, Care-Transfer
Surgeon	Operation, Treatment-Transfer, Care-Transfer
Therapist	Therapy, Treatment-Transfer, Care-Transfer
Registration staff	Admission, Discharge
Billing staff	Billing, Data transfer
Scientist	Statistical Analysis

Personal data objects are, for instance, processed by the following transformation procedures:

Table B.5: Transformation procedures

TP:	Used for:
pm_create	Creation of personal data file of a specified class
Append-only editor	Appending text to an existing file
Editor	Modifying a text file
Display program	Reading a text file and displaying it on the screen
Deletion program	Deletion of a file
Transfer program	Encrypted data transfer by interprocess communication
Statistic program	Reading files, calculating and writing statistics

The next step is the definition of authorised transformation procedures for tasks:

Table B.6: Authorised transformation procedures for tasks

Task:	Authorised TPs:
Diagnosing	pm_create, Append-only editor, Editor, Display program
Operation	pm_create, Append-only editor, Editor, Display program
Therapy	Append-only editor, Display program
Treatment-Transfer	Transfer program
Care-Transfer	Transfer program
Admission	pm_create, Editor
Discharge	Append-only editor
Billing	Editor, Display program
Data transfer	Transfer program
Statistics	pm_create, Editor, Statistics program

Finally, necessary accesses are defined. Possible accesses are read, write, delete, create and append.

Table B.7: Necessary accesses

Task:	Object class:	TP:	Accesses:
Diagnosing	Diagnosis	pm_create	create
"	"	Editor	read, write, append
"	"	Display program	read
"	Treatment protocol	Append-only editor	append
"	Treatment request	pm_create	create
"	"	Editor	read, write, append
Operation	Treatment request	Display program	read
"	Operational treatment data	pm_create	create
"	"	Editor	read, write, append
"	Treatment protocol	Append-only editor	append
Therapy	Treatment request	Display program	read
"	Treatment protocol	Append-only editor	append
Treatment-transfer	Diagnosis	Transfer program	read
"	default-class(MT)	Transfer program	create, write, append
"	Treatment request	Transfer program	read
"	default-class(MT)	Transfer program	create, write, append
Care-transfer	Diagnosis	Transfer program	read
"	default-class(CAR)	Transfer program	create, write, append
"	Treatment request	Transfer program	read
"	default-class(CAR)	Transfer program	create, write, append
Admission	Admission data	pm_create	create
"	"	Editor	read, write, append
"	Treatment protocol	pm_create	create
"	"	Append-only editor	append
Discharge	Admission data	Append-only editor	append
"	Treatment protocol	Append-only editor	append
Billing	Treatment protocol	Display program	read
"	Billing data	pm_create	create
"	"	Editor	read, write, append
Data transfer	Billing data	Transfer program	read
"	default-class(AD)	Transfer program	create, write, append
Statistical analysis	Statistics	pm_create	create
"	"	Editor	read, write, append
"	"	Deletion program	delete
"	"	Statistic program	write, append
"	Diagnosis	Statistic program	read

"	Treatment instruction	Statistic program	read
"	Operational treatment data	Statistic program	read

All access control information must be entered by a security officer with *pm-privileged-function* (called *rsbac_pm* in the implementation), using tickets provided by a data protection officer with the same program. Currently, all object classes, tasks, purposes, etc. must be entered as numbers, leaving the encoding for humans.

From the system's point of view, during and after the patient´s stay in hospital the patient´s data is processed by the following steps:

1. A registration staff member (by performing the task "Admission") creates a file for the patient´s admission data with *pm-create*, collects administrative, social, demographic and insurance information about the patient and writes it into the patient´s admission data file by using an editor. He creates a treatment protocol file with *pm_create* and appends the action "admission" to the treatment protocol.

2. The examination specialist (by performing the task "Diagnosing") creates a diagnosis file and uses the editor to write and change his diagnosis. Then he creates a treatment instruction file for this patient and writes into it with an editor, changing it when necessary. Finally he appends his actions to the treatment protocol file.
   If necessary, he can transfer a patient to another specialist, medical treatment centre or care ward (by performing the task "Treatment-transfer" or "Care-transfer"). For a patient transfer he can transfer diagnosis and treatment instruction data by using the transfer programs.

3. The surgeon (by transforming the task "Operation") reads the treatment instruction with the display program and operates on the patient. Afterwards he creates and edits the operational treatment data file, writing a protocol of the operation. As before, all actions are appended to the treatment protocol file.
   Like the examination specialist, the surgeon can transfer patients to another specialist, medical treatment center or care ward. For this he can also transfer diagnosis and treatment instruction data by the transfer programs.

4. The therapist (by performing the task "Therapy") reads the treatment instructions, treats the patient and appends his treatment actions to the treatment protocol.

5. When the treatment has been completed, the patient is discharged by a registration staff member (by performing the task "Discharge"), who makes last entries to the patient´s admission data and treatment protocol data by using the append editor.

6. At last, a billing staff member (by performing the task "Billing") reads the treatment protocol and creates and edits the billing data file, which he transfers to the patient's medical insurance company by using the data transfer program.

7. By performing the task "Statistical Analysis" diagnoses, treatment instructions and operation data can be read by the scientist's statistic program in order to calculate statistical data. However, access to these files for research purposes is only permitted if the patients in question have given their consent. Statistical data files can only be created, changed and deleted by users performing the current task statistical analysis.

References

[Abrams et al. 1990] M.Abrams, K.Eggers, L.LaPadula, I.Olson, "A Generalized Framework for Access Control: An Informal Description", *Proceedings of the 13th National Computer Security Conference*, Washington, October 1990.

[Abrams et al. 1991a] M.Abrams, J.Heaney, O.King, L.LaPadula, M.Lazear, I.Olson, "Generalized Framework for Access Control: Towards Prototyping the ORGCON Policy", *Proceedings of the 14th National Computer Security Conference*, Baltimore, October 1991.

[Abrams et al. 1991b] M.Abrams, L.LaPadula, M.Lazear, I.Olson, "Reconciling a Formal Model and Prototype Implementation – Lessons Learned in Implementing the ORGCON Policy", Mitre Corporation, Bedford, Mass.01730, November 1991.

[Abrams 1993] M.Abrams, "Renewed Understanding of Access Control Policies", *Proceedings of the 16th National Computer Security Conference*, Baltimore, September 1993.

[Abrams et al. 1993] M.Abrams, E.Amoroso, L.LaPadula, T.Lunt, J.Williams, "Report of an integrity research study group", *Computers&Security*, 12 (1993), Elsevier Science Publishers, pp. 679-689.

[Abrams/Zelkowitz 1994] M.Abrams, M.Zelkowitz, "Belief in Correctness", *Proceedings of the 17th National Computer Security Conference*, Baltimore, 11-14 October 1994.

[Amoroso 1994] E. Amoroso, "Fundamentals of Computer Security Technology", Prentice&Hall, 1994.

[Anderson/Frivold/Valdes 1995] D.Anderson, T.Frivold, A.Valdes, "Next-Generation Intrusion Detection Expert System (NIDES) - A Summary", SRI International, Computer Science Laboratory, SRI-CSL-95-07, May 1995.

[Atluri/Huang 1996] V. Atluri, W.-K- Huang, "An Authorization Model for Workflows", in: *Proceedings of Computer-Security-ESORICS'96*, Eds.: E.Bertino et al., Rome, September 1996, Springer-Verlag.

[Aura 1999] T.Aura, "Distributed Access-Rights Management with Delegation Certificates", in: J.Vitek, C.Jensen: Secure Internet Programming: Security Issues for Distributed and Mobile Objects", LNCS Vol. 1603, Springer-Verlag, 1999.

[Bach 1986] M.Bach, "The Design of the Unix Operating System", Prentice Hall, 1986.

[Bangemann 1994] "Europe and the global information society , Recommendations to the European Council", 26 May 1994, Brussels.

[Barkely et al. 1997] .J.F.Barkley, V.Cincotta, D.Ferraiolo, S.Gavrilla, R.Kuhn "Role Based Access Control for the World Wide Web", *Proceedings of the 20th National Information Systems Security Conference*, Baltimore, MD, 7-10 October 1997.

[BDSG-Referentenentwurf 1997] Novellierung des Bundesdatenschutzgesetzes, Referentenentwurf der Bundesregierung, 8 December 1997.

[BDSG Novellierungsentwurf 2000] BDSG-Novellierungsentwurf vom 25.5.2000, Kabinettsbeschluß vom 14.6.2000.

[Bell LaPadula 1973] D.E.Bell, L.LaPadula, "Secure Computer Systems: A Mathematical Model", Mitre Corporation, Bedford, Mass.01730, January 1973.

[Bell LaPadula 1976] D.E. Bell, L.LaPadula, "Secure Computer Systems: Unified Exposition and Multics Interpretation", Mitre Cooperation, Bedford, Mass. 01730, January 1976.

[Bennett 1997] C.Bennett, "Convergence Revisited: Toward a Global Policy for Protection of Personal Data ?", in: P.Agre, M.Rotenberg : Technology and Privacy: the New Landscape, MIT Press, 1997, pp.99-124.

[Berthold/Federrath/Köpsel 2000] O.Berthold, H.Federrath, S.Köpsel, "Web MIXes: A System for anonymous and unobservable Internet access", in: Federrath (Ed.), *Proceedings of the Workshop on Design Issues in Anonymity and Unobservability*, International Computer Science Institutes (ICSI), Berkeley, California, July 2000.

[Bertino/Origgi/Samarti 1994a] E.Bertino, F.Origgi, P.Samarti, "A New Authorization Model for Object-Oriented Databases", *Proceedings of the IFIP WG 11.3 8th Annual Working Conference on Database Security*, Eds.: J. Biskup, M.Morgenstern, C.Landwehr, Bad Salzdetfurth/Germany, August, 1994.

[Bertino/Weigand 1994b] E.Bertino, H.Weigand, "An Approach to Authorization Modelling in Object-Oriented Database Systems", Data and Knowledge Engineering, Vol. 12(1), North Holland, February 1994.

[Biba 1977] K.J. Biba, "Integrity Considerations for Secure Computer Systems", USAF Electronic Systems Division, Bedford, Mass., April 1977.

[Biham/Shamir 1990] E.Biham, A.Shamir, "Differential Cryptanalysis of DES-like Cryptosystems", *Advances in Cryptology, Proceedings Crypto 1990*.

[Biskup/Brüggemann 1988] J.Biskup, H.Brüggemann, "The Personal Model of Data: Towards a Privacy-Oriented Information System", *Computer&Security*, 7, 1988, pp.575-597.

[Blaze et al. 1996] M.Blaze, W.Diffie, R.Rivest, B.Schneier, T.Shimomura, E.Thompson, M.Wiener, "Minimal Key Lengths for Symmetric Ciphers to Provide Adequate Commercial Security", A Report by an Ad Hoc Group of Cryptographers and Computer Scientists, January 1996.

[BMI 1999] Bundesdatenschutzgesetz (BDSG) -Entwurf des Bundesministeriums des Inneren (BMI) vom 6.7.1999.

[Boyan 1997] J.Boyan, The Anomyzer: Protecting User Privacy on the Web. *Computer-Mediated Communication Magazine*, 1997.

[Bräutigam/Höller/Scholz 90] L.Bräutigam, H.Höller, R.Scholz, "Datenschutz als Anforderung an die Systemgestaltung", Westdeutscher Verlag, 1990.

[Brands 1995] S.Brands, "Electronic Cash on the Internet", *Proceedings of the Internet Society 1995 Symposium on Network and Distributed System Security*, San Diego, California, 16-17 February, 1995.

[Brands 1999] S.Brands, "Rethinking public key infrastructures and digital certificates --- building in privacy", MIT Press, August 2000, http://www.xs4all.nl/~brands/

[Brewer/Nash 1989] D.Brewer, M.Nash, "The Chinese Wall Security Policy", *Proceedings of the 1989 IEEE Symposium on Security and Privacy*, Oakland, May 1989.

[Brüggemann 1992] H. Brüggemann, "Rights in an Object-Oriented Environment", in: *Database Security V: Status and Prospects*, Eds.: C.Landwehr, S.Jajodia, North Holland, 1992, pp.99-115.

[Brunnstein/Fischer-Hübner 1990] K.Brunnstein, S.Fischer-Hübner, "Risk Analysis of 'Trusted' Computer Sytems", *Proceedings of the 6th International IFIP TC-11 Conference on Information Security, Sec'90*, Helsinki, May 1990.

[Brunnstein/Fischer-Hübner/Swimmer 1991] K.Brunnstein, S.Fischer-Hübner, M.Swimmer, "Concepts of an Expert System for Virus Detection", in: D.Lindsay, W.Price (Eds*.): Information-security- Proceedings of the 7th International IFIP TC-11 Conference on Information Security, Sec'91*, Brigthon, May 1991, North Holland, 1991.

[Brunnstein /Fischer-Hübner 1992] K.Brunnstein, S.Fischer-Hübner, "Möglichkeiten und Grenzen von Kriterienkatalogen" (Opportunities and Limitations of Security Evaluation Criteria), in: *Wirtschaftsinformatik*, Vieweg-Verlag, Vol. 4, August 1992.

[Brunnstein/Schier 1997] K.Brunnstein, K.Schier, "Global digital commerce: Impacts and Risks for developments of global information societies", ', in: J.Berleur and Diane Whitehouse, Eds., 'An ethical global information society: culture and democracy revisited', *Proceedings of the IFIP WG 9.2 Corfu international conference*, May 8-10, 1997, Chapman&Hall, 1997, pp. 75-82.

[Brunnstein 1997] K.Brunnstein, "Towards an holistic view of enterprise ICT security and safety", in: *Information Security in Research and Business-Proceedings of the IFIP TC11 13th International conference on Information Security (Sec'97)*, 14-16 May 1997, Copenhagen, Chapman&Hall, 1997.

[Brunnstein/Fischer-Hübner/Schaar 1998] K.Brunnstein, S.Fischer-Hübner, P.Schaar, "Verbraucherbefragung & Globale Informationsgesellschaft", in: Computer und Recht aktuell, *Computer und Recht*, February, 1998, Verlag Dr. Otto Schmidt, pp. 125-126.

[BT-Drucksache 1998] Schlußbericht der Enquete-Kommission "Zukunft der Medien in Wirtschaft und Gesellschaft" zum Thema "Deutschlands Weg in die Informationsgesellschaft", Bundestags-Drucksache 13/11004 vom 22.6.1998.

[Budapest Draft 1996] International Working Group on Data Protection in Telecommunications, ´Data Protection on the Internet, Report and Guidance´ (Budapest Draft), 1996.

[Bündnis 90/die Grünen 1997] Entwurf eines Bundesdatenschutzgesetzes (BDSG), Gesetzentwurf des Abgeordneten Manfred Such und der Fraktion Bündnis 90/die Grünen, 14 November 1997, BT-Drucksache 13/9082.

[Canada 1995] Connection Community Content: The Challenge of the Information Highway, Final Report of the Canadian Information Highway Advisory Council, September 1995.

[Castano et al. 1995] S.Castano, M.Fugini, G.Martella, P.Samarti, "Database Security", Addison-Wesley / ACM Press, 1995.

[CC 1996] Common Criteria Editorial Board, Common Criteria for the Information Technology Security Evaluation, Version 1.0, February 1996.

[CC 1998] The Common Criteria Project Sponsoring Organisations, Common Criteria for the Information Technology Security Evaluation, Version 2.0, May 1998.

[CC 1999] The Common Criteria Project Sponsoring Organisations, Common Criteria for the Information Technology Security Evaluation, Version 2.1, August 1999.

[CC-Project] Common Criteria Project, http://csrc.nist.gov/cc/.

[CESG 1989] UK Systems Security Confidence Levels, CESG Memorandum No.3, Communications-Electronics Security Group, UK, January 1989.

[Chaum 1981] D.Chaum, "Untraceable Electronic Mail, Return Addresses, and Digital Pseudonyms", *Communications of the ACM*, 24 (2). 1981, pp. 84-88, http://world.std.com/~franl/crypto/chaum-acm-1981.html

[Chaum 1985] D.Chaum, "Security without Identification: Transaction Systems to Make Big Brother Obsolete", *Communications of the ACM*, 28 (10). 1985, pp.1030-1044.

[Chaum 1987] D.Chaum, "Privacy-Protected Payments - Unconditional Payer and Payee Untraceability", *SMARD CARD 2000: The Future of IC Cards,* Proceedings of the IFIP WG 11.6 International Conference, Laxenburg, October 1987, North Holland, pp. 69-93.

[Chaum 1988] D.Chaum, "The Dining Cryptographers Problem: Unconditional Sender and Recipient Untraceability", *Journal of Cryptology*, 1, 1988, pp. 65-75.

[Chaum/Fiat/Naor 1988] D.Chaum, A.Fiat, M.Naor, "Untraceable Electronic Cash", Proceedings: *Advances in Cryptology - Crypto'88*, S.Goldwasser (Ed.), 1988, Lecture Notes in Computer Sciences, Springer Verlag.

[Chaum 1992] D.Chaum, "Achieving Electronic Privacy", Scientific American, August 1992, pp.76-81.

[Clark/Wilson 87] D.D.Clark, D.R.Wilson, "A Comparison of Commercial and Military Computer Security Policies", *Proceedings of the IEEE Computer Society Symposium on Security and Privacy*, Oakland, April 1987.

[Cooper/Birman 1995] D.A.Cooper, K.P.Birman, "Preserving Privacy in a Network of Mobile Computers", *Proceedings of the IEEE Symposium on Research in Security and Privacy*, IEEE Computer Society Press, 1995, pp. 26-38.

[CPSR 19934] Computer Professionals for Social Responsibilities, "Serving the Community: A Public-Interest Vision of the National Information Infrastructure, *The CPSR Newsletter*, Winter 1994.

[Cottrell 1995] L.Cottrell, "Mixmaster and Remailer Attacks", 1995 http://www.obscura.com/~loki/remailer/remailer-essay.html

[CTCPEC 93] The Canadian Trusted Computer Product Evaluation Criteria, Canadian System Security Centre, Version 3.0e, January 1993.

[Davies 1994] S.Davies, "TOUCHING BIG BROTHER-How biometric technology will fuse flesh and machine", *"Information Technology & People"*, Vol 7, No. 4, 1994.

[Davies 1997] S.Davies, "Re-Engineering the Right to Privacy: How Privacy has been transformed from a Right to a Commodity", in: P.Agre, M.Rotenberg: Technology and Privacy: the New Landscape, MIT Press, 1997, pp. 143-165.

[Denning 1976] D.Denning, "A Lattice Model of Secure Information Flow", *Communications of the ACM*, May 1976, Vol.19, No.5, pp. 236-143.

[Denning 1980] D.Denning, "Secure Statistical Databases Under Random Sample Queries", *ACM Transactions on Database Systems*, Vol.5(3), September 1980, pp.291-315.

[Denning 1982] D.Denning, "Cryptography and Data Security", Addison-Wesley, 1982.

[Denning 1986] D.Denning, "An Intrusion Detection Model", *Proceedings of the IEEE Symposium on Security and Privacy*, Oakland, April 1996.

[Denning/Neumann/Parker 1987] D.Denning, P.Neumann, D.Parker, "Social Aspects of Computer Security", *Proceedings of the 10th National Computer Security Conference,* Baltimore, 1987.

336

[Denning/MacDoran 1996] D.Denning, P.MacDoran, "Location-based Authentication: Grounding Cyberspace for Better Security, *Computer Fraud and Security*, Elsevier Science, Ltd., February 1996.

[Dierstein 1997] R.Dierstein, "Duale Sicherheit – IT-Sicherheit und ihre Beonderheiten", in: G.Müller, A.Pfitzmann (Eds.): Mehrseitige Sicherheit in der Kommunikationstechnik, Addison-Wesley, 1997.

[Diffie/Hellmann 1976] W.Diffie, M.Hellmann, "New Directions in Cryptography", *IEEE Transactions on Informtion Theory*, Vol. IT-22 (6), November 1976, pp.644-654.

[Dittrich/Hartig/Pfefferle 1989] K.Dittrich, M.Hartig, H.Pfefferle, "Discretionary Access Control in structurally Object-Oriented Database Systems", in: *Database Security II: Status and Prospects*, Ed.: C.Landwehr, North Holland, 1989, pp.105-121.

[Dowell/Ramstedt 1990] C.Dowell, P.Ramstedt, "The ComputerWatch Data Reduction Tool", *Proceedings of the 13th National Computer Security*, Washington, October 1990.

[DS-Beauftragte 1998] Arbeitsgruppe "Datenschutzfreundliche Technologien" der Datenschutzbeauftragten des Bundes und der Länder, Arbeitspapier "Datenschutzfreundliche Technologien, 1998, http://www.datenschutz-berlin.de/to/datenfr.htm

[DTI 1989a] DTI Commercial Security Centre Evaluation Manual, V22; Department of Trade and Industry (DTI), UK, February 1989.

[DTI 1989b] DTI Commercial Security Centre Functionality Manual, V21; Department of Trade and Industry (DTI), UK, February 1989.

[EFGA] Electronic Frontiers Georgia, Anonymous Remailer Information, http://anon.efga.org/Remailers

[El Gamal 1984] El Gamal, A. "Public Key Cryptosystem and Signature Scheme Based on Discrete Logarithms", *Advances in Cryptology, Proceedings Crypto 1984*, Plenum Press 1985, pp.10-18.

[EPIC 1998] Electronic Privacy Information Center, ´Surfer Beware: Personal Privacy and the Internet´, June 1997, http://www.epic.org/reports/surfer-beware.html

[Essmayr/Pernul/Tjoa 1997] W.Essmayr, G.Pernul, A.M. Tjoa, "Access Controls by Object-Oriented Concepts", *Proceedings of the IFIP WG 11.3 Annual Working Conference on Database Security"*, Lake Tahoe, California, USA, August 11-13, 1997, Chapman&Hall.

[EU Directive 1995] Directive 95/46/EC of the European Parliament and of the Council of 24 October 1995 on the protection of individuals with regard to the processing of personal data and on the free movement of such data, http://europa.eu.int/eur-lex/en/lif/dat/1995/en_395L0046.html

[EU Telecommunications Directive 1997] Directive 97/66/EC of the European Parliament and of the Council of 15 December 1997 Concerning the Processing of Personal Data and the Protection of Privacy in the Telecommunications Sector, http://www2.echo.lu/legal/en/dataprot/protection.html

[EU Commission 1998] EU Commission, Working Document: Platform for Privacy Preferences (P3P) and the Open Profiling Standard (OPS), Draft Opinion of the Working Party: OPINION 1/98, adopted by the Working Party on 16 June 1998, http://europa.eu.int/comm/dg15/en/media/dataprot/wpdocs/wp11en.htm

[EU Commission 2000] Opinion of the Working Party: Opinion 4/2000 on the level of protection provided by the "Safe Harbor Principles", adopted on 16th May 2000, http://europa.eu.int/comm/internal_market/en/media/dataprot/wpdocs/wp32en.htm

[Everett 1992] D.Everett, "Identity Verification and Biometrics", in: Computer Security Reference Handbook, Eds.: K.M.Jackson, J.Hruska, D.Parker, Chapter 10, Butterworth-Heinemann Ltd., 1992.

[FC 1992] National Institute of Standards and Technology (NIST) & National Security Agency (NSA), Federal Criteria for Information Technology security – Draft Version 1.0, December 1992.

[Federrath/Jerichow/Pfitzmann 1996] H.Federrath, A.Jerichow, A.Pfitzmann, "Mixe in Mobile Communication Systems: Location Management with Privacy", in: R.Anderson (Ed.): *Information Hiding*, LNCS 1174, Springer-Verlag, Berlin 1996, pp.121-135.

[Federrath/Pfitzmann 1997] H.Federrath, A.Pfitzmann, "Bausteine zur Realisierung mehrseitiger Sicherheit", in: Mehrseitige Sicherheit in der Kommunikationstechnik - Verfahren, Komponenten, Integration, G.Müller, A.Pfitzmann (Eds.), Addison-Wesley, 1997.

[Fernandez/Gudes/Song 1989] E.Fernandez, E.Gudes, H.Song, "A Security Model for Object-Oriented Databases", *1989 IEEE Computer Society Symposium on Security and Privacy*, Oakland / California, 1.-3. May 1989.

[Fernandez/Gudes/Song 1994] E.Fernandez, E.Gudes, H.Song, "A Model for Evaluation and Administration of Security in Object-Oriented Databases", *IEEE Transactions on Knowledge and Data Engineering*, Vol. 6, No.2, April 1994, pp.275-292.

[Ferraiolo/Kuhn 1992] D.Ferraiolo, R.Kuhn, "Role-Based Access Controls", *Proceedings of the 15th National Computer Security Conference*, Baltimore MD, October 1992.

[Ferraiolo/Gilbert/Lynch 1993] D.Ferraiolo, D.Gilbert, N.Lynch, "An Examination of Federal and Commercial Access Control Policy Needs", *Proceedings of the 16th National Computer Security Conference*, Baltimore, September 1993.

[Ferraiolo/Cugini/Kuhn 1995] D.Ferraiolo, J.Cugini, R.Kuhn, "Role-Based Access Control (RBAC): Features and Motivations", *Proceedings of the 11th Computer Security Application Conference*, New Orleans, Louisiana, December 11-15, 1995.

[Ferraiolo/Barkley/Kuhn 1997] D.Ferraiolo, J.Barkely, R.Kuhn, "A Role-Based Access Control Model and Reference Implementation Within a Corporate Intranet", *ACM Transactions on Information and System Security*, Vol.2, No.1, February 1999, pp. 34-64.

[Fischer-Hübner 1987] S.Fischer-Hübner, "Zur reidentifikationssicheren statistischen Auswertung personenbezogener Daten in staatlichen Datenbanken", Diplomarbeit, Universität Hamburg, December 1987.

[Fischer-Hübner/Brunnstein 1990] S.Fischer-Hübner, K.Brunnstein, "Combining Verified and Adaptive System Components towards More Secure System Architectures", in: J.Rosenberg, L.Keedy, 'Security and Persistence', *Proceedings of the International Workshop on Computer Architectures to Support Security and Persistance of Information*, Bremen, May 1990, Springer-Verlag.

[Fischer-Hübner/Yngström/Holvast 92] Fischer-Hübner, L.Yngström, J.Holvast, "Addressing Vulnerability and Privacy Problems generated by the Use of IT-Security Mechanisms", *Proceedings of the IFIP 12th World Computer Congress*, Volume II: Education and Society, Madrid, September 1992, Ed.: R.Aiken, North Holland.

[Fischer-Hübner 1993] S.Fischer-Hübner, "IDA (Intrusion Detection and Avoidance System): Ein einbruchsentdeckendes und einbruchsvermeidendes System", Shaker-Verlag, Aachen, 1993.

[Fischer-Hübner 1994a] S.Fischer-Hübner, "Ein Konzept eines formalen Datenschutz-Modells" (A Concept of a Formal Privacy-Model), in: Sicherheit in Informationssystemen, *Proceedings of the SIS'94-Con*ference, Zürich, March 1994, Eds.: K.Bauknecht, S.Teufel, vdf-Verlag.

[Fischer-Hübner 1994b] S.Fischer-Hübner, "Towards a Privacy-Friendly Design and Use of IT-Security Mechanisms", *Proceedings of the 17th National Computer Security Conference*, Baltimore, 11-14 October 1994.

[Fischer-Hübner 1995] S.Fischer-Hübner, "Considering Privacy as a Security-Aspect: A Formal Privacy-Model", DASY PAPERS No.5/95, Institute of Computer and System Sciences (DASY), Copenhagen Business School, 1995.

[Fischer-Hübner 1996a] S.Fischer-Hübner, "Teaching Privacy as a Part of the Computer Science Curriculum", *Proceedings of the IFIP TC-3/TC-9 Conference "The Impact of IT - From Practice to Curriculum"*, Israel, March 18-21, 1996, Eds: Y.Katz, D.Millin, B.Offir, Chapman & Hall.

[Fischer-Hübner/Schier 1996a] S.Fischer-Hübner, K.Schier, "Der Weg in die Informationsgesellschaft - Eine Gefahr für den Datenschutz ?",in: Britta Schinzel (Ed.), "Schnittstellen - Studien zum Verhaeltnis zwischen Informatik und Gesellschaft", Vieweg-Verlag, 1996.

[Fischer-Hübner/Schier 1996b] S.Fischer-Hübner, K.Schier, "Risks on the Way to the Global Information Society", *Proceedings of the IFIP-TC-11 Sec'96-Conference*, Samos, May 1996, Eds: S.Katsikas, D.Gritzalis, Chapman & Hall.

[Fischer-Hübner 1997a] S.Fischer-Hübner, "Privacy at Risk in the Global Information Society", in: J.Berleur and Diane Whitehouse, Eds., *'An ethical global information society: culture and democracy revisited', Proceedings of the IFIP WG 9.2 Corfu international conference*, May 8-10, 1997, Chapman&Hall, 1997.

[Fischer- Hübner 1997b] S.Fischer-Hübner, "A Formal Task-based Privacy Model and its Implementation: An updated Report", in: Arto Karila, Timo Aalto (Eds.), *Proceedings of the Second Nordic Workshop on Secure Computer Systems NORDSEC'97*, Helsiniki, November 6-7, 1997.

[Fischer- Hübner/Ott 1998] S.Fischer-Hübner, A.Ott, "From a Formal Privacy Model to its Implementation", *Proceedings of the 21st National Information Systems Security Conference*, Arlington, VA, October 5-8, 1998.

[Fischer- Hübner 1998] S.Fischer-Hübner, "Privacy and Security at Risk in the Global Information Society", *Information, Communication & Society (iCS)*, Vol. 1 (4), Winter 1998, Routledge, pp. 419-441.

[Fischer-Hübner 2000] S.Fischer-Hübner, "Privacy and Security at Risk in the Global Information Society", in: Th. Douglas, Brian Loader (Eds.), Cybercrime – law enforcement, securit6y and surveillance in the information age, Routledge, 2000, pp. 173-192.

[Flink/Weiss 1988] Ch.Flink, J.D.Weiss, "SystemV/MLS Labelling and Mandatory Policy Alternative", *AT&T Technical Journal*, May/June 1988, pp 53-64.

[Foti 1998] J.Foti, "Status of the Advanced Encryption Standard (AES) Development Effort", *Proceedings of the 21st National Information Systems Security Conference, Arlington, VA*, October 5-8, 1998.

[Franz/Jerichow/Pfitzmann 1997] E.Franz, A.Jerichow, A.Pfitzmann, "Systematisierung und Modellierung von Mixen", *Proceedings GI-Fachtagung 'Verlässliche Informationssysteme' VIS'97*, Eds.: G.Müller et al., Freiburg, 30.9.-2.10.97, Vieweg-Verlag.

[Franz/Jerichow/Wicke 1998] E.Franz, A.Jerichow, G.Wicke, "A Payment Scheme for Mixes Providing Anonymity", *Proceeding of the International IFIP-GI working conference TREC'98* (Trends in distributed systems for Electronic Commerce) Hamburg, 3-5 June 1998, Springer-Verlag.

[Franz/Pfitzmann 1998] E.Franz, A.Pfitzmann, "Einführung in die Steganographie und Ableitung eines neuen Stegoparadigmas", *Informatik-Spektrum*, Vol.21 (4), August 1998, Springer-Verlag.

[Freedom] Zero-Knowledge-Systems, Inc., Freedom Papers, http://www.freedom.net/info/freedompapers/index.html

[Gabber et al. 1999] E.Gabber, P.Gibbons, D.Kristol, Y.Matias, A.Mayer, "Consistent, Yet Anonymous, Web Access with LPWA", *Communications of the ACM*, Vol.42, No.2, February 1999, pp.42- 47.

[Garfinkel/Spafford 1997] S.Garfinkel, G.Spafford, Web Security & Commerce, *O'Reilly & Associates*, Inc., 1997.

[Gasser 1988] M.Gasser, "Building a Secure Computer System", van Nostrand Reinhold, 1988.

[Gendler-Fishman/Gudes 1997] M.Gendler-Fishman, E.Gudes, "A Compile-time Model for safe Information Flow in Object-Oriented Databases", in: Information Security in Research and Business- *Proceedings of the IFIP TC11 13th International conference on Information Security (Sec'97)*, 14-16 May 1997, Copenhagen, Chapman&Hall, 1997.

[Gerhardt 1992] W.Gerhardt, "Zur Modellierbarkeit von Datenschutzanforderungen im Entwurfsprozeß eines Informationssystems", *Datenschutz und Datensicherung (DuD)* 3, 1992, S.126-136.

[GISA 1989] German Information Security Agency, IT-Security Criteria, Criteria for the Evaluation of the Trustworthiness of Information Technology (IT) Systems, *Bundesanzeiger-Verlag*, January 1989.

[Gollmann 1999] D.Gollmann, "Computer Security", *John Wiley & Sons*, 1999.

[Goguen/Meseguer 1982] J.Goguen, J.Meseguer, "Security Policies and Security Models", *Proceedings of the IEEE Symposium on Security and Privacy*, Oakland, May 1982.

[Goldberg/Wagner/Brewer 1997] I.Goldberg, D.Wagner, E.Brewer, "Privacy-Enhancing Technologies for the Internet", *Proceedings of COMPCON'97*, San Jose, February, 1997, http://www.cs.berkeley.edu/~daw/privacy-compcon97-www/privacy-html.html

[Goldschlag/Reed/Syverson 1996] D.Goldschlag, M.Reed, P.Syverson, "Hiding Routing Information", in: R.Anderson (Ed.): *Information Hiding*, LNCS 1174, Springer-Verlag, Berlin 1996.

[Goldschlag/Reed/Syverson 1999] D.Goldschlag, M.Reed, P.Syverson, "Onion Routing for Anonymous and Private Internet Connections", *Communications of the ACM*, Vol.42, No.2, February 1999, pp. 39-41.

[Greenleaf 1995] G.Greenleaf, "The 1995 EU Directive on Data Protection - An Overview", *The International Privacy Bulletin*, published by Privacy International, 3 (2).

[Gülcu/Tsudik 1996] C.Gülcu, G. Tsudik, "Mixing E-Mail with Babel", *Proceedings of the IEEE Symposium on Network and Distributed System Security*, 1996.

[Holvast 1993] J.Holvast, "Vulnerability and Privacy: Are We on the Way to a Risk-Free Society?", in: J.Berleur et al. (Eds.): Facing the Challenge of Risk and Vulnerability in an Information Society, *Proceedings of the IFIP-WG9.2*

Conference, Namur May 20-22, 1993, Elsevier Science Publishers B.V. (North-Holland), 1993.

[Hosmer 1992a] H.Hosmer, "Metapolicies II", *Proceedings of the 15th National Computer Security Conference*, Baltimore, 13-16 October 1992.

[Hosmer 1992b] H.Hosmer, "The Multipolicy Paradigm*", Proceedings of the 15th National Computer Security Conference*, Baltimore, 13-16 October 1992.

[IDA 1990] J.E.Roskos, S.Welke, J.Boone, T.Mayfield, "Integrity in the Department of Defense Computer Systems", Draft IDA Paper P-2316, Institute for Defence Analysis, Virginia, July 1990.

[IITF 1995] Information Infrastructure Task Force - Privacy Working Group: Privacy and the National Information Infrastructure: Principles for Providing and Using Personal Information, Final Version, June 1995.

[IITF 1997] Information Infrastructure Taskforce - Information Policy Committee, *Options for Promoting Privacy on the NII*, Executive Summary, April 1997.

[Irving/Higgins/Safayeni 1986] R.H.Irving, C.A.Higgins, F.R.Safayeni, "Computerized Performance Monitoring Systems: Use and Abuse*"; Communications of the ACM*, Vol.29, Nr.8, 1996, pp.794-801.

[ITSEC 91] Information Technology Security Evaluation Criteria (ITSEC), Provisional Harmonised Criteria, June 1991.

[Jajodia/Kogan/Sandhu 1995] S.Jajodia, B.Kogan, R.Sandhu, "A Multilevel Secure Object-Oriented Data Model, in: Information Security – An Integrated Collection of Essays, Eds.: M.Abrams, S.Jajodia, H.Podell, *IEEE Computer Society Press*, 1995.

[Japan 1994] Ministry of International Trade and Industry (MITI), Programme for Advanced Information Infrastructure, May 1994.

[Johnson] N.Johnson,"Steganography", http://www.jjtc.com/stegdoc/

[Johnson/Jajodia 1998] N.Johnson, S.Jajodia, "Steganalysis of Images Created Using Current Steganographic Software*", Proceedings of the Workshop on Information Hiding, Portland,* Oregon/USA, 15-17 April 1998, http://www.jjtc.com/ihws98/jjgmu.html

[Jonscher/Gerhardt 1991] D.Jonscher, W.Gerhardt, "A Role-Based Modelling of Access Control with the Help of Frames", in: Information Security*, Proceedings of the IFIP TC11 / Sec'91 Conference*, Brighton, UK, 15-17 May 1991, Eds.: D.Lindsay, W.Price, Elsevier Science Publishers B.V. (Nort Holland), 1991.

[Karger et al. 1990] P.Karger, M.Zurko, D.Bonin, A.Mason, C.Kahn, "A VMM Security Kernel for the VAX Architecture", *Proceedings of the IEEE Symposium on Security and Privacy*, Oakland, May 1990.

[Kesdogan et al. 1996] D.Kesdogan, H.Federrath, A.Jerichow, A.Pfitzmann, "Location Management Strategies increasing Privacy in Mobile Communication

Systems", *Proceedings of the IFIP TC11 SEC '96 Conference* , Chapman & Hall, London 1996, 39-48.

[Ketelaar/Fischer-Hübner 93] R.Ketelaar, Fischer-Hübner, "On the Cutting Edge between Security and Privacy", *Proceedings of the IFIP WG 9.6 Conference 'Security and Control of IT in Society'*, Stockholm-St.Petersburg, August 1993, Eds.: R.Sizer et al., North Holland.

[Koch 1995] F.Koch "European Data Protection - Against the Internet?", *Privacy International Conference on Advanced Surveillance Technologies*, Copenhagen, September 1995.

[Köhntopp/Köhntopp 1996] K.Köhntopp, M.Köhntopp, "So einfach geht das !", First Surf, Computer&Net, 10.June 1996, http://www.firstsurf.com/koehn1.htm

[Kohnfelder 1978] L.Kohnfelder, "A Method for Certification", MIT Laboratory for Computer Science, Acmbridge, Mass., May 1978.

[Kühnhauser 1995] W.Kühnhauser, "On Paradigms for Security Policies in Multipolicy Environments", in: Eloff, Jan H.P., von Solms, Sebastiaan H.(Eds), Information Security - the Next Decade, *Proceedings of the IFIP TC11 11th International Conference on Information Security, IFIP/Sec'95*, May 1995, Chapman & Hall.

[Lai/Massey 1990] X.Lai, J.Massey, "A Proposal for a New Block Encryption Standard", *Advances in Cryptology – EUROCRYPT'90 Proceedings*, Springer-Verlag, 1991, pp.157-165.

[LaPadula 1995] L.LaPadula, "Rule-Set Modelling of Trusted Computer System", Essay 9 in: M.Abrams, S.Jajodia, H. Podell, "Information Security - An integrated Collection of Essays", *IEEE Computer Society Press*, 1995.

[Larrondo-Petrie/Gudes/Song 1990] M.Larrondo-Petrie, E.Gudes, H.Song, "Security Policies in Object-Oriented Databases", in: *Database Security III: Status and Prospects*, Eds.: D.Spooner, C.Landwehr, Elsevier Science Publishers B.V. (North Hollad), 1990.

[Lee 1988] Th.Lee, "Using Mandatory Integrity to Enforce 'Commercial' Security", *Proceedings of the IEEE Symposium on Security and Privacy*, Oakland, May 1988.

[Lipner 1982] S.B.Lipner, "Non-Discretionary Controls for Commercial Applications", *Proceedings of the IEEE Symposium on Security and Privacy*, Oakland, May 1982.

[LPWA] The Lucent Personalized Web Assistant, A Bell Labs Technology Demonstration, http://lpwa.com:8000/overview.html

[Lubinski 1993] A.Lubinski, "Ein Rollen-Normen Modell für den konzeptionellen Entwurf von Sicherheitsanforderungen in Unternehmensinformationssystemen", *GI_Fachtagung Verlässliche Informationssysteme VIS'93*, Munich, Vieweg Verlag, 1993, pp.68-79.

[Lukat/Pfitzmann/Waidner 1991] J.Lukat, A.Pfitzmann, M.Waidner, "Effizientere fail-stop Schlüsselerzeugung für das DC-Netz" *Datenschutz und Datensicherung (DuD)* 15/2 (1991), pp.71-75.

[Lundheim/Sindre 1993] R.Lundheim, G.Sindre, 'Privacy and Computing: a Cultural Perspective', in: R. Sizer *et al.* (Eds.): *Security and control of Information Technology in Society, IFIP WG 9.6 Working Conference*, St.Petersburg, August 1993, Elsevier Science Publishers.

[Lunt et al. 1992] T.Lunt, A.Tamaru, F.Gilham, R.Jagannathan, C.Jalali, P.Neumann, H.Javitz, A.Vales, Th.Garvey, "A Real-Time Intrusion Detection Expert System (IDES)", A Final Technical Report, SRI Project 6784, SRI International, February 1992.

[Madsen 1992] W.Madsen, *Handbook of Personal Data Protection*, Stockton Press, 1992.

[Madsen 1995] W.Madsen, "Securing Access and Privacy on the Internet", in: *Proceedings of the COMPSEC-Conference*, London, October 1995, Elsevier Science Publishers.

[Mayer-Schönberger 1997] V.Mayer-Schönberger, "The Internet and Privacy Legislation: Cookies for a Threat?", *West Virginia Journal of Law & Technology* 1, 1, Http://www.wvjolt.wvu.edu/wvjolt/current/issue1/articles/mayer/mayer.htm

[Mavridis et al. 1999] I.Mavridis, G.Pangalos, M.Khair, L.Bozios, "Defining Access Control Mechanisms for Privacy Protection in Distributed Medical Datebases", in: S.Fischer-Hübner, G.Quirchmayr, L.Yngström (Eds.): *Proceedings of the IFIP WG 8.5/9.6 Working Conference "User Identification & Privacy Protection - Applications in Public Administration and Electronic Commerce"*, Stockholm University/KTH, June 14-15, 1999, DSV Report-Series 99-007.

[McCollum, Messing/Notargiacomo 1990] C.McCollum, J.Messing, L.Notargiacomo, "Beyond the Pale of MAC and DAC – Defining New Forms of Access Controls", *Proceedings of the IEEE Symposium on Security and Privacy*, Oakland, May 1990.

[McCullough 1988] D.McCullough, "Specifications for Multi-Level security and a Hook-Up property", Proceedings of the IEEE Symposium on Security and Privacy, Oakland, May 1987.

[McLean/Landwehr/Heitmeyer 1984] J.McLean, C. Landwehr, C.Heitmeyer, "A formal statement of the MMS security model", *Proceedings of the IEEE Symposium on Security and Privacy*, May 1984, Oakland.

[McLean 1990] J.McLean, "The Specification and Modelling of Computer Security", *IEEE Computer*, Vol.23, No.1, (1990), 9-16.

[Millen 1992] J.Millen, "A Resource Allocation Model for Denial of Service", *Proceedings of the IEEE Symposium on Security and Privacy*, Oakland, May 1992.

344

[Millen/Lunt 1992] J.Millen, T.Lunt, "Security for Object-Oriented Database Systems", *Proceedings of the IEEE Symposium on Security and Privacy*, Oakland, May 1992.

[Mounji et al. 1995] A. Mounji, B. Le Charlier, D. Zampuniéris, N. Habra, "Distributed Audit Trail Analysis", *Proceedings of the ISOC '95 Symposium on Network and Distributed Systems Security*, San Diego, California, February 1995.

[MSFR 1992] National Institute of Standards and Technology (NIST), Minimum Security Requirements for Multi-User Operating Systems – Issue 2, August 1992.

[NBS 1977] National Bureau of Standards, "Data Encryption Standard", FIPS PUB 46, Washington, D.C., January 1977.

[NCSC 1987] National Computer Security Center, "A Guide to Understanding Audit in Trusted Systems", NCSC-TG-001-87, Fort George G. Meade, MD, July 1987.

[Neumann 1990] P.G. Neumann, "Rainbows and Arrows: How the Security Criteria Address Computer Misuse", *Proceedings of the 13th National Computer Security Conference*, Washington D.C., October 1990.

[Nikander/Viljanen 1998] P.Nikander, L.Viljanen, "Storing and Retrieving Internet Certificates", in: S.Knapskog, T.Brekne, *Proceedings of the Third Nordic Workshop on Secure IT Systems*, Trondheim, 5-6 November, 1998.

[NIST-AES] National Institute of Standard and Technology (NIST), Advanced Encryption Standard Development Effort, http://csrc.nist.gov/encryption/aes/aes_home.htm

[NIST-RBAC] National Institute of Standard and Technology (NIST), Role-Based Access Control (RBAC), http://csrc.nist.gov/rbac/

[NIST-SHA 1995] National Institute of Standard and Technology (NIST), "Secure Hash Standard", FIPS PUB 180-1, 17.April 1995.

[Notargiacomo 1995] L.Notargiacomo, "Role-Based Access Control in Oracle7 and Trusted Oracle7", in: *Proceedings of the First ACM Workshop on Role-Based Access Control*, Editors: Ch.Youman, R.Sandhu, E.Coyne, Gaithersburg, Maryland, USA, November/December 1995.

[Nothdurft 1994] K.Nothdurft, "Datenschutzrechtliche Anforderungen an die Systemgestaltung und die deutsche universitäre Ausbildung", Diplomarbeit, Studiengang Informatik, Universität Bremen, 1994.

[OPS] Proposal for an Open Profiling Standard, submitted to W3C on 2 June 1997, http://www.w3.org/TR/NOTE-OPS-FrameWork.html

[Oracle 1994] Oracle White Paper, "Database Security in Oracle7", Oracle Corporation, January 1994.

[Ott] A.Ott, "Rule Set Based Access Control in Linux", RSBAC-Home Page, http://www.rsbac.de/

[Ott 1997] Amon Ott, "Regel-basierte Zugriffskontrolle nach dem 'Generalized Framework for Access Control'-Ansatz am Beispiel Linux", Diplomarbeit Universität Hamburg, November 1997.

[Ott/Fischer-Hübner/Swimmer 1998] A.Ott, S.Fischer-Hübner, M.Swimmer, "Approaches to Integrated Malware Detection and Avoidance", *Proceedings of the 3rd Nordic Workshop on Secure IT Systems*, Trondheim, November 5-6, 1998.

[P3P] World wide Web Consortium (W3C), Platform for Privacy Preferences (P3P)Project, http://www.w3.org/P3P/

[Pangalos/Khair 1996] G.Pangalos, M.Khair, "Design of Secure Medical Database Systems", *Proceedings of the IFIP-TC-11 Sec'96-Conference*, Samos, May 1996, Eds: S.Katsikas, D.Gritzalis, Chapman & Hall.

[PGP] http://web.mit.edu/network/pgp.html or http://www.ifi.uio.no/pgp/

[PI 1999] Privacy International, Private Part Online 1999, http://www.privacy.org/pi/parts/parts99.html

[PI/EPIC 1999] Privacy International, Electronic Privacy Information Center, "Privacy and Human Rights - An International Survey of Privacy Laws and Developments", 1999, http://www.privacy.org/pi/survey/

[Picciotto 1987] J.Picciotto, "The Design of an Effective Auditing Subsystem", *Proceedings of the IEEE Symposium on Security and Privacy*, Oakland, May 1987.

[Pfitzmann/Waidner 1987] A.Pfitzmann, M.Waidner, "Networks without User Observability" *Computers & Security* 6/2 (1987), pp. 158-166.

[Pfitzmann 1990] A.Pfitzmann, "Diensteintegrierende Kommunikationsnetze mit teilnehmerüberprüfbarem Datenschutz", Informatik-Fachberichte 234, Springer-Verlag, 1990

[Pfitzmann/Waidner/Pfitzmann 1990] B.Pfitzmann, M.Waidner, A.Pfitzmann, "Rechtssicherheit trotz Anonymität in offenen digitalen Systemen", *Datenschutz und Datensicherheit (DuD)*, No.6, 1990, pp.243-253 (part 1), No.7, 1990, pp.305-315 (part 2).

[Pfitzmann/Pfitzmann/Waidner 1991] A.Pfitzmann, B.Pfitzmann, M.Waidner, "ISDN-MIXes - Untraceable Communication with very small Bandwidth Overhead", in: Information Security, *Proceedings of the IFIP TC-11 International Conference Sec'91*, May 1991, Brighton, D. T. Lindsay, W. L. Price (eds.), North-Holland, Amsterdam 1991.

[Pfitzmann/Rannenberg 1993] A.Pfitzmann, K.Rannenberg, "Staatliche Initiativen und Dokumente zur IT-Sicherheit - eine kritische Würdigung, *Computer und Recht*, Vol.9 (3), March 1993, pp.170-179.

[Pfleeger 1997] Ch.Pfleeger, "Security in Computing", 2nd Edition, Prentice Hall, 1997.

[Podlech 1988] A. Podlech, "Die Transformation des für Informationssysteme geltenden Informationsrechts in die Informationssysteme steuerndes Systemrechts", August 1988, in: L.Bräutigam, H.Höller, R.Scholz, "Datenschutz als Anforderung an die Systemgestaltung", Westdeutscher Verlag, 1990.

[Porras/Neumann 1997] P.Porras, P.Neumann, "EMERALD: Event Monitoring Enabling Responses to Anomalous Live Distrubances", *Proceedings of the 20st National Information Systems Security Conference*, Baltimore, 7.-10.October 1997.

[Price 1998] K.Price, Intrusion Detection Resources, http://www.cs.purdue.edu/coast/ids/ids-body.html

[Rabitti et al. 1991]. F.Rabitti, E.Bertino, W.Kim, D.Woelk, "A Model of Authorization for Next-Generation Database Systems", *ACM Transactions on Database Systems*, Vol.16, No.1, March 1991, pp.88-131.

[Ramaswamy/Sandhu 1998] Ch.Ramaswamy, R.Sandhu, "Role-Base Access Control Features in Commercial Database Management Systems", *Proceedings of the 21st National Information Systems Security Conference*, Arlington/VA, 5.-8.October 1998.

[Rannenberg 1994] K.Rannenberg, "Recent Development in Information Technology Security Evaluation, - The Need for Evaluation Criteria for Multilateral Security", *Proceedings of the IFIP WG 9.6 Conference Security and Control of IT in Society*, Stockholm-St.Petersburg, August 1993, Eds.: R.Sizer et al., North Holland.

[Rannenberg 1996] K.Rannenberg, "Common Criteria Observation Reports", November 1996 (not published officially).

[Rauterberg 1984] M.Rauterberg, "Wie anonym sind Datensätze wirklich?", *Datenschutz und Datensicherung (DuD)*, 1984, No.3, pp. 174-181.

[Registratiekamer 1995] Registratiekamer, the Netherlands and Information and Privacy Commissioner, *Privacy-Enhancing Technologies: The Path to Anonymity*, Volume II, Achtergrondstudies en Verkenningen 5B, Rijswijk.

[Registratiekamer/IPC 1995] Registratiekamer, the Netherlands and Information and Privacy Commissioner/ Ontario, Canada, *Privacy-Enhancing Technologies: The Path to Anonymity*, Volume I, Achtergrondstudies en Verkenningen 5A.

[Reiter/Rubin 1997] M.Reiter, A.Rubin, "Crowds: Anonymity for Web Transactions", DIMACS Technical Report 97 -15, 1997.

[Reiter/Rubin 1998] M.Reiter, A.Rubin, "Crowds: Anonymity for Web Transactions", *ACM Transactions on Information and System Security*, Vol.1, No.1, November 1998, pp. 66-92.

[Reiter/Rubin 1999] M.Reiter, A.Rubin, "Anonymous Web Transactions with Crowds", *Communications of the ACM*, Vol.42, No.2, February 1999, pp. 32-38.

[Rijndael] The Block Cipher RiJndael,
http://www.esat.kuleuven.ac.be/~rijmen/rijndael/

[Rindfleisch 1997] Th.Rindfleisch, "Privacy, Information Technology, and Health Care", *Communications of the ACM*, August 1997 / Vol.40, No.8, pp. 92-100.

[RIPEMD-160] The hash function RIPEMD-160,
http://www.esat.kuleuven.ac.be/~bosselae/ripemd160.html

[Rivest/Shamir/Adleman 1978] R.Rivest, A.Shamir, L.Adleman, "A Method for Obtaining Digital Signatures and Public-Key Cryptosystems", *Communications of the ACM*, Vol. 21(2), February 1978, pp. 120-126.

[Roberts 1972] L.Roberts, "Extensions of Packet Communication Technology to a Hand Held Personal Terminal", *Proceedings Spring Joint Computer Conference*, AFIPS, 1972.

[Rosenberg 1992] R.Rosenberg, The Social Impact of Computers, *Academic Press*, 1992.

[Rosenberg 1997] R.Rosenberg, "The Politics of privacy on the Global Information Highway", in: J.Berleur and Diane Whitehouse, Eds., *'An ethical global information society: culture and democracy revisited'*, Proceedings of the IFIP WG 9.2 Corfu international conference, 8.-10. May 1997, Chapman&Hall.

[Samarti et al. 1996] P.Samarti, E.Bertino, A.Ciampichetti, S.Jajodia, "Information Flow Control in Object-Oriented Systems, *IEEE Transactions on Knowledge and Data Engineering*, 1996.

[Sandhu 1992] R.Sandhu, "Lattice-Based Enforcement of Chinese Wall", *Computers&Security*, 11 (1992), Elsevier Science Publishers, pp.753-763.

[Sandhu et al. 1994] R.Sandhu, E.Coyne, H.Feinstein, CH.Youman, "Role-Based Access Control: A Multi-Dimensional View", *Proceedings of the 10th Computer Security Applications Conference*, Orlando, December 1994.

[Sandhu et al. 1996] R.Sandhu, E.Coyne, H.Feinstein, Ch.Youman, "Role-Based Access Control Models", *IEEE Computer*, 29(2), February 1996, pp.38-47.

[Sandhu 1996a] R.Sandhu, "Access Control: The Neglected Frontier", in: J.Pieprzyk, J.Seberry (Eds.), Information Security and Privacy, *Proceedings of the 1st Australasian Conference*, ACISP'96, Wollongong, NSW, Australia, June 1996, Springer-Verlag.

[Sandhu 1996b] R.Sandhu, "Role Hierarchies and Constraints for Lattice-Based Access Controls", in: *Proceedings of Computer-Security-ESORICS'96*, Eds.: E.Bertino et al., Rome, September 1996, Springer-Verlag.

[Sandhu/Ferraiolo/Kuhn 2000] R.Sandhu, D. Ferraiolo, R.Kuhn, "The NIST Model for Role-Based Access Control: Towards A Unified Standard", 5th ACM Workshop on Role-Based Access Control, Berlin, 26-28 July 2000.

[Schier/Fischer-Hübner 1998] K.Schier, S.Fischer-Hübner, "The Global Information Society and Electronic Commerce: Privacy Threats and Privacy Technologies",

Proceedings of the 5th IFIP TC-9 World Conference HCC-5, Geneva, 25-28 August 1998.

[Schlörer 1975] J.Schlörer, "Identification and retrieval of Personal Records from a Statistical Database", *Methods of Info. in Medicine*, Vol. 14(1), January 1975, pp.7-13.

[Schlörer 1976] J.Schlörer, "Confidentiality of statistical Records: A Threat Monitoring Scheme for On-line Dialogue", *Methods of Info. in Medicine*, Vol.15(1), January 1996, pp.36-42.

[Schlörer 1982] J.Schlörer, "Outputkontrollen zur Sicherung statistischer Datenbanken", *Informatik-Spektrum*, 1982/5, Springer-Verlag, pp. 224-236.

[Schneier 1996] B.Schneier, "Applied Cryptography – Protocols, Algorithms, and Source Code in C", John Wiley & Sons, Inc., 2nd Edition, 1996.

[SCSSI 1989] Catalogue de Critéres Destinés á évaluer le Degré de Confiance des Systémes d'Information 692/SGDN/DISSI/SCSSI, Service Central de la Sécurité des Systémes d'Information, July 1989.

[Sebring et al. 1988] M.Sebring, E.Shellhouse, M.Hanna, R.Whithurst, "Expert Systems in Intrusion Detection: A Case Study", *Proceedings of the 11th National Computer Security Conference*, Baltimore, October 1988.

[Seelos 1991] H.J. Seelos, "Informationssysteme und Datenschutz im Krankenhaus, DuD-Fachbeiträge 14, *Vieweg-Verlag*, 1991.

[Seiden/Melanson 1990] K.Seiden, J.Melanson, "The Auditing Facility for a VMM Security Kernel", *Proceedings of the IEEE Symposium on Security and Privacy*, Oakland, May 1990.

[Shannon 1948] C.Shannon, "A Mathematical Theory of Communication", Bell System Technical Journal, Vol. XXVII, No.3, July 1948, pp. 379-423.

[Shannon 1949] C.Shannon, "Communication Theory of Secrecy Systems", *Bell Systems Technical Journal*, Vol 28, October 1949, pp.656-715.

[Shockley 1988] W.R.Shockley, "Implementing the Clark Wilson Integrity Policy Using Current Technologies", *Proceedings of the 11th National Computer Security Conference*, Baltimore, 1988.

[Singapore 1991] National Computer Board (NCB)/ Singapore, *IT2000 - A Vision of an Intelligent Island*, August 1991.

[Smaha 1988] S.Smaha, "Haystack: An Intrusion Detection System*", Proceedings of the 11th National Computer Security Conference*, Baltimore, October 1988.

[Smaha/Winslow 1994] S.Smaha, J.Winslow "Misuse Detection Tools", *Computer Security Journal* 10(1994) 1, Spring, pp.39 – 49.

[Sobirey/Richter/König 1996] M.Sobirey, M., B.Richter, H.König, "The Intrusion Detection System AID. Architecture, and experiences in automated audit analysis", in P. Horster (Ed.): Communications and Multimedia Security II,

Proceedings of the IFIP TC6 / TC11 International Conference on Communications and Multimedia Security, Essen, Germany, September 1996, Chapman & Hall.

[Sobirey/Fischer-Hübner 1996] M.Sobirey, S.Fischer-Hübner, "Privacy-Oriented Auditing", *Proceedings of the 13th Annual CSR Workshop 'Design for Protecting the User',* Burgenstock/Switzerland, 11.-13.September 1996.

[Sobirey/Fischer-Hübner/Rannenberg 1997] M.Sobirey, S.Fischer-Hübner, K.Rannenberg, "Pseudonymous Auditing for a Privacy-Enhanced Intrusion Detection", *Proceedings of the IFIP TC-11 Sec'97-Conference "Information Security in Research and Business",* Copenhagen, 14.-16.May 1997, Eds: L.Yngström, J.Carlsen, Capman&Hall.

[Sobirey] Michael Sobirey's Intrusion Detection Systems Page, http://www-rnks.informatik.tu-cottbus.de/~sobirey/ids.html.

[von Solms/Naccache 1992] S.v Solms, D.Naccache, "On blind signatures and perfect crimes", *Computers and Security* 11 (1992), pp. 581-583.

[SPD-Bundestagsfraktion 1998] SPD Bundestagsfraktion: "Modernes Datenschutzrecht für die (globale) Wissens- und Informationsgesellschaft", Entwurf für ein Eckwertepapier der SPD-Bundestagsfraktion (Ute Vogt, MdB; Jörg Tauss, MdB, 08.12.1998).

[SPKI] C.Ellison, B.Frantz, B.Lampson, R.Rivest, B.Thomas, T.Ylonen, "Simple Public Key Certificate", Internet-Draft, draft-ietf-spki-cert-structure-06.txt, July 1999,

[Stiegler 1998] H.Stiegler, "Alternativen zur heutigen Evaluations- und Zertifizierungspraxis", *Datenschutz und Datensicherung* 22, April 1998, Vieweg-Verlag, pp.211-214.

[Syverson/Goldschlag/Reed 1997] P. Syverson, D. Goldschlag, M. Reed, "Anonymous Connections and Onion Routing", *Proceedings of the 1997 Symposium on Security and Privacy,* IEEE Computer Society Press, Oakland, 1997, http://www.itd.nrl.navy.mil/ITD/5540/projects/onion-routing/OAKLAND_97.ps , http://www.onion-router.net/Publications.html

[TACD 2000] TACD (Transatlantic Consumer Dialog) Statement on U.S. Department of Commerce Draft International Safe Harbor Privacy Principles and FAQs, http://www.tacd.org/press_releases/state300300.html

[TCSEC 1985] DoD Trusted Computer Systems Evaluation Criteria, DoD 5200.28-STD, Washington D.C., Department of Defence, 1985.

[Thees/Federrath 1995] J.Thees, H.Federrath, "Methoden zum Schutz von Verkehrsdaten in Funknetzen", *Proceedings der GI-Fachtagung 'Verläßliche Informationssysteme' (VIS'95),* Vieweg-Verlag, 1995, pp. 181-192.

[Thomas/Sandhu 1997] R. Thomas, R. Sandhu, "Task-based Authorisation Controls (TBAC): A Family of Models for Active and Enterprise-oriented Authorization

Management", *Proceedings of the IFIP WG 11.3 Workshop on Database Security*, Lake Tahoe, California, August 11-13, 1997, Chapman&Hall.

[Troy 1996] E.F.Troy, "Breakthroughs in Standardisations of IT Security Criteria", in: J. Pieprzyk, J.Seberry (Eds.): *Proceedings of the First Australian Conference "Information Security and Privacy"*, Wollongong, NSW, Australia, June 1996, Springer-Verlag.

[US Department of Commerce 1997] US Department of Commerce, "Privacy and Self-Regulation in the Information Age", Washington D.C., June 1997, http://www.ntia.doc.gov/reports/privacy/

[US Dept. Commerce 1998] International Safe Harbor Privacy Principles, issued by the Department of Commerce in November 1998, http://www.ita.doc.gov/td/ecom/menu.html

[US Dept. Commerce 1999] International Safe Harbor Privacy Principles, Department of Commerce, June DRAFT, 1999.

[US Dept. Commerce 2000] International Safe Harbor Privacy Principles, issued by the Department of Commerce on July 21, 2000, http://www.ita.doc.gov/td/ecom/menu.html

[US Government 1993] US-Government, *The National Information Infrastructure: Agenda for Action*, 1993.

[Vaccaro/Liepens 1989] H.S.Vaccaro, G.E.Liepens, "Detection of Anomalous Computer Session Activity", *Proceedings of the IEEE Symposium on Security and Privacy*, Oakland, May 1989.

[Waidner 1990] M.Waidner, "Unconditional Sender and Recipient Untraceability in spite of Active Attacks", *Eurocrypt '89*, LNCS 434, Springer-Verlag, Berlin 1990.

[Waidner/Pfitzmann 1989] M.Waidner, B.Pfitzmann, "The Dining Cryptographers in the Disco: Unconditional Sender and Recipient Untraceability with Computationally Secure Serviceability", Universität Karlsruhe 1989; Abstract in: *Eurocrypt '89*, LNCS 434, Springer-Verlag, Berlin 1990.

[Walz 1998] S.Walz, "Datenschutz-Herausforderung durch neue Technik und Europarecht", *Datenschutz und Datensicherung* (DuD) 22 (1998) 3, Vieweg-Verlag, pp. 150-180.

[Warren/Brandeis 1890] S.D. Warren, L.D.Brandeis, "The Right to Privacy", *Harvard Law Review*, 1890-91, No.5, pp.193-220.

[Wasik 1994] M.Wasik, "Foreword", *Proceedings of the IFIP WG 9.6 Conference Security and Control of IT in Society*, Stockholm-St.Petersburg, August 1993, Eds.: R.Sizer et al., North Holland.

[Westin 1967] A.Westin, Privacy and Freedom, New York, 1987.

[**Zöllner et al. 1997**] J.Zöllner, H.Federrath, A.Pfitzmann, A.Westfeld, G.Wicke, G.Wolf, "Über die Modellierung steganographischer Systeme", *Proceedings GI-Fachtagung 'Verlässliche Informationssysteme' VIS'97*, Eds.: G.Müller et al., Freiburg, 30.9.-2.10.97, Vieweg-Verlag.

Lecture Notes in Computer Science

For information about Vols. 1–1964
please contact your bookseller or Springer-Verlag

Vol. 1958: S. Fischer-Hübner, IT-Security and Privacy. XIII, 351 pages. 2001.

Vol. 1965: Ç. K. Koç, C. Paar (Eds.), Cryptographic Hardware and Embedded Systems – CHES 2000. Proceedings, 2000. XI, 355 pages. 2000.

Vol. 1966: S. Bhalla (Ed.), Databases in Networked Information Systems. Proceedings, 2000. VIII, 247 pages. 2000.

Vol. 1967: S. Arikawa, S. Morishita (Eds.), Discovery Science. Proceedings, 2000. XII, 332 pages. 2000. (Subseries LNAI).

Vol. 1968: H. Arimura, S. Jain, A. Sharma (Eds.), Algorithmic Learning Theory. Proceedings, 2000. XI, 335 pages. 2000. (Subseries LNAI).

Vol. 1969: D.T. Lee, S.-H. Teng (Eds.), Algorithms and Computation. Proceedings, 2000. XIV, 578 pages. 2000.

Vol. 1970: M. Valero, V.K. Prasanna, S. Vajapeyam (Eds.), High Performance Computing – HiPC 2000. Proceedings, 2000. XVIII, 568 pages. 2000.

Vol. 1971: R. Buyya, M. Baker (Eds.), Grid Computing – GRID 2000. Proceedings, 2000. XIV, 229 pages. 2000.

Vol. 1972: A. Omicini, R. Tolksdorf, F. Zambonelli (Eds.), Engineering Societies in the Agents World. Proceedings, 2000. IX, 143 pages. 2000. (Subseries LNAI).

Vol. 1973: J. Van den Bussche, V. Vianu (Eds.), Database Theory – ICDT 2001. Proceedings, 2001. X, 451 pages. 2001.

Vol. 1974: S. Kapoor, S. Prasad (Eds.), FST TCS 2000: Foundations of Software Technology and Theoretical Computer Science. Proceedings, 2000. XIII, 532 pages. 2000.

Vol. 1975: J. Pieprzyk, E. Okamoto, J. Seberry (Eds.), Information Security. Proceedings, 2000. X, 323 pages. 2000.

Vol. 1976: T. Okamoto (Ed.), Advances in Cryptology – ASIACRYPT 2000. Proceedings, 2000. XII, 630 pages. 2000.

Vol. 1977: B. Roy, E. Okamoto (Eds.), Progress in Cryptology – INDOCRYPT 2000. Proceedings, 2000. X, 295 pages. 2000.

Vol. 1978: B. Schneier (Ed.), Fast Software Encryption. Proceedings, 2000. VIII, 315 pages. 2001.

Vol. 1979: S. Moss, P. Davidsson (Eds.), Multi-Agent-Based Simulation. Proceedings, 2000. VIII, 267 pages. 2001. (Subseries LNAI).

Vol. 1980: M. Agosti, F. Crestani, G. Pasi (Eds.), Lectures on Information Retrieval. Proceedings, 2000. XI, 311 pages. 2001.

Vol. 1981: J.M.L.M. Palma, J. Dongarra, V. Hernández (Eds.), Vector and Parallel Processing – VECPAR 2000. Proceedings, 2000. XVI, 580 pages. 2001.

Vol. 1983: K.S. Leung, L.-W. Chan, H. Meng (Eds.), Intelligent Data Engineering and Automated Learning – IDEAL 2000. Proceedings, 2000. XVI, 573 pages. 2000.

Vol. 1984: J. Marks (Ed.), Graph Drawing. Proceedings, 2001. XII, 419 pages. 2001.

Vol. 1985: J. Davidson, S.L. Min (Eds.), Languages, Compilers, and Tools for Embedded Systems. Proceedings, 2000. VIII, 221 pages. 2001.

Vol. 1987: K.-L. Tan, M.J. Franklin, J. C.-S. Lui (Eds.), Mobile Data Management. Proceedings, 2001. XIII, 289 pages. 2001.

Vol. 1988: L. Vulkov, J. Waśniewski, P. Yalamov (Eds.), Numerical Analysis and Its Applications. Proceedings, 2000. XIII, 782 pages. 2001.

Vol. 1989: M. Ajmone Marsan, A. Bianco (Eds.), Quality of Service in Multiservice IP Networks. Proceedings, 2001. XII, 440 pages. 2001.

Vol. 1990: I.V. Ramakrishnan (Ed.), Practical Aspects of Declarative Languages. Proceedings, 2001. VIII, 353 pages. 2001.

Vol. 1991: F. Dignum, C. Sierra (Eds.), Agent Mediated Electronic Commerce. VIII, 241 pages. 2001. (Subseries LNAI).

Vol. 1992: K. Kim (Ed.), Public Key Cryptography. Proceedings, 2001. XI, 423 pages. 2001.

Vol. 1993: E. Zitzler, K. Deb, L. Thiele, C.A.Coello Coello, D. Corne (Eds.), Evolutionary Multi-Criterion Optimization. Proceedings, 2001. XIII, 712 pages. 2001.

Vol. 1995: M. Sloman, J. Lobo, E.C. Lupu (Eds.), Policies for Distributed Systems and Networks. Proceedings, 2001. X, 263 pages. 2001.

Vol. 1997: D. Suciu, G. Vossen (Eds.), The World Wide Web and Databases. Proceedings, 2000. XII, 275 pages. 2001.

Vol. 1998: R. Klette, S. Peleg, G. Sommer (Eds.), Robot Vision. Proceedings, 2001. IX, 285 pages. 2001.

Vol. 1999: W. Emmerich, S. Tai (Eds.), Engineering Distributed Objects. Proceedings, 2000. VIII, 271 pages. 2001.

Vol. 2000: R. Wilhelm (Ed.), Informatics: 10 Years Back, 10 Years Ahead. IX, 369 pages. 2001.

Vol. 2001: G.A. Agha, F. De Cindio, G. Rozenberg (Eds.), Concurrent Object-Oriented Programming and Petri Nets. VIII, 539 pages. 2001.

Vol. 2002: H. Comon, C. Marché, R. Treinen (Eds.), Constraints in Computational Logics. Proceedings, 1999. XII, 309 pages. 2001.

Vol. 2003: F. Dignum, U. Cortés (Eds.), Agent Mediated Electronic Commerce III. XII, 193 pages. 2001. (Subseries LNAI).

Vol. 2004: A. Gelbukh (Ed.), Computational Linguistics and Intelligent Text Processing. Proceedings, 2001. XII, 528 pages. 2001.

Vol. 2006: R. Dunke, A. Abran (Eds.), New Approaches in Software Measurement. Proceedings, 2000. VIII, 245 pages. 2001.

Vol. 2007: J.F. Roddick, K. Hornsby (Eds.), Temporal, Spatial, and Spatio-Temporal Data Mining. Proceedings, 2000. VII, 165 pages. 2001. (Subseries LNAI).

Vol. 2009: H. Federrath (Ed.), Designing Privacy Enhancing Technologies. Proceedings, 2000. X, 231 pages. 2001.

Vol. 2010: A. Ferreira, H. Reichel (Eds.), STACS 2001. Proceedings, 2001. XV, 576 pages. 2001.

Vol. 2011: M. Mohnen, P. Koopman (Eds.), Implementation of Functional Languages. Proceedings, 2000. VIII, 267 pages. 2001.

Vol. 2012: D.R. Stinson, S. Tavares (Eds.), Selected Areas in Cryptography. Proceedings, 2000. IX, 339 pages. 2001.

Vol. 2013: S. Singh, N. Murshed, W. Kropatsch (Eds.), Advances in Pattern Recognition – ICAPR 2001. Proceedings, 2001. XIV, 476 pages. 2001.

Vol. 2015: D. Won (Ed.), Information Security and Cryptology – ICISC 2000. Proceedings, 2000. X, 261 pages. 2001.

Vol. 2016: S. Murugesan, Y. Deshpande (Eds.), Web Engineering. IX, 357 pages. 2001.

Vol. 2018: M. Pollefeys, L. Van Gool, A. Zisserman, A. Fitzgibbon (Eds.), 3D Structure from Images – SMILE 2000. Proceedings, 2000. X, 243 pages. 2001.

Vol. 2020: D. Naccache (Ed.), Topics in Cryptology – CT-RSA 2001. Proceedings, 2001. XII, 473 pages. 2001

Vol. 2021: J. N. Oliveira, P. Zave (Eds.), FME 2001: Formal Methods for Increasing Software Productivity. Proceedings, 2001. XIII, 629 pages. 2001.

Vol. 2022: A. Romanovsky, C. Dony, J. Lindskov Knudsen, A. Tripathi (Eds.), Advances in Exception Handling Techniques. XII, 289 pages. 2001

Vol. 2024: H. Kuchen, K. Ueda (Eds.), Functional and Logic Programming. Proceedings, 2001. X, 391 pages. 2001.

Vol. 2025: M. Kaufmann, D. Wagner (Eds.), Drawing Graphs. XIV, 312 pages. 2001.

Vol. 2026: F. Müller (Ed.), High-Level Parallel Programming Models and Supportive Environments. Proceedings, 2001. IX, 137 pages. 2001.

Vol. 2027: R. Wilhelm (Ed.), Compiler Construction. Proceedings, 2001. XI, 371 pages. 2001.

Vol. 2028: D. Sands (Ed.), Programming Languages and Systems. Proceedings, 2001. XIII, 433 pages. 2001.

Vol. 2029: H. Hussmann (Ed.), Fundamental Approaches to Software Engineering. Proceedings, 2001. XIII, 349 pages. 2001.

Vol. 2030: F. Honsell, M. Miculan (Eds.), Foundations of Software Science and Computation Structures. Proceedings, 2001. XII, 413 pages. 2001.

Vol. 2031: T. Margaria, W. Yi (Eds.), Tools and Algorithms for the Construction and Analysis of Systems. Proceedings, 2001. XIV, 588 pages. 2001.

Vol. 2032: R. Klette, T. Huang, G. Gimel'farb (Eds.), Multi-Image Analysis. Proceedings, 2000. VIII, 289 pages. 2001.

Vol. 2033: J. Liu, Y. Ye (Eds.), E-Commerce Agents. VI, 347 pages. 2001. (Subseries LNAI).

Vol. 2034: M.D. Di Benedetto, A. Sangiovanni-Vincentelli (Eds.), Hybrid Systems: Computation and Control. Proceedings, 2001. XIV, 516 pages. 2001.

Vol. 2035: D. Cheung, G.J. Williams, Q. Li (Eds.), Advances in Knowledge Discovery and Data Mining – PAKDD 2001. Proceedings, 2001. XVIII, 596 pages. 2001. (Subseries LNAI).

Vol. 2037: E.J.W. Boers et al. (Eds.), Applications of Evolutionary Computing. Proceedings, 2001. XIII, 516 pages. 2001.

Vol. 2038: J. Miller, M. Tomassini, P.L. Lanzi, C. Ryan, A.G.B. Tettamanzi, W.B. Langdon (Eds.), Genetic Programming. Proceedings, 2001. XI, 384 pages. 2001.

Vol. 2039: M. Schumacher, Objective Coordination in Multi-Agent System Engineering. XIV, 149 pages. 2001. (Subseries LNAI).

Vol. 2040: W. Kou, Y. Yesha, C.J. Tan (Eds.), Electronic Commerce Technologies. Proceedings, 2001. X, 187 pages. 2001.

Vol. 2042: K.-K. Lau (Ed.), Logic Based Program Synthesis and Transformation. Proceedings, 2000. VIII, 183 pages. 2001.

Vol. 2043: , D. Craeynest, A. Strohmeier (Eds.), Reliable Software Technologies – Ada-Europe 2001. Proceedings, 2001. XV, 405 pages. 2001.

Vol. 2044: S. Abramsky (Ed.), Typed Lambda Calculi and Applications. Proceedings, 2001. XI, 431 pages. 2001.

Vol. 2045: B. Pfitzmann (Ed.), Advances in Cryptology – EUROCRYPT 2001. Proceedings, 2001. XII, 545 pages. 2001.

Vol. 2048: J. Pauli, Learning Based Robot Vision. IX, 288 pages. 2001.

Vol. 2051: A. Middeldorp (Ed.), Rewriting Techniques and Applications. Proceedings, 2001. XII, 363 pages. 2001.

Vol. 2052: V.I. Gorodetski, V.A. Skormin, L.J. Popyack (Eds.), Information Assurance in Computer Networks. Proceedings, 2001. XIII, 313 pages. 2001.

Vol. 2053: O. Danvy, A. Filinski (Eds.), Programs as Data Objects. Proceedings, 2001. VIII, 279 pages. 2001.

Vol. 2054: A. Condon, G. Rozenberg (Eds.), DNA Computing. Proceedings, 2000. X, 271 pages. 2001.

Vol. 2055: M. Margenstern, Y. Rogozhin (Eds.), Machines, Computations, and Universality. Proceedings, 2001. VIII, 321 pages. 2001.

Vol. 2056: E. Stroulia, S. Matwin (Eds.), Advances in Artificial Intelligence. Proceedings, 2001. XII, 366 pages. 2001. (Subseries LNAI).

Vol. 2057: M. Dwyer (Ed.), Model Checking Software. Proceedings, 2001. X, 313 pages. 2001.

Vol. 2059: C. Arcelli, L.P. Cordella, G. Sanniti di Baja (Eds.), Visual Form 2001. Proceedings, 2001. XIV, 799 pages. 2001.